World Yearbook of Education 2007

This 2007 volume of the *World Yearbook of Education* considers the challenges of understanding and providing work-related education arising from the rapid expansion of the global economy. It looks at the impact of these challenges on both workers and labour markets and considers the current global context from a wide variety of theoretical, political and cultural perspectives.

Educating the Global Workforce brings together debates on what knowledge means and how it is enacted in different work spaces of the global knowledge economy with issues that are prominent in vocational education, organizational studies and business/management debates. Contributors with perspectives from Africa, Asia, South America and the Middle East as well as the most exciting thinkers in western industrialized countries look at:

- how multiple meanings of knowledge, work, workers and learning are emerging in challenging new configurations in global arrangements of production
- how workers and work-related education are shaped by the intersections of the global/local, and how they shape global/local relations
- how different social and cultural groups have differential access, and differential benefits, from work-related education
- how different communities confront the challenge of educating the global workforce.

This volume addresses a wide variety of work contexts ranging from industrial to professional to self-employment. With an emphasis on the interdependence of elements of the global economy and particularly the mediation of new technologies, it provides exciting, provocative and timely perspectives on work-related education in the globally networked, knowledge-based economy.

Lesley Farrell is Associate Professor at the Faculty of Education, Monash University, Victoria, Australia.

Tara Fenwick is a Professor of Education at the University of British Columbia, Canada.

World Yearbook of Education Series
Series editors: Terri Seddon, Jenny Ozga and Evie Zambeta

World Yearbook of Education 2007

Educating the global workforce: knowledge, knowledge work and knowledge workers

**Edited by
Lesley Farrell and
Tara Fenwick**

Routledge
Taylor & Francis Group

LONDON AND NEW YORK

First published 2007
by Routledge
2 Park Square, Milton Park, Abingdon, Oxon OX14 4RN

Simultaneously published in the USA and Canada
by Routledge
270 Madison Ave, New York, NY 10016

Routledge is an imprint of the Taylor & Francis Group, an informa business

Typeset in Palatino by
HWA Text and Data Management, Tunbridge Wells
Printed and bound in Great Britain by
Antony Rowe Ltd, Chippenham, Wiltshire

British Library Cataloguing in Publication Data
A catalogue record for this book is available from the British Library

Library of Congress Cataloging-in-Publication Data
World yearbook of education 2007 : educating the global workforce :
knowledge, knowledge work and knowledge workers / edited by
Lesley Farrell and Tara Fenwick.
    p. cm. – (World yearbook of education series)
    Includes bibliographical references and index.
    1. Education–Economic aspects–Cross-cultural studies. 2. Education
    and globalization–Cross-cultural studies. I. Farrell, Lesley, 1953–
    II. Fenwick, Tara J.
LC65.W698 2007
338.4'7370973–dc22   2006032946

ISBN10: 0–415–41603–5 (hbk)
ISBN10: 0–203–96266–4 (ebk)

ISBN13: 978–0–415–41603–0 (hbk)
ISBN13: 978–0–203–96266–4 (ebk)

Contents

Contributors

Farizah Ahmad is currently pursuing her PhD programme at the Department of Professional and Continuing Education, Faculty of Educational Studies, Universiti Putra Malaysia (UPM). She has worked as a Principal Assistant Secretary at the Prime Minister's Department, and Assistant Secretary at the Ministry of Information, and Ministry of Home Affairs, Malaysia. Her keen interests are in lifelong learning, transformative learning and spirituality.

Stephen Billett has worked within the Australian vocational education system and more recently as a teacher and researcher at Griffith University, Australia. His research interests include the social and cultural construction of vocational knowledge, and learning in and through working life, particularly how vocational practice can be developed in workplace settings. Publications include *Learning Through Work: Strategies for Effective Practice* (Allen & Unwin 2001) and *Work, Change and Workers* (Springer 2006).

Shauna Butterwick is an Associate Professor in Adult Education in the Department of Educational Studies at the University of British Columbia, Canada. Her research projects have focused generally on women's learning and more particularly on women's learning experiences in relation to paid work as well as women's learning in feminist social movements.

Clive Chappell is Associate Dean Research and Development in the Faculty of Education, University of Technology Sydney, Australia and former Director of OVAL Research, a key university research centre investigating issues of organizational, vocational and adult learning. He is co-author of the book *Reconstructing the Lifelong Learner: Pedagogies on Individual, Organizational and Social Change* (Routledge 2003).

Anita Devos teaches in adult and workplace learning in the Faculty of Education at Monash University, Australia. In her research, Anita applies feminist and Foucauldian analyses to a consideration of the relationship between work, learning and identity. She is the editor of a collection entitled *Shifting the Boundaries: Feminist Practices in Adult Education* (Posst Pressed 1999), and is currently working on a project exploring the role of workplace mentoring in shaping identity.

Marianne Döös is Associate Professor of Education at Stockholm University, Sweden. Her research deals with the processes of experiential learning in contemporary settings, on individual, collective and organizational levels. Recent projects concern shared leadership, conditions for competence in work-life, and organizational development, the aims of which are to generate theory within organization pedagogies and to subject outcomes to empirical investigation. Her recent publications include 'Functioning at the edge of knowledge', *Journal of Workplace Learning*, 17(8) (2005).

Richard Edwards is Professor of Education at the University of Stirling, UK. He has researched and written extensively of lifelong learning, adult education and workplace learning, drawing upon conceptual framing from post-structuralism. His most recent book is *Signs of Learning*, with Robin Usher (Springer 2007).

Lesley Farrell is Associate Professor at the Faculty of Education, Monash University, Australia. Her research is concerned with language and social change in work-related educational contexts, especially the construction of knowledge and learning in globally networked communities. Her recent publications include *Making Knowledge Common: Literacy and Knowledge at Work* (Peter Lang 2006).

Tara Fenwick is Professor of Education and Head of the Education Studies Department at the University of British Columbia. Her research focuses on learning and education in workplaces. Her most recent books include *Learning through Experience* (Kreiger 2003) and *Work, Subjectivity and Learning* (co-editors S. Billett and M. Somerville, Springer 2006).

Maria Clara Bueno Fischer is a Brazilian researcher in adult, popular and vocational education. She works at the University of UNISINOS (Universidade do Vale do Rio dos Sinos/Rio Grande do Sul), Brazil where she teaches and researches in the postgraduate programme on issues related to education, work and social exclusion. She has worked with social movements and workers' cooperatives to support them in the process of legitimizing their learning from experience and has published several articles about these issues.

Keith Forrester works in the Lifelong Learning Institute in the School of Education, University of Leeds, UK. He has a long-standing interest in conceptions and practices of workplace learning and in particular, to issues relating to labour learning.

Ram Ashish Giri, a Reader in the Faulty of Education at Tribhuvan University, Nepal, has been involved in English language education (ELE) in Nepal for the last 15 years. He has completed a number of projects in the field and has published research reports and articles in Nepali and international journals. His notable works include establishment of the first ELT resource centre in Nepal, and the Nepal English Language Teachers' Association. For his doctoral project at Monash University, he is exploring Nepali ELE policy.

Bernard Holkner is a Senior Lecturer in the Faculty of Education at Monash University, Australia and Director of the Centre for Educational Multimedia. He has research and teaching interests in the areas of telecommunications, multimedia and information technology. In a career which has encompassed teaching and researching at all educational levels, Bernard has initiated a range of significant applications of technology into learning settings. Recently, he has been researching ethical issues in information technology and the social impacts of information technologies in global settings. He has published in the areas of values and moral perspectives on ICT and is known for research on socio-technical networks and the global workforce.

Glynda A. Hull is Professor of Education at the University of California, Berkeley, CA. Her research examines adult literacy and changing contexts and requirements for work; writing, digital technologies and students at-risk; and urban education. Her books include *Changing Work, Changing Workers: Critical Perspectives on Language, Literacy, and Skill* (SUNY Press 1997) and *The New Work Order: Education and Literacy in the New Capitalism* (Westview 1996)

Knud Illeris holds a PhD in Psychology and is Professor of Lifelong Learning at Learning Lab Denmark, the Danish University of Education, and Adjunct Professor of Adult Learning and Leadership at Teachers College, Columbia University, New York. Three of his books have been published in English: *The Three Dimensions of Learning* (Krieger 2004), *Adult Education and Adult Learning* (Krieger 2004) and *Learning in Working Life* (Roskilde University Press 2004).

Kaela Jubas is a doctoral student in the Department of Educational Studies at the University of British Columbia, Canada. In addition to her research and teaching on work and learning, her doctoral project explores shopping as a site and process of learning about the links between consumption, citizenship, globalization and resistance.

Zane Ma Rhea is an experienced organizational development consultant to the corporate, government and education sectors in Australia, specializing in the leadership and management of diversity. She has developed an innovative teaching tool, *The Diversity Game*. She is a Senior Lecturer in the Faculty of Education, Monash University, Australia.

Srabani Maitra is a doctoral student in the Department of Adult Education at the Ontario Institute for Studies in Education of the University of Toronto. Her research interests are on home-based work, immigrant women and contingent work. She has also published and presented on adult learning, contingent work and transnational telework.

André Elias Mazawi is an Associate Professor in the Department of Educational Studies, Faculty of Education, University of British Columbia, Canada. He is also associate researcher at the UBC Centre for Policy Studies in Higher Education and Training (CHET). A sociologist of education, he is interested in higher education policies and the stratification of the academic workplace. Currently, he is editing a special issue on globalization and knowledge policies in the Arab states. He serves as French editor and associate editor of the *Canadian Journal of Higher Education* and as member of the International Board of Editors of the *Mediterranean Journal of Educational Studies*.

Kiran Mirchandani is an Associate Professor at the Ontario Institute for Studies in Education of the University of Toronto, Canada. She has published on home-based work, telework, contingent work, entrepreneurship, transnational service work and self-employment. She teaches in the Adult Education and Community Development Program, and offers courses on gendered and racialized processes in the workplace; critical perspectives on organizational development and learning; and technology, globalization and economic restructuring.

Mazanah Muhamad is a Professor of Adult Education and Chair of Cancer Education and Outreach Services at Universiti Putra Malaysia (UPM). Her research focuses on adult education and lifelong learning. Her most recent books are *Adult and Continuing Education in Malaysia* (UPM Press and UNESCO Institute for Education 2001) and *Designing and Facilitating Adults Learning* (co-author with G.L. Carter, UPM Press 2002).

Kathy Nicoll is a Senior Lecturer in Education at the University of Stirling, UK. She has worked in a number of universities in Australia and the UK and researches in the fields of professional development and policy. Her most recent book is *Flexibility and Lifelong Learning: Policy, Discourse, Politics* (Routledge 2006).

Othman Omar is a Project Manager, UPM-Cornell University Cancer Education and Research Project. He has diversified experience at various levels during separate careers in government, private and civil society sectors, including executive and academic leadership roles in private higher education. His ongoing interest is on continuing education and lifelong learning.

Fazal Rizvi is a Professor in the Department of Educational Policy Studies at the University of Illinois, USA, where he directs its Global Studies in Education program. His current research interests include theories of globalization and culture, postcolonialism and education, internationalization of higher education and student mobility. His next book, *Globalizing Educational Policy*, will be published by Routledge in late 2007.

Peter Rule is a Senior Lecturer in the Centre for Adult Education at the University of KwaZulu-Natal in Pietermaritzburg, South Africa. He recently completed his doctorate in adult education with a thesis on the history of adult education projects in and around Johannesburg. He has experience of working with NGOs in KwaZulu-Natal in the fields of adult literacy, disability, gender, early childhood development and HIV/AIDS. His research interests are in the history of adult education in South Africa, adult education and disability, and dialogue in adult education.

Peter H. Sawchuk teaches and carries out research in the areas of work, learning, technology and labour movement development. He is currently cross-appointed to the Department of Sociology and Equity Studies in Education, and the Centre for Industrial Relations and Human Resources (University of Toronto, Canada). His latest works include *Adult Learning and Technology in Working-class Life* (Cambridge University Press 2003) and *Critical Perspectives on Activity* (co-edited with Newton Duarte and Mohamed Elhammoumi, Cambridge University Press 2006).

Hermine Scheeres leads the Changing Practices Research Cluster in the Faculty of Education, University of Technology Sydney, Australia. Hermine uses ethnographic and discourse analytic approaches to research culture, communication, identity and learning, particularly in post-bureaucratic workplaces and organizations. She publishes across disciplinary areas and fields of practice in journals including *Studies in Continuing Education, Organisation Studies* and *Applied Linguistics*.

Nicky Solomon is a Professor and Head of Education and Lifelong Learning at City University, London. Her research interests focus on knowledge construction and identity work in contemporary workplaces. Her recent publications include *Persuasive Texts? Rhetoric and Educational Discourse* (co-authored with R. Edwards, K. Nicoll and R. Usher, Routledge 2004) and *Reconstructing the Life-long Learner: Pedagogies of Individual, Social and Organisational Change* (co-authored with C. Chappell, C. Rhodes, M. Tennant and L. Yates, Routledge 2003).

Makere Stewart-Harawira is an Associate Professor at the University of Alberta, Canada. She writes on globalization, global order and indigenous peoples. Makere is the author of the recently published *The New Imperial Order: Indigenous Responses to Globalization* (Zed Books/ Huia Books 2005). Her recent research focuses on the intersection of the revitalization of traditional languages and culture, global citizenship and postmodern imperialism.

Jeffery Taylor is Professor of Labour Studies at Athabasca University, Alberta, Canada. He is a labour historian and his publications include *Union Learning: Canadian Labour Education in the Twentieth Century* (Thompson 2001) and *Fashioning Farmers: Ideology, Agricultural Knowledge and the Manitoba Farm Movement, 1890–1925* (Canadian Plains Research Center 1994).

Özlem Ünlühisarcıklı is an Assistant Professor in the Faculty of Education at Boğaziçi University, Turkey. She holds an MA from that university and a PhD from the University of Manchester, UK. Her research interests are education and development, adult continuing education, teacher training and vocational skills acquisition.

Rui Yang is a Senior Lecturer at the Faculty of Education, Monash University, Australia. He has taught and researched at the universities of Shantou, Sydney, Western Australia, Hong Kong and Monash. He is particularly interested in cross-culturalism in education policy, higher education, and sociology of education, and has written extensively in these fields.

Wuhu Yao works at the International Office at Northcote High School in Melbourne, Australia. His educational background includes a Bachelor of Arts in English from Hunan Normal University in China and a Master of Education from Monash University in Australia. He has worked in China, the United States and Australia.

Jessica C. Zacher is an Assistant Professor of Teacher Education and Liberal Studies at the California State University, Long Beach, CA. Her research involves issues of multiculturalism and identity in and out of classrooms. Her current project investigates the ways second-language learners experience highly structured language arts curricula in urban schools.

Hong Zhu has a PhD in Second Language Education from Ontario Institute for Studies in Education at the University of Toronto, Canada, with a focus on recent immigrants from the People's Republic of China to Canada. Her research interests include language, education, citizenship and multiculturalism in Canada.

Clair Ribeiro Ziebell is a Brazilian teacher working at the University of UNISINOS (Universidade do Vale do Rio dos Sinos/Rio Grande do Sul), Brazil where she teaches in the undergraduate social work course. She has also developed extramural activities with the local womens' movement and undertaken research projects related to it.

Series editors' introduction

This 2007 volume of the *World Yearbook of Education* takes up the question of *Educating the global workforce*. It extends the work begun in the 2005 and 2006 volumes, which interrogated the effects and implications of globalisation and education in relation to nationalism and education research and policy, by considering knowledge in the context of changing relationships between work, education and work-related learning.

The volume editors, Lesley Farrell and Tara Fenwick, centre the volume by drawing attention to the way knowledge in work is being redefined alongside the changes in economies, work and working-lives which underpin the sense that, today, we live in a globalised knowledge economy. These widely held understandings, relayed through global policy discourses and the practical experiences of changing work-learning places, problematise accepted and established relationships between work and education. These changes drive a preoccupation with knowledge as a key factor in economic development and puts a premium on developing workers for the new economy. They privilege work-related learning over other educational purposes – what the editors define as the 'spaces and activities intentionally planned to mobilise particular practices, behaviours and ideas related to paid work' (p. 14). Yet, the editors argue, this commonsense narrative of contemporary global economic development begs questions about what counts as 'knowledge' in the 'the knowledge economy'. Who are the 'knowledge workers' in this new global economy? What is the 'working knowledge' that workers must enact? And how might education and educators respond to this drive towards work-related learning?

The editors open up these questions by considering the way the idea of the global knowledge economy, and its associated practical effects in work and learning, have challenged established education and training arrangements and encouraged alternative ways of doing learning. Yet in explaining these developments and their effects, the editors caution us against a too-uncritical acceptance of the knowledge economy discourse and an overemphasis on globalisation from above. They argue, instead, that it is necessary to look beyond deterministic notions of globalisation, which emphasise worldwide standardising and homogenising processes and consider the way global processes inflect local spaces in which actors retain a capacity for agency. This focus on 'globalisation from below' reveals ways in which ordinary people work together to develop localised ways of responding to, dealing with, and re-directing processes of learning and patterns of work that accompany everyday reconfigurations of work practices, work organisations and cultures, and working knowledges and identities. Their message is that this orientation to globalisation not only highlights the diversity of practice and effects, and the tensions and contradictions that are entailed in what global policy discourse calls 'the knowledge economy', it also reveals the way large-scale economic, social and cultural processes and transformations generate practical politics that operate across scales and spatialities.

The chapters collected together in this volume provide windows into these themes related to changes in knowledge, knowledge work and knowledge workers. The authors are drawn from around the world, making this a truly global collection framed by a global sensibility. The detailed analyses presented through the chapters are organised thematically. The first three parts address: 'What counts as working knowledge?'; 'Knowing and working the global economy'; 'Work, working life and working identities'. The final part looks back towards work-related learning because, as the editors argue, this is a volume in a *World Yearbook of Education* that has been written by education researchers not economists. This part presents chapters that consider 'Challenges for work-related education'. And again, this shift in nomenclature is significant. Just as educators and education researchers have framed this volume, it is written in order to speak to educators about education and the 'vital' contribution that education makes to 'worker and knowledge development' (p. 9). In this the volume speaks clearly, asserting the need for education and educators to find (better) ways of engaging with contemporary economic reform and the work-related learning trajectory, now and for the future.

As series editors of the *World Yearbook of Education*, we are delighted that scholars with the insight and imagination of Lesley Farrell and Tara Fenwick have taken up the challenge of preparing the 2007 volume. They have brought their distinctive expertise in language and social change (framed from Australia) and work and learning (framed from Canada), and their different academic networks, together in productive ways to produce this collection across time-spaces and research orientations. In this work they have enacted the ambition of the *World Yearbook of Education* series, which is not just to document worldwide developments in education but to map a significant and emerging educational issue with a view to framing up a serious research agenda at the cutting edge of the field. Moreover, they have achieved this in a special way that makes a significant contribution to knowledge and debate about contemporary education. Importantly, they have offered a framework for thinking about contemporary changes in education and their interfaces with work and the economy. This framework brings the question of knowledge in work into the frame of education research. The collection reminds us that in all the hype and racy talk of knowledge economy, learning society, and lifelong learning, it is important to continue working on old questions – like 'what counts as knowledge?', 'whose knowledge is it?', 'how is it defined?' and 'who ?' – that have long informed educational debates and mobilised the practical politics of education. The volume challenges us as educators, policy makers and education researchers to think, all over again, about what counts as 'really useful knowledge' for worker-learners and how it can be enacted through work-related *education*. As the volume editors note:

> What educators and policy makers at national, regional and international levels need to do now is to cast a critical eye over the past and to consider, with far greater clarity than we have managed in the past, what role work-related education should play in the future. As part of those deliberations we need to consider who work-related education is intended to benefit and what kinds of knowledge-based economies it should be helping to build (p. 24).

Terri Seddon, Jenny Ozga and Evie Zambeta
Melbourne, Edinburgh and Athens, 2006

Introduction

Lesley Farrell and Tara Fenwick

[K]nowledge is now the driver of productivity and economic growth
(OECD, *The Knowledge-Based Economy*, 1996: 4)

A knowledge-based economy relies primarily on the use of ideas
rather than physical abilities and on the application of technology
rather than the transformation of raw materials or the exploitation of
cheap labour.
(World Bank, *Lifelong Learning for the Global Knowledge
Economy*, 2003: 1)

We live in a time when the popular belief – reinforced in boardrooms,
newspapers and policy pronouncements alike – is that any region's
long-term growth is fundamentally linked with knowledge. This belief
is nurturing a gnawing anxiety that we may not be producing enough
knowledge or the right kind of knowledge to survive in this global economy.
In the West, the labour force is ageing and shrinking rapidly in numbers
while younger workers sustain relatively high levels of unemployment.
Severe trades-skill shortages erupt annually alongside massive job layoffs
in different sectors depending on commodity supplies, fast-shifting
labour sites, and emerging industries in global markets. Peter Sawchuk
(this volume) shows that while some argue that existing workers need
to be 'upskilled' in technological competencies needed for a knowledge
economy, others claim that technologies have deskilled existing work
beyond the point of recognition. Debates rage about what knowledge,
exactly, is most valuable in different groups of the global workforce.

Meanwhile, dramatic global imbalances persist around the world in
trading capacity, trained workers and knowledge production. So, while the
so-called West worries about what forms of university education are likely
to improve the employability of their young people, many developing
countries struggle to provide primary education and increase literacy to
provide the literate workforce that global industries demand. But such
binaries – developed/developing – prove misleading when considering
issues like literacy, where sites of low literacy flourish in wealthy regions,

and demands increase for new literacy practices particularly in tandem with new technologies. In this volume, Glynda Hull and Jessica Zacher offer case studies showing the struggles of low literate workers in the US, and the ways that new literacies recruit powerful new worker identities.

Given the generally accepted proposition that education systems are the key levers for knowledge production and thus for ensuring survival of individuals, firms and nations in a global economy, it is not surprising that a highly critical gaze has turned to educational provision at all levels, in most regions around the world. Major challenges have been issued to the compulsory K-12 schooling system for not providing the appropriate experiences that will prepare young people to enter a fast-moving technologised and mobile global labour market. Vocational systems of apprenticeships and training have been found woefully inadequate in preparing sufficient numbers of tradesworkers to meet fast-shifting industry demands, or for preparing workers to navigate complex practices and always-emerging technologies. Higher education institutions have been attacked for their disconnection from labour market needs, their unimaginative discipline-bound theories and their lack of innovative initiative focused on the here-and-now. Both the Organisation for Economic Co-operation and Development (OECD) and the World Bank have been issuing key policy documents calling for the redesign of education for human capital formation in a rapidly changing economy, albeit purporting different visions for this educational reform (in contrast to the World Bank's focus on market and individualism, the OECD focuses more on social inclusion, social cohesion and knowledge distribution through sharing).

This book addresses central questions around this intersection of education with the multiple meanings of knowledge in a global economy. For starters, the preceding paragraphs embed assumptions that appear commonly in policy documents about the knowledge economy, assumptions that need to be picked apart. What does 'knowledge' mean, and what does it mean when it is understood as a commodity of, and an enactment constituting, a 'global knowledge economy'? What precisely are the changing enactments of 'knowledge' in different work sectors, activities and geo-political areas of the economy? How does knowledge become legitimated in these different spaces of work, and by whom? For that matter, what is 'work' in a global economy, and who are the workers? And how can we think about education, in all its forms and provisions, in relation to these questions? The authors in this collection each take up these questions in relation to specific issues and regions of work. But before we say more about the authors and the actual development of the book, we want to pause and address these foundational issues of knowledge, economy, work and education. We have our own peculiar understandings of these concepts and their relationships. In the following paragraphs we endeavour to locate our perspectives and definitions, which may help illuminate our reasons for stitching this book together in the way that we have.

What is work in a global economy, and who are the (knowledge) workers?

Without entering the complex debates about how to understand globalisation or the extent to which nation-states and other borderings have dissolved or transformed amidst the global shifts in movements of capital, labour and culture, we venture some modest assertions about how work is changing in a globally networked economy. Here we tread carefully among physical characteristics of work activity variously observed and recorded, the images and meanings attributed to contemporary work in the collective imaginary of different societies, and the interaction between the material and the ideational. In the studies and examples presented by authors in this collection, we see work organisations becoming more fluid and distributed. Work sites in some cases are nodes of complex activity, people and technical practice that are far removed from the organisations they serve. Transient work units such as those described by Shauna Butterwick, Kaela Jubas and Hong Zhu are technology-based and bounded by digital communication. Standardisation across these units is critical. In the call centres described by Kiran Mirchandani and Srabani Maitra, the distributed work sites are compelled to articulate culturally with those they serve, through accent, network-building and identity modification. In all, there is primary emphasis on building networks and maintaining continuous, sometimes relentless 24/7, communication, largely through ICT-enabled fields of interaction. In all of these contexts, education is recruited, sometimes explicitly, often implicitly, to the task of creating the global networks that generate and sustain global economic activity. Tumultuous flows and speed of information in new modalities (video conferencing, podcasts, text messaging) described by Bernard Holkner are demanding new literacies and reducing the value of information, but also opening opportunities for new alliances and sites for producing knowledge.

Yet within all the global patterns of distributed networking, standardisation, digital communication and general accelerations in work, we believe it is vital to retain a clear focus on the actual experiences of actual workers. People are not patterns: they are idiosyncratic actors. They work in particular places, at particular moments, using tools and practices that have meanings in those places, interacting with other people who have evolved ways of being together that are unique and local, within the possibilities and constraints inscribed in those places. These material workplaces can be distinguished from the broader networks of work sites across which ideas and texts flow, but as Kathy Nicoll and Richard Edwards show, both are connected and animated through globalising processes. Farrell (2006) calls these broader networks in which workplaces are encompassed 'workspaces'. Both embed and produce the dynamics of the global economy, and both must be examined to understand how knowledge is understood and where education is/might be positioned.

And among these workplaces and spaces, who are considered to be the knowledge(able) workers? For some commentators like Robert Reich (former US Secretary of Labor), knowledge workers form the ranks of the professional-technical middle class: the accountants, lawyers, journalists and engineers (2003). Those knowledge workers occupying the top tiers of status and income are the global dealmakers: transnational CEOs and executives of global investment banks. All others are, for Reich, 'left behind' through increasing gaps of income, opportunity and symbolic-analytic knowledge. Certainly some individuals and groups are particularly vulnerable in a global economy, and their struggles deserve special support, as Knud Illeris argues. However the blurrings among workers' knowledge advantage and capacity to negotiate their work and worth is far more complex than Reich portrays, as Ram Giri and Peter Rule illustrate in their case studies showing how English language shapes work and workers in Nepal and how HIV/AIDS is woven through work education in South Africa respectively.

A strong emphasis on 'skill' development continues to label workers as categorically 'skilled' or 'unskilled', based on assumptions that the ability to perform certain activities can be standardised, measured and added where missing. The politics of who knows what is 'skill' becomes buried in such practices. This affects most profoundly not only those moving from one vocation to another as employment opportunities shift, but also the vast groups of migrant professional workers seeking credentialisation in host countries. In the West, a panoply of invisible barriers typically prevent these immigrants from being recognised as appropriately 'skilled' to take jobs that, in some cases, the host countries are desperate to fill. A further irony is that the entire codification of skills, worked out in extensive detail for assessment and educational delivery in most OECD countries, is based on what has passed for knowledge in the past – in structures of limited relevance for the fast-changing fluid workplaces/workspaces and jobs that are continually emerging. Fazal Rizvi argues that the much-celebrated networks that putatively permit migrant workers to negotiate these knowledge spaces and places are in fact highly circumscribed and problematic, reinforcing multiple barriers and prejudices determining what constitutes skill and who wields it.

All of these influences fundamentally affect workers' identities, and their efforts in performing identity create knowledge that also deserves recognition, as Clive Chappell, Hermine Scheeres and Nicky Solomon explain. How workers negotiate a sense of self amidst globally-induced work pressures that is not disempowered or dehumanised is the focus of Stephen Billett's chapter. Statements from organisations and governments stress the need for flexible, resilient, innovative workers, throwing responsibility onto individuals to manage their own survival and create pegs for their own identities as knowledge workers. As people take up this compulsion, 'the' worker in 'the' global economy increasingly becomes characterised as enterprising, autonomous and mobile, marketing an image and angling a knowledge, learning continuously and urgently while scanning all surroundings for clues, trends and warnings. Workers' desires, including desires to know, to transgress or to fly free, become assembled into these expectations – and the economic project of self-improvement turns into a lifelong obsession or a line of flight, or both (Fenwick, 2002). A corollary decline in organised labour in developed countries, as Jeff Taylor shows, has eroded both workers' collective affiliations and the resulting critical voice that historically has exposed the politics of work knowledge and fought the naturalisation of unfettered markets.

What does knowledge mean, and how is it part of a 'global knowledge economy'?

Robert Reich has argued that the global economy depends upon elite symbolic-analytic knowledge – the capacity to generate, design, manipulate and translate ideas, moving them across languages and audiences. The OECD also emphasises the need for mediation and management of knowledge (1996). As work groups become split apart and distributed in time and place, the central need is to somehow ensure that they remain linked, that information moves efficiently among them, and that they work within consistent standards and processes. But more, organisations now compete through 'value-adding' – unique goods, new solutions or resources enhanced with new information, design or service. Further, with the decline in manufacturing jobs in wealthy industrialised countries through technologisation, governments are looking to knowledge-based, Research and Development industries as the way to diversify their economies. Therefore it is no surprise that innovative knowledge above all, particularly techno-scientific innovation, is promoted through government incentives. Governments are also promoting knowledge mobilisation or 'transfer', fostering knowledge networks, multi-sector knowledge partnerships and international collaborations in an effort to increase their knowledge advantage through sharing.

But knowledge-connecting and knowledge-making occurs in varying levels of work activity. While, say, the R&D labs of a multinational pharmaceutical firm innovate new products to be implemented through software innovated by their university partner, at the level of a local worksite the workers must find a way to make this new procedure work. They must problem-solve the software glitches, translate product specifications and improvise ways to organise their own groups and processes to adapt the corporate directives to local culture and resources. They also must develop multiple modes and networks of communication – across diverse regions and communities within and without the organisation, across levels of knowledge abstraction, across company hierarchies and across new textual forms ranging from ISO 9000 reports to email and cell phone transmissions.

This is the important 'common knowledge' of improvisation and connection (Farrell, 2006) that unfolds in the microprocesses of workers' everyday activities. This knowledge is *enacted* and not necessarily codified or even recognised – it is embodied, situated in action, and mediated by local preferences, tools and values. In fact this knowledge is so provisional and pragmatic that everyone who participates in it tends to simply accept it as mundane everyday activity. And yet this knowledge, existing alongside formally codified professional knowledge, certifiable vocational skill, and bodies of innovative, technical and scientific knowledge, could be viewed as a central animator of much work activity in the global economy.

So, recognition of knowledge emerges as a clear problem in determining exactly what knowledge is required in the workplaces of a global economy. And relations of power within workplaces, across regions and globally are worked through in terms of what counts as knowledge and who can say so. For developing countries seeking integration in the global economy to fight poverty and survive, as Andre Mazawi shows, double binds await. The Western hegemony of knowledge and meanings of 'knowledge economy' become the yardstick measuring all other regions, challenging their own knowledge and traditions of vocational education along with their foundations in religion and historical culture. A 'structural leap' into West-dominated knowledges profoundly affects cultural practices and policies in education: Makere Stewart-Harawira explains the dramatic conflicts sustained by indigenous peoples caught in globalising, colonising knowledge webs. Overall, the understanding of how knowledge is produced and circulated in the global knowledge economy is highly ambiguous, and the notion of what forms of knowledge are most valuable in various exchange relationships are far more nuanced than present policy declarations would imply.

How can we think about education in a global knowledge economy?

Education is never innocent, for it is always embedded in particular spaces and cultural practices at every level – policy, social structures, institutional norms and regulations, curriculum, and local interactions. In this way education has been, as Simon Marginson (1999) put it, 'a primary medium of globalisation, and an incubator of its agents' (p. 4).

The relationship between education, employment and labour markets is changing. Whereas vocational education and training (VET) in the past has been treated as a supplier of skilled labour to industry, the perception now is that this locked relationship cannot meet the fast-changing patterns of a global knowledge economy. According to Keith Forrester, vocational education in Europe and the UK must shift more to develop entrepreneurism, autonomy, citizenship and sustainability: fostering critical capacity in new workers. But here again, different regions interpret differently the dilemma of just what to make of the 'knowledge economy', and how to position vocational education accordingly. In Malaysia, argue Farizah Ahmad, Othman Omar and Maznah Muhamad, VET has played a key role serving rapidly changing social reform policies, from eradicating poverty in the 1960s, to creating national unity and fuelling heavy industrial export in the 1970s–80s. Now, in trying to maintain its position as a serious player in global trade, Malaysia accepts the knowledge economy discourse unproblematically and focuses VET on generating 'creativity and cognitive skills', managerial capacity, entrepreneurism and the value of lifelong learning. By contrast in Turkey, as Özlem Ünlühisarcıklı explains, VET is firmly rooted in a historical apprenticeship system. While recent changes have enabled greater flexibility, there is still strong emphasis on systematic progression through particular training levels, matching individual to job and standardising all through a national qualifications framework driven by European Union priorities.

A growing distrust that compulsory school systems or even vocational training institutions can prepare the right knowledge workers for unpredictable production needs has helped fuel an emphasis on 'lifelong learning' for work. This has spawned a slew of work-related education providers among NGOs and non-profit organisations, private agencies, government-funded initiatives, occupation-specific networks, self-styled consultants, blogs, industry spinoffs, or just about anyone who has learned to pitch learning. In some iterations, the responsibility for wading through these billboards to find appropriate work education is awarded entirely to individuals. They must choose carefully to ensure their own, their organisation's and their nation's economic growth, and they shall choose regardless of income, location, prior educational opportunity, access to or awareness of their so-called choices. With the growing expectation that individuals will seek and self-fund their own knowledge development for work purposes, these providers have bent their programmes to offer flexible, accelerated learning opportunities – often with very little external evaluation beyond industry and individual consumers' satisfaction. Providers can capitalise upon fashionable issues or promise to fix those surface ripplings that mask deeper currents and contradictions. One example are the popular cross-cultural training programmes in workplaces which, as Zane Ma Rhea points out, manage to essentialise culture, reduce it to individual behaviours and assert Western norms, all under the flag of inclusion. It is little wonder that some commentators regard the individualised re-scripting of education in these movements as deeply problematic.

Education as learning outside institutions is increasingly apparent, according to authors in this volume: in the emphasis on knowledge networks and mentoring (Anita Devos), relational knowledge connections (Marianne Döös) and community-based coalitions (Maria Clara Bueno Fischer and Clair Ribeiro Ziebell). Questions are raised about the conflict between such informal knowledge development and a system based on credentialism, as well as the contradictions of expecting collaborative knowledge-sharing in organisations and open markets where knowledge-exchange determines competitive position.

Globally, education is re-shaping patterns of knowledge development. Migrating students and educational programmes marketed to developing countries by the wealthy West continue to create a small knowledge elite in poorer nations, with networks cutting across borders. Rui Yang and Wuhu Yao show the resulting complex negotiations in a case of higher education based in China. The problem for Mazawi, writing about Saudi Arabia, is the resulting homogenisation/cultural standardisation, colonisation, cultural dependence of developing countries on the West, and a general acceptance of the global knowledge economy as current reality that education needs to address by remedying the country's deficit. Tikly (2001) shows how in regions as poor as sub-Saharan Africa, a 'crippling brain drain' of potential knowledge workers is pervasive. Education capacity is so far from being able to provide skills required by business and the public sector, that enrolments are declining and drop-outs increasing. At this rate, shows Tikly, 50 per cent in low-income countries can expect to be permanently excluded from employment with another 20 per cent in low-income, insecure employment within nations with low literacy rates.

These issues and global power imbalances are almost overwhelming to contemplate. But for educators, education in its various forms is not (only) about legitimising a particular global order by helping workers to accommodate to its demands and find employability, but also about challenging it, fostering thoughtful participation in it and fuelling resistance to its excesses – while building the knowledge recognition, social capital and social inclusion that can begin to address the many inequities generated by the current emergences of the global knowledge economy.

About this book

Within all of these issues, the focus of this book is on education and learning rather than economics, and on workers rather than employers, organisations and states. Authors have been selected who maintain a critical position on issues of the 'global economy' as well as assumptions about knowledge and the economy's needs for knowledgeable human capital. Overall, our belief is that education in various forms is a vital dynamic in worker and knowledge development, alongside sharp questions about who defines knowledge and development, and for what purposes.

The book is intended to be an international collection, and we are fortunate to have authors writing from contexts of work and education in regions characterised by wide diversity in income, historical culture, colonial inheritances, political constraints and regulatory frameworks: including Indigenous Peoples, South America, Southeast Asia, Africa and China as well as North America, Australia, the UK and various regions of Europe. However, given the complexity and diversity of issues and perspectives in any region, these voices will at best gesture towards contextual variation being experienced globally, and cannot be understood to 'represent' these regions. Further, we have chosen to limit contributions to English. And like any language, English grammar shapes one particular perspective and entirely prevents others. So, while authors have endeavoured to be sensitive to the hegemony of Western perspectives on education and globalisation, this volume in many ways re-enacts this hegemony.

Amidst such wide-ranging issues as knowledge, work and education in a global economy, the book does not attempt to be comprehensive, nor to fully represent this historical moment. We have gathered together leading authors, all university-based researchers who have been studying and thinking about work-related issues for some time and have something to say. We did not attempt to represent the extensive research on work and education occurring in popular education, human resource and management development, or the college system involvement in VET: these complex areas each have accumulated their own large volumes of literature. Issues of ecology/sustainability, racism, gender, youth workers, migrant and precarious labour are all important and have been addressed in various chapters as layers and dynamics within complex systems. That is, these issues and groups are not treated as natural, boundaried categories that are allowed to define the terms of the debate while denying questions as to their own constitution. Overall, most authors here work against such boundaries, to unsettle established categories and notions about what is knowledge in work, how it is produced and circulated, and what this might mean for education and educators.

This volume is typical of global knowledge production in that it has involved a close collaboration between Lesley and Tara, as well as between the authors and the editors, to painstakingly construct shared knowledge over space and time. As editors we brought our distinct disciplinary and cultural backgrounds (Tara in work and learning, from Canada, Lesley in language and social change in globalising contexts, from Australia) to bear on questions about knowledge, knowledge work and knowledge workers. With the generous help of Miriam Faine, our editorial assistant, we worked mostly on Skype and email to conceptualise the volume, contact potential authors all over the world, negotiate with authors and publishers, and shape our own arguments and writing. Our meetings collapsed our time-spaces in ways that often felt bizarre: a summer holiday Monday evening for Tara in Vancouver was a wintry Tuesday morning in the middle of a busy term for Lesley in Melbourne. The challenges and the potential of the global workspace we inhabited were always in the foreground of our thinking – it could not be otherwise. For us this volume represents a true and entirely equal collaboration that instantiates the very best of what the global knowledge economy has to offer.

References

Farrell, L. (2006) *Making Knowledge Common*. New York: Peter Lang.

Fenwick, T. (2002) 'Transgressive desires: new enterprising selves in the new capitalism', *Work, Employment and Society*, 16 (4), 703–24.

Marginson, S. (1999) 'After globalization: emerging politics of education', *Journal of Education Policy*, 14, 19–31.

OECD (1996) *The Knowledge-based Economy*. Paris: OECD.

Reich, R. (2003) 'Nice work if you can get it', *Wall Street Journal*, December 26.

Tikly, L. (2001) 'Globalisation and education in the postcolonial world: towards a conceptual framework', *Comparative Education*, 37, 22, 151–71.

World Bank (2003) *Lifelong Learning for a Global Knowledge Economy*. Washington, DC: World Bank.

Part I

What counts as working knowledge?

1   Educating a global workforce?

Lesley Farrell and Tara Fenwick

In the public rhetoric, at least, education is the answer to most, if not all, the questions raised by the global knowledge-based economy. In this chapter we begin an examination of what education promises the global workforce, and what the global workforce, and the knowledge-based economy, might reasonably ask of education. Different perspectives on the knowledge-based economy imply different constructions of 'knowledge'. Workers are characterised within these frameworks as 'knowledge workers' (an elite), or, perhaps, 'knowledgeable workers' (the non-elite majority) and questions arise around what they are required to learn, to know and to be able to do. The global knowledge-based economy produces profound challenges to work-related education at every level. While these challenges manifest themselves in uniquely local ways at specific local sites, they are produced, and must be addressed, in contexts that are uncompromisingly global. If work-related education is to contribute to positive outcomes for people and for local communities we (workers, corporations, educators, researchers, policy makers, politicians and international organisations) must find new ways to pay attention to the ways in which a workforce in the knowledge-based economy can be understood to be 'global' as well as 'local', and what workers need to be able to know and be able to do to move across and within these spatial and temporal domains.

Introduction

What is involved, and what is at stake, in educating a global workforce for a knowledge-based economy? In this chapter we examine current rhetoric of education in a knowledge-based economy – what is work-related education, what roles does it play and who it is for? What does it mean to identify a global workforce, and what kinds of workers comprise such a workforce? We begin with the growing emphasis placed on education as a 'driver' of the knowledge-based economy and move to a discussion of the knowledge implied in such education. We then consider the circumstances under which the (or even a) workforce can be characterised as global (or local) and what the implications might be for the education of the people and communities and organisations that make up that workforce. For our purposes here, when we talk about work-related education we mean spaces and activities intentionally planned to mobilise particular practices, behaviours and ideas related to paid work.

Education as a 'key driver'

The global economy is generally understood to be a high-skills economy. By this we mean that, in many parts of the world, mental labour is viewed as replacing or substantially augmenting physical labour and natural resources as the basis of economic productivity (e.g. de Ferranti *et al.* 2002). Aside from the problem of separating mental from physical as though these are distinct domains of activity, in this context education is viewed as a primary driver of economic transformation, becoming a (in some cases *the*) fundamental plank of national and international economic and social policy:

> When European leaders set the goal for Europe of becoming the number one knowledge economy, they declared that what was needed was 'not only a radical transformation of the European Economy, but also a challenging programme for the modernization of social welfare and education systems'. In 2002 they added that, by 2010, Europe should be the world leader in terms of the quality of its education systems
>
> (OECD 2005: 3)

In comparing the economic performance of the United States with that of the European Union, the OECD argues that an emphasis on education clearly confers benefits, not only on national economies, but also on society more generally and on individuals specifically. Since the US is purportedly 'underperforming' on global tests of educational achievement like the PISA (Program for International Student Assessment) managed by the OECD, its place as the leading performer in the global knowledge economy is considered to be under threat (OECD 2005).

While competition between the economic superpowers of the West is nothing new, the World Bank (2003) maintains that developing countries are now enmeshed in the same competition, requiring radical reform of education and training systems for their economic development. This entails not just greater financial investment in education and training, but wholesale transformation of social, cultural and pedagogical assumptions underpinning local education systems:

> developing countries and countries with transition economies risk being further marginalized in a competitive global knowledge economy because their education systems are not equipping learners with the skills they need. To respond to the problem, policymakers

need to make fundamental changes. They need to replace the information-based, teacher-directed rote learning provided with a formal education system governed by directives with a new type of learning that emphasizes creating, applying, analyzing, and synthesizing knowledge and engaging in collaborative learning across the lifespan.

(World Bank 2003: xvii–xviii)

Clearly for some countries, perhaps for many, this implies a complete reconfiguration, not only of vocational education and training but also of schooling, higher education and professional education. In some critical senses, all education comes to be understood as work-related education.

It is difficult to overestimate the fundamental changes that such a reconfiguration implies. For good or ill, it challenges traditional relationships between students and teachers (and, thereby, traditional understandings of the relationships between parents and children, the individual and the community, the individual and the state) and it challenges traditional understandings of what counts as legitimate knowledge and who is authorised to legitimate it. The economic and policy demands of transformations on this scale can be profound. In some cases comprehensive new approaches to technical and vocational education have been developed that incorporate explicit demands of global corporations and international standards frameworks. Slowinski (1998) demonstrates that global corporations exert influence over European national education policies both directly, through their corporate training demands, and less directly through their effective lobbying of the European Union (EU) to shape regional educational policies. However, while the EU has a specific education policy mandate, other regional trade agreements like the North American Free Trade Agreement (NAFTA) and the Asia Pacific Economic Co-operation (APEC), exert influence over the education and training policies of their regions obliquely by implying certain levels and kinds of skills. Dale and Robertson argue that the International Monetary Fund, Organisation for Economic Co-operation and Development and the World Trade Organisation

play the role of the collective capitalist state. They are able, through conditionality, loans, debts and other strategies, to impose the model not only on the leading nations, but on the whole world.

(Dale and Robertson 2002: 14)

In some cases, especially in countries which are reliant on international aid for the development of mass education systems, these demands have relocated control of education outside the local national community. In the case of Africa, for instance, Brock-Utne (2000) considers the role of Norwegian funding channelled through UNICEF and argues that 'the partnership [between the African countries and the donor agencies] is as unequal as it can be' and results in education focusing on literacy (usually in a European language) and ignoring local, work-related, skill development which might conceivably lead to self-employment or employment in the local community.

One prominent sign of these transformations is the promotion of English as the language of instruction in many developing countries. This has the dual advantage of making English language curriculum materials instantly available to help transform education systems and at the same time produce the English-literate workforce required for participation in the global economy. There is, however, a price to pay. In sub-Saharan Africa children are often taught in English from the beginning of their schooling, despite national Government policies to the contrary and the fact that teachers in rural areas have little experience in using English and little teacher training (Brock-Utne 2000; Grov 1999). The policy of the Complementary Opportunity for Primary Education (COPE) programme, funded by UNICEF, requires English to be the language of instruction. Imam (2005) reports a similar situation in Bangladesh. As Chase-Dunn (1999) argues, Western imports of education have included values of individualism, rationalism, efficiency, and emphasis on science and progress as well as on (individual) human rights. Framing education in English seems to help standardise Western measures of skill, technology, innovation and productivity in ways that are quickly recalibrating regional economic and political relationships.

Education can, however, be viewed as a driver of globalisation in quite a different sense, one in which Western views and values about education are as available to disruption as any others. Edwards and Usher (2000) argue that contemporary forms of Open and Distance Learning favoured by many Western universities drive globalisation precisely because they disrupt (rather than reinforce) common understandings of Western educational institutions (like training colleges and universities) and of what counts as established knowledge. Open and Distance Learning programmes detach the student from their local community, creating a virtual community in a 'diaspora space'. In non-formal educational spaces, the import of English also enables counter-globalisation discourses to unfold and find support in developing countries, and provides opportunities for labour and civil rights activists to link with global resources and networks.

A significant feature of claims about the critical role of education and training in national and individual advancement is the way economic and social well-being are conflated. In policy rhetoric at least, educational reform is presented as the solution to all kinds of persistent social problems including gender inequality, race and ethnic inequality, social fragmentation, and growing gaps between rich and poor posed by a global economy. As Brown and Lauder (2006) argue,

Not only is education seen to hold the key to a competitive economy but it is also seen to be the foundation of social justice and cohesion.

(Brown and Lauder 2006: 25)

The World Bank supports this view with regard to the simultaneously economic and socially transformative potential of education in developing countries:

By improving people's ability to function as members of their communities, education and training increase social cohesion, reduce crime, and improve income distribution.

(World Bank 2003: xvii)

Claims like these are sometimes based more on pious intention than on firm social and economic data. Some kinds of education can be argued to increase social cohesion and, presumably, therefore reduce crime, but it is very difficult to say the extent to which even the best education and training programmes improve income distribution, under what circumstances, and for which groups. Brown and Lauder contend that current approaches to education policy-making focus on lifting standards as a whole, not on reducing the gaps between performance and reward for particular groups of people. In the USA, for instance, the census data reveal that university graduates earn on average 91 per cent more than people who have only completed their secondary education (OECD 2005). However, since averages can be misleading, it is important to disaggregate the data. When that is done it seems that longstanding gender and racial inequalities are far from being eradicated:

White men with a bachelors degree earn about $10,000 a year more than Black or Hispanic men with the same qualification. The difference between White men and Hispanic females widens to virtually $20,000.

(Brown and Lauder 2006: 39)

In this case at least, it seems that traditional race and gender disparities persist despite the global knowledge economy and, while education is without doubt increasingly necessary for any kind of employment, it will not, of itself, improve income distribution within nations.

The knowledge-based economy has had a similarly complex effect on regional income disparity. While some, like Friedman (2006), argue that 'the world is flat' by virtue of ubiquitous internet access, allowing India and China (amongst other nations) to become major players in global supply chains, others argue that the Information and Communication Technologies (ICT) serve only to make disparities more difficult to see. They point out that nations which have invested heavily in the technological education and training of their workforce, but with less economic and political power in the global arena, tend to engage in high technology industries in a subordinate role:

> they revolve at the will (and mercy) of the leading regions, working on problems delegated from the hub that have little or no local significance.
>
> (Brown and Duguid 2002: 431)

The core-periphery relation in the global division of labour has been transformed. Labour-intensive manufacturing has shifted to poor and developing regions, while accelerated innovation and the focus on 'value-adding' in wealthy regions (as well as trade agreements favouring their own commodities) has undermined the market for primary commodities on which many developing economies have depended (Tikly 2001). The problem for such countries is complex and difficult to solve. If they train a highly skilled workforce in a local context which does not have the specific history and economic and political support of the major players (the right 'ecology') then they may find that these high-value, expensively trained workers are 'poached' by the major players and the local skill base is depleted. If they do not train their local workforce for new industries then they will not be players at all.

Education is, then, critically important in the knowledge-based economy but the outcomes it provides for individuals, social groups or national regional economies are neither obvious nor predictable. As Tikly (2001) argues, different sectors within education can have positive or negative correspondences with the global economy at different times. Elite education producing high skills development and social capital, can increase integration and participation in global economic activity, but may also promote worker migration from poorer to wealthy regions. Basic education and low-skills training can improve conditions for the poor but also create wider exclusionary divides within and across regions. Education generally can legitimise an existing global order that, as Stiglitz (2002) claims forcefully, garners a disproportionate share of benefits for the West at the expense of the developing world, but education also fuels resistance by providing forum and focus for critical correspondence with the status quo. Tikly suggests, for example, that 'post-colonial elites of sub-Saharan Africa may also use their participation in global forums to form a bulwark against Western economic and political hegemony' (Tikly 2001: 162).

What education, what knowledge?

While there seems to be almost universal agreement that we all operate in a knowledge-based economy, there is no clear agreement over what such an economy might be, or how it might be different from the economies that have gone before. There is, indeed, no clear agreement about what constitutes the 'knowledge' that drives the knowledge economy, about who or what (the people, the technologies, the organisations) participates in such knowledge, or about how they make it or about how they use it.

Broadly speaking, as Powell and Snellman (2004) argue, there has been a fundamental shift in the way we understand the knowledge-based economy: from being a *subset* of economic activity to functioning as a *dimension* of economic activity. For some time, in popular rhetoric as well as in academic literature, 'the knowledge economy' was treated as a discrete economy, a subset of global, networked economic activity. It was marked by a heavy emphasis on scientific theory building, on technical forms of technological innovation, and on 'knowledge intensive' industries like biotechnology, nanotechnology, certain kinds of engineering, etc. in which productivity growth was unquestionably rapid. Within this framework, knowledge intensive industries were understood to drive profound economic and social changes on a global scale well beyond their industry sectors. This understanding supported the view that the knowledge economy operated in ways that were substantially different from other sectors of the economy, and from the way that economies were understood to function in the past. Some argued that these industries created new kinds of jobs for the elite few, notably Reich's (1991) 'symbolic analysts', and these highly valued workers demanded and developed new kinds of work practices and new kinds of work organisation marked by personal mobility and autonomy.

The academic debate (and, to some extent, the policy debate) has moved away from this characterisation of a knowledge economy to focus on what is understood to be a new orientation to all economic activity. Fundamental to this approach is the view that economic activity is differentially globally networked, linking people and organisations and practices in distributed production and supply chains. These networks make new demands on the capacity of people and organisations to produce new knowledge. Powell and Snellman adopt this perspective when they define the knowledge economy as:

> production and services based on knowledge-intensive activities that contribute to an accelerated pace of technological and scientific advance as well as rapid obsolescence. The key components of a knowledge economy include a greater reliance on intellectual capabilities than on physical inputs or natural resources, combined with efforts to integrate improvements in every stage of the production process, from the R&D lab to the factory floor to the interface with customers.
>
> (Powell and Snellman 2004: 201)

This approach, now articulated in policy documents of the OECD, suggests that the most fundamental shift in economic activity is the erasure of established categories like industry or high-tech sectors and even the previously undisputed distinction between products and services:

> increasingly, knowledge and related intangibles not only make businesses go but are all or part of the 'products' firms offer. Old distinctions between manufactured objects, services and ideas are breaking down.
>
> (Davenport and Prusak 1998: 47)

From this perspective, economic activity has not so much been transformed as it has been hybridised. Powell and Snellman draw our attention to 'new economy' businesses like Amazon.com that rely on complex applications of ICT to figure out what their customers are buying and, in doing so, produce new trends: at the same time they utilise an industrial-era warehousing system (albeit one that is globally distributed) to store and track their products. Similarly, eBay utilises sophisticated internet technologies to tap into a range of global niche markets and relies heavily on a postal system developed centuries ago. In the same way, 'old economy' businesses, like automotive manufacture and mining for instance, exploit the design possibilities of digital technologies to simultaneously develop and produce goods, and rely on the communicative potential of email in a globally distributed supply chain.

The shift in understanding of the knowledge-based economy has altered notions of what constitutes knowledge, who needs to know it and how it might be learned. From an emphasis on technical knowledge there is now a greater emphasis on capacity to make and use new knowledge in collaboration, that is, to view knowledge as a social production. While technical knowledge remains important, its rapid obsolescence makes technical training precarious. More critical are skills associated with integrating new technical knowledge into existing work practices, and with problem solving more generally. Associated with this shift is increasing emphasis on what have been called 'soft skills', especially communication skills and, more contentiously, skills of self-presentation, self-marketing and self-management (Thompson *et al.* 2001). Communication skills are self-evidently necessary when workers operate in distributed environments (when they are not in physical proximity) but are also fore-grounded when knowledge is understood to be social – to be produced by people in collaboration. At a more fundamental level, literacy, especially in English, is critical if workers are to be able to participate in many of the international and corporate quality assurance practices that require documentation. The Quality Manuals of global corporations, for instance, often extend to the work practices of local companies that supply the global corporation. They may require that workers on the factory floor work in teams to solve problems and document their problem-solving practices. If the problem is solved, but the team fails to document its processes, then the company may be in danger of losing its preferred supplier status (Farrell 2006, Hull 2000, Jackson 2004).

This is not say that all workers are now, or can be, knowledge workers in the generally accepted sense of the term, released from the burden of physical labour to solve problems and innovate, autonomous in their organisations and mobile at their own initiative across corporations and geographical boundaries. Several commentators argue that for most people, in most parts of the world, the technical aspects of work are standardised and that little innovation at the technical level is required or even permitted (Thompson *et al.* 2001, Brown and Lauder 2006). People comprising the bulk of the global workforce may rarely use the technical knowledge they have learned but they will use all the communicative strategies they have developed, in formal education as well as on (and off) the job. It is in this arena that routine knowledgeable workers will be required to innovate. In short, most work involves knowledge production of new and different kinds and even the most relentless physical labour is caught up in a web of documentation demanded by the global knowledge economy.

Who is the 'global workforce'?

While it is certainly true that a relatively small group of elite knowledge workers are innovators and designers trading their skills on a global market, the rest of us tend to live and work in the same location in relatively routinised activities that may appear to have far more to do with local concerns and relationships than with global linkages. So how can we think about a global workforce? While certain segments of the workforce (elite knowledge workers, 'guest workers') are global in the sense that they are increasingly mobile across national boundaries, it is also true that far more workers are affected by the mobility of work itself. In short, companies outsource work. As capital seeks the cheapest and least regulated production zones, and the most lucrative markets, certain kinds of work activity move rapidly around the globe. From this mobility and distribution of work springs demand for greater standardisation of knowledge, greater coordination and control of supply chains, and tighter connections threading together far-flung communities and individuals.

As we were finalising this chapter, Australian newspapers were reporting two stories about globally mobile workers. The first story was concerned with fast-food chain McDonald's recruitment of staff from the Philippines, Britain, the Middle East and India to work in remote towns in Western Australia. McDonald's management argued that they had tried to recruit locally but had failed because the resources boom in Western Australia had created a labour shortage as potential workers took up comparatively much more highly paid positions with mining companies. However, while there is certainly a skilled labour shortage in most parts of Western Australia, the indigenous population (about 15 per cent of the total population in this area) is suffering from massive unemployment – about 40 per cent of indigenous people in the area cannot find work. A local government official offered the view that international corporations had to be prepared to put effort into training local indigenous people if they were to keep their promise to employ locally.

The second story was concerned with the meat industry's attempt to extend the importation of temporary workers under a special visa program. The meat industry argued that there were not enough skilled workers to supply the industry, and that workers had to be imported. The union argued that there was no skill shortage in the area – the industry simply wanted to hire workers satisfied with lower wages, workers who had had fewer or ambiguous industrial rights under their temporary visa arrangements. The Government was reportedly reluctant to offer permanent residence (and the associated rights) to these workers, arguing that temporary visas allowed for a more flexible workforce in the meat industry.

These two instances illustrate one way that workers can be considered global. In each case migrant workers were imported because of a real or perceived local skill shortage, while the option of training a potential local workforce was not pursued. In each case the workers reside in Australia under a special visa and their rights as residents (and as workers) are thereby restricted. This practice is hardly exclusive to Australia – the category of 'guest worker' or 'migrant worker' has been a vexed one for many years in Europe, and recently in Canada, where vigorous debates rage about the extent to which the position of worker should confer the full entitlements of citizen, or at least of permanent resident.

A global workforce is not, however, necessarily composed only of workers (whether they are at the top end or at the bottom end of the food chain) who move around the globe. The outsourcing of production and functions like accounting or customer service is now a ubiquitous organisational practice. In these arrangements it is the work which is mobile – the workforce which may be considered global but relatively stationary. The work practices and even conditions are subject to such highly prescriptive internationally standardised protocols, procedures and documentation that local policies and practices matter less. These processes and protocols can be part of individual corporate deals, like the Quality Manuals of the major global automotive companies (Scholtz and Prinsloo 2001). At other times they are part of international quality assurance certifications programmes like QS or ISO. Whatever is the case they require that workers, whether they are located in Boston, in Banglaore or in Bermuda, fill out the same forms, observe the same quality assurance practices and sometimes adopt the same problem-solving practices.

From this perspective, a significant part of work-related education is global too, and work-related education is critical to creating a global workforce that is, nonetheless, geographically and temporally distributed. Motorola's 'Six Sigma' training programme, for instance, is undertaken by Motorola workers all over the world, and is syndicated to other global corporations. It is also part of some universities' MBA programmes. Its pervasiveness means that Motorola has a pool of managers at any location who have learned the Motorola way and the Motorola value system. In important respects we can say that education and training, organised on a global scale, are core networks through which a global workforce is created.

We must, however, avoid the temptation to simplify and trivialise the importance of location – local knowledge, local history and geography, local people and local problems – in claiming that workforces are global. Global workforces are local workforces too. Clearly certain kinds of economic activity cluster in certain physical locations despite the 'death of distance' sometimes attributed to ICT, faster transportation and open global markets. As Porter (1998) asks:

> if location matters less why then is it true that the odds of finding a world-class mutual-fund company in Boston are much higher than in most any other place?
>
> (Porter 1998: 77)

If the finance industry, with its heavy reliance on ICT and on open global markets, is tied so firmly to place it can hardly be surprising if other industries are also tethered in sometimes invisible ways to their specific locations. While the idea that knowledge, economic activity and workforces are all globally networked is important, it can also be misleading. Knowledge is embedded in local communities and economic activity shapes local and regional development. For example the hub of ICT, Silicon Valley, relies on people who choose to relocate there physically from all over the world, even though the cost of living is very high and the lifestyle stressful. The place itself has a history of over 90 years' involvement in technological innovation, with the immediate presence of a depth and breadth of highly experienced people, expertise and infrastructure, and close material links to complementary industries. So in all,

> the networked economy is not just a technological network carrying digital information, but a social network supporting the creation of human knowledge.
>
> (Brown and Duguid 2002: 436)

Silicon Valley is uniquely situated – geographically, socially, economically and historically. Those conditions cannot be replicated elsewhere, or at least not without resulting in economic servitude. The lesson to be learned from Silicon Valley, argue Brown and Duguid, is to exploit the local. Their point is that, for many countries, local, historically and culturally embedded knowledge and economic activity may be at least part of the solution as well as the problem. Brazil is often cited as an example of a country that has successfully developed a lucrative niche market in the very high-tech, highly productive biotech industry by exploiting local knowledge ecologies (Ferrer *et al.* 2004, da Silveira and Borges 2005). The knowledge of agriculture workers, as well as the biochemists and the ICT experts, has been critical to the development of biotechnology in the fields of health and agriculture, producing an ecology that could not be replicated in the most well-resourced high-tech environment. In that sense at least, the individuals, the industry and the national economy are all less vulnerable than they might otherwise be to appropriation.

Education and the global workforce

We began this chapter by asking what education promises the global workforce, and what the global workforce, and the knowledge economy, might reasonably ask of education. So far we have argued that debates around the knowledge-based economy (however it is understood) have offered a generally uncritical rationale for the development of work-related education. Clearly all aspects of education and training are being recruited to support and develop a knowledge-based economy. What educators and policy makers at national, regional and international levels need to do now is to cast a critical eye over the past and to consider, with far greater clarity than we have managed in the past, what role work-related education should play in the future. As part of those deliberations we need to consider who work-related education is intended to benefit and what kinds of knowledge-based economies it should be helping to build. A first step in this process is to view economic globalisation in a less deterministic way than is often the case in education research and debate, and to view workers and work-related educators as having some agency in the complex and contradictory processes of economic globalisation we have referred to above. Appadurai's invitation (2001) to educators is to worry less about globalisation from above, with its standardisations and homogenisation, and to focus more on globalisation from below – the problems of ordinary people in the global everyday. This focus is upon the potential that global networks offer for the circulation of ideas – human imaginations – and resources that can generate collective patterns of dissent and new designs for collective life. These alternative imaginings and possibilities can feed directly into the immediate and specific needs of local communities. Globalisation from below involves local and global players collaborating in internal criticism and debate, horizontal exchange and learning, and vertical collaborations and partnerships with more powerful persons and organizations together form[ing] a mutually sustaining cycle of processes.

(Appadurai 2002: 24)

This kind of process invokes powerful non-nation actors of all sorts – NGOs, institutions, firms, transnational advocates, academics, international agencies, public intellectuals – in a relationship of dialogue rather than one of domination with local and regional communities. For Appadurai the main problem is the growing disjuncture between the globalisation of knowledge and the knowledge of globalisation. He proposes that this dialogue, this education, needs to open spaces: to bridge languages, to study globalisation from below (its institutions, its horizons, its vocabularies), and to share knowledge about globalisation drawing on multiple global resources. Local workforces can operate more powerfully in local economies when connected with, not just used by or sold, the flow of capital, ideas, technologies and strategies circulating in global knowledge economies. If we think about work-related education from this perspective we may view its challenges somewhat differently. We may direct our attention much more to the skills and knowledge that people and communities enact to leverage global networks at local sites, and less to the urgent calls fitting people to standardised processes, migration routes, consumption patterns and knowledge protocols.

References

Appadurai, A. (2001) 'Grassroots globalization and the research imagination', in A. Appadurai (ed.) *Globalization*. Durham, NC: Duke Press.

Appadurai, A. (2002) 'Deep democracy: urban governmentality and the horizon of politics', *Public Culture*, 14 (1): 21–47.

Brock-Utne, B. (2000) *Whose Education for All? The colonization of the African mind*. New York: Falmer Press.

Brown, J.S. and P. Duguid (2002) 'Local knowledge: innovation in the networked age', *Management Learning*, 33 (4): 427–37.

Brown, P. and H. Lauder (2006) 'Globalisation, knowledge and the myth of the magnet economy', *Globalisation, Education and Societies*, 4 (1): 25–57.

Chase-Dunn, C. (1999) 'Globalization: a world-systems perspective', *Journal of World-Systems Research*, 2: 187–215.

Dale, R. and S. L. Robertson (2002) 'The varying effects of regional organizations as subjects of globalization of education', *Comparative Education Review*, 46: 1–36.

da Silveira, J.M.F.J. and I.C. Borges (2005) *An Overview of the Current State of Agricultural Biotechnology in Brazil*. Bellagio, Italy: Belfer Centre, STTP Kennedy School of Government, Harvard University.

Davenport, T.H. and L. Prusak (1998). *Working Knowledge: How Organizations Manage What They Know*. Boston: Harvard Business School Press.

de Ferranti, D., G.E. Perry, D. Lederman and W.F. Maloney (2002) *From Natural Resources to the Knowledge Economy*. Washington, DC: World Bank Latin American and Caribbean Studies.

Edwards, R. and R. Usher (2000) *Globalisation and Pedagogy: Place, Space and Identity*. London and New York: Routledge.

Farrell, L. (2006) *Making Knowledge Common: Literacy and Knowledge at Work*. New York: Peter Lang & Co.

Ferrer, M., H. Thorsteinsdottir, U. Quach, P.A. Singer and A.S. Daar (2004) 'The scientific muscle of Brazil's health biotechnology', *Nature Biotechnology Supplement*, 22: 8–12.

Friedman, T.L. (2006) *The World is Flat*, New York: Farrer Straus and Giroux.

Grov, H. (1999) 'Cope and non-formal education – strategies toward education for all. A Focus on Relevance and Learning', Master (hovedfag) thesis. Oslo: Institute for Educational Research

Hull, G. (2000) 'Critical literacy at work', *Journal of Adolescent and Adult Literacy*, 43 (7): 648–52.

Imam, S.R. (2005) 'English as a global language and the question of nation-building education in Bangladesh', *Comparative Education*, 41 (4): 471–86.

Jackson, N. (2004) 'Introduction', in M.E. Belifore, T.A. Defoe, S. Folinsbee, J. Hunter and N.S. Jackson (eds) *Reading Work: Literacies in the New Workplaces*. Mahwah, NJ: Lawrence Earlbaum Associates: 1–15.

OECD (2005) *Education at a Glance 2005*. OECD Education.

Porter, M.E. (1998) 'Clusters and the new economics of competition', *Harvard Business Review*, Nov–Dec: 77–90.

Powell, W. and K. Snellman (2004) 'The knowledge economy', *Annual Review of Sociology*, 30: 199–220.

Reich, R. (1991) *The Work of Nations: Preparing Ourselves for 21st Century Capitalism*. London: Simon and Schuster.

Scholtz, S. and M. Prinsloo (2001) 'New workplaces, new literacies, new identities', *Journal of Adolescent and Adult Literacy*, 44 (8): 710–13.

Slowinski, J. (1998) 'SOCRATES invades Europe', *Education Policy Analysis Archives*, 6 (9): 1–26.

Stiglitz, J.E. (2002) *Globalization and its Discontents*. New York/London: Norton.

Thompson, P., C. Warhurst and G. Callaghan (2001) 'Ignorant theory and knowledgeable workers: interrogating the connections between knowledge, skills and services', *Journal of Management Studies*, 38 (7): 923–42.

Tikly, L. (2001) 'Globalisation and education in the postcolonial world: towards a conceptual framework', *Comparative Education*, 37 (22): 151–71.

World Bank (2003) 'Lifelong learning in the global knowledge economy: challenges for developing countries: a World Bank report'. Washington, DC: World Bank.

2 Globalisation, work and indigenous knowledge in the global marketplace

The New Zealand experience

Makere Stewart-Harawira

Since the completion of the economic architecture for global governance in the mid-1990s, we have seen the overt emergence of an imperialist agenda that has been long in the making. As in the past, the construction of new hierarchies of knowledge and the reshaping of society is central to this agenda. Allied to this is the emergence of new forms of social Darwinism associated with universalist notions of an enterprise culture and the knowledge economy.

The reshaping of knowledge and society is a phenomenon that, from an indigenous perspective in particular, has long and familiar roots. At the local level, the impact of globalisation on the role of the nation state and the recasting of its role as mediator between local policy and capital and the global economy, has shaped indigenous peoples' relationships with globalisation in often contradictory ways.

This chapter explores the implications of these developments for indigenous peoples' knowledge and aspirations in the twenty-first century and the importance of traditional indigenous worldviews in revisioning the meaning of "being in the world".

Introduction

In Canada recently, at the formal signing of a Memorandum of Understanding between Blue Quills Tribal College in Saddlelake Reserve and the University of Alberta, the Provincial Minister for Advanced Education spoke with eloquence about the role of higher education in promoting the knowledge economy and the responsibility of graduates to contribute back to the Province and facilitate provincial engagement in the global economy, thus contributing to their responsibility to become good citizens. There is of course nothing new in these laudable ambitions. The function of education in creating good citizens and in honing the competitive economic edge has been one of the markers of high modernity since the Enlightenment. In the contemporary moment, the intertwining of citizenship with the economic good has become a key signifier of "good" educational policy.

The extent to which these ambitions have coherence with the aims and goals of the graduates from tribal colleges whose aims include enhanced self-determination in a province in which they are consistently unrepresented in positive socio-economic statistics, may be questionable. There are additional problems with these articulations and it is these that I intend to comment on in addressing the overall focus of this chapter. The first problem is the impoverished view of both knowledge and citizenship that is represented in such articulations. The second is the employment of education as a means of reordering society. The third is the ongoing marginalisation of particular kinds of ontologies, in this case, indigenous knowledge.

The primary objective of this chapter is to argue that in the market-driven climate of adult education and a world increasingly preoccupied with terrorism, commodities, power and greed, the values, world views, and understandings of our place in the world which are expressed within indigenous ontologies have a critical role to play in the articulation of a different vision for global society. Yet despite policies such as those which purport to "infuse" indigenous values into mainstream educational curriculae, indigenous ontologies are under renewed attack as neoclassical economics and neoliberal ideologies tighten their hold over the drivers of socio-economic policies, interpretations of sustainability and resiliency, and, of course, education. At the same time, ironically, the same forces that formerly decried the validity and value of indigenous traditional knowledge now actively mine it for its economic value and marketability.

It is true to say, I think, that there has never been a time when the eco-centred humanism and spiritual connectedness that is broadly represented in many indigenous belief systems and world views has been more urgently needed. In making this claim, I want to make it clear that I do not argue for an essentialist view of indigenous knowledge, neither do I suggest that the kinds of values and world views represented in this discussion are unique to indigenous peoples, for that is demonstrably not the case. My intention is to demonstrate the ways in which such values and perspectives are currently endangered by ideologically driven policies manifest notably within education, and to emphasise the urgency of the imperative for intervention. The backdrop for this discussion is the role of education in promoting Maori[1] educational and economic development in New Zealand since the 1980s.

The impacts of strongly assimilationist policies for Native education by missionaries and other emissaries of Christianity in the first instance, and colonial governments in the second instance, have been well documented. The extinguishments of aboriginal land rights, the denial of the validity of treaties signed between indigenous nations and the colonial powers, the discursive construction of sovereign indigenous nations as "populations" within colonial states and the disestablishment of indigenous social and religious systems accompanied the disciplining of indigenous minds and bodies. The recruitment, training, education and employment of indigenous peoples were fundamental to achieving the colonial goal of constructing them as docile and productive providers of labour.

Like other indigenous peoples who have experienced colonisation, Maori in New Zealand were subjected to a plethora of measures by first, missionaries who paved the way for colonisation, and second, the colonial apparatus of the British Empire. From the time of first contact in the early eighteenth century culminating in the signing of a formal treaty between heads of some Maori tribes and the British Crown in 1840, Maori were subjected to increasingly radical methods of domination. As elsewhere, warfare, and when that failed, education, were the primary tools of suppression, assimilation and social control. And again as elsewhere, access to land and resources was the underlying agenda. By 1868, the numbers of settlers had surpassed the Maori population. By 1867 and the involvement of the colonial state in the provision of formal education and training for Maori, the alienation of Maori land, language and culture was well under way.

Impelled by the threat of imminent language loss combined with the continuing state appropriation of Maori language, by the mid-1970s Maori had developed strong and effective interventions that sought to reassert the legitimacy of Maori knowledge, the revitalisation of Maori language and culture, and a transformation of Maori social, economic and political positioning in New Zealand society. Currently 15 per cent of the total population of New Zealand (a figure that is expected to increase to 17 per cent by 2021), Maori have since made significant gains in reducing their over-representation in negative social indices including education and employment. The appointment in the mid-1970s of a tribunal to oversee the hearing of Maori grievances stemming from the betrayal by the Crown of the promises given in the Treaty of Waitangi and the ongoing confiscation of Maori land, has also played a key role in facilitating Maori social and economic development. Today however, under the impact of neoliberal policies and a Conservative drive to regain the popular vote, Maori are experiencing a significant backlash and retrenchment of proactive government policies. Even more worrying is a renewed attack on traditional Maori knowledge forms and values – an attack that comes from both without and within. At the heart of this attack are fundamental questions of what constitutes knowledge, the kind of knowledge that is required to move society forward, and our vision of the future.

Power, knowledge and the reordering of society

The production of knowledge as the most important form of global capital has taken centre stage in the advancement of global capitalism, altering the basis of economic activity in fundamental ways (Burton-Jones 1999 cited in Peters 2002). Nebulous and ambiguous, the knowledge economy discourse operates as a new form of socio/economic exclusion/ inclusion which is driven by the exigencies of the competitive state and the global market. Underpinning these new social divisions is the construction of new hierarchies of knowledge that are determined by market value. Historically, the reordering of knowledge and the legitimating of sets of ideas that occur within particular historical conjunctures have been allied to profound changes in the shape of the society. Today they are aligned to "changes in the international institutions, social movements and technology and the knowledge economy" (Popkewitz 1997: 37).

Fundamental parallels can be drawn between the developments of modernity that directly reshaped the politico/economic structural framework of the former imperial world and the reformulation of knowledge and being in the context of globalisation and new forms of imperialism (cf. Hardt and Negri 2000; Stewart-Harawira 2005). In the fifteenth and sixteenth centuries, the developments of modernity led to a radical transformation in the nature of knowledge and the meaning of being such that the understanding of the unity of "One" promulgated in Renaissance humanism was relinquished in favour of Cartesian rationality based on division and separation and a reconstruction of the nature and goals of "science" (Stewart-Harawira 2005: 43–5). In the developments of today's postmodern imperialism, the meaning of knowledge and being and the nature of society are again being reformulated by capitalism's most powerful allies.

The administrative apparatuses of territorial monarchies and government apparatuses that were developed during the period of modernity were linked to the development of particular forms of knowledge. The shift in the nature of governance was accompanied by a radical transformation in the conceptualisation of nature and existence accompanied by an equally radical shift in the nature of knowledge. Despite challenges by thinkers such as Pascal, Leibniz and Spinoza in the seventeenth century and Rousseau and Kant in the eighteenth century, the empiricism of Cartesian thought converged with the shift towards the economy in governance, and gave birth to new forms of disciplinarity and social control for which education was a primary vehicle.

It was this period that saw the development of mechanisms concerned with the exercising of power over "human bodies and their operations" (Foucault 1980: 104), in particular the extraction of time and labour for the production of wealth. During the eighteenth century, the notion of the population emerged in ways that "interconnected the science of government, the recentring of the theme of the economy … and the problem of population" (Foucault 1991: 98–9). This was the point at which the introduction of the economy into political practice became seen as the epitome of good government and citizenship as a tool for the production of capital, rather than an end in itself. The conditions by which states were finally able to exert absolute rule over populations were reached in the period of the late nineteenth to early twentieth centuries. These conditions were fulfilled in the combining of "aspiration to the administrative ordering of nature and society", described as "high modernism", "the unrestrained use of the power of the modern state" as the instrument for achieving these ends, and "a weakened … civil society that lacks the capacity to resist" (Scott 1998: 88–9).

The re-engineering of social life as a means of transforming society has a long history in which elites from both ends of the political spectrum sought to shape the world according to their own dreams and ambitions. Visionary elites of the past have included Henri Comte de Saint-Simon, the Shah of Iran, Vladimir Lenin, Leon Trotsky and Julius Nyere, to name but a few. They shared a conviction in the ability to transform society through a sweeping re-engineering of social life, yet came from both ends of the political spectrum. What is important about these grand experiments in social engineering is the authoritarian high-modernist environments in which they took root (Scott 1998), the role of the state and the political economy, and the dominance of particular forms of knowledge as universal epistemes in the remoulding of society, cloaked to be sure, in egalitarian notions of equality, citizenship, and in our time, democracy. Today's critical moment is marked by a clash between new and increasingly dangerous forms of state authoritarianism and the increasing loss of civil liberties, and the resurgence of strong civil resistance. Fundamental to this latter process is the recovery of local subjugated knowledges and a revisioning of the nature of society.

New formations of liberalism and the reconstruction of citizenship

During the 1970s and 1980s, the resurgence of indigenous activism in the local, national and international arenas coalesced around the politicising of indigenous identity and demands for a recognition of indigenous peoples' collective and inherent rights. Foucault (1980: 81–2) defined subjugated knowledges in two ways; first, as "historical contents" which functionalism and/or formal systemisation buried or disguised, and second, as whole sets of knowledges that have been disqualified from the hierarchy of knowledge and sciences on the basis of their alleged naiveté or irrelevance.

The insurrection of subjugated indigenous knowledges was central in the development of indigenous counter discourses at the global and local levels and became a vehicle for reaffirming the importance of indigenous spiritual and cultural traditions as well as rights. Fundamental commonly held indigenous spiritual principles include the notion of deep interconnectedness and the intermeshing of the material and spiritual worlds. Other concepts speak to issues of reciprocity and balance, to the particular and spiritual significance of indigenous peoples' relationship with their lands, rivers, mountains, forests, lakes, and other elements of the natural world, a relationship based on belonging and stewardship, and compassion as the fundamental attribute of "the indigenous mind". The reassertion of many of these principles was in part the basis of political and cultural interventions by which indigenous peoples sought to regain measures of self-determination. These principles were also fundamental to education strategies developed by and for indigenous peoples in some parts of the colonised world as a critical means of intervening in the negative social statistics in which indigenous peoples were grossly over-represented.

The counter-discourses and strategies of resistance of indigenous peoples impacted on the reshaping of international human rights instruments and on the development of new forms of engagement at the national and international level. Within the structures and institutions of international order, the right of indigenous peoples to self-determination became one of the most hotly contested principles in international law. Significantly, no sooner was this right affirmed within the UN Human Rights Commission framework, than it became discursively reframed as a "right to development". Likewise, the particular nature of the relationship of indigenous peoples to their traditional lands and territories has been increasingly recognised within various international instruments. In most cases, these too are framed within discourses of a "right to development".[2] For instance, in a "written statement of some significance", one of the five members of the UN Working Group on Indigenous Peoples (1987) suggested that indigenous peoples' requests for "autonomy" could be usefully interpreted as an "instrument necessary for their development and the development of their members, as well as the state as a whole" (Turk 1987 cited in Kingsbury 1989: 140). This, he suggested, would lead to autonomy for indigenous peoples being reinterpreted, "not as an end in itself or a first step to political independence but rather an instrument necessary for their development and for the development of the state as a whole" (Kingsbury 1989: 141).

States responded to indigenous peoples' interventions and the resultant changes within international law in a variety of ways. In New Zealand, the strength and effectiveness of Maori political and cultural interventions drove the Crown's recognition that failure to develop new relationships with New Zealand's indigenous peoples would undermine investment confidence and actively inhibit the ability of the state to carry out its business (Fleras and Spoonley 1999). By the 1980s and under the driving force of neoliberalism and economic restructuring, policies which arose out of the recognition of rights and responsibility were being reshaped by a much more pragmatic agenda, that of removing barriers to foreign investment. The appointment of a tribunal body to oversee and facilitate claims by Maori against the Crown on the basis of breaches of the 1840 Treaty of Waitangi[3] led to Maori–state relationships renegotiated largely on the basis of grossly under-valued monetary compensations based on treaty claims. Outcomes have been varying and often problematic.

The worst effects of the Treaty settlement approach to redressing the disenfranchisement, and in some cases, genocidal policies that characterised indigenous peoples' relationships with coloniser states has been the impact of liberalist ideologies and the extinction of aboriginal customary rights through treaty settlements in which land is exchanged for money and in which such land as remains within indigenous ownership becomes subject to the imposition of state legislation. This new form of assimilation by the state (Tully 2000) has seen the construction of indigenous peoples as participants in "the consumptive commercial mentality shaped by state corporatism" (Alfred 1999: 114) through a "divide and rule" process which compels indigenous groups who have frequently shared boundaries and territories for specific purposes, to compete against one another in the monetary marketplace.

Indigenous education and the cultural-political project of resistance

Of the interventions by indigenous peoples that occurred during the 1970s and 1980s, one of the most significant occurred in the arena of education, notably in places such as Canada and New Zealand. In the case of the latter, Maori interventionist strategies in the education arena were given impetus by the 1960 Hunn Report which revealed the enormous disparities in educational achievement between Maori and non-Maori (Hunn 1960) and a report which showed Maori language to be facing imminent extinction (Benton 1978). The increasing disparity between Maori and non-Maori across all social indices combined with grave concerns regarding the identified loss of Maori language and culture, became a catalyst for Maori development of proactive responses which operated from within multiple sites including the education system. Coupled with political interventions which included demands for the cessation of the alienation of Maori land and for the return of some measure of self-determination, these strategies ultimately played a significant role in the transformation of the political landscape in New Zealand.

Intervention movements in education by Maori which were initiated in the early 1980s were fuelled by the ongoing failure of state initiatives to successfully intervene in what was seen as "the crisis of Maori education". Calls for the revitalisation of Maori language and culture were predicated on the legitimacy and validity of Maori knowledge, language, world-views, and self-determination. Initially developed and funded by Maori at the grass-roots level, the first immersion education system developed by and for Maori was the *Kohanga Reo* or preschool "language nest". This was followed within a few years by the establishment of total immersion schools at the primary level, later followed by immersion secondary schools. Today there are also three Maori tertiary education institutions.

In these initiatives that emerged somewhat falteringly in the early 1980s and grew rapidly during the 1990s, the recentring of Maori knowledge and language at the centre of a broad range of strategic responses was profoundly important. By 2001, 45 per cent of all Maori children of less than five years of age were enrolled in early childhood education services, and of those, nearly one-third were in Maori immersion preschools. With the revitalisation of Maori language and culture coupled with the advancement of Maori economic and social development as their main objective, these institutions all operate from within a paradigm in which the validity and legitimacy of being Maori and of Maori ways of knowing, is taken for granted (Smith 2002).

Human Capital Theory and neoliberalism

The radical restructuring of states into neoliberal forms that engulfed first, developing, and second, developed countries in the 1980s impacted strongly on states' indigenous peoples' relationships. It also profoundly impacted the nature of education as revived neoclassical forms of Human Capital Theory which made its first appearance in the second half of the nineteenth century became popularised throughout OECD countries (Marginson 1993 cited in Olssen *et al.* 2004).

The influence of Hayekian neoclassical economics promoted firstly by the Austrian School of Economics and promulgated somewhat differently within the Chicago School of Economics in the post-World War II years saw development become aligned with Human Capital Theories that sought to maximise labour and productivity through targeting education. Its re-emergence in the 1960s, influenced by the work of Theodore Schulz and Gary Becker (who declared education to be "the most important single determinant of economic growth"; Becker 1964 cited in Olssen *et al.* 2004: 147), saw the popularising of technical-functionalist theories of education concerned with demonstrating the correlation between levels of education and economic growth measured by GDP. This model sees all rational human action as purposeful, goals-oriented and underpinned by economic self-interest. In the 1980s, economic restructuring coupled with a renewed emphasis on technology saw a resurgence in investment in human capital, albeit in a form adapted to the free market model which has dominated education and other critical policy areas since the mid-1980s. This ideological climate dominated the politico/economic landscape in the years immediately following the resurgence of indigenous resistance initiatives.

The dramatic ideological sea-change in New Zealand's national politics was initiated in 1984 following the snap election of the fourth Labour government. Unlike previous Labour governments, this particular government was dominated by Hayekian ideologues and members of the right-wing lobby group, the New Zealand Business Roundtable, who were pivotal in the reforms that swept the country. Widely referred to as "Rogernomics", named thus after Roger Kerr, the principle architect of New Zealand's restructuring, the reforms involved the dismantling of the Keynesian welfare state, the privatisation and subsequent sale of national assets held within state-owned enterprises, the introduction of a rational choice model into the public health system, and the attempted privatisation of schooling. Recommendations by the Treasury Department became increasingly influential in government policy.

The ideological shift in the nature of education strengthened the transformation and commodification of knowledge and the further marginalisation of non-marketable pedagogies and epistemologies. The 1987 Brief by Treasury to the incoming government became essentially the charter for the dismantling of the centralised education system, the devolution of responsibility for funding to local Boards of Trustees and a competitive funding system through the introduction of bulk funding policies. Perpetual training and the doctrine of "infinite reskilling" as the motivator of "both policy and practice", a model which is underpinned by the neoclassical economic doctrine that individuals are "rational utility maximisers" (Olssen *et al.* 2004: 150), became seen as the solution to economic woes and thus the objective of post-secondary education. This was the climate in which the first Maori economic development summit took place, also, coincidentally, in 1984.

Called to set a platform that would lead to a cultural and economic renaissance for Maori and to find a way forward to the achievement of social and economic parity with non-Maori New Zealanders, the objectives defined for the 1984 Maori Economic Development Conference included devolution of the responsibility for Maori development to Maori themselves. This became the foundation for the first decade of Maori development. It is significant that the new direction for Maori articulated at that first summit was congruent with the goals for reduced state dependency, devolution and privatisation that were being driven by the government's New Right agenda (Durie 2005). Devolution opened the way for Maori to become major service deliverers within the health, education, welfare and labour sectors, despite "disquieting signals that it was a government manoeuvre for economic reform and cost cutting at Maori expense" (Durie 2005: 4). The establishment of the first Maori immersion preschool programme, initially without state funding, the subsequent development of Maori immersion primary and secondary schools and the opening of the first of three Maori post-secondary educational institutions in New Zealand in 1992 were the visible expression of these goals. The corporatisation of Maori governance structures followed.

Economic development for the global market

Twenty years after the first Maori economic summit and the development of the first Maori immersion education programmes, the 2005 Maori Economic Development Conference took as its credo three broad objectives: developing assets, developing people, developing enterprise (Hui Taumata 2005). The background papers and presentations prepared for the 2005 Maori Economic Development Conference are instructive.

In 1998, the Ministry of Development report, "Closing the Gaps" (Ministry of Education 1998), concluded that mainstream education for Maori had resoundingly failed to address the disparities between Maori and non-Maori. Until 1999, according to the Ministry in 2005, Maori continued to be under-represented at all levels of tertiary education (Ministry of Education 2005). Since 2002, Maori have moved to having the highest participation rate in tertiary education of any ethnic group in New Zealand. Most of this, however, occurs at the lower levels. At the higher levels, Maori continue to be under-represented and to have lower retention and completion levels.

In the last eighteen years, Maori have experienced substantial change in the labour market (Department of Labour 2005). Despite having been the most adversely affected by the economic restructuring policies of the late 1980s and early 1990s, by 2003 Maori had the lowest rate of unemployment ever recorded. Yet Maori are still more than two and a half times more likely to be unemployed than non-Maori. Responses to the background reports presented at the Maori Economic Development Conference are equally interesting. In a number of influential papers, the application of Human Capital Theories was seen as the only viable pathway to Maori economic development.

In his keynote address to the 2005 Maori Economic Development Conference, the Chair of the New Zealand Business Roundtable, Ron McLeod, compared data regarding wealth by ethnicity produced by Statistics New Zealand showing the net worth of Pakeha or non-Maori New Zealanders to be three times that of Maori (McLeod 2005). Taking the aggregate value of Maori-collectively owned land held in various forms of trust, McLeod argued for the restructuring of collective models of Maori land ownership into one which would provide for shares in a land-owning company which would "enable land to be transacted by an agent for a group of owners based on a creed of maximising the interests of all owners" as a means of increasing Maori-held assets.

A keynote address by the Chief Executive Officer of Te Runanga o Ngai Tahu, the corporation responsible for managing the affairs of one of the now wealthiest tribes in New Zealand, advocated a similar approach. In Potiki's view, the ideology of "not one more acre", meaning no further loss of Maori land for any reason whatsoever, has "contaminated [Maori] ability to think outside the box" (Potiki 2005: 7). According to both perspectives, rather than being spiritually and ideologically bound, Maori should adopt a rational utility maximiser approach, both to education and training, and to their relationship with the lands and waters. This approach in many cases now drives the translation of deeply valued genealogical links not only to ancestors but also indeed to the whole of creation, into economic beneficiaries as stakeholders in corporatised tribal trustboards.

Indigenous knowledge – challenge and opportunity in the global imperium

The reshaping of education policy within the framework of the global economy saw the entry of market-oriented discourses of "flexibility and cutting-edge innovation into the lexicon of education" (Blackmore 2000: 133–56). For Maori, these discourses have impacted in two notable ways; in an increased demand for the development of human capital largely through skills-based training and education, and in an increasing trend towards the commodification of knowledge and resources traditionally held sacred. Against these trends, however, is an alignment of Maori scholars and activists committed to the preservation and strengthening of traditional knowledge and values as the foundation for future Maori social and economic development.

The critical question facing indigenous educationalists is that of an effective response to the challenge of the rational utility maximiser model of knowledge and development. One such approach based on an analysis of pre-European Maori political economy is an "economy of affection" model (Henare 1997) developed from Maori traditional knowledge systems. Based on "kinship, solidarity, spirituality and guardianship", these knowledge systems were underpinned by beliefs that "exemplified the connectivity between all living things, the ancestral linkages to the gods from whom we all originate, and the intrinsic sacredness of all things animate and inanimate". This view that "all things are sacred and all things are connected" implies a model of relationality that is based on "the need for mutual respect and care, 'humanism' based on humanity and humility" (Henry 2000).

In today's dangerously divided neo-imperial world, there is an urgent need for a re-examination of how we construct the nature of knowledge and being, and critically, the ways in which we construct and interpret "other". In indigenous epistemologies and ontologies, deep interconnectedness is the paramount principle governing all relationships. In today's imperialism, the "other" includes any and all who express difference and opposition – difference from the goals of capitalism's imperial masters and knowledge as its tool; opposition to a politics which constructs difference and the longing to have one's homeland intact and whole – as "terrorism". The spiritual and cultural principles that underpin traditional indigenous knowledge bases are indeed under renewed attack, so too is the nature of being human, and compassion as its deepest expression.

There is, however, hope; hope that the development of effective and principled educational practices can and will model alternative and effective ways of successfully "being in the world" in deep and compassionate interrelationship. Indigenous peoples have a great deal to contribute to that process. The will and responsibility to do so, however, rests with all of us, with indigenous educators, with communities and with all individuals of good heart.

Notes

1 The term "Maori" is a generic term applied in the post-contact period to the indigenous or first peoples of New Zealand.
2 For a detailed discussion of the elaboration of international legal norms concerning indigenous rights to their lands and territories, see Anaya (1996: 104–7).
3 An agreement between Maori tribes and the British Crown which in the Maori version guaranteed Maori full British citizenship and the retention of Maori sovereignty while according the Crown the right to govern. The English version in contrast states that Maori ceded sovereignty to the British Crown. These two clearly differing versions have been a source of considerable controversy.

References

Alfred, T. (1999) *Peace, Power, Righteousness: An Indigenous Manifesto*. Ontario: Oxford University Press.

Anaya, S. James (1996) *Indigenous Peoples in International Law*. New York: Oxford University Press.

Benton, R. (1978) "Results of sociolinguistic survey of language use in Maori households". Wellington: New Zealand Council for Educational Research.

Blackmore, J. (2000) "Globalization: a useful concept for feminists rethinking theory and strategies in education?" in N.C. Burbules and C.A. Torres (eds) *Globalization and Education: Critical Perspectives*. London and New York: Routledge, 133–56.

Burton-Jones, A. (1999) *Knowledge Capitalism: Business, Work and Learning in the New Economy*. Oxford: Oxford University Press.

Department of Labour (2005) "Trends in Maori Labour Market Outcomes 1980–2003". Available at: http://www.huitaumata.maori.nz/pdf/labour.pdf (accessed April 2006).

Durie, M. (2005) "Te Tai Tini. Transformations 2025". 2005 Hui Taumata. Available at: http://www.huitaumata.maori.nz/pdf/speeches/Keynotes_Durie.pdf (accessed April 2006).

Fleras, A. and Spoonley, P. (1999) *Recalling Aotearoa: Indigenous Politics and Ethnic Relations in New Zealand*. Auckland: Oxford University Press.

Foucault, M. (1980) "Two lectures", in C. Gordon (ed.) *Power/Knowledge: Selected Interviews and Other Writings 1972–1977*. New York and London: Harvester Wheatsheaf.

Foucault, M. (1991) "Governmentality", in G. Burchell, C. Gordon and P. Miller (eds) *The Foucault Effect: Studies in Governmentality*. Chicago: University of Chicago Press, 87–104.

Hardt, M. and Negri, A. (2000) *Empire*. Cambridge, MA: Harvard University Press.

Henare, M. (1997) "Tapu, mauri, hau, mana: a Maori philosophy of vitalism and the cosmos". Presented at the Conference on Indigenous Traditions and Ecology, 13–16 November, Centre for the Study of World Religions, Divinity School, Harvard University.

Henry, E. (2000) "International trade – APEC and Maori development". Paper presented at the UN Commission on Sustainable Development. CSD-8: Panel on Trade and Indigenous People: Statements. Available at: http://www.un.org/esa/sustdev/mgroups/mgipday3.htm (accessed December 2005).

Hui Taumata (2005) "A brief backgrounder". Background stimulus paper prepared by the Hui Taumata. Available at: http://www.huitaumata.maori.nz/pdf/hui_paper.pdf#search= per cent22Hui per cent20Taumata per cent20objectives per cent201984 per cent22 (accessed 4 April 2006).

Hunn, J.K. (1960) "Report on Department of Maori Affairs with statistical supplement", 24 August 1960 [1961]. Appendices to the Journal of the House of Representatives, G-10 [Hunn Report].

Kawharu, I.H (1989) *Waitangi: Maori and Pakeha Perspectives of the Treaty of Waitangi*. Auckland: Oxford University Press, 121–57.

Kingsbury, B. (1989) "The Treaty of Waitangi: some international law aspects", I. H.

Marginson, S. (1993) *Education and Public Policy in Australia*. Melbourne: Cambridge University Press.

McLeod, R. (2005) "Developing assets". Keynote address, Hui Taumata 2005. Available at: http://www.huitaumata.maori.nz/pdf/speeches/Keynote-McLeod.doc (accessed March 2006).

Ministry of Education (1998) "Closing the gaps". Wellington: NZ Government Printer.

Ministry of Education (2005) "Maori in tertiary education: a picture of the trends". Available at: http://www.huitaumata.maori.nz/pdf/tertiary.pdf (accessed April 2006).

New Zealand Business Roundtable (2005) Available at: http://www.huitaumata.maori.nz/pdf/businessnz.pdf (accessed April 2006).

Olssen, M., Codd, J. and O'Neill, A. (2004) *Education Policy: Globalization, Citizenship and Democracy*. London and New Delhi: Sage.

Peters, M. (2002) "Education policy in the age of knowledge capitalism". Keynote address to the World Comparative Education Forum, Economic Globalization and Education Reform, Bejing Normal University, 14–16 October 2002.

Popkewitz, T.S. (1997) "A social epistemology of educational research", in T.S. Popkewitz and L. Fendler (eds) *Critical Theories in Education: Changing Terrains of Knowledge and Politics*. New York and London: Routledge, 17–44.

Potiki, T. (2005) "Developing assets". Keynote address, Hui Taumata 2005. Available at: http://www.huitaumata.maori.nz/pdf/speeches/Keynotes_Potiki.doc (accessed 21 April 2006).

Scott, J.C. (1998) *Seeing Like a State: How Certain Schemes to Improve the Human Condition Have Failed*. New York: Yale University.

Smith, G. (2002) "Kaupapa Maori theory: transformative praxis and new formations of colonisation". Presented at "Cultural Sites, Cultural Theory, Cultural Policy", Second International Conference on Cultural Policy Research, Wellington, New Zealand.

Statistics New Zealand (2005) "Maori population: looking out to 2021". Available at: http://www.huitaumata.maori.nz/pdf/population.pdf (accessed April 2006).

Stewart-Harawira, M. (2005) *The New Imperial Order: Indigenous Responses to Globalization*. New Zealand and Australia: Huia Books; London: Zed Books.

Tully, J. (2000) "The struggles of indigenous peoples for and of freedom", in D. Ivison, P. Patton and W. Sanders (eds) *Political Theory and the Rights of Indigenous Peoples*. Cambridge: Cambridge University Press.

3 Whose knowledge counts?

A case study of a joint MBA programme between Australia and China

Rui Yang and Wuhu Yao

Over the past decade, MBA education in China has experienced drastic growth triggered by the unprecedented economic development. With the adoption of the 'open-door' policy and the introduction of the market, Chinese government welcomes foreign universities from developed countries to offer MBA programmes jointly with Chinese institutions in China. While such programmes expose Chinese students to global practices, issues related to curriculum adaptability to the local contexts remain little studied in the literature. Meanwhile, trans-national provision of higher education has increased dramatically during the past decade. Some providers even advocate the 'global template' – a generic product that has no trace of local character of knowledge – in current trans-national higher education courses. Through a case study of a China–Australia joint MBA programme, and based on empirical data, this chapter investigates curriculum adaptability from a perspective of the global–local nexus. It shows how Western-based knowledge is perceived by Chinese students, and analyses how educators, both Australian and Chinese, are influenced by global forces while struggling with local relevance. It delineates an unequal power relationship between foreign (Western) and indigenous knowledge, and questions what counts as 'scholarship'.

Introduction

Over the past decade of rapid economic growth, there has been a surging demand for qualified business administration personnel in China. Master of Business Administration (MBA) education has thus received unprecedented attention. With China's entry into the World Trade Organisation, the government welcomes foreign universities offering joint MBA programmes with Chinese institutions. It is expected that through these programmes Chinese students would broaden their perspectives and familiarise themselves with the global business environment and practices.

In line with the dramatic increase of trans-national higher education provision, foreign institutions are partnering with the Chinese to export their education to China. Some providers even advocate the 'global template', a generic product that has no trace of local character of knowledge, in current trans-national higher education courses (Luke, 2005). On the one hand, this is a continuation of the long-standing 'sanctioned ignorance' that enables an individual discipline or nation to proceed without reference to others, and without fully acknowledging the legacies of colonialism and imperialism (Appadurai, 2001). There is a need to question this in order to reveal hidden colonial influences in past and current beliefs and practices.

On the other hand, there is a miscalculation of global dominance. The interplay between the global and the local often sees forces from both directions collide and exogenous forces adapt to local conditions as the result. This global–local nexus is a twofold process of give-and-take, an exchange by which global trends are reshaped to local ends, and a dynamic interaction between global trends and local responses. The local becomes an expression of the global (Robertson, 1995). It is thus increasingly misleading to set up oppositions between the global and the local.

This has great implications for the trans-national provision of higher education. With accelerated knowledge circulation and dependence of education on the development of technological capability and a radical reconfiguration and cultural re-articulation taking place in educational and social life (McCarthy *et al.*, 2003) under the influence of globalisation, Chinese students are required to have knowledge of both the global and the local. Unique perspectives and values based on rich local experience and awareness of the society and culture would allow people to seize the initiative in identifying the real needs of their local societies and in setting up their own agendas and targets. However, it is the local perspective that is overshadowed by the dominant, hegemonic global.

Furthermore, pedagogies are culturally situated knowledge. As pointed out long ago, "the greatest error educators can make is to assume that education is an isolated or cloistered institution to be interpreted by itself without regard to the cyclonic forces sweeping the earth" (Brameld, 1961: 22). Business administration is deeply rooted in culture. MBA education was initiated a century ago in the West and remains underdeveloped in China with a short history of two decades. As China is a country with a very different culture and history, issues related to curriculum adaptability to the local context loom large. Yet, this has been little researched.

This chapter aims to fill the gap in the literature by reporting findings of an in-depth case study of an Australia–China joint MBA programme. It is based on empirical data gathered by questionnaires and interviews. Questionnaires were distributed to all 74 students who were studying for their six-month/one-year course in Melbourne. Sixty-eight (92 per cent) were returned. The target interview informants included 15 students from China, three teachers (one from China, two from Australia) and two administrators (one each from China and Australia). It shows how Western-modelled knowledge is perceived by Chinese students, and analyses how educators, both Australian and Chinese, are influenced by global forces while struggling with local relevance. It also delineates an unequal power relationship between Western and indigenous knowledge, and questions what counts as 'scholarship'.

The case study programme

As part of Australian proactive higher education export to China, by 2004, four joint MBA programmes had been accredited in China. Dozens of others were officially approved but not registered with the Ministry of Education. Our case study programme was one of the four, offered jointly by La Trobe University (LTU) in Melbourne and Zhejiang University of Technology in Hangzhou. Established in 1964, LTU is the third university in Victoria, with 15,000 students at its Melbourne campus and over 7,000 at six other campuses in regional Victoria, and 3,000 staff members in 2004.

LTU began its China MBA programmes in 1994. It did not have a school of management until its joint MBA programmes in China grew much faster than expected and it decided to establish the Graduate School of Management (GSM) in 1997 within the Faculty of Law and Management. As pointed out by its China Project Director, it was the prosperity of LTU's joint MBA programmes in China that gave birth to the GSM (Interview LTCP-A-02).

After ten years' development of its MBA programmes with China, LTU is now one of the largest Australian MBA education providers in China with partnerships based on a twinning model with Chinese institutions. In 2004 alone, some 1,500 Chinese students in 14 cities across 8 provinces were enrolled in its programs. Annually over 400 Chinese students enrolled in its joint programmes which are taught at LTU's Melbourne campus. Its partner institutions in China include Fuzhou Cadre Training Institute, Beijing Institute of Industry and Commerce, and Zhejiang University of Technology. It has also developed good relationships with some Chinese companies and government agencies. Its MBA programme claims to be designed to meet the needs of Chinese nationals who are interested in pursuing or advancing their management career. Many students enrolled in the programme are senior managers in government or joint ventures in China.

In order to respond to the different market situations in China, LTU takes a flexible approach as to the location and length of the course. Its joint MBA programme usually ranges from 18 months to 2 years, incorporating 12–18 months part-time study in China and 6 or 12 months full-time study in Australia. Students are required to complete 16 subjects. Most of them are taught in English by Melbourne-based faculty. A few specialised ones are taught in Chinese by teachers from the Chinese partner. In many cases, especially when most students are working for and supported by the government with sufficient financial resources, 6 of the 16 subjects are taught in China within 6 months, and the other 10 are conducted in LTU's Melbourne campus for another 12 months. In some less affluent areas, where most students are studying at their own expense, usually 10 subjects are delivered in China and 6 in Australia. The duration is reversed to 12 months in China and 6 months in Australia.

One respondent from LTU made the following comments:

> The program is consistent with our aim to provide courses of high academic standards and attractive to students, well taught and relevant to the needs of the market. At the GSM, we offer a recognised MBA course designed to meet the needs of modern managers. In this joint program, students have the opportunity to develop skills and gain valuable experience that can be used in pursuing their career goals, and be better prepared to tackle problems faced by businesses today in an increasingly competitive global market. Another exciting initiative is to link our graduates with international recruiting groups, giving them access to a wide range of employment opportunities once their studies are completed.
>
> (Interview-LTCP-A-02)

The curriculum designed by the GSM has been described as the most suitable for Chinese students. It is composed of eight specialist streams with six core subjects, characterised by its strong emphasis on an international perspective, and its intention to avoid too much focus on China-specific issues. With its different streams, it is intended to attract a wide range of students with demands in different areas of management. Teaching staff in the programme are selected on the basis of their teaching and research experience and their exposure to international business practices. There is an additional component of an industry programme, facilitating interactions and exchanges of information between the students and some company managers and organisations based in Australia. Building on such a corporate network, LTU claims it provides students with a range of industry contact options including business forums, company site tours and industry contact assistance.

Major findings

Borrowing views of tasks and levels in curriculum development developed by Wiles and Bondi (1998) and Prideaux (2003), and based on the information collected by questionnaires and interviews, this section reports the major findings of our study in terms of three aspects: course content, teachers and teaching strategies, and the needs of industry.

Course content

Decisions about course content in a business curriculum reflect its planners' assumptions about the nature of business administration, skills and theories necessary to manage business, as well as the most essential elements in management, and how these elements can be organised as an efficient basis for students to learn (Thanopoulus, 1986).

Course content is the most important factor that attracts Chinese students to enroll in the programme. Among the 68 survey respondents, 60 (88.2 per cent) students chose course content as the most important factor for them to enrol in the programme. They held strongly that the recognition and integration of Chinese culture into the curriculum was essential in making the programme adaptive for their needs (scaled 4.43 out of 5), and recognised the connection between MBA curriculum and national culture (scaled 4.5 out of 5). This view was confirmed repeatedly by our interview participants who expressed their willingness to choose a joint programme that tailors course content to suit their social, cultural and managerial needs in China, as illustrated by the following quote from a student:

> The Chinese culture has a profound impact on the beliefs and values of individuals and thus has great influence on their styles of management.
>
> (Interview-LTCP-S-11)

The programme has a 'cocktail' curriculum that incorporates current Western-style business courses with some management subjects that reflect the business environment in China. Some measures have been taken to ensure the attraction of the programme to Chinese students. For example, while the subjects are largely based on business modes in Western countries, especially the USA and Australia, they also cover a variety of practices in different parts of the world, especially East and South Asia, which are the most intensely developing markets over the last decade. Instead of only following the so-called 'Harvard Mode' of MBA curriculum, which focuses only on American market and business, the programme allows some flexibility in terms of the course content.

While this helps to avoid an entire divorce of the curriculum from the Chinese context, it still lacks the ability to bring together the different Chinese and Western course contents to allow students to integrate them. Teaching materials are predominantly Western. Often, when the teachers decide to go without a formal textbook, the content focuses more on Asia-Pacific areas and issues, despite the fact that most of the theories and concepts are still based on North American and European markets and businesses. Some students complained that the course content were not adaptive enough to their experience and background.

When asked about the content they thought was particularly inadequate and not adaptive, most students mentioned *Intellectual Property Management*, *Human Resource Management*, *Marketing*, and *Entrepreneurial Business Planning*. This is not surprising as they are some of the typical areas in which business operates differently in China, as commented by one student:

> While the course contents certainly familiarise us with some international practices and theories in different areas of business administration, without taking the actual situation in China into consideration, all these are no more than engaging in idle theorising.
>
> (Interview-LTCP-S-08)

However, the measures taken by the programme to enhance its curriculum adaptability to Chinese students are questionable. Although the programme has been offered in China for years, it is not exclusively designed for Chinese students. Its curriculum is almost the same as those offered within Australia and elsewhere, except for a few subjects taught by the teachers from the Chinese partner. When questioned, the organiser claims the superiority of the global Western to the Chinese local by arguing that this way of operating is for the benefit of Chinese students, as expressed by the following comments by its director:

> In the current situation, the fact is that business in China is trying to learn from the international or Western mode of administration. There is still a long way to go if they want to catch up. Take Haier (the largest business producing electric and electronic appliances in China) as an example, as one of the top companies in China, its administrative style is very similar to those in the West, but in a global context, it cannot even get into the top 500. The objective of our program is to equip our students with advanced managerial experience, skills and perceptions from Western countries, so that they can serve a leading role in the process of globalisation of business in China. Presumably, at least at the current stage, there is not much necessity to adapt our curriculum to Chinese culture and Chinese business, though there are some successful stories of business administration in China.
>
> (Interview-LTCP-A-02)

A few Chinese students had similar views, stressing the impact of the irreversible trend of globalisation on MBA education. For example, one student made the following observation:

> MBA education and the business in China are, and will continue to be, merging into the global movement of economy, politics and culture across national borders. If MBA education is to provide the students

with practical skills and methods, its curriculum has to be built up with a global vision, instead of only focusing on individual countries or regions.

(Interview-LTCP-S-8)

However, according to the overwhelming majority of the students, MBA education, as an important aspect of social practices and professional training, should never be divorced from its recipients' living and working environment and culture. When all students are from China, the integration of Chinese culture into the curriculum becomes inevitable.

While some administrators and teachers from LTU particularly emphasise the necessity of exposing Chinese students to the increasingly enormous impact of globalisation to keep pace with the accelerating global tide of movement of culture, values and beliefs across national borders, most students in the programme express their discontent with the curriculum for its lack of account of Chinese society/culture. Such a shortage has led to gaps between the curriculum and what industries in China require.

Teachers and teaching strategies

Teaching staff are the centre of the programme and responsible for the progression of the field of MBA education. Items related to teachers and teaching strategies of the programme were also considered seriously by the students. They expected their teachers to possess abundant experiences in real business environments in addition to theoretical knowledge, and preferably with familiarity with the culture and business operations in China and knowledge of Chinese students' learning and thinking styles.

The provider seems to understand this demand. In terms of selecting teaching staff for the programme, experience in real business environment and appreciation of cultural diversity are considered, as explained by the director:

Although we are not going to make changes to our course content specifically for Chinese students, the teachers have long been doing this by deliberately adding contents related to culture, business and markets in China ... Through the academic and social interactions with the teachers from our Chinese partners, Australian teachers learn to adapt their teaching strategies to the needs of Chinese students.

(Interview-LTCP-A-02)

The Chinese students in the programme see first-hand and personal business experiences as the most important attributes of good teachers of MBA programmes. Because of their focus on the practicability of the MBA curriculum, they strongly appreciate more interactive instructional approaches other than traditional 'chalk-and-talk' teaching methods. Overall, they are satisfied with the strategies their teachers have taken in the programme, as shown by the following quote from a student:

> One of the most important advantages of this program is that the lecturers, except those local teachers at the partner university in China, are usually engaged in different businesses in Australia, or at least have extensive experience in the area of business administration. In this way, some seemingly very academic contents in the curriculum can be integrated into their previous experience and thus make their lectures more vivid, attractive and easier for us to understand, especially when our English skills are very limited. To Chinese MBA students, what we need most is not the knowledge facts in the textbooks, but the problems, solutions, methods, and principles that emerge in our working life.
>
> (Interview-LTCP-S-08)

Chinese MBA students are relatively weak in practical communication skills in terms of public speaking and professional writing. In the traditional Chinese learning environment, the teacher is the source of 'correct' knowledge, and the right answer is generally 'knowable' and should be memorised by a 'good' student. Students only feel comfortable to speak out their opinions when they consider they know the 'right answer' (Thompson, 2002).

Our fieldwork shows most of the students in the programme have realised this, and prefer the teaching approaches taken by their lecturers. In line with Haight and Kwong's (1999) argument, skills related to analytical thinking and professional communication should be emphasised to Chinese MBA students, and should be considered related to the influence of Western learning approaches. One student respondent expressed his progress after studying in the programme:

> The main gain from this study is that I feel more comfortable to express my opinions in different situations, in both written and spoken form. Personally, I think the progress came from the interactive teaching strategies used by our Australian teachers, which did not rely much on textbooks, but instead encouraged us to state our opinions on various business topics and situations by applying the concepts and theories learned in class.
>
> (Interview-LTCP-S-11)

However, a serious problem is that the teachers generally have little understanding of Chinese culture, not to mention the business environment and practices in China. The perceptions these teachers have on Chinese culture and business are often superficial, inaccurate and outmoded. For example, 'teamwork' is perceived differently in the Chinese business world; it is more like considering the business as a big family and every 'family member' (employee) needs to work together to contribute to the prosperity of the family. Therefore, great importance is attached to employees' recognition of the 'family'. One of our respondents recalled he once asked an Australian teacher about how to develop employees' stronger sense of belonging to the 'family' and was told that such a concept of 'family' was not compatible with ideas of modern business management.

The following comments by students illustrate this further:

> Although I know that Australian teachers encourage us to ask questions, I became reluctant to do so after several times, because they just could not give satisfactory answers, especially when these questions are related to doing business in China.
>
> (Interview-LTCP-S-9)

> I feel that some of the teachers are not at all familiar with the business environment in China, not to mention Chinese culture. Probably they have never been to China and have no idea of how business administration is conducted there.
>
> (Interview-LTCP-S-13)

Like their comments on the course content of the curriculum, Chinese students also expect their teachers to be familiar with Chinese culture and understand the business environment in China.

Obviously, one major obstacle that impairs the curriculum adaptability of China–Australia joint MBA programmes is the shortage of qualified teachers who understand Chinese culture and society. Most Australian MBA lecturers, with experience of business administration coming mainly from working in Australian business, are trained to teach local students within Australia, and some of them had not even visited China before. They have little knowledge of the contemporary business world in China, and still rely on their past knowledge of Chinese management, largely from outmoded resources.

Needs of industry

In the context of educational debate, it is commonplace for industry to express its needs in terms of a trained workforce as well as morality and social responsibility (Tasker and Packham, 1991). Within MBA education, the practicability of its curriculum has long been a central focus. Many educators argue that business schools need to closely watch their curriculum to prepare students for employment that meets the needs of employers (Lucas, 1980; Miller, 1980).

Despite the long-standing controversy as to whether the MBA curriculum should be more academic or practical, there has been a common recognition that the current MBA education curriculum has failed to respond to the requirements of the industry (Mangan, 2003). Students studying for their MBA degree expect the education to provide them with access to greater competency in the business world and consequently facilitate them to be more employable (Meyer and Lehew, 2001).

This has been a long-standing issue in MBA education, especially for international students. Previous studies showed that the needs of international students from developing countries at US universities were not being met with regard to practical experience and anticipated postreturn employability (Lee *et al.*, 1981). The education they receive is narrow-minded and often irrelevant to situations in their home countries (Fasheh, 1984; White and Griffith, 1998).

Chinese enterprises are becoming increasingly 'picky' about employing MBA graduates, despite the obvious shortage of such professionals in the labour market. The Chinese business world expects MBA graduates to have extensive practical experience in China's market, sound professional knowledge in her/his own field and multiple skills in other related areas, exquisite observation and prediction of China's market, excellent professional attitude and spirit, and the ability to bring in benefits right away (Zhou, 2003).

Understandably, some of these expectations are different from those in the West. Some of these 'unique' requirements are the result of the immature market mechanism in China, but many are due to the cultural differences between the two. The needs of the industry in China could be hard for Westerners to understand.

However, in the reforming era, industry in China is seeking to catch up with international standards of both products and management. The intensified globalisation has also moulded the respondents in the study to perceive the needs of industry in a particular way, as one teacher from the Chinese partner university pointed out:

> In the process of globalisation, many companies in China have felt the pressures it brings about. They also realise the unilateral focus on China's domestic market is no longer appropriate. Therefore learning the management patterns from Western countries is definitely necessary at this stage.
>
> (Interview-LTCP-T-01)

The incorporation of the needs of industry in China into the curriculum was not taken into consideration because it was the understanding of the developer that the objective of the programme was to teach students Western modes of business administration. Indigenous Chinese knowledge has not been given opportunities to influence the programme. Fundamental assumptions of local Chinese knowledge have been excluded by the very nature of the dominant Western paradigm. However, the students viewed this differently. Generally they were discontented with the ability of the curriculum to meet the needs of local industry.

Our study found that 63 (92.6 per cent) of the 68 surveyed respondents selected practicability as the reason to choose the programme and 45 (66.2 per cent) placed high value on the relevance of the programme to local industry. The majority of them, however, disagreed with the adaptability of the curriculum to the needs of Chinese industry. According to them, most of the case studies employed in teaching were overwhelmingly confined to Western business experience, with little direct applicability to the industrial environment in China. The Western-modelled business strategies and methodologies could not give them real-life guidance in China. Moreover, there were not sufficient opportunities for them to establish connections with local Australian business, although they thought the internships, company tours and seminars with business administrators organised by LTU during their study in Melbourne were very helpful in obtaining direct experience of Australian business.

Concluding remarks

In an increasingly globalised world, some commonly held assumptions about education and knowledge are constantly in question, due to economic, cultural and social transformations. International joint MBA programme developers need to be sure that both the contents and structures appropriately reflect the attributes and demands of their local students. This is particularly true in programmes designed for Chinese students (Thompson, 2002), as illustrated by our case study, which shows Chinese students regard curriculum adaptability to their local context as a key aspect.

Our case study could be better understood in the contemporary trend of trans-national higher education provision. While the export of the foreign (often Western) into China has been viewed positively within the corporatisation of higher education, many critical perspectives raise a number of problematic issues (Dunn and Wallace, 2004), including the commodification of knowledge and the hegemony of Western knowledge and pedagogies. There are a number of pedagogical issues in achieving high quality of trans-national higher education courses in China. The danger with the 'global template' is its dissociating education from China's social, cultural and political origins. Such decontextualised, 'globalised' curricula reflect a particular view of what is claimed to be 'universal' and informed by the geographical and social location of the curriculum developer, which is typically the Western (English-speaking) world. The implicit social values of these exporting countries inform the curriculum, and Chinese social and cultural context in which students live is largely ignored by such courses.

This links closely to the long-standing issue in Chinese education that indigenous Chinese wisdom and imported Western knowledge have never been on an equal footing. It raises the question of what counts as 'scholarship'. It reminds us that real/proper knowledge is only produced by some particular countries in a particular way (Appadurai, 2001). It warns us that Western educational systems and structures continue to define education for the rest of the world (Goodman, 1984), and by extension, they define what knowledge is and who may claim competence in it.

References

Appadurai, A. (2001) 'Grassroots globalisation and the research imagination', in A. Appadurai (ed.) *Globalisation*, Durham, NC: Duke University Press, 1–21.

Brameld, T. (1961) *Education for the Emerging Age*, New York: Harper and Row.

Dunn, L. and Wallace, M. (2004) 'Australian academics teaching in Singapore: striving for cultural empathy', *Innovations in Education and Teaching International*, 41, 3: 291–304.

Fasheh, M. (1984) 'Foreign students in the United States: an enriching experience or a wasteful one?' *Contemporary Educational Psychology*, 9: 313–21.

Goodman, N. (1984) 'The institutionalisation of overseas education', in E. Barber, P. Altbach, and R. Myers (eds) *Bridges to Knowledge: Foreign Students in Comparative Perspective*, Chicago, IL: University of Chicago Press, 7–18.

Haight, G.T. and Kwong, K.K. (1999) 'Future of the MBA in China', *Business Forum*, 24, 2: 33–6.

Lee, M.Y., Abd-Ella, M., and Burke, L. (1981) *Needs of Foreign Students from Developing Countries at US Colleges and Universities*, Washington, DC: National Association for Foreign Students Affairs.

Lucas, J.A. (1980) 'Identifying regional and community markets', in P. Jedamus and M. Peterson (eds) *Improving Academic Management*, San Francisco, CA: Jossey-Bass, 238–62.

Luke, C. (2005) 'Capital and knowledge flows: global higher education markets', *Asia Pacific Journal of Education*, 25, 2: 159–74.

Mangan, K.S. (2003) 'The new MBA: business-school professors shift programs to emphasise relevance flexibility', *Chronicle of Higher Education*, 49, 33: 12–17.

McCarthy, C., Giardina, M.D., Harewood, S.J. and Park, J. (2003) 'Contesting culture: identity and curriculum dilemmas in the age of globalisation, postcolonialism, and multiplicity', *Harvard Educational Review*, 73, 3: 449–59.

Meyer, D. and Lehew, M. (2001) 'The professional Master's degree: addressing the changing needs of textiles and apparel students and industry', *Journal of Family and Consumer Sciences*, 93, 4: 75–8.

Miller, R. (1980) 'Appraising institutional performance', in P. Jedamus and M. Peterson (eds) *Improving Academic Management*, San Francisco, CA: Jossey-Bass, 406–31.

Prideaux, D. (2003) 'Curriculum design', *British Medical Journal*, 326: 268–70.

Robertson, R. (1995) 'Globalisation', in M. Featherstone, S. Lash and R. Robertson (eds) *Global Modernities*, London: Sage, 25–44.

Tasker, M. and Packham, D. (1991) 'What are the "needs of industry"?', *Industry and Higher Education*, 5, 2: 124–30.

Thanopoulus, J. (1986) *International Business Curriculum: A Global Survey*, Cleveland, OH: Academy of International Business.

Thompson, E.R. (2002) 'Chinese perspectives on the important aspects of an MBA teacher', *Journal of Management Education*, 26, 3: 229–58.

White, D.S. and Griffith, D.A. (1998) 'Graduate international business education in the US – comparisons and suggestions', *Journal of Education for Business*, 74, 2: 103–15.

Wiles, J. and Bondi, J. (1998) *Curriculum Development: A Guide to Practice*, New York: Macmillan.

Zhou, P. (2003) 'Development of MBA education in China: opportunities and challenges for Western universities', *International Journal of Business and Management Education*, 11, 2: 1.

4 Work and the labour process

'Use-value' and the rethinking of skills and learning

Peter H. Sawchuk

The multiple traditions of sociological analysis of work can make important contributions to understandings of the relationships between knowledge and work. This chapter seeks to renew an interest in the labour process specifically. Criticizing the ongoing 'up-skilling/de-skilling impasse', I offer discussion of several alternative conceptual resources that may contribute to a more robust appreciation for skill, knowledge, learning and human development as phenomena in their own right, potentially unified under a suggested 'Use-value Thesis' of the labour/learning process. It is argued that recognizing 'use-value' sets the stage for a broader systemic understanding of the contradictory interests and practices (e.g. up-skilling/de-skilling, engagement/alienation, cooperation/conflict) that occur simultaneously in all workplaces under capitalism, and in turn offers a means to more coherently assess the full range and variation of human learning.

Introduction

This chapter builds from questions posed within a large-scale empirical project looking at the changes in work, learning and technological design of welfare work in Ontario (2002–06) (Hennessy and Sawchuk, 2003; Sawchuk, 2003a). Simply put, this research demanded answers that were not forthcoming from existing literature. Therefore, drawing on sociology of work and Labour Process Theory (LPT), I explore current theoretical models of skill, knowledge and work with the goal of opening a new level of integrated analysis.

Of course, one of the key arguments of this volume is that, more so than other forms of learning, work-based learning is particularly shaped by global economic pressures. Though originating in a specific sector and country, I argue that the chapter addresses a global phenomenon. That is, the patterns of work, learning and technological-based change continue to be mirrored around the world wherever neo-liberal governments and capitalism flourishes. The chapter presumes the juxtaposition of global homogenization, economic rationalization, heightened control and de-skilling, on the one hand, and the local, culturally specific, everyday struggle of workers to create parallel, and not infrequently competing, labour processes and knowledge work on the other. This chapter offers further conceptual resources for identifying the generally poorly understood, worker-centred dimensions of knowledge work and the contradictions that shape it to contribute to a broader understanding of what counts as working knowledge.

Our research asked: is a simple recovery of the 'de-skilling' thesis as suggested in our research team's earlier analyses, adequate to describe the processes we were seeing amongst welfare workers? Likewise, should various competing models of work change, such as Daniel Bell's post-industrial thesis, Manuel Castells' network society thesis, post-Fordism, flexible specialization, lean production, high performance production, up-skilling or re-skilling theses be substituted, appended or referenced? In light of the emergent findings of the 'Working IT' research,[1] a number of models were re-assessed for their ability to illuminate, in particular, the contradictory nature of labour/learning processes. Our evidence forced us to consider the ideas of de-skilling and up-skilling, their mutual constitution and their simultaneity. In our project's search for answers, we viewed paid work as definitively historical and social; and that the most powerful conceptualizations recognize that work entails both a process of change and human development/learning. In this sense, the separation of analyses of work and analyses of learning was deemed an important barrier to be overcome.

Below, I briefly summarize the past and current status of sociology of work and LPT, and make the case for the need to find a unifying conceptual framework which treats knowledge, skill and human development adequately as phenomena in their own right, while never losing sight of the need for a critical political economic perspective on the nature of paid work. Toward this end, below I present several additional theoretical resources, and what I refer to as the 'Use-value Thesis' on the labour/learning process.

The need for new resources for a critical perspective on the labour/learning process

Research in sociology of work and LPT has continued to evolve since World War II. It was in the late 1950s that the 'industrialism thesis' (e.g. oriented to technical-rational progress, mass production/consumption and labour–management cooperation) first became established. Later, it was further extended as the 'post-industrialism thesis' (e.g. oriented to the displacement of industrial work through technology, the emergence of service and knowledge work, better quality products and work, and the leisure society). Challenging it in the 1970s was Marxist LPT inspired by the work of Harry Braverman (e.g. oriented to reclaiming the relevance of class-conflict *vis-à-vis* de-skilling, social polarization and the struggle for control) which was followed by further critiques: feminist and post-structuralist development of LPT, as well as Regulation Theory, Institutional Economics and Contingency Theory (see Sawchuk, 2006a). Throughout the industrialism/post-industrialism approaches continued, and what has now emerged, I argue, can be referred to as the 'de-skilling/ up-skilling impasse': roughly equal proportions of persuasive work/ skills research demonstrating that disempowerment and resistance occur, new forms of technological and socio-emotional control occur, rising educational requirements continues to occur, de-skilling occurs, and up-skilling occurs – all with little agreement as to their inter-relations. In Sawchuk (2006a) I register the need to conceptualize these inter-relations, and go on to say that in doing so there is a major risk of losing the critical Marxist observations that largely fuelled the original challenge to the industrialism/post-industrialism theses in the first place.

My argument in this chapter is that despite the development of vital new concepts and expansive programmes of empirical research, our broader understanding of work and learning, and specifically the LPT tradition, has advanced only modestly. To be sure, there can be many ways of thinking about this, and several contributions within this collection provide vital starting points. Nevertheless, in the remainder of this section I review several key works that, in my view, make a fundamental contribution to the breaking of the up-skilling/de-skilling impasse. Most do so by articulating Marxist principles explicitly, but all point toward key contradictory relationships within work and learning environments that in my view are central to creating critical, integrated analysis.

We can begin with a look at the work of Paul Adler. Adler (2005) summarizes a good deal of his substantial past work on LPT, highlighting the confusion that surrounds the up-skilling/de-skilling debates. In particular he takes the LPT corpus to task for both failing to account for aggregate upgrading trends in education and work-based skill requirements, and for the drift toward an apolitical, contingency approach and the abandonment of Marxist analysis. Citing the work of Spenner and others, Adler highlights evidence of persistent, if gradual, up-skilling trends drawing on the *Dictionary of Occupational Titles* tracking as well as the massive growth in educational participation over the last 50 years. Though there are some significant clarifications[2] to be made in this regard, nevertheless, drawing on detailed analysis of global software design work, Adler's goal is more fundamental. He offers a 'paleo-Marxist' (his term) solution to the up-skilling/de-skilling impasse – able to reconcile *both* a broad pattern of upgrading *and* a multitude of counter-examples of de-skilling – with a focus on the *socialization of the forces of production* in a contradictory relationship with the profit-motive of capital. In other words, an aggregate socialization of work processes (i.e. the expansion of the complexity of the social division of labour) on the one hand, and the expansion of the privatized relations of production (i.e. private ownership and its requirements for capital accumulation) on the other, continually act on one another to produce the types of skill changes Marx originally identified with the transformation of capitalism. In Adler's case, he contrasts the apparent 'de-skilling' of software design work through modularization, profit-maximization and globalization, with the overall socialization and growing interdependence that such global production systems necessarily produce, raising the potential of communication, decreasing the 'idiocy' of isolated and particularistic design. In doing this, Adler adds a vital, forsaken component of LPT by reclaiming the argument that, according to Marx, the forces and relations under capitalism create conditions for historical change because they are contradictory. A reading of either the up-skilling or de-skilling research demonstrates an all too infrequent recognition of this dialectical element; and hence its tendency to under-achieve as an overall analysis of a social, political system in motion. At the same time, however, Adler (2005) shares with so much of the debate to date little conceptual/empirical attention to the processes of skill development and knowledgeability themselves.

In response to some of these concerns, we can look toward the work of Nancy Jackson. She presents a fundamental critique of the presumptions that pervade dominant understandings of vocational skill which can serve as an orienting backdrop to the types of gaps produced both in the context of the up-skilling/de-skilling impasse and the otherwise expansive critique offered by Adler. She comments that these dominant understandings,

> [treat] knowledge and skill as naturally occurring phenomena, locatable empirically by examination of work processes in the world around us. In this mode, vocational knowledge and skills are constructed as stable objects which stand outside the learner, and can be discovered in the form of 'tasks' to be mastered. Such tasks and their mastery are seen to be unambiguously definable and accessible to evaluation in a systematic and unambiguous manner … 'Performance' becomes a form of action from which the 'knowing subject' has been removed for all practical purposes. It is a moment of abstraction, a separation of subject and object, a rupture in the internal continuity of knowledge and action. It is precisely this separation that provides for the possibility of external definition and control – it creates a position for authority outside the moments of teaching and learning from which these activities may be defined, measured, and evaluated for someone else's purposes … But I will argue here that it [also] has the effect of disorganizing vocational activity for the purposes of the individuals whose 'need' is to master it as a form of practical action.
>
> (Jackson, 1994: 344)

The key issues raised by Jackson, for our discussion, are (i) the dearth of conceptual means to draw distinctions between managerial/designer based understandings of vocational knowledge and actual, practical work, skill and knowledge activity; (ii) the persistent, fundamental epistemological denial of the acting and knowing subject; and finally (iii) the socially reproductive effects that these dominant presumptions actually have in 'disorganizing' the potential of workers to individually/ collectively work, learn and develop in their own terms. Jackson argues for an analysis that recovers people as subjects of their labour, rather than merely objects of managerial control. She concludes by advocating a variety of socio-cultural schools of thought – among them 'situated learning' and 'activity theory' – as an important foundation for more adequate analysis of skill and knowledge development.

While hardly a comprehensive response to the issues raised by either Adler or Jackson, one hopeful contribution toward a substantive model of skill itself is found in the work of A. Aneesh where it's argued that,

> [t]here is a need to reconceptualize [Braverman's] thesis about skills and develop new criteria for the understanding of skills. I seek to lift the debate out of the de-skilling vs. re-skilling confusion, developing an alternate set of analytical tools to make sense of skills, especially in view of the transformations associated with information technologies. I attempt to focus on deeper structures of skills independent of the question of whether de-skilling plagues all industries … The concept of skill saturation seeks to evaluate skills solely on the basis of their grammar and structures … It does not allude to the consciousness – obscure or obvious – of the manager or the worker, nor does it refer skills to the will of the work designers
>
> (Aneesh, 2001: 365–6)

This analysis of *saturated* versus *unsaturated* skill is well worth noting. Skill saturation is defined by Aneesh as the closure of the space for play, leading to predictability of procedure and outcome 'resulting from the exhaustive ordering of various components of skill and the elimination of all irregular spaces of work' (Aneesh, 2001: 363–4). Unsaturated skills, on the other hand,

> tend to contain multiple bonds with the job and certain unanalyzed dimensions to allow enough room for action to take place, an action based on long and intuitive understanding. It implies engagement that is implicit, inherent, and defies clear visibility. Michael Polanyi's concept of 'tacit dimension' may allow us to understand how the unqualified process of the formalization of skills leads to complete predictability, and eliminates the elements of creative freedom and discovery. Polanyi explained tacit dimension as something that remains unanalyzable in action … Many creative skills are performed

and learned by 'indwelling' and 'interiorization,' rather than by explicit, formalized knowledge.

(Aneesh, 2001: 373–4)

Importantly, Aneesh's model helps us break open some of the contradictory claims that permeate the up-skilling/de-skilling impasse, providing a means of theorizing Jackson's acting/knowing subject. Aneesh's model helps us see, for example, that the type of skilled, semi-skilled and unskilled categorizations of a coding system like the *Dictionary of Occupational Titles* may in fact miss a crucial point. Many jobs, conventionally defined, may exhibit unexpected levels of *both* closure and openness as defined by the 'saturated–unsaturated' continuum, particularly when actual work activity is looked at closely. This breaking up of conventional, presumed hierarchies of skill/knowledge is helped further by challenging the arbitrary straight-jacket that defines *legitimatized* goals, interests and activity from a strictly organizational standpoint.[3] Thus, highly skilled work may at moments exhibit enormously 'saturated' elements, just as apparently unskilled, routinized work frequently obscures enormous evidence of play, hidden 'tricks-of-the trade' and subversion. This is a point Jackson (1994: 342–3) makes in her discussion of the need to account for the specific subject standpoints. At the same time, it should be apparent that there is an instructive contrast between Aneesh's and Jackson's assessments: Aneesh's claim of saturation, a more substantive means of identifying de-skilling, and its effect of regularizing work on the one hand, and Jackson's assessment that such levels of managerial control may actually disorganize work/learning activity on the other. How are we to reconcile these seemingly contradictory accounts from the perspective of a critical, political economic perspective that, broadly speaking, Adler calls for?

From the field of educational studies comes a unifying conceptualization that begins to help us address such questions. Glenn Rikowski (e.g. 2002a, 2002b) begins from Marxist theory and expands the issue of skill, education, training and informal learning to all work-based activity as examples of a singular phenomenon: the development and application of *labour-power* and personhood:

labour-power is a complex phenomenon with inherent contradictions and tensions that become incorporated within personhood – given labour-power's fusion with the person of the labourer … However, as well as these diverse aspects of the unified social force that is labour-power, there is a deeper rift that de-stabilises labour-power and the person within which its force flows. Labour-power, which takes the form of human capital, is at odds with the person (de facto with itself) as not-labour-power; the person with interests, desires, motives (with dreams even) that run counter to the subsumption of the self as labour-power. The antagonistic labour–capital relation is a relation within personhood too in capitalist society. Our existence as labour against capital (as opposed to labour within and as capital) places a limit on the capitalisation of our souls ...

(Rikowski, 2002a: 15–16)

Rikowski (2002b) goes on to list an exhaustive series of what he calls qualities, attributes and aspects of labour-power, and recovers Marx's original claims of its singularly unique ability (against all other commodities) to create value, and in the process helps us identify another contested, core relationship: 'The labour-power of the labourer is under the sway of a potentially hostile will, a will that also exists against capital as well as within it. The labourers also have the capacity to use their precious commodity in non-capitalist productive forms as labour beyond capital, which is the capitalist's dread' (Rikowski, 2002a: 8).

Unifying the critique: a 'Use-value Thesis'

Rikowski's recovery of core principles of Marxist analysis appears to contribute to the type of 'paleo-Marxist' goals identified by Adler in his critique of LPT and de-skilling. It contributes recognition of the dialectic nature of skill/knowledge under global capitalism that might help break the impasse of the up-skilling/de-skilling debates without the abandonment of a critical Marxist perspective. A *Use-value Thesis* begins with this dialectic, rooted in analysis of the basic building block of capitalist society: the commodity form. We start, first, from the idea that central to understanding the functioning of (past, present or future) society is that people are both, as in Jackson's observations, subjects and objects of history; that societies are actively built. Through this building (or labour) process they satisfy their individual and collective (cultural, psychological and material) needs. In a capitalist society specifically these needs are met in two basic ways: either *directly* (the production of use-values) or *indirectly* (the production of exchange-values). Use-values are produced all around us, across all spheres of our daily lives, even though only a select portion of this production has 'economic' value (i.e. exchange-value). Use-value, of course, also provides the basis for commodity production in that consumers buy things that they want to (in some broad sense) use. One of the defining features of capitalist society, as Marx observed, is that as the system develops and expands, more and more of our use-value production is organized by the principle of exchange-value production. In other words, life activities are increasingly commodified.[4] My point here is that use-value production is the foundational activity, and must be reconfirmed to better understand the complexity and specificity of work/ learning practice.

Activity, skill and knowledge embedded in use-value production accounts for the pragmatic, shared *and* generally cooperative orientation by both workers and management to the intrinsic, practical usefulness of the service or product. Use-value orientation also explains much of the shared interest in maintaining a reasonable environment of human interrelation (i.e. use-value in terms of friendship, recognition, respect, identity formation, etc.). However none of this precludes conflict that necessarily emerges as use-value generation comes into relationship with the over-arching need to generate ever-increasing levels of exchange-value and profit, in the classic analysis of antagonistic relations of production, subversion, resistance, sabotage and so on. The Use-value Thesis, in this sense, places this type of contradictory 'parallel universe' that prevail in all capitalist workplaces at the centre of specific work/skill analysis. This central contradiction anticipates *both* cooperation *and* conflict, engagement *and* alienation, up-skilling *and* de-skilling simultaneously within the same work environment. As the summary of so much spilt ink attests, such dynamics simply are not mutually exclusive, and the Use-value Thesis, in this sense, contributes a unifying explanation why, under capitalism, this is necessarily the case.

The work of the four authors reviewed above can be understood in relation to this dialectic of use-value/exchange value. For this, we can pay particular attention to their discussions of key contradictory relations (roughly summarized for each author as follows):

- socialization of forces of production *versus* capitalist profitability (Adler)
- practical action/knowing subjects *versus* objectifying managerial control (Jackson)
- unsaturated skill/play *versus* saturated skill/rationalized procedure (Aneesh)
- labour-against-capital *versus* labour-as-capital (Rikowski).

Making the linkage between work and learning in keeping with a Use-value Thesis is inherent in, as Rikowski puts it, 'labour-power's fusion with the person'. *Learning*, as I comment elsewhere, is the *labour* we do on ourselves and labouring teaches us all the time whether those lessons are deemed legitimate or not. Moreover, given that labour is constituted by both use-value and exchange-value production we can speak in the same terms of learning. Of course, as valuable as it may be to raise the questions and issues above, there is still a good deal missing regarding tools for a coherent empirical programme. In this sense, both Jackson's (1994) and Adler's (2005) explicit suggestions for a turn toward socio-cultural approaches to learning are highly relevant. And indeed, work moving in this direction has continued to emerge with special attention to Cultural Historical Activity Theory (CHAT) specifically (see Sawchuk,

2003b, 2006b; Livingstone and Sawchuk, 2004; Sawchuk *et al.*, 2006; cf. Fenwick, 2001).

Nevertheless, the overwhelming lack of attention to actual processes of human development and activity, the recognition of the 'knowing and acting subject' (Jackson) within analyses of the labour process appears chronic; a condition which virtually assures the maintenance of the up-skilling/de-skilling impasse on the one hand, and the tendency to 'de-Marxify' LPT on the other. How does the Use-value Thesis open up new ground for LPT and research that articulates the juxtaposition of local/global effects? It does so by, first, inherently linking labour process and labour-power concepts to socio-cultural theoretical traditions such as CHAT or even Situated Learning that have the capacity to offer detailed, expansive, empirical analyses of the actual human developmental process. Second, it provides the capacity to identify and track interwoven 'trajectories of activity' (i.e. learning and human development; Sawchuk, 2003b) that always co-exist but which result in radically different expansive and/or contracted learning outcomes. Drawing on Aneesh's (2001) formulation, for example, while a set of occupational skills may be assessed as leaning toward the saturated end of his 'saturated–unsaturated' continuum model (leaving little room for discretion and play) this may simply be accurate for those activities defined as *organizationally legitimate*, that is involving processes that convert labour-power into exchange-value and ultimately surplus value and profitability. If we are to pay attention to Marx, as Adler and Rikowski do, we might recognize the dialectic of exchange-value and use-value production. Since the direct satisfaction of human needs (use-value) can be continuous with, tangential to and in opposition to the interests of capital, we discover a conceptual work/learning framework that can illuminate domination, accommodation as well as the often elusive dimensions of play, creativity, agency, and the learning that supports workers' resistance. That is, saturated and unsaturated skills, like use- and exchange-value always co-exist. What Adler (2005) refers to as the socialization of the relations of production and what Jackson (1994) argues is the 'disorganizing' effect of objectified vocational knowledge, are part and parcel of these other hidden dimensions of activity as well.

Conclusions

For the purposes of better understanding the global, homogenization of labour/learning processes and the local learning responses of workers, the practical-political value of this proposed marriage of ideas lies in encouraging the maintenance of a critical, political economic perspective which is deeply ingrained in a specific socio-cultural framework of the learning process. It theorizes the juxtaposition of widespread de-skilling, on the one hand, and, what becomes increasingly clear at another level, that both worker/management cooperation does exist and that, in fact, new skills are constantly emerging.

The notion of contradictory relations is central to the proposed mode of analysis. The approaches of Adler, Jackson, Aneesh and Rikowski each illuminate a key form, all of which contributes to an understanding of the 'parallel universes' that make up the labour process and human development within the capitalist workplace. Clearly, broader trends toward collective socialization occur even amidst modularized production; subjects reclaim their agency even under conditions of objectification; de-skilling undoubtedly occurs, even in professional settings where we might not conventionally expect it; up-skilling occurs, even within routine work where sometimes the only spaces for unsaturated knowledge are found in forms of resistance. More importantly, these contradictory trajectories of development can and do occur at the same time, amongst the same people, in the same workplace. This is the unity of use-value and exchange-value production as work-based learning.

Notes

1 Project funded by SSHRC-INE under the Working and Lifelong Learning Network, entitled the 'Working IT Project' (Principal Investigator, Peter H. Sawchuk).

2 These clarifications include the fact that the *Dictionary of Occupational Titles* (the latest version is 1991) is far from a definitive assessment of actual skill and knowledgeability of workers in practice, but rather the result of fairly cursory occupational analysis (indeed, the classification systems in the fourth, fifth and sixth digits of the codes are laughable if one were to compare them to even the most basic qualitative accounts of workers and work); and, as Livingstone (1999; and Berg 1970 before him) has demonstrated, increased educational participation may in fact be better termed 'credential inflation' in that there clearly exists a series of 'gaps' between skill/knowledge acquisition and application in the labour process.

3 Such 'organizational standpoints' would include a bloc of dominant interests, minimally based on gender and race as well as class positions.

4 The key examples here are, of course, the idea of 'human capital' as well as the notion of 'soft skills'. These concepts function to convert activities, skills and knowledge broadly conceived into things that have value in exchange (e.g. for a wage).

References

Adler, P. (2005) 'From Labour Process to Activity Theory', in P. Sawchuk, N. Duarte and M. Elhammoumi (eds) *Critical Perspectives on Activity: Explorations Across Education, Work and Everyday Life*, New York: Cambridge University Press.

Aneesh, A. (2001) 'Skill Saturation: Rationalization and Post-Industrial Work', *Theory and Society*, 30: 363–96.

Berg, I. (1970) *Education and Jobs: The Great Training Robbery*, New York: Praeger.

Fenwick, T. (2001) 'Tides of Change: New Themes and Questions in Workplace Learning', *New Directions for Adult and Continuing Education*, 92 (winter): 3–17.

Hennessy, T. and Sawchuk, P. (2003) 'Worker Responses to Technological Change in the Canadian Public Sector: Issues of Learning and Labour Process', *Journal of Workplace Learning*, 15, 7: 319–25.

Jackson, N. (1994) 'Rethinking Vocational Learning: The Case of Clerical Skills', in L. Erwin and D. MacLennan (eds) *Sociology of Education in Canada: Critical Perspectives on Theory, Research and Practice*, Toronto: Copp Clark Longman.

Livingstone, D. (1999) *The Education–Jobs Gap*, Toronto: Garamond.

Livingstone, D. and Sawchuk, P. (2004) *Hidden Knowledge: Organized Labour in the Information Age*, Toronto: Garamond.

Rikowski, G. (2002a) 'Methods for Researching the Social Production of Labour Power in Capitalism'. Paper presented at School of Education Research Seminar, University College Northampton, March 2002.

Rikowski, G. (2002b) 'Fuel for the Living Fire: Labour-Power!', in A. Dinerstein and M. Neary (eds) *The Labour Debate: An Investigation into the Theory and Reality of Capitalist Work*, Aldershot: Ashgate.

Sawchuk, P. (2003a) 'Coping with Change in the Ontario Public Sector: The Importance of Participatory Design'. Paper presented at the Work and Learning Network (WLN) Conference, University of Alberta, Edmonton, 25–28 September 2003.

Sawchuk, P. (2003b) *Adult Learning and Technology in Working-Class Life*, New York: Cambridge University Press.

Sawchuk, P. (2006a) 'The Labour/Learning Process: "Use-Value" and the Rethinking of Knowledge and Skill', *Journal of Industrial Relations*, 48, 5: 593–617.

Sawchuk, P. (2006b) 'Frameworks for Synthesis in the Field of Adult Learning Theory', in T. Fenwick, T. Nesbit and B. Spencer (eds) *Learning for Life: Canadian Readings in Adult Education*, Toronto: Thompson.

Sawchuk, P., Duarte, N. and Elhammoumi, M. (eds) (2006) *Critical Perspectives on Activity: Explorations Across Education, Work and Everyday Life*, New York: Cambridge University Press.

5 From union education to workers' education

Workers learning how to confront twenty-first-century capitalism

Jeffery Taylor

Workers and unions face considerable challenges as they confront a new phase of capitalist development in the twenty-first century. The structures that provided many workers in the developed world with a measure of security in the latter half of the twentieth century are being dismantled in the face of the internationalization of production, work intensification and employer pressure to reduce labour costs. Other workers, who never enjoyed those limited protections, struggle to establish basic workplace rights in a hostile climate. Labour educators, working for and with unions and other labour organizations, play a crucial role in helping workers to understand these processes and actively engage with them.

This chapter assesses the state of international labour education by defining key terms, reviewing the historical development of workers' and union education, distinguishing different strands and periods in this history, surveying current practice with examples from various parts of the world, and identifying methods and approaches that seem to be successful in assisting workers to develop the capacities required to meet their workplace and broader needs. It asks whether the union education that has recently dominated the field is sufficient to meet these challenges or whether older traditions of workers' education should be reclaimed.

Introduction

The first years of the twenty-first century have not been kind to unions and the workers they represent. Capital is continuing its global reorganization of production, distribution and exchange in a never-ending pursuit of profit maximization that gained a new lease of life with the collapse of the Soviet Union at the end of "the short twentieth century" (Hobsbawm, 1995). While capitalist expansion and reorganization have been features of global society for five centuries – and the theorists of globalization should remember this – there are departures as well as continuities in the current period. Each succeeding phase of capitalist development extends the spatial and social reach of commodity relations, but this phase is unique with its internationalization of production and re-engineering of an older model of industrial mass production. Workers, who sell their labour power to provide the essential fuel to produce profits, are confronted daily with incessant pressures from employers to work harder, be more productive (produce more output for less return), and accept the reality of managerial control whereby any notions of human equality or democratic decision-making are checked at the door. While the variety of legal regimes in the capitalist world mean that workers in the global north continue to enjoy relatively superior workplace protections to those in other regions, this basic workplace reality is the same for all workers (Moody, 1997; Munck, 2002; Yates, 2003).[1]

A central feature of capitalist workplaces is the struggle for control of knowledge. Workers know best how to do their jobs. This knowledge, however, gives workers power and autonomy in the workplace. It is in the interests of employers to assert control over this knowledge by, for example, introducing new technology in order to transfer the knowledge to machines that the employer owns or reorganizing work processes in order to extract productive knowledge from the workforce (Edwards, 1979). Some of the most important battles in the history of industrial capitalism have been over these issues. Indeed, the labour movements in the first industrial countries (notably northern Europe, the United States and the white settler societies of the British Empire) were forged in battles for control over knowledge of the production process, from weavers and farm workers in England and France during the early nineteenth century to various craft workers, machinists, miners and others in late-nineteenth-century Europe, North America and Australasia. The first unions emerged to defend skilled workers' customary controls over apprenticeship training, production knowledge, the pace and organization of work, and other workplace matters from employer encroachment. Most of the functions that are now taken for granted as "management rights" were wrested from the control of workers in struggle (Palmer, 1976). Unions, therefore, have a historic and fundamental interest in workplace knowledge, education and training.

While workers have struggled with employers over the control of knowledge and other matters, the workplace has also been their most important site for learning about the nature of work, capitalism, and the essential features of the broader class society. Every day workers deal with the reality that they must sell their labour power in order to survive in a legal, social and economic context in which employers have immense power over them. Unions, as part of their broader mandate to protect and enhance their members' interests, use workers' experiences as the basis upon which to conduct their own educational activities (Boughton, 2005).

What follows is a brief survey of this activity that situates current practice in its historical context. While the focus is primarily on English-speaking societies and the global north, there are references to other regions. After locating the origins of workers' education in the early stages of industrial capitalism, the emergence of a narrower union education in the mid-twentieth century is sketched. Some examples of current union educational provision in the global north and south are then discussed and placed in the context of the shift to a new stage of capitalist development, which began in the last quarter of the twentieth century. The chapter concludes by assessing the relationship between workers' and union education in light of the challenges that workers now face.

Before proceeding with the argument, however, categorical distinctions used in this chapter require some explanation. Labour education, labour studies, union education, trade union training and trade union studies are terms that are currently used in English to refer to various types of non-formal and formal educational activity for and about trade unionists. Union education and trade union training refer to educational programmes conducted by labour organizations (unions and their various federations or peak bodies) for their members. Labour and trade union studies refer to post-secondary or tertiary courses and programmes that focus on labour and the working class. Labour education encompasses union education/trade union training, labour/trade union studies and other non-vocational courses and programmes offered for trade unionists by educational and other social institutions. Union involvement in workplace learning or training (skills for immediate and future work requirements) is not normally considered to be union or labour education, although the distinction is becoming blurred as this involvement increases. Finally, workers' education is a historical term that is broader than union and labour education (Spencer, 2002; Taylor, 2001). In this chapter, I discuss workers' and union education.

The origins of workers' and union education

Organized education by and for the adult working class emerged from the workers' education movements of the late nineteenth and early twentieth centuries. In the United Kingdom (UK), for example, which spawned the first movement, the Workers' Educational Association (WEA) was formed in 1903 to offer lectures on a variety of university-level subjects for interested working-class students. The Plebs League and the National Council of Labour Colleges developed later to offer a more explicitly class-based and socialist analysis from the 1920s to the 1940s (McIlroy, 1999; Simon, 1990). Comparable movements emerged in Australasia during this period, while in Canada a WEA in the UK mould evolved into an organization offering more critical, working-class-focused education (Friesen and Taksa, 1996; Law, 1996; Newman, 1993; Taylor, 2001). Furthermore, a Swedish WEA was formed in 1912 to offer independent, working-class education (Hopkins, 1985: 101). In the United States, meanwhile, a militant labour college movement with a class perspective developed in the early twentieth century (Aronowitz, 1990).

By the middle of the twentieth century, however, the older workers' education in which workers and the working class were the natural constituency was being replaced in the global north by a narrower, union-controlled education that focused on industrial relations training and building the institutional capacity of labour organizations. This shift, which began in North America, occurred as part of the period of capitalist expansion that commenced at the end of the Second World War and continued until the middle of the 1970s. North American worker militancy in the 1930s and 1940s resulted in the organization of millions of workers in new industrial unions and the establishment of legal regimes that recognized the right of unions to exist, provided a framework for their formation, compelled employers to bargain with them and established administrative procedures for contract enforcement. As a result, labour organizations faced substantial educational challenges as they learned how to function in this new period. Most importantly, elected representatives of union locals had to be trained in union administration, collective bargaining, grievance handling and other tasks. By the 1950s most North American education specifically for the adult working class was union education designed to equip workers to perform roles in their labour organizations and to represent their fellow workers in the industrial relations systems.

These legal and institutional developments were not sufficient to account for the ideological change that was involved in the shift from worker to union education, however. Unions had been recognized as legitimate institutions in capitalist society and had been legally incorporated into it. In return for this legitimacy, union leaders were expected to act responsibly, which included keeping member militancy in check and allowing employers to manage their firms unencumbered. Furthermore, as part of the anti-communist hysteria that was a feature of North American society in the 1950s the most militant union leaders and activists were purged or marginalized, leaving movements that were led by individuals who accepted capitalism and the subordinate role that unions and workers played in it. Broad-based workers' education was marginalized as well (Aronowitz, 1990; Taylor, 2001).

While the North American system of plant-based certification, bargaining and grievance arbitration accounted for the breadth and depth of union courses there, labour movements in other parts of the global north developed similar educational programmes in the post-war period to teach their members how to function in their respective industrial relations systems. Continental European trade unionists, for example, were trained to participate in legislatively mandated works councils (workplace committees with representation from employees and managers). By the 1970s and 1980s, as the period of post-war capitalist stability began to crumble and worker militancy increased, liberal and social democratic governments in the United Kingdom, Australia, New Zealand, Canada and other countries provided monies to unions for internal education. Throughout the third and fourth quarters of the twentieth century, however, the subject matter was limited to industrial relations training. As a result, the broader-based and critical education that had been part of the older workers' education movements was suppressed (McIlroy, 1999; Stirling, 2002; Taylor, 2001).

Union education and capitalist reorganization

Union education in the global north at the beginning of the twenty-first century is a mix of structures and programmes that were established during the period of post-war capitalist stability and newer approaches that have developed to help workers cope with or resist the current capitalist reorganization. Noteworthy new departures include education linked to organizing campaigns, union attention to workplace (vocational) learning, and courses that draw connections between workplace and broader changes. In the vast majority of cases, however, participants in educational events are treated and addressed as union members rather than as part of a broader working class and the main focus continues to be on unions' institutional capacity. But is this sufficient in the new world order?

Employer attacks on workers in the global north accelerated by the late 1970s as a result of the crisis in global capitalist economies marked by the energy crisis, inflation and high unemployment. These attacks precipitated a general decline in union density (the percentage of workforce members in a country who are union members) during the 1980s and 1990s. Besides the impact on individual unorganized workers, who are denied the benefits of union membership, lower densities have a negative effect on the ability of unions to promote the wellbeing of their members and workers in general. As a result, organizing became a priority for labour movements in various countries during the 1990s.

Legislative amendments to the system of Australian industrial arbitration in the 1980s and 1990s, which resulted in a shift from industry-wide awards for wages and working conditions to enterprise-level bargaining and other changes, forced Australian unions to think about organizing in a serious way for the first time since the arbitration system was established at the turn of the twentieth century. One result was the formation of Organising Works in 1994 to provide organizer training for the Australian labour movement. For the previous 20 years, traditional union education had been provided through the government-funded and union-run Trade Union Training Authority (TUTA). When government funding was stopped, a "New TUTA" was formed with a mandate to do organizing training. New TUTA became the teaching core of Organising Works and provided a nine-month programme that was a combination of classroom instruction and field work (Widenor and Feekin, 2002).

The Trades Union Congress in the United Kingdom developed its own Organising Academy to train organizers and begin to address the dramatic decline in union membership in that country (Stirling, 2002: 31).

In the United States, meanwhile, where density is among the lowest in the world, a number of initiatives have been undertaken and education has played an important role in them. The AFL-CIO's Organizing Institute (OI), formed in 1989, was designed to train a new cadre of organizers and to contribute substantially to the creation of an organizing culture in the American labour movement. It recruited mostly young organizers, provided initial instruction in short courses, and then apprenticed them in the field with mentors (Widenor and Feekin, 2002). The programme was most successful when it partnered with unions or organizations with a central commitment to organizing the unorganized. The OI and the Asia-Pacific American Labor Alliance (APLA), formed in 1992 to organize and advance the interests of Asian-American workers, trained over a hundred Asian-American organizers during the 1990s, for example.

The APLA was part of a wave of immigrant organizing in the United States at the end of the twentieth century, with Los Angeles being a centre of vibrant activity. The Service Employees International Union organized 74,000 mostly immigrant and female home-health-care workers in 1999, for example, and the following year it led a successful strike of 8,000 janitors as part of its "Justice for Janitors" campaign. The janitors' struggle, for example, included a bilingual (Spanish and English) popular education programme for the general membership that was instrumental in the strike's success. More broadly, labour education has played an important role in allowing immigrant workers to understand their power and ability to take control of their working lives (Wong, 2002).

The labour movement, it will be recalled, was born in struggles over workplace knowledge in the early years of industrial capitalism, but this area was largely abandoned to employers during the period of mass industrial production in the twentieth century. As capital internationalizes production and shifts to global assembly lines, however, unions have been forced for a variety of reasons to confront the issue of workplace training (skills for immediate and future work requirements). For one thing, they have had to assist members who have lost their jobs due to economic restructuring to gain access to training opportunities. For another, this latest phase of capitalist development has been accompanied by an employer ideology that shifts responsibility for training to individual workers while extolling the virtues and importance of workplace knowledge and learning.

While unions in the nineteenth and early twentieth centuries struggled against ceding control of workplace knowledge to employers, the dominant approach now is to work jointly with employers in partnership agreements. Various employee development schemes in the United States, the United Kingdom, and other parts of the global north, for example, are joint employer–union endeavours to provide a range of educational opportunities for workers (from basic skills to career development), but with little union involvement other than the shared sponsorship with the employer. In other cases, unions have negotiated training trust funds as part of their overall compensation packages. The degree of union control is greater here, but the training offered is often traditional skill development that uncritically accepts the view that workers, rather than employers or governments, are responsible for training and employability. The danger of joint employer–union partnership schemes is that, in the absence of a strong countervailing union ideology that makes sense of workers' subordinate role in production, employer ideologies will be dominant (Holland and Castleton, 2002; Forrester, 2001, 2002a, 2002b; Scully-Ross and Chiera, 2005; Martin, 1995).

The best examples of union involvement in training in the global north are those in which a conscious learning strategy exists that links workplace training to union education and infuses both with a union perspective. UNISON's programme in the United Kingdom, for example, provides a range of educational opportunities for its members including basic literacy, vocational training, union education, and accredited university and college courses. By assisting its members to pursue educational opportunities that might not otherwise be available to them, the union hopes that learners will develop the confidence and skills to play roles in their communities, their union, and the wider labour movement (Sutherland, 1998; Forrester, 2002a).

Finally, some union educators in the global north are explicitly addressing the problem of global capitalist reorganization and its impact on workplaces in courses on the changing nature of work. European unions, for example, have a variety of programmes and courses that allow workers to understand this relationship. However, these are often accompanied by partnerships or "social dialogue" with employers, even though employers have initiated the changes against which workers have to mobilize (Bridgford and Stirling, 2000; Miller and Stirling, 1998; Miller, 2002; Stirling, 2002). In more militant unions, such as the Canadian Union of Postal Workers, or among rank-and-file militants who assemble at international labour gatherings such as the Detroit-based Labor Notes annual conferences, explicit analyses of capitalism and the necessity for international worker solidarity form part of the educational offerings (Spencer, 1994; Labor Notes, 2006).

The most promising educational challenges to capitalist reorganization and its impact on the world's workers have come from unions and workers' movements in the global south. South Africa's black unions, for example, were part of the revolutionary wing of the anti-apartheid movement and have continued that militant tradition in the post-apartheid period. Education in the Confederation of South African Trade Unions (COSATU) and its affiliates is explicitly socialist and anti-capitalist, assisting their memberships to understand that they are part of a larger national and international working class whose interests conflict with those of their employers. But COSATU's alliance with the African National Congress government, which accepts a capitalist South Africa, threatens to dull this revolutionary edge (Cooper, 1998, 2002, 2005). The Brazilian National Confederation of Metalworkers' Programa Integrar, meanwhile, provides union education and vocational training for union activists, rank-and-file members and the unemployed in a system that focuses on the whole working class and draws connections between workplace reorganization and the broader context of global capitalist restructuring (Lopes, 2002). And Korean workers, in the face of fierce authoritarian governments and employers, have established a militant labour movement (with significant female grassroots leadership) since the 1980s that embeds its educational activity in day-to-day struggle (Moody, 1997: 213–18).

Conclusion

The world's first trade unions were formed to defend workers against employer attacks on their customary rights and property, most notably their control of productive knowledge. Workers' education movements that emerged in the early years of industrial capitalism were dedicated to providing working people with a liberal education that would equip them with the critical skills to analyse the societies in which they lived. Workers' movements at the end of the nineteenth and the beginning of the twentieth centuries sharpened this critique to provide workers with an understanding of their class position within capitalism and the guideposts to their emancipation. With the general acceptance of the legitimacy of trade union organization in the global north in the middle of the twentieth century, and their incorporation into their respective countries' legal regimes, workers' education was narrowed to union education and focused increasingly on training trade union representatives to participate in industrial relations systems.

At the beginning of the twenty-first century, the world's workers are confronting a new phase of capitalist development in which employers are aggressively reorganizing and relocating production, dislocating workers and demanding various monetary and non-monetary concessions. The period of capitalist stability and apparent détente between workers and employers that characterized most of the latter half of the twentieth century in the global north has passed. Union educational responses to these changes are varied. Industrial relations training continues, but has been supplemented by the training of organizers, a broadening of focus from training in union functions to workplace learning, and courses and programmes that draw connections between workplace restructuring and international capitalist reorganization. Unions, however, continue to concentrate on building institutional capacity and empowering their members as trade unionists. While these functions are no doubt necessary for survival in a hostile climate, it is not clear that they are sufficient to meet the challenges mounted by capital.

Many unions in the global south, meanwhile, employ critical analyses of the position of the working class in capitalist society in their organizational and educational work that is more akin to an older workers' education than to what is currently practised in the global north. This is not surprising since these unions and the workers they represent face conditions similar to those that spawned the earlier movements in the north. Capital's global reach no doubt requires that workers' movements throughout the world need to cooperate and learn from each other in order to adequately confront the challenges they face. Movements in the global north would do well to acquaint themselves with what is happening in the global south, while those in the south might study the north's earlier workers' education movements. Experience does suggest that a narrower union-based education is not sufficient in today's climate and that different educational approaches, as part of a broader working-class resistance, are required.

Note

1 Capitalism has developed unevenly. It was born in western Europe and spread circuitously and over time to other parts of the world. Various binary categories – First and Third Worlds, developed and underdeveloped world, core and periphery, for example – have been used over the past 50 years to describe areas of greater and lesser capitalist development. There are no binary categories that can capture the complexity of this process. Nonetheless, for the sake of simplicity, in this chapter I use the terms "global north" to describe the historically developed capitalist world (western Europe, North America, Australasia [geographically in the global south]) and "global south" to describe the rest of the world (Asia, Africa, Latin America and eastern Europe [geographically part of the global north]).

References

Aronowitz, S. (1990) 'The new labor education: a return to ideology', in S. London, E. Tarr and J. Wilson (eds) *The Re-education of the American Working Class*, New York: Greenwood: 21–34.

Boughton, B. (2005) 'What does the working class learn when it works?', Paper presented at Researching Work and Learning conference, Sydney, Australia, December 2005.

Bridgford, J. and Stirling, J. (eds) (2000) *Trade Union Education in Europe*, Brussels: European Trade Union College.

Cooper, L. (1998) 'From rolling mass action to "RPL": the changing discourse of experience and learning in the South African labour movement', *Studies in Continuing Education*, 20, 2: 143–57.

Cooper, L. (2002) 'Union education in the new South African democracy', in B. Spencer (ed.) *Unions and Learning in a Global Economy*, Toronto: Thompson Educational Publishing: 37–49.

Cooper, L. (2005) 'Who or what "teaches" workers political consciousness?' Paper presented at Researching Work and Learning conference, Sydney, Australia, December 2005.

Edwards, R. (1979) *Contested Terrain: The Transformation of the Workplace in the Twentieth Century*, New York: Basic Books.

Forrester, K. (2001) 'Modernised learning: an emerging lifelong agenda by British trade unions?', *Journal of Workplace Learning*, 13, 7/8: 318–26.

Forrester, K. (2002a) 'Unions and workplace learning: the British experience', in B. Spencer (ed.) *Unions and Learning in a Global Economy*, Toronto: Thompson Educational Publishing: 138–48.

Forrester, K. (2002b) 'Work-related learning and the struggle for employee commitment', *Studies in the Education of Adults*, 34, 1: 42–55.

Friesen, G. and Taksa, L. (1996) 'Workers' education in Australia and Canada: a comparative approach to labour's cultural history', *Labour/Le Travail* 38, Fall: 170–97.

Hobsbawm, E. (1995) *Age of Extremes: The Short Twentieth Century, 1914–1991*, London: Abacus.

Holland, C. and Castleton, G. (2002) 'Basic skills and union activity in the UK and Australia', in B. Spencer (ed.) *Unions and Learning in a Global Economy*, Toronto: Thompson Educational Publishing: 89–97.

Hopkins, P.G.H. (1985) *Workers' Education: An International Perspective*, Milton Keynes: Open University Press.

Labor Notes (2006) 'Labor Notes Conference: Building Solidarity From Below', *Labor Notes*, 324, March: 5.

Law, M. (1996) 'Workers' education and training in a new environment' in J. Benseman, B. Findsen and M. Scott (eds) *The Fourth Sector: Adult and Community Education in Aotearoa/New Zealand*, Palmerston North: Dunmore Press: 166–72.

Lopes, F.A.M. (2002) '*Programa Integrar* in Brazil: union intervention in employment, development and education', in B. Spencer (ed.) *Unions and Learning in a Global Economy*, Toronto: Thompson Educational Publishing.

Martin, D. (1995) *Thinking Union: Activism and Education in Canada's Labour Movement*, Toronto: Between the Lines.

McIlroy, J. (1999) 'Making trade unionists: the politics of pedagogy, 1945–79', in A. Campbell, N. Fishman and J. McIlroy (eds) *British Trade Unions and Industrial Politics* (Vol. 1), Aldershot: Ashgate: 37–65.

Miller, D. (2002) 'Training transnational worker representatives: the European works councils', in B. Spencer (ed.) *Unions and Learning in a Global Economy*, Toronto: Thompson Educational Publishing.

Miller, D. and Stirling, J. (1998) 'European Works Council training: an opportunity missed?', *European Journal of Industrial Relations*, 4, 1: 35–56.

Moody, K. (1997) *Workers in a Lean World: Unions in the International Economy*, London: Verso.

Munck, R. (2002) *Globalisation and Labour: The New 'Great Transformation'*, London: Zed Books.

Newman, M. (1993) *The Third Contract: Theory and Practice in Trade Union Training*, Paddington, Australia: Stewart Victor Publishing.

Palmer, B.D. (1976) 'Most uncommon common men: craft and culture in historical perspective', *Labour/Le Travailleur*, 1: 5–31.

Scully-Ross, E. and Chiera, E. (2005) 'Learning to organize: unions, work and learning', paper presented at Researching Work and Learning conference, Sydney, Australia, December 2005.

Simon, B. (1990) 'The struggle for hegemony', in B. Simon (ed.) *The Search for Enlightenment: The Working Class and Adult Education in the Twentieth Century*, London: Lawrence and Wishart.

Spencer, B. (1994) 'Educating Union Canada', *Canadian Journal for the Study of Adult Education*, 8, 2: 45–64.

Spencer, B. (2002) 'Introduction', in B. Spencer (ed.) *Unions and Learning in a Global Economy*, Toronto: Thompson Educational Publishing: 17–24.

Stirling, J. (2002) 'Trade union education in Europe: emerging from the gloom', in B. Spencer (ed.) *Unions and Learning in a Global Economy*, Toronto: Thompson Educational Publishing: 26–36.

Sutherland, J. (1998) 'A trade union approach to learning strategies in a global economy', Paper presented at the Canadian Labour Congress/Ontario Federation of Labour Training Conference, Toronto, June 1998.

Taylor, J. (2001) *Union Learning: Canadian Labour Education in the Twentieth Century*, Toronto: Thompson Educational Publishing.

Widenor, M. and Feekin, L. (2002) 'Organizer training in two hemispheres: the experience in the USA and Australia', in B. Spencer (ed.) *Unions and Learning in a Global Economy*, Toronto: Thompson Educational Publishing: 100–11.

Wong, K. (2002) 'Labour education for immigrant workers in the USA', in B. Spencer (ed.) *Unions and Learning in a Global Economy*, Toronto: Thompson Educational Publishing: 70–8.

Yates, M.D. (2003) *Naming the System: Inequality and Work in the Global Economy*, New York: Monthly Review Press.

6 Healing, hiding and hope(lessness)

HIV/AIDS and workplace education in KwaZulu-Natal, South Africa

Peter Rule

Given the high rates of mortality and illness in the South African adult population ascribed to HIV/AIDS, the pandemic poses particular educational challenges to the workplace and society as a whole. This chapter focuses on HIV/AIDS workplace education and training in the province of KwaZulu-Natal, South Africa, which is one of the global epicentres of the disease. It makes use of data from a review of the South African and international literature, a survey of South African workplace initiatives regarding HIV/AIDS, and qualitative data gathered from workplaces in Pietermaritzburg, the provincial capital. The chapter identifies and examines the various approaches and contending discourses that inform HIV/AIDS education in the workplace. It draws on Bourdieu's notion of 'habitus' in order to understand the challenges that confront HIV/AIDS education. Mezirow's transformative theory and his notion of perspective transformation provide a framework for engaging with adult learners on the issue of HIV/AIDS.

Introduction

HIV/AIDS is the quintessential other. At a biological level, it disguises itself as a retrovirus and weakens the immune system's resistance to opportunistic diseases. Many people, particularly in the South, die of AIDS without ever knowing that they are infected. At a social level, AIDS was initially associated with the 'homosexual and drug-using other' and later with marginalized groups such as sex workers and migrant workers. Its associations with 'suspect' moral conduct and, in Africa, with bewitchment, create stigma, silence and secrecy around the disease. This is reflected in language where all sorts of distancing euphemisms and conspiracy-laden acronyms confirm the otherness of the disease (Sontag 1990). At the macro-political level, AIDS is the other in relation to South Africa's fledgling democracy, threatening to roll back the socio-political and economic gains of the post-apartheid era by sapping government resources and destabilizing social structures.

In the workplace, HIV/AIDS raises the spectre, for workers, of stigmatization, discrimination and dismissal, and the ultimate otherness of death. For management, it connotes absenteeism, loss of productivity and high staff turnover. South African companies report stigma and discrimination as the biggest obstacles to effective HIV/AIDS programmes, bigger even than cost (Ellis and Terwin 2005). Confronting and dealing with the otherness of HIV/AIDS, and the fear that it evokes, is thus one of the central challenges of HIV/AIDS education in the workplace.

This chapter asks the question, how should workplaces in South Africa respond, with regard to education and training, to the challenges of HIV/AIDS? It makes use of data from a review of the South African and international literature, a survey of South African workplace initiatives regarding HIV/AIDS, and qualitative data gathered from workplaces in Pietermaritzburg, the provincial capital of KwaZulu-Natal. In order to provide a context, it begins by describing the extent of the epidemic in South Africa, with a focus on the province of KwaZulu-Natal, the epicentre of the disease, and on the workplace situation. It goes on to examine the economic impact of HIV/AIDS and to outline the legislative framework for HIV/AIDS in the workplace. The paper then shifts to HIV/AIDS education in the workplace. It identifies four foci within workplace education programmes and critically assesses their efficacy in relation to the changing social context of AIDS and the epidemiological progress of the disease. It draws on Bourdieu's notion of habitus, to understand the challenge of HIV/AIDS education in the workplace, and the links between workplace and community interventions. It concludes by linking habitus to the context of adult education and, in particular, Mezirow's transformative theory, to make a case for the centrality of perspective transformation in HIV/AIDS education.

Prevalence, incidence and mortality rates in South Africa

South Africa has the largest number of people living with HIV in the world, estimated at about 5.7 to 6.2 million people or approximately 15 per cent of the population (Department of Health 2005). HIV prevalence is highest in the province of KwaZulu-Natal, on the fertile and densely populated eastern seaboard. HIV prevalence among antenatal clinic attendees nationally rose from 0.7 per cent in 1990 to 27.9 per cent in 2003 (Gouws and Karim 2005: 56). By 2004 the prevalence rate at ante-natal clinics in KwaZulu-Natal had risen to 40.7 per cent with more than 50 per cent of young women in the 20–24 age group infected (Department of Health 2005).

A survey of educators released in 2005 found that KwaZulu-Natal had the highest rate of infection among educators, 21.8 per cent compared with a national average of 12.7 per cent (HSRC 2005). Infection rates are much higher among certain other categories of work such as truck drivers, sex workers and mine workers (Campbell 2003; Gouws and Karim 2005). Men and women are differentially affected, with more women infected, and at a younger age, than men (HSRC 2002; Bradshaw and Dorrington 2005).

While there are indications that the disease is levelling in South Africa and that the rates of incidence are beginning to decline, the rate of mortality continues to rise because of the existing prevalence rate. Bradshaw and Dorrington (2005) comment in particular on the rapid increase in the young adult mortality rate. The social implications of this high young adult mortality rate are manifold, including increasing numbers of orphans and child-headed households, reduced household income and care, leading to increasing household impoverishment, as well as consequences at a macroeconomic level.

The economic impact of HIV/AIDS

HIV/AIDS has a powerful economic impact on government, business and ordinary households. At the level of government, the pandemic takes a huge chunk of the national health budget, which could otherwise be allocated to preventive medicine and to tackling other critical diseases such as tuberculosis and cancer, or reallocated to development spending in other departments such as housing and education. HIV/AIDS also places a strain on the welfare system as more and more people apply for disability grants as a consequence of infection, and for child support grants to raise AIDS orphans.

The impact of HIV/AIDS on business is growing. For more than a decade, business responded to the disease either tardily or not at all on the fallacious premise that AIDS primarily affected unskilled labourers who were easily replaceable (Whiteside and Sunter 2000; Dickinson 2004a: 83). There is now evidence that AIDS has affected business much more severely than initially anticipated, and businesses in KwaZulu-Natal are hardest hit: 57 per cent of companies in KwaZulu-Natal indicated that HIV/AIDS had reduced labour productivity or increased absenteeism, a higher percentage than any other province (Ellis and Terwin 2005: 44).

Besides businesses, HIV/AIDS has a grievously destructive impact on households, families and communities. A household typically loses its breadwinners, is plunged into poverty and even disintegration as care-givers die and orphans are absorbed into other households or left to fend for themselves (Whiteside 2005). This places HIV/AIDS workplace programmes in perspective. As Jonathan Oppenheimer, managing director of De Beers Consolidated Mines, noted on receiving an award for the De Beers HIV testing programme: 'our sense of accomplishment is coupled with a growing understanding that the boundary between company and community is an artificial and tenuous distinction when it comes to combating a disease of the magnitude of AIDS' (Strategiy 2005: 2).

The legislative framework

South Africa has a progressive legislative framework for dealing with HIV/AIDS in the workplace. This framework includes clauses in the Bill of Rights, forming part of the South African Constitution (Act 108 of 1996), which guarantee the right of everyone to fair labour practices and to equal treatment. The Labour Relations Act (Act 66 of 1995) confirms this by stating that discrimination against employees on any grounds, including sexual orientation and disability, is an unfair labour practice. This legislation was tested and upheld in the Constitutional Court (Hoffman v. South African Airways 2000). The Employment Equity Act (Act 55 of 1998) explicitly protects employees against unfair discrimination on the basis of their HIV status regarding employee benefits, pre-employment testing and dismissal.

Dealing with HIV/AIDS in the workplace

Now that I have outlined the broader socio-economic and legislative context, I turn to four strategies for HIV/AIDS education in the workplace that are currently employed in South Africa: education for prevention; education for human rights; education for damage control; and education for community engagement. These strategies are not mutually exclusive. They often overlap and inform each other. However, they point to distinct foci in the struggle with the disease and represent contending interests. Ideally, an integrated education programme that embraces all interests would be optimal.

Education for prevention

This approach aims to equip the workforce to protect itself and thereby to reduce the rate of new infections, reduce costs for employees and impacts on workers' households. This approach is dominated by a technical discourse around safe sex, including condom use. It tends to ignore the moral and cultural issues around sex, and thus the 'habitus' of workers (see discussion of Bourdieu's notion of habitus below).

Prevention programmes are widely implemented in the workplace but do not always use the best methods. Mapolisa and Stevens (2003), in their national study of workplaces, found that two-thirds of shop stewards reported prevention programmes at their workplaces, but that these programmes were 'fairly passive and required few resources', using pamphlets and posters rather than training peer educators and providing treatment. They argue that 'the cheaper and easier activities had been chosen over the ones known as more effective and successful but more costly' (Mapolisa and Stevens 2003: 59).

Surveys indicate that most workers know about HIV/AIDS. However, there is a gap between awareness and behaviour change. Campbell's research among mine workers and sex workers in Gauteng shows that there are powerful social determinants of behaviour, such as economic subsistence and cultural assertions of masculinity, that obviate against behaviour change (Campbell 2003). Women in particular are often disempowered when it comes to negotiating safe sexual encounters because of their social status and dependence. While education for prevention is essential, it is not sufficient for addressing a context in which many workers are already HIV positive and knowledge interventions in themselves do not necessarily lead to behaviour change.

Education for human rights

The focus here is on programmes that raise awareness about rights to privacy, voluntary testing, equality of treatment and non-discrimination, and access to resources such as counselling, testing, medication and care. It finds expression in a rights-based discourse which refers to supporting legislation.

The emphasis on rights has been championed by legal advice agencies (Achmat 1997) and some trade unions who seek to protect their members against victimization by management on the basis of their HIV status. It has also been the focus of literacy programmes that deal with HIV/AIDS (Project Literacy 2001). Despite a progressive legislative environment, stigma associated with HIV/AIDS is still widespread in the workplace and takes the form, among employers, of termination of employment and refusals to offer employment. A national survey of companies found that stigma was the greatest single obstacle to the effectiveness of HIV/AIDS programmes (Ellis and Terwin 2005). Among workers it manifests in a refusal to discuss HIV/AIDS, since it is regarded as 'a private matter', and in a reluctance to disclose HIV positive status in the workplace (Mapolisa and Stevens 2003; Masindi 2003; Dickinson 2004b).

The rights discourse is critically important as a way of countering stigma. However, by itself it may be counterproductive since employees might permanently delay undergoing HIV testing because it is their right to refuse testing and treatment, and therefore never confront and deal with their potentially HIV-positive status.

Education for damage control

This is a management-driven approach which begins with a risk assessment and then implementation of AIDS awareness programmes, testing and even treatment. The focus here is on 'managing' the disease in order to reduce its harmful impact on company productivity and profitability. It is informed by a technical management discourse around risk analysis, strategy, implementation and evaluation.

This approach places primary emphasis on productivity and profitability rather than people. It courts failure by not securing the buy-in of employees and unions, and not convincing them that it has their interests at heart. In some instances, unions have opposed workplace testing for HIV because of suspicions that the results could be used to discriminate against HIV positive workers and undermine their rights (Dickinson 2004a) or simply not collected results of tests (AIDS Education Worker 2006).

Because of its cultural, moral and political overtones, HIV/AIDS cannot be viewed merely as a technical issue requiring appropriate management strategies. Trust is of critical importance: trust between management and unions; employers and employees; employees and medical practitioners. Involvement of both management and unions in developing and disseminating an AIDS policy is crucial, as is the visible participation of high-profile managers and union leaders, and a clear indication from the top of the importance of the programme. For example, Sasol's successful HIV/AIDS Response Programme (SHARP) involved the company stopping work for a compulsory, four-hour long workshop, with managers and union leaders setting an example by being tested first, and HIV positive workers playing a role in raising awareness and advocating testing and treatment (Geldenhuys 2005).

Education for community engagement

This approach identifies the cultural and social roles of workers, their sexual mores and expectations, generating discussion around these roles and their dangers; it sets up networks of support in and with communities. It is informed, on the one hand, by a discourse of corporate accountability with its notions of corporate citizenship, reputation management, and social and environmental responsibility (Burton 2002); and, on the other, by a discourse of community development which includes notions of participation, sustainability, community impact and education.

Larger companies in South Africa such as Sasol (Geldenhuys 2005) and De Beers (Strategiy 2005) have begun to move beyond employee-targeted programmes to include the communities from which employees come. Strategies have included making available Voluntary Counselling and Testing (VCT) and treatment, in the form of antiretroviral drugs, to the family members of employees. This has become more possible as the cost of drugs has fallen.

The challenges inherent in this approach have to do with defining the parameters of involvement (Dickinson 2004a). A company might become overextended in its provision of support to the community in a way that is not sustainable, with the consequent fall-out of a withdrawal of services. It might also confuse its own role with that of the state, whose responsibility it is ultimately to provide health services to the public. As one company director put it, 'we need to ask whether we're running a company or a province' (Dickinson 2004a: 85). Another challenge involves the disparity between corporate and community cultures and capacities, as the corporate and community sectors learn to speak each other's languages and develop effective partnerships in responding to the pandemic.

Habitus, sexual practices and HIV/AIDS education

The French sociologist Pierre Bourdieu's notion of 'habitus' provides a useful conceptual tool for understanding challenges facing HIV/AIDS education in South Africa. The habitus refers to 'systems of durable, transposable dispositions' which are 'principles of the generation and structuring of practices and representations' (Bourdieu 1977: 72). The habitus is embodied in members of a group or a class, manifesting in their speech, actions and postures. I understand the habitus as the embodied schemes or assumptions that lie behind the way people say and do things. These schemes are informed by family and class backgrounds, role models, typical ways of referring to phenomena in particular culture, prevailing attitudes and norms in society. The habitus is produced and internalized through experience rather than explicit discourse and pedagogy.

Bourdieu's notion of habitus is useful for understanding HIV/AIDS education because of its emphasis on the body and the way that the habitus is inscribed on the body. This moulding of the body happens at a pre-conscious level of practice and differs radically along gender lines. Males have a 'centrifugal' orientation which is directed towards the outside world of work, politics and war, whereas females have a 'centripetal' orientation directed towards the home, domestic work and child-rearing. Importantly, this sexual habitus includes an inscription of power relations between male and female.

There is a great deal of evidence in South Africa that the prevailing sexual habitus of men and women contributes to the growth of the HIV/AIDS pandemic (Karim 2005; Harrison 2005). In rural South Africa, twice as many women are infected as men and women generally acquire HIV at least five to ten years earlier than men (Karim 2005: 245). Women's inferior social and economic position makes them dependent on men and leads some to using sex as a commodity in order to make a living. In addition, the sexual habitus of women which casts them in a subordinate role makes them vulnerable, particularly as masculinity is cast in terms of 'aggression, dominance, independence' (Karim 2005: 253). The ensuing double standard links sexual practices with reproduction and morality for women, but endorses multiple sexual partners for men. Public health programmes promoting abstinence, fidelity and condom use run the danger of being ineffective because they ignore existing gender inequalities.

The prevailing sexual habitus also makes men vulnerable to HIV infection (Makahye 2005). Peer pressure constructs sexual liaison with multiple partners as evidence of manliness. In addition, women and girls expect males to fulfil 'traditional masculine behaviours', thus maintaining the gendered system despite their oppression within it because of their economic vulnerability and need (Makahye 2005).

In sum, a patriarchal society such as South Africa produces a certain kind of sexual habitus, comprising both conscious and unconscious dispositions, which generate the following practices and representations: unprotected sex; multiple sexual partners; taboos around talking openly about sex; power imbalances between men and women in making decisions around when, how and with whom to have sex. In its more pathological forms, patriarchy also contributes to a habitus in which the practice of rape and the belief that unprotected sex with a virgin will cure AIDS become possible. All of these conditions contribute to the AIDS epidemic. Set against the background of a South African society characterized by migrant labour, unemployment and poverty, and by a government that for a long time refused to acknowledge the link between the HIV virus and AIDS, a patriarchal sexual habitus becomes potentially lethal. This is the broader context of structural inequalities around class and gender which HIV/AIDS education initiatives in the workplace need to take into account.

What are the implications of the foregoing analysis for HIV/AIDS education in the workplace? First, the embodied and pre-conscious nature of the sexual habitus means that disseminating information will not, by itself, necessarily change sexual practices. Second, the sexual habitus entails power relations, arising from structurally determined and perpetuated gender inequalities, that need to be addressed within HIV/AIDS education programmes. Third, programmes need to be located in the community, where the sexual habitus is formed and perpetuated, and not only or primarily in the workplace (Frolich 2005; Makahye 2005). HIV/AIDS is not merely a problem of productivity and profitability, but a much wider societal challenge which has dire implications for society at large.

While the habitus provides a useful way of understanding challenges to HIV/AIDS education in South Africa, it does not offer any particular leads for the practice of workplace education. In the field of adult education, Jack Mezirow, the American theorist and practitioner, offers an approach to engaging with the sexual habitus through transformative learning.

Applying transformation theory: Mezirow and HIV/AIDS education

Mezirow views the construction of meaning as a key to understanding adult learning. He develops the concept of 'meaning perspectives' as 'frames of reference' or 'habits of expectation' that filter our sense perceptions'; they 'govern the activities of perceiving, comprehending, and remembering' and thus operate as 'perceptual and interpretive codes in the construal of meaning' (Mezirow 1991: 4). Mezirow's meaning perspectives are similar to the 'systems of durable, transposable dispositions' which constitute Bourdieu's habitus in that they are products of socialization and are largely naturalized and taken for granted. Meaning perspectives (rule systems governing perception and cognition) are manifest in particular 'meaning schemes' (specific knowledge, beliefs, value judgements or feelings involved in making an interpretation). In regard to the sexual habitus, an example of a meaning perspective might be 'patriarchy' and the meaning schemes associated with it could include 'woman as subordinate to man', 'woman as primary care-giver', 'man as initiator of sex' and so on. What Bourdieu adds to Mezirow is his emphasis on the embodied nature of these perspectives as ingrained dispositions of the bodily hexis.

> Meaning perspectives that are uncritically assimilated through socialization can distort our ways of knowing, believing and feeling. This is where the critically reflective process of adult learning can help to transform meaning perspectives and enable learners to develop a 'more inclusive, differentiated, permeable (open to other points of view), and integrated meaning perspective'.
>
> (Mezirow 1991: 7)

What Mezirow adds to Bourdieu's notion of habitus is the possibility of change and how change might happen through adult learning. 'Transformation theory contributes a needed and emancipatory dimension to socialization theory' (Mezirow 1991: 3). For Mezirow, transformative theory is particularly relevant to societies in transition as a result of modernization, where traditional norms and values, such as 'the place of women in the kitchen', are under strain. The HIV/AIDS pandemic arguably constitutes a 'disorienting dilemma', to use Mezirow's phrase, at both a personal and a collective level, which provides an opportunity for transformative learning. Such learning is often extremely difficult and adults are likely to resist change to deeply embedded and embodied norms and practices. However, in the lethal context of HIV/AIDS, transformative learning becomes a survival imperative.

Towards a holistic approach

Given the need for perspective transformation at both the individual and collective levels in relation to HIV/AIDS workplace education, the following guidelines drawn from the literature and best practice are pertinent:

- Development of clear AIDS policies in the workplace which are generated by and disseminated among all relevant stakeholders, including management and staff unions. This can create a climate in which the challenges of HIV/AIDS are formally recognized and addressed in the workplace, thus breaking the silence, secrecy and ignorance associated with the disease.

- Involvement of People Living with HIV and AIDS (PLHAs) in workplace programmes as role models, preferably people who are situated in the workplace itself. This makes the threat of the disease real to people in the workplace, as well as the possibility of dealing with the disease positively.
- PLHAs should play a role in the planning, implementation, evaluation and follow-up of programmes rather than making single appearances during a programme, but should also be deployed carefully in recognition of their particular strengths and limitations (Dickinson 2004b).
- Mainstreaming of gender as an integrated part of HIV/AIDS education programmes. According to UNESCO, gender mainstreaming is a process of 'assessing the implications for men and women of any planned action, including legislation, policies or programmes, in any area and at all levels'. The ultimate aim of such mainstreaming is 'gender equality' (UNESCO cited in Commonwealth Secretariat 2002: 14).
- Formation of partnerships between workplaces and communities, as well as with government at local, provincial and national levels. This is in line with the benefits of a multi-sectoral approach which recognizes that no single sector of society can deal with the disease on its own. Companies such as De Beers and Anglo Platinum in the mining sector, and Sasol in the fuel sector, have led the way in this regard (Ellis and Terwin 2005; Geldenhuys 2005; Strategiy 2005).

Given these general guidelines, what should HIV/AIDS programmes in the workplace, informed by Mezirow's transformation theory, Bourdieu's notion of habitus and emerging best practice in South Africa and elsewhere, look like?

What Mezirow and Bourdieu contribute to an understanding of HIV/AIDS education in the context of adult learning is that adults bring to the learning encounter their own habitus in relation to sexuality, and their own meaning perspectives through which they understand and interpret the phenomenon of HIV/AIDS. Simply providing adult learners with information is not likely to transform the meaning perspectives that govern their behaviour. A more thorough-going process of personal engagement and critical reflection is necessary. This could involve:

1   identifying HIV/AIDS as a 'disorienting dilemma' which confronts adult learners, whether they are infected or affected, at a personal and social level; because of the stigma and silence surrounding HIV/

AIDS, an explicit acknowledgement of the importance of dealing with the disease, in the form of an AIDS policy and management and union-sanctioned programmes, will help to create an environment that is conducive to open discussion of the issue;

2 critically reflecting on existing meaning perspectives that adults hold and feelings that they experience in relation to sexuality in general and HIV/AIDS in particular; the stimulus for critical reflection could be provided in a variety of non-threatening ways, including drama, testimony of people living with HIV and AIDS, role play and peer group discussion;

3 providing information on issues such as the causes of HIV infection, prevention and treatment as an aid to critical reflection; and on the rights of employees living with HIV and AIDS;

4 allowing participants to generate alternative ways of thinking, feeling, believing and behaving through peer discussion;

5 providing resources to support new meaning perspectives, including availability of condoms, treatment, counselling, testing, peer group support;

6 generating collective action in the communities of participants through engagement with local organizations such as support groups, home-based carers, women's organizations, schools and sports clubs.

In each of these steps, the importance of gender mainstreaming and a multisectoral approach should be integrated.

Conclusion

HIV/AIDS constitutes a major challenge to adult education globally, but particularly in sub-Saharan Africa where the epicentre of the disease resides. Programmes that simply transmit information have not been effective. A more thorough-going approach which acknowledges the deeply ingrained and gender-differentiated nature of the sexual habitus, and which critically engages adult learners in transforming their meaning perspectives in a supportive environment, holds out greater promise.

References

Achmat, Z. (1997) *HIV/AIDS and the Law: A Resource Manual*, Johannesburg: AIDS Law Project/Lawyers for Human Rights.
AIDS Education Worker (2006) Interviewed by Peter Rule in Pietermaritzburg, 29 March 2006.
Bourdieu, P. (1977) *Outline of a Theory of Practice*, Trans. R. Nice, Cambridge: Cambridge University Press.

Bradshaw, D. and Dorrington, R.E. (2005) 'AIDS-related mortality in South Africa', in S. Karim and Q. Karim (eds) *HIV/AIDS in South Africa*, Cape Town: Cambridge University Press.

Burton, L. (2002) 'In good company: why social and environmental responsibility is crucial for sustained business success', *People Dynamics*, September: 20–3.

Campbell, C. (2003) *'Letting Them Die': How HIV/AIDS Prevention Programmes Often Fail*, Cape Town: Double Storey.

Commonwealth Secretariat (2002) *Gender Mainstreaming in HIV/AIDS*, London: Commonwealth Secretariat.

Department of Health (2005) 'National HIV and Syphilis Antenatal Sero-Prevalence Survey in South Africa 2004'. Available at http://www.doh.gov.za (Accessed 27 March 2006).

Dickinson, D. (2004a) 'Corporate South Africa's response to HIV/AIDS: why so slow?', *South African Labour Bulletin*, 28 (6): 81–6.

Dickinson, D. (2004b) 'People living openly with HIV/AIDS in the workplace', *South African Labour Bulletin*, 28 (2): 59–62.

Ellis, L. and Terwin, J. (2005) *The Impact of AIDS on Selected Business Sectors in South Africa*, Stellenbosch: Bureau for Economic Research, Stellenbosch University.

Frolich, J. (2005) 'The impact of AIDS on the community', in S. Karim and Q. Karim (eds) *HIV/AIDS in South Africa*, Cape Town: Cambridge University Press.

Geldenhuys, H. (2005) 'Sasol hones its weapons to help workforce fight scourge', *Sunday Times*, 4 December: 12.

Gouws, E. and Karim, Q. (2005) 'HIV infection in South Africa: the evolving epidemic', in S. Karim and Q. Karim (eds) *HIV/AIDS in South Africa*, Cape Town: Cambridge University Press.

Harrison, A. (2005) 'Young people and HIV/AIDS in South Africa: prevalence of infection, risk factors and social context', in S. Karim and Q. Karim (eds) *HIV/AIDS in South Africa*, Cape Town: Cambridge University Press.

HSRC (2002) *First Nationally Representative Survey Results of HIV Prevalence*, Pretoria: Human Sciences Research Council.

HSRC (2005) 'HIV Prevalence among South African educators in public schools: Fact Sheet 6'. Available at http://www.hsrc.ac.za/media/2005/3/20050331FactSheet6.html (Accessed 21 March 2006).

Karim, Q. (2005) 'Heterosexual transmission of HIV: the importance of a gendered perspective in HIV prevention', in S. Karim and Q. Karim (eds) *HIV/AIDS in South Africa*, Cape Town: Cambridge University Press.

Makahye, G. (2005) 'Young men', in S. Karim and Q. Karim (eds) *HIV/AIDS in South Africa*, Cape Town: Cambridge University Press.

Mapolisa, S. and Stevens, M. (2003) 'Unions fall short on HIV/AIDS', *South African Labour Bulletin*, 27 (6): 58–60.

Masindi, N. (2003) 'Measuring HIV/AIDS related stigma: a literature review', Pretoria: Centre for the Study of HIV/AIDS, University of Pretoria.

Mezirow, J. (1991) *Transformative Dimensions of Adult Learning*, San Francisco, CA: Jossey-Bass.

Project Literacy (2001) *Positive People: Managing HIV/AIDS in the Workplace and Community*, Arcadia: Project Literacy; Cape Town: Kagiso Education.

Sontag, S. (1990) *Illness as Metaphor and AIDS and Its Metaphors*, New York: Doubleday.

Strategiy (2005) 'De Beers wins international HIV/AIDS award'. Available at http://www.strategiy.com (Accessed 11 November 2005).

Whiteside, A. (2005) 'The economic impact of AIDS', in Karim, S. and Karim, Q. (eds) *HIV/AIDS in South Africa*, Cape Town: Cambridge University Press.

Whiteside, A. and Sunter, C. (2000) *AIDS: The Challenge for South Africa*, Cape Town: Human and Rousseau and Tafelberg.

Part II

Knowing and working the global economy

7 Working life learning, young people and competitive advantage

Notes from a European perspective[1]

Keith Forrester

The progression of young people into the labour market remains a problematic area for policy-makers throughout the enlarged European Union. This chapter provides a selective and critical review of the human capital theory assumptions influencing policy initiatives affecting young people's transition into work. Particular attention is given to the emerging dominant neo-liberal views seen as necessary to 'high performance' labour markets. It is suggested that the vocational learning of young people is being distorted increasingly by long-standing contradictions between liberalisation and the tradition of the state intervention, social partnership model in most European countries. Against a background of revolt by young people and trade unions in France together with the rejection of the European Constitution, it is suggested that a deepening anger and political frustration characterises the current policy direction of skill formation strategies for young people in many parts of Europe.

Introduction

Fifteen hundred cars had to burn in a single night and then, on a descending scale, nine hundred, five hundred, two hundred, for the daily'norm' to be reached again, and for people to realise that ninety cars on average are torched every night in this gentle France of ours.

(Baudrillard 2006: 5) on the revolt of young French people burning their own banlieus in October/November 2005

Over the last decade or so, there has emerged in the UK, the European Union (EU) and other late capitalist economies, a widespread policy consensus that stresses the importance and pursuit of a high skill, knowledge-based economy and learning society. 'Skills, knowledge, education, training and learning are now seen as the answer to a multitude of economic and social problems, ranging from competitiveness, productivity and economic growth to unemployment and social exclusion' (Lloyd and Payne 2002: 365). Existing pathways from school to work, and vocational education and training (VET) arrangements more generally, acquire added importance. At the same time however, increasing doubts are raised about the simplistic notions of human capital theory underpinning claims for the vocational pathways seen as characterising a high skilled economy. At a political level and hot on the heels of the 'non' vote in France to the European Constitution, the revolt by young people from the suburbs of Paris against the neo-liberal labour market reforms of the de Villepin government provided graphic evidence of the deep anger and political frustration towards French in particular but EU economic strategies in general. Nationwide closures of the universities and many secondary schools together with a general strike denounced the solution of 'flexploitation' of young people in particular, to the problems of racism, unemployment and global capital.

This chapter will focus on the situation in Europe, with particular attention given to Britain. Apart from the historic failure to develop high quality apprenticeship pathways highlighted by Keep (2001), Britain is seen as representing a particular political direction within the strategic debates on 'the way forward' within the European Union. In contrast to the largely uncritical country and regional policy pronouncements of VET implicit in EU and member state policy documentation, this chapter argues that the present period is best characterised by doubt, uncertainty and wide-ranging debate. Some of the reasons behind this uncertainty – such as global economic and technological changes – are not particular to Europe and can be seen as important contextual features informing VET reform policies elsewhere, such as in Canada, Australia and South Africa (Keating *et al.* 2002). In other instances, such as the absorption of the new accession countries into the EU, there is obviously a particular regional dimension to the uncertainties. Wider socio-economic pressures together with new educational ideas are resulting in acute pressures for change but in directions that are unclear.

The first section of the chapter provides a brief overview of the policy context within Europe. The 'Lisbon Agenda', it will be suggested, is providing a framework, discipline and urgency for reform of vocational training rarely seen at a European level. It will be argued that this 'urgency' results from a marked turn within the region towards neo-liberal formulations that are resulting in profound socio-economic tensions. In the second section, examples of the vocational training experiences available to workers within Europe are discussed. Particular attention is given to apprenticeship schemes. The isolation at policy and conceptual levels of training schemes for young people from wider societal considerations, it will be argued, is a significant weakness in attempts to 'modernise' programmes. The third section will highlight two areas that, it is suggested, will ultimately contribute towards shaping the strategic nature and extent of the VET experienced by apprentices.

Methodologically, it is of course a hazardous task to discuss examples and to draw conclusions from a regional European perspective. As Attwell and Hughes note,

Until recently transitional research in VET has been focused primarily on the tasks of information gathering and exchange. Typically, experts from different countries agreed on a common format for information collecting and published what were often point to point mapping studies.

(Attwell and Hughes 2004: 1)

The numerous publications from the European Centre for the Development of Vocational Training (CEDEFOP) on European VET systems have been characterised by such an approach and have generated a wealth of cross-national, national country and sector studies in VET. However, instead of a descriptive comparative approach, this chapter focuses on a selective identification of key trends and developmental tasks. Such an approach avoids the largely deterministic and prescriptive stance that pervades much of the literature.

Vocational learning at the centre of policy developments

Around 80 million people aged between 26 and 64 years within the EU are seen as 'low skilled' (European Unit 2004). The variety of VET systems and programmes is great. When the proposed enlarging of the EU (through the 'acceding and candidate' countries) is included, this variety and diversity is daunting. In the Central and Eastern European acceding and candidate countries, for example, VET issues are low on the political agenda with often impoverished infrastructures (ETF 2004: 26). In the newer Mediterranean countries, the ETF survey suggests that current VET schemes are expensive, bureaucratically designed and ineffective. Coherent systemic reform is absent and few countries have adopted a comprehensive approach to VET reforms.

Partly as a response to the particular problems posed by the acceding and candidate countries, but more importantly as a response to perceived changes in the wider global economy, a number of important strategic policy issues dominate thinking and (in)activity across the EU. The Lisbon European Council summit of March 2000, for example, concluded with a number of recommendations committing the EU to becoming, by 2010, 'the most dynamic and competitive knowledge-based economy in the world capable of sustainable economic growth with more and better jobs and greater social cohesion, and respect for the environment'. Central to the grandiose claims of the Lisbon Strategy was the improvement of the quality and effectiveness of EU education and training systems. The 2002 'Copenhagen Declaration' continued this focus on the creation of 'a knowledge-based Europe'. A number of practical initiatives aimed at the development of a single framework for the transparency of competencies and qualifications ('Europass') were outlined. Annual member state obligations and progress on the Lisbon Strategy objectives are available for inspection together with periodic review reports (see Kok 2004). The 2004 Maastricht Communiqué (European Commission 2004), together with the 2004 Interim Report 'Education and Training 2010', again focused on the current and future priorities of VET within the expanding European Union. There is little doubt that education and training within a 'dynamic knowledge-based economy', as the Lisbon Strategy puts it, represents a key strategic concern at both a policy and a practice level. On the other hand, there are real doubts about whether such concerns are sufficient to address and engage with the dilemmas and tensions characterising national state provision. As will be argued below, the effectiveness and contribution of VET reside less with issues of qualifications, credentials, participation rates, retention data, curriculum and pedagogy (important as they are) and more with wider issues of a political economic nature.

Apprenticeship learning and the wider societal context

Apprenticeships have survived as an internationally understood structure within which young people can learn, demonstrate their abilities and potential and develop their identities. At a general level, apprenticeships can be seen as involving three broad and interrelated dimensions: the contractual framework between the employer and trainee, the cultural socialising aspects of introducing apprentices into work and adulthood, and the formal and informal aspects of the learning (Fuller and Unwin 2003). The nature and meaning of apprenticeship varies greatly, however, once historical and national particularities are included in any analysis. The historical weakness of the British apprenticeship arrangements, for example, through on-the-job training coupled with voluntary attendance in evening class provision, resulted in industrial training failing to become institutionalised within the national education system. As a recent analysis of UK skills and education development argues,

> The training infrastructure between ages 14–19 suffers from the poor standing of ill-financed colleges and an under-developed apprentice system. Britain is seen to fall between two stools; it has neither a fully-fledged employer-based apprentice system nor an established mix between formal colleges and informal on the job learning – the so-called dual system.
>
> (The Work Foundation 2005)

As Dessinger (2004: 44) suggests, 'the division of education and training typical (of nineteenth century Britain) paralysed the development of educational opportunities for the working classes and helped create a social pattern of industrial training being that of "boy labourers" rather than "boy learners"'.

The historical past continues to weigh heavily on both the content and debate of apprenticeships today. The much-publicised launch in 1986 of the National Vocational Qualifications (NVQs), for example, together with the family of Modern Apprenticeships (MAs) in 1995, radically separates the UK experience and thinking from most other countries in Europe. Absent in MAs is any minimum training period – such as a three-year programme for bakers – any need for a general education, any robust quality, relevance criteria or strong regulatory framework. It is hardly surprising that 'success' or 'completion' rates remain a continuing area of concern. Despite a number of recent reforms, worries continue to exist. As one commentator from the Social Market Foundation put it recently,

> The government spends about £7 billion on education and training for low skilled young people and adults. Many programmes do little to make the participants more employable.
>
> (Alakeson 2005: 17)

Central to the predominantly market-led Anglo-Saxon model of apprenticeships and to VET more generally is the primacy of employers and of the social partners. In Denmark, for example, labour is well organised with high levels of unionisation and a history of collaboration with employers over industrial training. Recent reforms to the apprenticeship programme have resulted in more time spent in school on theoretical teaching than in the German system and more in-company learning than in the Swedish system. However, the highly regarded German 'Dual System' (and to a lesser extent, the systems in Austria and Switzerland as well) is usually seen as demonstrating the advantages and effectiveness of the social democratic/social partner approach to apprenticeships when compared with the Anglo-Saxon/market driven model. In contrast to the social class divisions characterising the educational and vocational routes for young people in the UK, the German 'training culture' is based on a long-standing and widely accepted understanding of the importance of an underpinning pedagogical basis to apprenticeship learning, setting it apart from 'normal work'. German apprenticeships represent a system of training rather than a system of employment as in the market-driven economies.

However, commentators such as Attwell and Hughes (2004) talk of the 'crisis' facing the German dual system 'which partly stems from falling enrolment numbers and partially from the relative inflexibility of the system'. Others mention the difficulties of the dual system sufficiently covering new occupational areas that are emerging from recent economic and technological developments. In the UK, an extensive literature documents the historical failure of British employers to provide serious and high quality vocational learning opportunities for young people (Keep *et al.* 2002: 21).

Attempts to understand the continuing underperformance of apprenticeship schemes in Britain or the inflexibility of dual schemes are increasingly moving beyond the narrow policy rhetoric characterising much documentation. Isolating skill formation strategies from wider societal concerns for young people moving into work can easily result in prescriptive assertions that ignore the limits and constraints of possible practices. The importance of a wider societal framework becomes even more urgent given the policy direction of seeing skills as 'the mechanism through which countries will be able to sustain higher wages, reduce unemployment, pay for a decent welfare state and provide equality of opportunities' (Lloyd and Payne 2004: 5). Vocational learning, be it for young people or adults, ultimately, it is suggested, is a political choice about a fairer or more humane society. As such, it involves assumptions and views (often hidden) about gender, industrial democracy and political citizenship as well as strong labour and social rights, a more equal distribution of income and tolerance and respect for others. As Lloyd and Payne (2002) point out, young people making the transition from school to work within a more market-driven model of capitalism do so within high levels of social inequality, limited trade union and worker rights, long working hours, a polarised distribution of skills and relatively low wages (Guile 2004, Keep 2001).

Pressures for change?

As Fuller and Unwin (2003: 41) note, it is these wider societal changes that have resulted in 'several countries throughout Europe and beyond … attempting to reform their apprenticeship systems in response to a number of challenges'. A growing literature on recent changes in work and social life resulting from 'globalisation' now exists and provides a fruitful and imaginative means through which to critically re-examine VET understandings, institutions and practices. Increasingly, there is the realisation that ability and work in the period ahead are likely to be based on more than 'the bottom line'. What are some of the issues and 'challenges' that are influencing this rethinking and reform?

Employer engagement?

Late capitalist economies today share the view that global economic pressures are forcing governments to assume responsibility for speeding the transition towards the adoption of a high skills pathway and for reforms within the education and training systems that will increase the supply of these skills. However, instead of a high skills, high value added strategy allied to a supportive apprenticeship and VET system to produce a national workforce, there are other equally attractive routes to competitive advantage within advanced capitalist economies. These include protected markets, economic growth through company mergers or acquisitions, cost-cutting strategies, seeking monopoly power and new forms of Fordism. Given that skills and vocational knowledge are only a means to an end in the dominant late capitalist visions of economic survival, these alternative pathways contribute towards understanding the low importance, status and performance of apprenticeships and VET in particular countries (Ackroyd and Procter 1998).

Such a poor record and performance on the recognition and development of 'vocational knowing' amongst employees may not be particular to the British economy. It may be instead a characteristic of the Anglo-American variety of development and of countries adhering to the 'flexibility' advice of agencies such as the OECD. As Keep (2001) points out, when considering the issue of 'skills', there is a central paradox at the heart of the Anglo-Saxon model of capitalism. The rejection of the stakeholder model of capitalism with its regulated apprenticeship environment and labour involvement, in favour of a deregulated shareholder perspective with a heavy emphasis on 'high performance' through skills resulting from high trust, high involvement and high discretion work systems, is failing to deliver. Instead of a shift towards high performance, the Anglo-Saxon model has instead witnessed the decline of job security and increase of work intensification and stress levels.

Such business practices, irrespective of the contrary policy rhetoric, help to explain the continuing low status and performance of apprenticeship schemes within such countries competing on price, quantity and low specification (Green 1998).

A significant challenge, then, exists within particular varieties of late capitalist economies of resolving this paradox between ideals of a high performance nature and the investment and development of a knowledgeable workforce. In some countries such as the UK, there is the persuasive argument that apprenticeship schemes remain a prisoner and casualty of this paradox.

Competences?

A second cluster of issues that impinge on the discussion and reform of apprentice training in Europe, Australia, North America and elsewhere, is greater understanding of what constitutes competence at work. Instead of an emphasis on the worker and then on the work, there is now a unified conception of the workers' lived experience of work (Sandberg 2000). Competences are situational and context-dependent. Performing better than others has less to do with possessing a superior set of attributes and more to do with different ways of understanding the work through interactions with others at work. The use of the term 'work-related knowledge', to some extent, is an attempt to capture some of the new thinking or the 'dynamic equilibrium between the know-what of theory and the know-how of practice' (Brown and Keep 1999: 5). Encompassed within conceptions of work-related knowledge is recognition of the tacit dimension of knowing and second, a recognition of the social context underpinning our ability to know i.e. within particular communities of practice whose members develop ideas about how knowledge should be acquired, applied and shared. Fuller and Unwin, for example, have used critically the insights of Lave and Wenger (1991) in their studies of Modern Apprenticeships. Their empirical studies have explored a variety of learning environments or cultures experienced by apprentices within an 'expansive–restrictive' continuum (Fuller and Unwin 2003: 53).

Exploring changing and differing conceptions of competence then has resulted in a number of wide-ranging discussions that ultimately challenge many taken-for-granted assumptions about the nature of vocational learning. In part, these debates reflect recognition of the increased importance of VET and the need for a more sustained and analytical discussion on the relationship between work and learning. Tomassini (2004b) mentions the 'paradigm change' from 'first you learn, then you do' i.e. the prior certification via qualifications and formal training pathways to an approach based not on formal qualifications but on competencies obtained through workplace learning. Similar to Attwell and Hughes, Tomassini sees the notion of professional or occupational identities as a crucial focus of attention (Tomassini 2004a).

An emphasis on learning, for example, begins to address the socio-cultural, social relations and situated context of young people learning in the workplace (Fenwick 2001). Exploring differing conceptions and practices of a 'learning', 'knowing', 'developing' or 'knowledgeable' work-force suggests more complicated but varied pathways that engages with the socialisation function traditionally associated with apprenticeship schemes.

Young people and the neo-liberal crisis in the EU

The increasing adoption of neo-liberal strategies and solutions within the EU (Bohle 2006, Van Der Pijl 2006) is having a profound impact on the politically acceptable and tolerated frameworks and prescriptions to a variety of 'problems', including the issue of young people's vocational learning. The rapid enactment of 'market reforms' is exacerbating long-standing contradictions between liberalisation and the tradition of state intervention in several European countries (Van Der Pijl 2006: 11). Increasingly driven by the European employers' organisation (UNICE) and the European Round Table of Industrialists (and enshrined in the socially destructive Maastricht Treaty of 1991 and endorsed in the 1999 European Employment Strategy) the consequences of dismantling the post-war class compromise has resulted in the biggest political crisis within the EU since its inception. The dramatic revolt in the French *banlieues* in autumn of

2005 signalled a profound European apprehension and anger toward the rigid and narrow market solutions offered by the employers to 'becoming the most dynamic and competitive knowledge-based economy in the world'. Similarly, the rejection of the proposed European Constitution – the clinching mechanism for locking in neo-liberalism at the EU level, argues Van Der Pijl (2006: 37) – not only raised important questions about European governance but also indicated the depth of dissatisfaction and fears for the future direction of the EU. The structural crisis characterising the EU today is likely to strongly shape the solutions to the complex problems facing young people's transition from schooling to work. As Hodkinson and Bloomer (2002: 42) conclude after qualitatively examining the 'learning careers' of a number of young people in the UK,

> significant improvement of learning and learning opportunities, for people like Luke, depends on ameliorating some of the major social, cultural and economic difficulties/disadvantages that they face.

The events and revolts of 2005 seem to demonstrate the increasing distance between the experiences and aspirations of young people with the current direction and nature of policy concerns within the EU.

Conclusions

While not all commentators might share the analysis underpinning Tomassini's 'paradigm change', there is widespread agreement on the difficulties on making this happen. This chapter has focused on the situation in Europe and has suggested some of the reasons why arrangements for young people entering the labour market remain an area of considerable concern and worry. The situation in the UK was given particular attention due to historical failure to satisfactorily resolve this problem. Paradoxically, the growing uncertainties around particular 'skill formation' strategies within the EU is matched by a growing interest amongst a variety of stakeholders and professionals in the general area of vocational learning. The growing realisation that the issue of 'skills' is too important to be left to dedicated professional and policy circles has begun to widen the issues and agendas seen to impact on existing arrangements. This chapter has raised some of these wider societal issues and suggested that any future reforms of particular training schemes need to engage with this socio-economic environment.

Note

1   This chapter is based on a paper presented at the conference, The Future of Lifelong Learning and Work, University of Toronto, 20–22 June 2005.

References

Ackroyd, S. and Procter, S. (1998) 'British manufacturing organisation and workplace relations: some attributes of the new flexible firm', *British Journal of Industrial Relations*, 36(2): 163–83.

Alakeson, V. (2005) 'Opinion', *Education Guardian*, 10 May: 17.

Attwell, G. and Hughes, J. (2004) 'Collaborative and comparative approaches to researching VET' (www.theknowxnet.com): 1–12.

Baudrillard, J. (2006) 'The pyres of autumn', *New Left Review*, 37: 5–8.

Bohle, D. (2006) 'Neoliberal hegemony, transitional capital and the terms of the EU's eastward expansion', *Capital and Class*, 88: 57–86.

Brown, A. and Keep, E. (1999) *Competing Perspectives on Workplace Learning and the Learning Organisation*, Coventry: Institute for Employment Research.

Dessinger, T. (2004) 'Apprenticeship cultures: a comparative view', in S. Roadhouse and D. Hemsworth (eds) *Apprenticeships: An Historical Re-invention for a Post-industrial World*, Proceedings of a conference by the University Vocational Awards Council, London.

European Commission (2004) *Maastricht Communique on the Future Priorities of Enhanced European Cooperation in Vocational Education and Training*, Brussels: European Commission.

ETF (2004) *ETF Yearbook 2004: Learning Matters*, Turin: European Training Foundation.

European Unit (2004) *Vocational Education and Training* (www.europeunit.ac.uk).

Fenwick, T.J. (2001) *Socio-Cultural Perspectives on Learning through Work*, San Francisco, CA: Jossey Bass/Wiley.

Fuller, A. and Unwin, L. (2003) 'Fostering workplace learning: looking through the lens of apprenticeship', *European Educational Research Journal*, 2(1): 41–55.

Green, A. (1998) 'Core skills, key skills and general culture: in search of a common foundation for vocational education', *Evaluation and Research in Education*, 12(1): 23–43.

Guile, D. (2004) 'Evolving concepts of apprenticeships', in S. Roadhouse and D. Hemsworth (eds) *Apprenticeships: An Historical Re-invention for a Post-industrial World*, Proceedings of a conference by the University Vocational Awards Council, London.

Hodkinson, P. and Bloomer, M. (2002) 'Learning careers: conceptualising lifelong work-based learning', in K. Evans, P. Hodkinson and L. Unwin (eds) *Working to Learn: Transforming Learning in the Workplace*, London: Kogan Page.

Keating, J., Medrich, E., Volkoff, V. and Perry, J. (2002) *Comparative Study of Vocational Education and Training Systems: National Vocational Education and Training Systems across Three Regions under Pressure of Change*, Adelaide: National Centre for Vocational Education Research.

Keep, E. (2001) *Globalisation, Models of Competitive Advantage and Skills*, Warwick: University of Warwick: SKOPE Research Paper No. 22.

Keep, E., Mayhew, K. and Corney, M. (2002) *Review of the Evidence on the Rate of Return to Employers of Investment in Training and Employer Training Measures*, Warwick: University of Warwick: SKOPE Research Paper No. 34.

Kok, W. (2004) *Facing the Challenge: The Lisbon Strategy for Growth and Employment*, Luxembourg: Office for Official Publications of the European Communities.

Lave, J. and Wenger, E. (1991) *Situated Learning: Legitimate Peripheral Participation*, New York: Cambridge University Press.

Lloyd, C. and Payne, J. (2002) 'Developing a political economy of skill?', *Journal of Education and Work*, 15(4): 365–90.

Lloyd, C. and Payne, J. (2004) *'Idle Fancy' or 'Concrete Will'? Defining and Realising a High Skills Version for the UK*, Warwick: University of Warwick: SKOPE Research Paper No. 74.

Sandberg, J. (2000) 'Competence: the basis for a smart workforce', in R. Gerber and C. Lankshear (eds) *Training For a Smart Workforce*, London: Routledge.

The Work Foundation (2005) *Where are the Gaps? An analysis of UK Skills and Education Strategy in the light of the Kok Group and European Commission Midterm Review of the Lisbon Goals*, London: The Work Foundation.

Tomassini, M. (2004a) 'Identifying the professional identity: models of evolution of professional identities and the impact on VET' (www.theknownet.com).

Tomassini, M. (2004b) 'Knowledge dynamics, communities of practices: emerging perspectives on training' (www.theknownet.com).

Van der Pijl, K. (2006) 'A Lockean Europe?', *New Left Review*, 37: 19–38.

8 Meeting the challenges of global economy in vocational education and training

The case of Malaysia

Farizah Ahmad, Othman Omar and Mazanah Muhamad

The forces of the global economy and technological changes have made a highly trained, skilled and well-educated workforce essential in order for any country to progress, prosper and remain competitive. The successes of nations are now dependent on the capacity of the available workforce to respond to the fast-changing needs of the global environment. The aim of this chapter is to present how the goal and purposes of vocational education and training is meeting the global challenges and the new demands of the workplace in a developing country like Malaysia. Analysis is based on content analysis of the country's national agenda through its Five-year Plans and other related documents. Analysis showed that Malaysia has always been abreast of the global trends and is adapting very well to the newly emerging knowledge-based and global market economy. Vocational education and training has evolved from task-oriented training of a psychomotor nature to training which encompasses broad-based knowledge and competencies which include computer literacy, communication skills, managerial abilities, discipline, entrepreneurial spirit, self-improvement and, most importantly, is no longer terminal in nature. However, data indicates the results are still far below the desired targets. Issues and challenges encountered include cultural attitudes, gender, curriculum relevancy, lifelong learning and technological changes. It is argued that continued strong governmental support and equal commitment from the private sector, especially in terms of investments in education, training and skill development, will determine the capacity of a nation to rise above the challenges.

Introduction

Human resource development has been identified as the most critical factor in enabling Malaysia to take the quantum leap from a production-based economy to a knowledge-based economy and becoming a fully developed nation by the year 2020. The knowledge-based economy is one where the generation and utilization of knowledge contribute significantly to economic growth and wealth creation. The critical factor needed in the new economy is therefore the capacity of human capital to create, innovate and generate new ideas as well as apply technology and exercise superior entrepreneurial skills in order to compete well in a global environment. For this capacity to be acquired, the skill intensity of the workforce population has to be increased significantly. More funding and programmes for education and training are also required. This chapter examines Malaysia's preparation for a knowledge-based economy in terms of producing a trained, skilled and well-educated workforce. It presents the general trends in terms of the goal and purposes of vocational education and training in Malaysia as reflected in the country's national agenda through its Five-year Plans. The analysis is based on content analysis of the Malaysian Government Five-year Plans and other related documents.

Malaysia is strategically located in Southeast Asia, connecting trading routes between East and West. Given such geography, trade has been its lifeblood since historical times. Today Malaysia is the fourth most open economy in the world with imports and exports accounting for over 200 per cent of its total gross domestic product. Economic openness has made Malaysia inevitably globally integrated. Another of Malaysia's global features is its multiracial and multilingual workforce and its cultural linkages with many countries in the region such as Indonesia, China, India and Japan.

The population of Malaysia in 2005 was 26.75 million and the median age was 23.3 years, reflecting a young population (Malaysia, 2006). With a declining fertility rate, the population in the 14 years and below age group is expected to grow at a slower rate. On the other hand, those in the working age group, that is, 15–64 years, will increase from 62 per cent in 2000 to 63.6 per cent in 2010. Similarly, the proportion of the 65 years and above age group will also increase due to better life expectancy resulting from improved quality of life. The growth in the working-age population implies the need to create more employment opportunities as well as increased provision of education and training facilities.

Malaysian vocational education and training system

Vocational education refers to vocational education and skills training provided in the secondary and post-secondary school system to prepare youths for employment in various industrial trades. The objectives of the vocational education system as outlined by the Ministry of Education (2005) were as follows:

- to provide the industrial and commercial sectors with manpower equipped with basic skills and knowledge;
- to provide a flexible and broad-based curriculum to meet not only the immediate needs but also future needs and changes in industries;

- to provide basic education in science, mathematics, and languages to enable students to adapt themselves to new methods of work and achieve greater proficiency in their future work;
- to provide the foundation for skills and knowledge on which to build subsequent education and training.

Most vocational education and training providers are run by government agencies; however, in recent years the government has adopted a policy of involving private initiatives to complement the government's efforts in producing the skilled workers needed by industry. The government agencies involved in training are:

- the *Ministry of Education* which provides technical and vocational courses at secondary school level. School leavers from the technical schools can either seek employment at entry level or pursue their post-secondary education at certificate or diploma level in polytechnics or community colleges which are under the purview of the Ministry of Higher Education or other training institutions under the supervision of other ministries.
- the *Ministry of Higher Education* is responsible for post-secondary education which includes vocational education and training at polytechnics and community colleges. Graduates of polytechnics and community colleges fulfil the demand for manpower at the semi-professional level in engineering, commerce and services sectors. More polytechnics and community colleges are being planned for establishment under the Ninth Malaysia Plan (2006–10).
- the *Ministry of Human Resources* runs industrial training institutes that offer industrial skills training programmes at basic, intermediate and advanced levels for pre-employment or job entry level. These include apprenticeship programmes in the mechanical, electrical, building and printing trades as well as programmes to train instructors. The Ministry also operates the Centre for Instructors and Advanced Skills Training (CIAST), the Japan–Malaysia Technical Institute (JMTI) and four advanced technology centres (ADTEC).
- *Majlis Amanah Rakyat (MARA)* or the *Council of Trust for the Indigenous People* under the purview of the Ministry of Entrepreneur and Cooperative Development, is a public agency responsible for the development of the indigenous people. The courses provided are targeted for the development of these ethnic groups. There are 12 skills training institutes in different parts of the country which offer programmes at basic, intermediate and advanced levels. MARA also co-ordinates the operations of three advanced skills training institutions, i.e. the German–Malaysian Institute (GMI), British–Malaysian Institute (BMI) and Malaysia–France Institute (MFI).

- the *Ministry of Youth and Sports* develops training infrastructure so that school dropouts between the ages of 17 and 25 can be given the opportunity to acquire skills that can put them into the employment market. The Ministry provides basic, intermediate and advanced levels of industrial skills training through its seven youth skills training centres and the Youth Advanced Skills Training Centre.

The Ministry of Human Resources established The National Vocational Training Council (NVTC) as the sole awarding body for the Malaysian Skill Certificate. The NVTC evaluates and approves an organization as an accredited centre for undertaking training and assessment leading to the award of the Malaysian Skill Certificate, the national skill qualification. The Malaysian Skill Certificate (MSC), a government skill qualification, is awarded for five skill levels: L1 (semiskilled level), L2 (skilled level), L3 (advanced skill level), L4 (advanced skill/supervisor level) and L5 (advanced skill/manager level). The MSC is obtainable through (i) completing an accredited programme at an accredited training centre, (ii) acquiring credits required for certification, or (iii) obtaining recognition of actual work performance. The primary focus of the MSC awards is to provide a nationally recognized skill qualification for the purpose of gaining employment in Malaysian industry.

National agenda on vocational education and training

Malaysia's development policies are based on the Five-year Malaysia Plans (MPs) beginning with the first plan in 1966. Malaysia has just embarked on the Ninth Malaysia Plan (9MP) which covers the period 2006–10. This section briefly traces the development of the national agenda for vocational education and training from 1966 to the current situation.

The 1960s (1st Malaysia Plan)

This period covers the 1MP (1966–70). In terms of its economic phase, Malaysia was entering import-substitution industrialization. In terms of education, the primary objectives were nation building, eradicating poverty among the *bumiputera* (the Malays and other indigenous groups) and widespread education (Malaysia, 1965). During this period, there was a great need for technical level, craftsmen and artisan personnel (Othman, 2001). The main players were Industrial Training Institutes for industrial training and the National Productivity Centre for management training. In-service training was handled by the Development Administration Unit of the Prime Minister's Department.

The 1970s (2nd and 3rd Malaysia Plans)

During this period Malaysia was entering the export-oriented industrialization phase. In terms of education, the prevailing emphasis was on national integration and unity. The Malay language was made the medium of instruction at public schools. The New Economic Policy was introduced to 'restructure' the society of Malaysia. It was intended to create national unity through state intervention in terms of economic distribution programmes. Courses in entrepreneurial and management studies were introduced to prepare the *bumiputera* for greater participation in business and industry. According to the Plans (Malaysia, 1971, 1976), the government's primary goal was also to increase the number of *bumiputera* in technical and professional occupations. One of the highlights of this period was the reorientation and expansion of the education and training system to meet national manpower needs, specifically in science and technology. In terms of vocational training, measures were taken to ensure training meets industrial needs. The National Advisory Council of Industrial Training (NACIT) was set up in 1972, consisting of representatives from both public and private sectors. The National Industrial Training and Trade Certification Board under the Ministry of Labour and Manpower in cooperation with the private sector, developed national standards at basic, intermediate and advanced level for 19 industrial trades.

The 1980s (4th and 5th Malaysia Plans)

During this period Malaysia was venturing into heavy industries. The manufacturing sector was at its peak. In the 1980s the government had introduced privatization, Malaysia Incorporated and Look East policies. The overall objective of education and training was to promote national unity and prepare Malaysians for full and active involvement in the expanding industrial and business sectors by giving priority to courses in business, commerce, science, technical and related fields (Malaysia, 1981, 1986). In line with this, the facilities for vocational education were expanded. During this period, 53 industrial trades at basic, intermediate and advanced level were offered in vocational education and training. Secondary education was revamped into a system of streaming into general and vocational education, and no new technical schools were established during the period. In skills training, emphasis was given to promoting attitudinal change towards blue collar jobs, as well as promoting discipline and work ethics to follow the Japanese and Korean models. In this respect, trainees were sent for on-the-job training in Japan and South Korea. Othman (2001) indicated that during this decade, private training institutions were also established to provide various commercial, agricultural and engineering trade courses. Another focus for human capital development was on skills training for employment, self-employment, creativity and innovation.

The 1990s (6th and 7th Malaysia Plans)

Vision 2020, the way-forward initiative for Malaysia was one of the major highlights of the early 1990s. Vision 2020 provided the national agenda for attainment of the status of fully developed nation by the year 2020. With that vision, the 7MP positioned the education and training agenda to produce a workforce that is knowledgeable, highly-skilled and computer literate, strongly motivated, disciplined, with high moral and ethical values, as well as being instilled with a set of industrial values essential for maintaining a productive and competitive edge (Malaysia, 1996).

Consequently the 6MP and 7MP (1991–2000) were to address the shortages in skilled and technical labour brought about by rapid industrialization and technological development in Malaysia (Malaysia, 1991a, 1996). During this period the government made a significant move to upgrade technical education, mainly to increase science and technical human resources (Economic Planning Unit, 2005). In this regard, secondary vocational schools were restructured into secondary technical schools to increase numbers of students in technical schools, hence preparing them to continue their studies in various science and technical related fields at post-secondary level. As skills training programmes were affected by a shortage of instructors, trainees were sent to Germany, Japan and the United Kingdom to acquire the new emerging technologies. Advanced skilled training institutes with the cooperation of Germany, France and Japan were also established in Malaysia to offer advanced skill training, particularly in production technology and industrial electronics. With the increasing globalization of the world economy, the ability to communicate in a second language, for example English, which is an international language of commerce, was emphasized. Vocational education and training also shifted from conventional methods to competency-based education. The National Vocational Training Council (NTVC) adopted a new five-level skills qualification. The accreditation system was critical not only in producing highly skilled workers but also in developing career paths parallel to the existing academic-based career development.

At this time it was recognized that enrolment in technical and vocational education was lower than regional standards. Furthermore the transition from an assembly-based manufacturing economy to a knowledge-based economy needed better trained and technically proficient graduates from the technical and vocational system. This in turn required various reforms to improve the preparation of students for employment, as well as for students intending to pursue higher education. To support these moves, four major pieces of legislation were enacted:

- *the Education Act 1996*, which defines a national education system for schools;

- *the Private Higher Educational Institutions Act 1996*, which makes provision for a broad range of higher education providers;
- *the National Council on Higher Education Act 1996*, which provides for the setting up of a national body to determine policy and co-ordinate the development of post-school education in Malaysia;
- *the National Accreditation Board Act 1996*, which provides for the establishment of a board to ensure that high standards are maintained in higher education institutions, particularly in the private sector.

The 6MP and 7MP (1991–2000) were to lay the foundation for a knowledge-based economy with the launching of the National IT Agenda (NITA) and the Multimedia Super Corridor.

The new millennium (2001–10)

During the 8MP, 2001–5, human capital development emphasized nurturing creativity and cognitive skills to provide the impetus for the knowledge-based economy. Education and training was aimed at producing multi-skilled and knowledgeable manpower that would be versatile, willing to learn continuously, technopreneurial as well as having the ability to acquire and apply knowledge, particularly in modern technology (Malaysia, 2001a). At the same time, the lifelong learning process was finally acknowledged in the education and training agenda (Othman and Mazanah, 2003). In the 9MP, 2006–10, the thrust is to produce sufficient knowledge workers that are needed by the nation to achieve a knowledge-based economy (Malaysia, 2006). Of significance was the focus on learning rather than teaching and special references were made to lifelong learning in the context of developing Malaysia into a knowledge-based economy. The concept of lifelong learning for the first time was linked to productivity and employability (Navi Bax and Abu Hassan, 2003).

> A system of lifelong learning will be promoted to ensure that workers can continuously upgrade their skills and knowledge in order to remain relevant in the environment of rapidly changing technology and work processes as well as to nurture a learning society.
>
> Malaysia, Government of (2001b: 134)

Beginning in 2000, vocational education and training was expanded and introduced in the Malaysian education system earlier than before. Life Skills became one of the core subjects at both primary and secondary levels. The subject is aimed at preparing students with basic knowledge and skills, promoting interest, and developing positive work culture in technology and entrepreneurship. This curriculum was introduced at Grades 4–6 at primary school level and Forms 1–3 (Grades 7–9) at secondary level. At the primary level, major components include technology and design, trade, and entrepreneurship. At the secondary level, major components include technology and design, technical skills (technical drawing, electric, electronic, electromechanical and engineering), home economics (food and catering, cookery, tailoring, etc), agriculture (plants, landscape, pets, etc), and trade and entrepreneurship (Curriculum Development Centre, Ministry of Education, 2001).

During 8MP and 9MP, the size of the country's workforce is estimated to increase to reach 12.4 million in 2010. The growth of the labour force is attributed to the increase in the size of the working-age population. Two-thirds of unemployment comes from the 15–24 age group. There is also an increase in the number of job seekers with tertiary education from 13.9 per cent in 2000 to 20.0 per cent in 2005 (Malaysia, 2006). During the 9MP, the participation rate of the 17–23 years age group in tertiary education is targeted at 40 per cent in 2010. There are more education and training opportunities for women during 9MP to increase their employability. By the same token, more educational and training opportunities are provided to school leavers and the unemployed.

Over four decades, the national education and training agenda has moved from being task-oriented to being technology-driven and focused on holistic human capital development. The current agenda is to develop human capital that is knowledgeable, skilled, innovative, progressive in thinking and attitude, with strong ethics and universal values, to drive a knowledge-based economy.

It is realized that there is still a significant shortage of workforce supply in the managerial, professional and technical categories; only 13.9 per cent of the population in the labour force in 2000 (Malaysia's *Third Outline Perspective Plan*, 2001b) and 20.0 per cent in 2005 respectively, have the tertiary education that is critical to drive a knowledge-based economy. The enrolment at the tertiary level of the age cohort 17–23 years increased to 25.0 per cent following the substantial allocation provided for tertiary education, but it is still lower compared with many of the newly industrialized economies (NIEs). The targeted enrolment in science and technical fields was also still below the targeted 60 : 40 science to arts ratio. As of 1999, enrolment in science and technical fields constituted only 31.0 per cent.

Economic growth is contingent upon capacity for keeping abreast of fast technological changes. Technology development is determined by human capital involved in research and expenditure allocated for R&D. During 1985–95 there were only 500 R&D scientists and engineers per million population in Malaysia which is below the target of 1,000 scientists and engineers per million population by the year 2000 as outlined in Malaysia's Second Outline Perspective Plan (Malaysia, 1991b). The ratio of R&D scientists and technologists of 7 per 10,000 labour force in 2000 (Third Outline Perspective Plan, OPP3) puts Malaysia in the 17th position relative to 21 other countries, described in Table 8.1 (Malaysia, 2001b) with regard to Infostructure and Computer Infrastructure.[1]

With respect to information and communication technology (ICT), Malaysia has made significant headway in terms of becoming a global ICT hub. The Multimedia Super Corridor concept created in 1996 aimed to transform Malaysia into an IT-cultured and knowledge-based society. The ICT expenditure for education and research in 2000 was at least double the expenditure in 1995. However compared with other NIEs, there is still much to be achieved by Malaysia in terms of access and equity of communications infrastructure, ICT penetration rates, development of local content and security of ICT networks. Access is still mostly concentrated in urban areas, resulting in disparity between the urban and rural areas and a digital divide.

Issues and challenges

Although in terms of policies, Malaysia has a well-charted pathway towards producing a trained, skilled and well-educated workforce to drive the nation into a knowledge based economy, the results are yet to achieve the desired targets and Malaysia lags behind when compared with the performance of newly industrialized economies like Singapore

Table 8.1 Country position by components of knowledge development index 2000

Country	Knowledge index	Computer infrastructure	Infostructure	Education and training	R&D and technology
United States	1	1	10	8	3
Japan	2	8	3	10	1
Sweden	3	5	2	3	2
Finland	4	2	4	4	4
Norway	5	4	1	1	10
Denmark	6	7	5	2	9
Australia	7	6	6	6	11
Switzerland	8	13	7	9	5
Canada	9	3	12	5	15
Netherlands	10	10	9	13	8
United Kingdom	11	9	8	11	14
Germany	12	12	13	12	7
New Zealand	13	11	14	7	17
Ireland	14	15	15	15	12
South Korea	15	16	11	16	13
Singapore	16	14	16	19	6
Malaysia	17	17	17	17	16
Thailand	18	19	21	14	19
China	19	18	19	18	20
Philippines	20	22	18	20	18
Indonesia	21	21	20	21	21
India	22	20	22	22	22

Source: Malaysia (2001b)

and South Korea. This section examines some of the issues and challenges encountered: cultural attitudes, gender, curriculum relevancy, lifelong learning and technological challenges.

Cultural attitudes

Traditionally, parents in Malaysia aspire for their children to make it to university. It is seen as the path to high wages, prestige and success. As a result, cultural attitudes towards vocational education are not encouraging in Malaysia. Vocational education and training is usually perceived as a system of education for the poor, and for the educationally inferior groups that are not eligible for admission into higher education. To maximize the potential of the population workforce, this old cultural perception must change. There is a critical need to highlight that all pathways of education and training are equally important in developing a robust educational system. Vocational education and training must be given due recognition and importance for its value as an integral part of the national agenda to become a knowledge-based society and a fully developed nation by the year 2020.

Gender

As the enrolment rates of girls are equal to, or exceed, those of boys at all levels of schooling, the key challenge now is to promote female participation in technical and vocational education. There is a critical need to attract female students particularly by expanding facilities available for them and for occupational areas favoured by female students such as computers and commercial subjects. There is also a critical need to encourage more female enrolment in technical subjects such as engineering.

Curriculum relevancy

An important challenge is how best to reposition the vocational education and training system in a global environment of rapid changes in technology, pervasive use of ICT and the knowledge-based economy. In this respect, a relevant curriculum, which addresses the need of students, community and workplace, should replace the curriculum that is overloaded and mismatched between what is learnt and what is demanded by the community or workplace. There is a critical need for vocational and training institutions to reform their curriculum to meet the needs of industries. Linkages and close networking with industries are crucial to ensure the curriculum is developed using a contextual approach. Equally important for the new economy are the values for lifelong learning and employability skills such as communications, interpersonal skills, planning, organization, problem solving, teamwork, leadership, innovation and entrepreneurship. Vocational courses should be practice-oriented and skills-based. The teaching approach should adopt interactive and processed-based methods.

Lifelong learning

In a knowledge-based employment environment, it is estimated that 50 per cent of what is learnt becomes obsolete in five years. Training and retraining is crucial for multi-skilled and versatile workers to cope with these changes. Lifelong learning can be enhanced when education and training programmes are available and accessible to the learners. The global information revolution that is happening today can take learners beyond access and into inquiry, interest groups and problem solving. However, issues pertaining to access and equity of ICT and its infrastructure need to be resolved to an adequate level and capacity. Informatization is an essential resource for the development of knowledgeable human capital. Lifelong learning programmes and the infrastructure need to be in place and the workforce and society have to be nurtured as knowledge and information seekers.

Technological changes

In a global environment of rapid changes in technology, pervasive use of ICT and the knowledge-based economy that we are moving towards as an industrialized nation, the ability to understand and use technology is greatly needed. There is a crucial need to move to an ICT-based teaching and learning environment which will change the way people learn, plan and manage their learning independently.

Conclusion

This chapter has put the case that in meeting the challenges of a competitive global market and the pursuit of a knowledge-based economy, which requires a workforce with high level skills, the government continues to emphasize vocational education and skills training. This is seen in the upgrading and expansion of the sector to meet market demand. Vocational education and training has also moved from being task-oriented to broad-based knowledge and competencies which include computer literacy, communication skills, managerial abilities, discipline, entrepreneurial spirit, self-improvement and most importantly it is no longer terminal in nature. The system now provides for an alternative and an attractive career development path that promotes lifelong learning, continuous skill advancements for the skilled workforce. The national discourse on the concept of vocational education and training thus has moved from one that focuses on employability and economic concerns to a broader definition that includes lifelong learning.

Note

1 Infostructure includes newspaper circulation, telephone subscribers, and mobile phones while indicators of computer infrastructure include number of computers per 1,000 population, computer power per capita and connections to the Internet.

References

Curriculum Development Center, Ministry of Education (2001) *Integrated Curriculum for Primary Schools: Mathematics.* Available at: <http://www.ppk.kpm.my> (accessed 11 May 2006).

Economic Planning Unit, Prime Minister's Department (2005) *Malaysia Achieving the Millennium Development Goals.* Kuala Lumpur, United Nations Country Team, Malaysia. Available at: <http://www.undp.org.my> (accessed 11 May 2006).

Malaysia, Government of (1965) *First Malaysia Plan: 1965–1970.* Prime Minister's Department. Kuala Lumpur: National Printing Department.

Malaysia, Government of (1971) *Second Malaysia Plan: 1971–1975.* Prime Minister's Department. Kuala Lumpur: National Printing Department.

Malaysia, Government of (1976) *Third Malaysia Plan: 1976–1980.* Prime Minister's Department. Kuala Lumpur: National Printing Department.

Malaysia, Government of (1981) *Fourth Malaysia Plan: 1981–1985.* Prime Minister's Department. Kuala Lumpur: National Printing Department.

Malaysia, Government of (1986) *Fifth Malaysia Plan: 1986–1990.* Prime Minister's Department. Kuala Lumpur: National Printing Department.

Malaysia, Government of (1991a) *Sixth Malaysia Plan: 1991–1995.* Kuala Lumpur: National Printing Department.

Malaysia, Government of (1991b) *The Second Outline Perspective Plan, 1991–2000.* Kuala Lumpur: Government Printers.

Malaysia, Government of (1996) *Seventh Malaysia Plan: 1996–2000.* Prime Minister's Department. Kuala Lumpur: Percetakan Nasional Malaysia Berhad.

Malaysia, Government of (2001a) *Eighth Malaysia Plan 2001–2005.* Prime Minister's Department. Kuala Lumpur: Percetakan Nasional Malaysia Berhad.

Malaysia, Government of (2001b) *The Third Outline Perspective Plan, 2001–2010.* Prime Minister's Department. Kuala Lumpur: Percetakan Nasional Malaysia Berhad.

Malaysia, Government of (2006) *Ninth Malaysia Plan 2006–2010.* Prime Minister's Department. Kuala Lumpur: Percetakan Nasional Malaysia Berhad.

Ministry of Education (2005) *Brief Info: Technical Education Department.* Kuala Lumpur: Percetakan Nasional Malaysia Berhad.

Navi Bax, M.R and Abu Hassan, M.N (2003) 'Lifelong learning in Malaysia'. Paper presented at International Policy Seminar co-organized by IIEP/UNESCO and KRIVET on Making Lifelong Learning a Reality, Seoul, South Korea, June 2003.

Othman Omar. (2001) 'What adults learn', in M. Muhamad and Associates (eds) *Adult and Continuing Education in Malaysia*. Kuala Lumpur: UNESCO Institute for Education, Germany and Universiti Putra Press.

Othman Omar and Mazanah Muhamad. (2003) 'Life skill development in Malaysia: post secondary education and workplace learning scenario'. Paper presented at International Conference 2003 on the Role of Adult and Continuing Education for Life Skill Development organized by the ACE of Korea, Seoul, South Korea, 26–27 September 2003.

9 Vocational training through the apprenticeship system in Turkey

Özlem Ünlühisarcıklı

This chapter explores the processes of vocational training through the apprenticeship system from its inception before the Republic (1923) to the present day in Turkey.

The Ahi Associations

When nomadic Turks came to Anatolia from Central Asia in the eleventh century they settled in villages, towns, and cities which changed their tribal lifestyle. At that time all commerce was controlled by the Armenian and Greek traders who had a strong guild system among themselves. The changes in the social structure and the need to compete with the Armenian and Greek traders led the Turkish traders and artisans to organize. The organization of Ahi was founded by Ahi Evran towards the middle of the thirteenth century.

The Ahi Associations became the major economic, social and cultural power in the Islamic Turkish society for centuries. The word *ahi* means 'brother', however, some argue that the word *'ahi'* comes from *'akı'* which means 'generous' (Ekinci, 1990; Çağatay, 1989). There were several moral and social rules an Ahi should obey, as well as regulations which determined almost everything ranging from who should be accepted for membership in the associations to supervision and discipline. These rules and regulations were called the Ahi System. The main philosophy of the Ahi System was to help the individual to have peace of mind both in this world and the next. This was to be achieved through a balanced way of living by investing both in this world, where one leads one's present life, and in the next world where one is supposed to go after death. The Ahi way of thinking flourished among the artisans. Each trade had its own Ahi Association; in smaller towns they would either organize in groups of trades or all the trades would organize under the same association. Women were not allowed to become members of the Ahi. This restriction of women from economic activities in the society was part of Islamic culture. Women were perceived as responsible for the house duties, child rearing, and looking after their husbands. Therefore, the Ahi Associations were fraternity associations (Çağatay, 1989).

In the Ahi System, society was perceived as an integral whole. People were not discriminated against on the grounds of their occupation, social class or wealth. Everybody worked for the betterment of the whole society and each individual living in that society. Society was built on the principle of solidarity rather than competition. As a matter of fact, it was a moral obligation for an Ahi to spend all their personal savings for the benefit of people in need. This was called the 'solidarity of life and wealth', and was exercised to such an extent that high levels of profit and increase in capital were discouraged because of the fear that they would destroy solidarity. The Ahi System depended on a paternalistic authority. At the top of the hierarchy was the *Ahi Baba* who was the vocational, political, moral, and religious leader, yet perceived as a father by all Ahi members. Similarly, the master was the role model for the apprentice and the journeyman.

Vocational training in the Ahi System

In the Ahi System, vocational training, general education, and social life were interwoven. Therefore, there were two types of education in the Ahi System: vocational training and social education. The vocational skill acquisition process was long and highly structured: one would start as an assistant apprentice, would become first an apprentice and then a journeyman, and finally a master.

Assistant apprenticeship, the first step towards becoming a master, started about the age of ten when parents requested a master to accept their son. Assistant apprentices would work in the workshop to acquire vocational skills but would also attend a dervish lodge – a religious school – to get a general education in religion, music, literature, and similar subjects. After serving two years as an assistant apprentice, one would become an apprentice.

An apprentice was obliged to obey the master and the master was obliged to train the apprentice in all the details and subtleties of the vocation. In addition, an apprentice would learn the etiquette of the trade from the master. The apprentice would continue to go to the dervish lodge and there would learn manners in order to be a socially acceptable person. There were 740 principles to be obeyed which formed moral and religious life. The length of an apprenticeship would change from trade to trade but it was in general 1,001 days. When the time serving as an apprentice had finished, an apprentice would be expected to accomplish a task and if the performance satisfied the master and the journeyman, then the apprentice would become a journeyman.

The length of service as a journeyman was three years in all trades. A journeyman was bound to learn some military skills like riding a horse, fighting with a sword, and archery, besides continuing on-the-job training in the workshop. After three years of service, a journeyman would attend a ceremony where he was expected to prove his competence in his specific trade to a council of masters. If the journeyman was found to be successful, he would become a master (Ekinci, 1990). In the Ahi System, nobody could establish his own business without first becoming a master.

Vocational skill acquisition in this system was highly related to life. The apprentice was not treated as a pupil learning something that is taught but as a person who was 'working with responsibility'. If an apprentice could not perform a given task successfully that would mean loss of time and material, therefore the apprentices were expected to be responsible for their progress.

In the late sixteenth century, imports from Western countries, which were cheaper, created marketing problems; and there was an increase in the number of artisans in urban centers because of migration (Taşpınar, 1992). The most important reason for the collapse of the Ahi System was because it was an Islamic-oriented association. It excluded traders and artisans from other religions. The Ottoman Empire consisted of heterogeneous ethnic minorities who had their own laws and regulations, and who were functioning generally in trade and commerce. Ahi Associations lost their influence gradually and as the numbers of minority traders and artisans increased, new regulations were needed (Çağatay, 1989).

The Gedik

In 1727, the number of master artisans who could have a license to establish a business was restricted to prevent inflation of trade establishments. The permission or license to act as a trader or artisan was called '*Gedik*'. The 'license' could only be held by those who had been through the apprenticeship system (Ekinci, 1990). The Gedik had close links with religious fraternities and apprentices would be questioned on religious matters besides vocational ones during graduation ceremonies (Evren, 1999). The vocational training and social education continued the strong influence of the Ahi System (Çağatay, 1989). An apprentice would work beside the master and would become a journeyman and then would have to wait for his master to quit working or to die; then the journeyman would inherit the license of his master and would become a licensed master. Another way to obtain a license was to buy it. A journeyman whose master was still in business and had no intention to quit would negotiate with another master who wanted to quit the trade and would buy the license.

Consequently, those who did not have a license could not establish their own business and were obliged to work as a journeyman under a master artisan who had a license. Thus, problems arose between the masters and journeymen and the system weakened. In the nineteenth century, trade with foreign countries increased. However, the monopolistic Gedik system was a drawback in the competitive international trade and the monopolistic requirement for licenses was abolished in 1860 (Çağatay, 1989; Ekinci, 1990) and the Gedik was restructured. The Gedik enabled the Muslim and non-Muslim Ottoman traders and artisans to come together in places called 'lonca', which meant 'room'. The Lonca in the nineteenth-century Ottoman Empire corresponded to the guild system in medieval Europe. At that time, factory production had begun in Europe and the Ottoman traders and artisans could not compete with their European counterparts. The Ottoman Empire imported many goods but was unable to export goods, and thus weakened (Taşpınar, 1992). These organizations were abolished altogether in 1912 (Ekinci, 1990; Çağatay, 1989).

The initial establishment of vocational education schools was begun in the nineteenth century by local administrations which financed and managed these schools (Akpınar, 2004).

The apprenticeship system in the Turkish Republic

The rest of this chapter covers apprenticeship training from the early days of the Turkish Republic to the present day. The majority of elementary school graduates do not continue their education in Turkey. Table 9.1 provides the numbers of students in the formal education system in Turkey for the 2003–4 academic year. Therefore, the training of apprentices and journeymen in a systematic way through non-formal education could be considered as a panacea for providing the much-needed qualified workforce. Moreover, in Turkey, many artisans still learn their skills on-the-job through the traditional methods, although, since the beginning of the Republic there have been efforts to complement practical and theoretical training to increase quality.

The enactment of the Law on Unification of Education in 1924, after the establishment of the Turkish Republic (1923), brought all the schools in Turkey under the management of the central authority (Ministry of Education) including vocational schools. In the late 1940s, vocational courses were initiated as an important means for the training of a skilled labor force. Mobile courses were also initiated to provide vocational skills to people in villages. In addition to vocational courses, by the 1960s importance was also placed on one- to two-year practical trade schools which primary school graduates could attend. In the 1960s, vocational high schools were established as schools of five years duration after

Table 9.1 Numbers of schools, teachers, and students in 2003–4

Educational institutions	Schools	Teachers	Students
Elementary education	36,117	384,029	10,479,538
General high schools	2,831	86,051	1,963,998
Vocational and technical high schools	3,681	73,998	1,050,394

Source: DIE, 2006

the completion of five years of primary school. The duration was later extended to six years. Four-year technical high schools were included in the system in the 1970s. The system was restructured in 1973 with the National Education Basic Law No. 1739. According to the law, preparing individuals for an occupation, higher education or the labor market was the objective of vocational and technical education (Akpınar, 2004).

The first law concerning apprenticeship training was issued in 1977 as the Law of Apprenticeship, Journeymanship and Mastership No. 2089, which enabled the acquisition of a profession through apprenticeship training within the Turkish national education system. The vocational training model for apprentices was adapted from the German dual system which enabled apprentices to receive training both in the workplace and in school. This law defined the status of apprentices, journeyman, and masters; regulations for the work hours and work conditions; and social security and payment. However, there have been many arguments around the inclusion of this training within the system:

> According to the Article 18 of the National Education Basic Law No. 1739, the Turkish national education system is divided into two major sections, namely, 'formal' and 'non-formal' education. The place of apprenticeship training (also within Law No. 2089) within this system has caused argument. Some have argued that the organization foreseen in Law No. 1739 prevails and thus apprenticeship training should be evaluated as coming under non-formal training. While others argued that with Law No. 2089, apprenticeship training has been added as a different subsystem to formal and non-formal training in the Turkish national education system.
>
> (Akpınar and Ercan, 2002: 80)

In line with the second part of the above arguments the General Directorate of Apprenticeship Training was established in the central organization, but later this directorate was combined with the General Directorate of Non-formal Education to form the General Directorate of Apprenticeship and Non-formal Education. The expected development of apprenticeship training did not occur and from 1977 to 1986, only some 20,000 apprentices were provided with contracts in line with the regulations, whereas about one million apprentices and their masters did not apply for a contract. Thus, 98 percent of the apprentices in Turkey were working informally (Erder Köksal and Lordoğlu, 1993).

Considering the failure of this law, a new one was prepared and issued in 1986 as the Law of Apprenticeship and Vocational Training No. 3308, to organize apprenticeship, formal and non-formal vocational and technical education in an integrated system. The aims of the law are: to provide qualifications via education, to protect the young who work with no social security, to provide opportunity for the young to re-enter the educational system, and to regulate the master–apprentice relationship. Thus, this law considers apprenticeship as part of formal education and aims to provide training to apprentices in schools.

According to Law No. 3308, the basic aims of apprenticeship training are:

a. To provide the same studentship rights to the apprentices as the students in formal education system have. In accordance with the aims and principles of the formal education system, the participants in apprenticeship training are expected to: acquire the attitudes of a good citizen, learn the common tasks and procedures in different vocations, comprehend the meaning and importance of work discipline, learn the general principles of work security, acquire a common general culture, acquire behaviors and attitudes to help to accustom trainees to working life.

b. To help those seeking apprenticeships, who have finished primary education and are above the age of 14 and below the age of 19, to choose a vocation appropriate to their interests and aptitudes.

c. To prepare apprentices for the journeymanship examination through the acquisition of vocational knowledge, skills and work habits.

d. To prepare journeymen for the mastership examination through the acquisition of the knowledge, skills and work habits to perform the vocational tasks alone and to run a workshop.

(MEB, 1990)

There are 46 articles in this law. Article 13 makes clear that without a written apprenticeship contract, the owner of a workshop cannot employ an apprentice. In Article 14, it is explained that a probation period of not less than a month and not more than three months, is allowed before the written contract becomes binding. The Ministry decides the duration of the probation period. If neither the employer nor the apprentice has applied to the relevant Apprenticeship Training Center for abolition within ten days after the probation period, the written apprenticeship contract becomes binding. The duration of the apprenticeship is two to four years. Apprenticeship training offers both theoretical and practical training to the young who work at enterprises in order to acquire vocational skills.

Law No. 3308 was amended in 2001 and the name of the law was changed to the Vocational Education Law No. 4702. With the amendments, the Vocational Training and Education Law gives apprenticeship training opportunities not only to those below 19 years of age but also to those over 19 years of age. In general, the goal of the Law is to orient more students to vocational training, and to offer principles of vocational training that would be applied in schools and enterprises for apprentices, journeymen, and masters. Furthermore, the new law enables vocational and technical secondary education graduates

> to progress to 2 year vocational higher education institutions that are in line with the students' prior education, without taking the university entrance examination. The Law envisages the establishment of vocational and technical education regions consisting of vocational and technical secondary institutions and vocational higher education schools. The Law grants the right to foundations to establish vocational education institutions provided that they will not be profit-seeking organizations, and requires the enterprises, which fall within the context of this Law to employ people who have vocational training relevant with the nature of the business.
>
> (Secretariat General for EU Affairs, 2006: 552)

Law No. 3308 conveys that the principles related to training and certification in unrecognized occupations is in the Trades and Craftsmen Law No. 507:

> In accordance with the regulation related to 'Provision of Certificates in Occupational Fields and Provinces Where Apprenticeship Training is Not Applied' brought out according to Law No. 507, chambers may organize preparatory courses for those who are going to enter journeymanship and mastership examinations. In this context, it could be said that there are no widespread and systematic activities ...
>
> (Akpınar and Ercan, 2002: 89)

Therefore, those who have written apprenticeship contracts are obliged to attend educational activities organized by the Ministry, either in the Vocational Training Centers, or in the training units established at enterprises which have master trainers, or supra training centers which are established and run by the Turkish Confederation of Trades and Craftsmen. Apprentices in small enterprises go to Vocational Training Centers and these centers comprise the main medium for apprenticeship training.

Vocational Training Centers

Vocational Training Centers, which were named Apprenticeship Centers when they were established in 1979, and were renamed with the amendments made to Law No. 3308 in 2001, provide vocational education for those who have dropped out from the formal education system and are working in workshops to acquire vocational skills. In these centers, apprentices, journeymen, and masters receive education and training in many crafts like carpentry, textiles, shoe-making, electricity, construction, tailoring, automotives, and so on. Depending on the specific craft to be acquired, apprenticeship training takes three or four years in these centers. The apprentices attend the courses in the centers one day (not less than eight hours) each week. In these centers, the general knowledge subjects (such as Turkish, mathematics and vocational mathematics, administration and cooperatives, total quality management) comprise 40 percent of the program while vocational subjects are 60. Practical skills are gained on-the-job while working at the enterprises. After finishing the program the apprentices take the 'experienced apprenticeship exam' for a certificate and to become a journeyman.

The journeymanship training is in a condensed format (240 hours). Of this, 176 hours are allocated to courses related to the management of a workplace (such as economics, administration, workers' health and work security, accountancy, insurance and tax regulations, labor law, advanced occupational information). At the end of the courses, the journeymen take an examination and those who pass it become masters. Journeymen who have not attended a Vocational Training Center but have worked for at least five years as a registered journeyman may also take the relevant examination and become a master.

Masters are expected to attend courses in the Vocational Training Centers to get a 'Master Trainer Certificate'. They attend courses which last 40 hours in total. The courses they attend include: principles of apprenticeship and vocational training, training psychology, communication and communication tools in training, occupational analysis and preparation of training programs, workshop and occupational course teaching methods, work security, work quality and cost relationships, testing and assessment in training, testing and assessment. A 'Master Trainer Certificate' is required from masters in order for them to recruit apprentices and journeymen for their workshops; otherwise the law does not allow an artisan to recruit an apprentice or a journeyman under social security.

Those who want to establish their own business have to take another proficiency exam after five years of work experience. There are different regulations for those who start apprenticeship training after graduating from secondary school, and vocational and technical secondary school (Akpınar and Ercan, 2002).

Table 9.2 provides some data on apprenticeship training in Turkey. Recent statistics indicate that in the 2004–5 school year there were 359 Vocational Training Centers in 81 cities offering training in 110 different crafts (Directorate General of Press and Information, 2006).

In Turkey today apprenticeship training is implemented in different ways. The first one is the apprenticeship training carried out by the Ministry of National Education; the second type of education is the apprenticeship training provided by professional organizations in occupational branches where the Ministry of National Education does not offer such training; and third, vocational education and orientation courses in educational centers.

Table 9.2   Apprenticeship training in Vocational Training Centers

Academic year	Organiz-ations	Teachers	Student/participants				
			Candidate apprentice	Apprentice	Journeymen	Master trainer	Total
1989–1990	220	1,359	6,714	*	*	13,523	121,596
1994–1995	292	3,142	10,036	144,126	29,748	15,173	199,083
1999–2000	330	5,084	6,792	133,551	64,274	13,959	218,576
2003–2004	292	4,604	2,501	119,996	73,413	13,460	209,370

* no information available.

Source: Akpınar (2004: 27)

However, traditional apprenticeship training is also taking place in the informal sector which is not approved by the Ministry (Ünlühisarcıklı, 1999). The following provides the background of traditional apprenticeship training in Turkey.

Traditional apprenticeship training in the informal sector

There is another form of apprenticeship training in Turkey that is still observed and which would be called a traditional apprenticeship system in the informal sector. In simple terms, the informal sector is the name for economic activities generated by people who have no or only limited access to highly organized public or private sector employment opportunities.

The findings of a research study conducted in 1997 reveal that although it is a legal requirement for an apprentice or journeyman to attend a Vocational Training Center, only 10.8 percent of the apprentices and 29.6 percent of the journeymen had ever attended one of these centers in Istanbul, Turkey (Ünlühisarcıklı, 2001). Recent studies estimated that there are around one million children aged between 12 and 18 who are working in the industry sector in Turkey and of these children only about 250,000 are enrolled in Vocational Training Centers (UNICEF, 2006). There are various reasons for not attending these centers:

> Since their workshops have a semi-legal basis – the masters are either tax evaders or had not registered their workshops – they cannot attend the centers or send their apprentices and/or journeymen; the masters do not want their apprentices and/or journeymen to be away from work for one day each week; the apprentices have no information about (these centers), so the masters do not bother; the apprentices do not want to take courses; and so on.
>
> (Ünlühisarcıklı, 2001: 453)

The traditional hierarchy of relations still exists to some extent among artisans. However, in traditional apprenticeships there is no systematized, organized way of training. The main mode of skill acquisition for an apprentice is observing the master or the journeyman on-the-job.

> The master also explains what to do to an apprentice, shows the errors an apprentice has made while performing a specific task, helps the apprentice if he asks for help, and supervises the apprentice on-the-job. During the initial stages of apprenticeship, much depends on the apprentice acquiring the vocational skills he seeks.
>
> (Ünlühisarcıklı, 2001: 452)

The complexity of the tasks performed increases as the apprentice acquires more skills. The apprentice learns while working on-the-job. In the traditional apprenticeship training in the informal sector there are no pre-determined rules and regulations for an apprentice to become a journeyman. Generally, when apprentices get older, and become more autonomous while working (needing less supervision and help from the journeymen or the master), their payment increases and they are referred to as journeymen, and later, after becoming experienced they are called 'master'. But these people need to attend Vocational Education Centers and get the relevant certificates to be able to legalize their business; otherwise they function illegally in the informal sector.

Conclusion

Since 1997, basic education in Turkey lasts for eight years. Upon completion of basic education students have three options for continuing their education: general secondary education, vocational and technical secondary education, and non-formal education including apprenticeship training. Since only about 30 percent of elementary school graduates continue their education, providing apprenticeship training to provide young people with vocational skills proves to be crucial and important. For the time being, government policy focuses on providing theoretical and practical skills, which complement each other, to prepare the young artisans for their prospective mastership.

The apprenticeship training system has been formalized over the years by the Ministry of National Education so that elementary school graduates would attend a Vocational Training Center or another approved program by the Ministry while working as an apprentice. However, one can also see the remnants of the Ahi System in the traditional apprenticeship system that has been carried through by the master artisans who set up their own small-scale businesses.

With the amendments made to Law No. 3308 in 2001 there have been major changes in vocational education which enabled higher flexibility.

The system now allows individuals over 19 to attend apprenticeship training. Furthermore, after remedial training, transition from non-formal education to formal vocational and technical education and finally to post-secondary vocational schools is possible without sitting the university entrance examination. There are also efforts to create a national qualification framework for quality assurance, teaching and management which will produce a skilled workforce in line with European Union priorities. There is cooperation among various agencies such as the Employment Organization (İŞKUR), the Small and Medium Sized Enterprises Support Administration Directorate (KOSGEB), the Turkish Confederation of Employer Associations (TİSK) and the like, to synchronize non-formal apprenticeship training activities with labor market policies.

The challenge is in placing each apprentice in just the right branch of vocational training depending on the skill of the individual, and providing appropriate job placement as their skills enhance. Increasing coordination among the related state and private sector institutions, and non-governmental organizations would also contribute to optimizing the use of educational facilities and sources. The apprentices work hard and there is not much time for leisure; therefore, providing opportunities and means for socializing would be an important contribution to their lives. Another challenge is reaching to those apprentices who are working in the informal sector and acquiring their vocational skills traditionally.

References

Akpınar, A. (2004) *Initial Vocational Education and Training in Turkey*. Available at: <http://www.iskur.gov.tr> (accessed 2 May 2005).

Akpınar, A. and Ercan, H. (2002) *Report on the Vocational Education and Training System in Turkey*, Ankara: National Observatory Network (established by the European Training Foundation).

Çağatay, N. (1989) *Bir Türk Kurumu Olan Ahilik* (The Ahi: A Turkish Organization), Ankara: Türk Tarih Kurumu Basımevi.

DIE (2006) *Turkey's Statistical Yearbook 2004*. Available at: <http://www.die.gov.tr/yillik/06_Egitim.pdf> (accessed 24 April 2006).

Directorate General of Press and Information (2006) *The Structure of the Turkish Educational System*. Available at: <http://www.byegm.gov.tr/REFERENCES/EDUCATION-system.htm> (accessed 24 April 2006).

Ekinci, Y. (1990) *Ahilik ve Meslek Eğitimi* (Ahi System and Vocational Training), Istanbul: Milli Eğitim Bakanlığı.

Erder Köksal, S. and Lordoğlu, K. (1993) *Geleneksel Çıraklıktan Çocuk Emeğine: Bir Alan Araştırması* (From Traditional Apprenticeship to Child Labor: A Fieldwork), Istanbul: Friedrich-Ebert-Stiftung.

Evren, B. (1999) *Ottoman Craftsman and Their Guilds*, Istanbul: Doğan Kitap.

MEB (1990) *Çıraklık Eğitimi Yönetmeliği* (Regulations for Apprenticeship Training), Ankara: Milli Eğitim Bakanlığı.

Secretariat General for EU Affairs (2006) 'Education, Training and Youth'. Available at: < http://www.abgs.gov.tr/NPAA/up_files/doc/IV-18(eng).doc> (accessed 11 April 2006).

Taşpınar, M. (1992) 'Elazığ ve Malatya'da Çıraklık Eğitimi ve Sorunları' (Apprenticeship Training and Problems in Elazığ and Malatya), unpublished MA Thesis, University of Fırat.

UNICEF (2006) 'Child-to-Child Training in Apprenticeship Centers Project'. Available at: <http://www.die.gov.tr/CIN/got-unicef/apptraining/app-training.htm> (accessed 11 April 2006).

Ünlühisarcıklı, Ö. (1999) 'Pathways to Employment and Vocational Skill Acquisition: Apprentices, Journeymen, and Masters in the Informal Sector in Istanbul, Turkey', unpublished PhD Dissertation, University of Manchester.

Ünlühisarcıklı, Ö. (2001) 'Training on the Job in Istanbul: A Study of Skills Acquisition in Carpentry and Car-repair Workshops', *International Review of Education*, 47, 5: 443–58.

10 Where the global meets the local

Workforce diversity education

Zane Ma Rhea

In organisations around the world there has, since the 1960s, been a growing focus on the leadership and management of workforce diversity. As globalisation has increasingly impacted on economic systems, enabling both the rapid growth of global organisations and human mobility, coupled with a greater demand for locally skilled workers, the consequence of such turbulence is that workforce supply and demand systems have experienced dramatic change. The human resource requirements of global capitalism, the sheer diversity of its needs, have caused organisations to fundamentally rethink human resource planning and training.

This chapter traces the development of organisational responses to the emerging requirement that the leadership and management of an increasingly heterogeneous workforce is an essential part of doing business in the twenty-first century. Diversity training programmes have been, by far, the most common tool by which organisations have attempted to meet this new need. This chapter examines the approaches to diversity over the past 25 years that have been formulated through global discourses about the leadership and management of workforce diversity. It assesses their ability to deliver ongoing human resource development in a constantly changing global market and assesses their contribution to the education of the global workforce. This chapter argues that the provision of diversity training continues to be shaped by the market rather than by a sustained educational approach to pedagogy, curriculum, assessment and evaluation that is the norm in established fields of professional practice.

Introduction

A large percentage of the new growth in the labor market will be women, minorities and immigrants. What that means is that over the course of 20 to 30 years, the workforce will become more heterogeneous from a race standpoint, from a skills standpoint and from an experience standpoint

(Jones *et al.*, 1989: 13)

In organisations around the world there has, since the 1960s, been a growing focus on the leadership and management of workforce diversity. As globalisation has increasingly impacted on economic systems, enabling both the rapid growth of global organisations and increasing the reach of nationally based markets, human workforce mobility has also increased. Many nations have proactive migration programmes designed to attract skilled labour and everywhere people are moving around the globe looking for improved financial opportunities for themselves and their families. In this same period, previously nationally based organisations and industries have expanded to become global in their reach, taking their organisational cultural expectations into new places, creating a demand for new skills and attitudes. Domestically, in economically developed nations, the available pool of skilled labour has changed dramatically, as predicted by analysts. The demands by women, minorities and immigrants for right of access to work in what had been relatively homogenous white male enclaves shifted dramatically into a need for the previously excluded to come into the workforce to enable organisations to meet the challenges of a rapidly globalising world. The consequence of globalisation is that workforce supply and demand systems have experienced dramatic change. The requirements of global capitalism, and its sheer diversity, have caused many organisations to rethink human resource planning and training.

This chapter traces the development of diversity leadership and management courses as one of the major organisational responses to the globalisation of the workforce and of corporate life. It argues that, as organisations began to be affected by increased workforce diversity there developed an awareness that the leadership and management of such a diversity had become an essential part of doing business in the twenty-first century. A number of 'globalisation' drivers have caused this awareness to impact on strategic workforce planning. Over the period of this review (1980–2005), a flurry of literature has served to promote what is taken to be the need to think about and plan for the leadership and management of human workforce diversity. As an example, Cox and Tung (1997) identify the following:

> A variety of high impact business trends are converging to create this growing diversity in critical constituencies, and as a result, make understanding and managing diversity central to organizational effectiveness. Four such trends are: (a) the increasing formation of global strategic alliances; (b) the increasing globalization of the workforce and the markets for products and services; (c) the emergence of the network structure; and (d) the increasing diversity of gender and racio-ethnic background of labor and consumer markets.
>
> (Cox and Tung, 1997: 8)

The work of Taylor Cox and colleagues, spanning 1990–2002, was extremely influential during the late 1990s. Until that time, and especially during the 1980s, the field was led predominantly by internal human resource development personnel working in a relatively parochial way with external consultants in particular organisations to solve their particular issues.

The 1990s saw the development of a number of more generalisable approaches to diversity leadership and management. Harrington (1993) for example, argued that three approaches to diversity management were being adopted in corporations. She described them as Affirmative Action, responding to new employment laws; Valuing Diversity, focusing on social justice arguments; and Managing Diversity, changing organisational structures (Harrington, 1993). The approaches, broadly described, are not mutually exclusive and the mid-1990s to mid-2000s witnessed a jockeying between approaches as globalisation drivers continued to impact upon and shape diversity within organisations and organisations strove to mobilise their workforces into greater productivity to capture and secure market share.

Regardless of the approach to human resource diversity adopted by an organisation, diversity training programmes have been, by far, the most common tool by which organisations have attempted to manage and optimise the output of the changing workforce. Organisations have incorporated diversity into their strategic workforce development planning, relying on the education of leaders, managers and workers to accommodate, integrate and capitalise on diversity.

This chapter examines the development of the diversity leadership and management field and critiques the conceptual limits of the approaches taken to diversity in organisations. It is argued that the framework used by an organisation will directly shape the way that organisation will undertake ongoing human resource training and development in a constantly changing global market. Arguably, the provision of diversity training continues to be shaped by the market rather than by a sustained educational approach to pedagogy, curriculum, assessment and evaluation that is the norm in established fields of professional practice.

The meaning of diversity

Diversity at its simplest means 'variety, a variety of something such as opinion, colour, or style or discrepancy, or a difference from what is normal or expected' (Encarta: Diversity). An evocative term that signals the *zeitgeist* of globalisation, the social articulation of a changing world, where the authority, the rules and the structures of the 'majority' (aka Western, white, middle class heterosexual, able bodied, men) were giving way to questions about identity, power, representation, rights, and at its most optimistic, an impassioned reminder of the value and beauty of human diversity.

> Amongst humans, particularly in a social context, the term diversity refers to the presence in one population of a (wide) variety of cultures, ethnic groups, languages, physical features, especially if they are recognized by members of that population to constitute characteristics of a race, socio-economic backgrounds, opinions, religious beliefs, sexuality, gender identity, and neurology.
>
> (Wikipedia: Diversity)

Wikipedia also records the use of 'diversity' in the business context:

> In a business context, diversity is approached as a strategy for improving employee retention and increasing consumer confidence. The 'business case for diversity', as it is often phrased, is that in a global and diverse marketplace, a company whose makeup mirrors the makeup of the marketplace it serves is better equipped to thrive in that marketplace than a company whose makeup is homogeneous. Another part of the business case is how well a company utilizes its diversity ... Diversity issues change over time, depending on local historical conditions.
>
> (Wikipedia: Diversity – Business Context)

Nancy Adler (1983) gives an early example of a discussion of diversity in the business sense at a time when there was a growing awareness of the need to take cultural diversity seriously in organisations, particularly in the management of cultural diversity. She found that, 'most organizations that had more than one culture represented in their membership were characterized by cultural diversity: a diversity of socio-cultural perspectives, world views, life-styles, social skills, languages, management styles, and cognitive styles' (Adler, 1983: 13). She was one of the first to recognise that 'this diversity leads to greater complexity within the organization' (Adler, 1983: 16).

Thomas (1996), a leading figure in the field of diversity management and training, undertook the task of redefining diversity, as his book by the same title indicates. He suggested that beyond simplistic definition 'diversity is not synonymous with difference, but encompasses similarities and differences; that diversity refers to collective (all-inclusive) mixtures of similarities and differences along a given dimension; and, that the component elements in diversity mixtures can vary, so a discussion of diversity must specify the dimensions in question' (Thomas, 1996: 6).

Leaders and managers of organisations were looking for answers in response to the changes in the demographics of their available labour pool and there was an implicit threat in the emerging data that an organisation that did not respond to the new workforce diversity was, at a minimum, going to miss an opportunity to position itself in new global markets, and at worst was going to fail as an organisation. As outlined above, a variety of responses to this perceived threat were developed.

Context of diversity training

Economic globalisation, both castigated and praised, has provided the *raison d'être* for diversity training. Wikipedia provides an extensive discussion of 'Globalization', saying:

> A typical definition can be taken from the International Monetary Fund, which defines globalization as the growing economic interdependence of countries worldwide through increasing volume and variety of cross-border transactions in goods and services, free international capital flows, and more rapid and widespread diffusion of technology. All definitions appear to agree that globalization has economic, political, cultural, and technological aspects that may be closely intertwined.
>
> (Wikipedia: Globalization)

Economic globalisation was of primary concern at the United Nations sponsored 'We the Peoples' Millennium Forum held in New York in 2000. Section C: *Facing the challenge of globalization: equity, justice and diversity* explicitly links diversity and globalisation stating that:

> To most, globalization is a process of economic, political and cultural domination by the economically and militarily strong over the weak. For example, the combined assets of the top 200 corporations in the 1960s were 16 per cent of world gross domestic product. This increased by the early 1980s to 24 per cent and in 1995 had risen to 34 per cent. In this process, not only does the gap between the 'haves' and 'have nots' widen but the ranks of the poor are swelling, civil societies are being threatened, pushing an increasing number into extreme poverty, and Governments are becoming dependent. The current globalization process is not inevitable; it is the result of decisions taken by human beings.
>
> (United Nations: Millennium Forum)

The foundational aspects of the diversity field in organisations are to be found in the civil rights movement of the 1960s in the United States of America. As the nation where civil rights struggles influenced the world alongside the consolidation of big business muscle, the impact of the way the United States has articulated its commitment to equality of opportunity at work alongside the business case for effective diversity management cannot be understated.

Significant contribution to the field was also made by social and organisational psychology, sociology and human rights law. Hofstede's (1980, 1983, 1984, 1985) research in the late 1970s and early 1980s was significant in the way that it opened up discussion specifically about ethnic cultural differences within corporations globally. Similarly, Harrington (1993), discussed above, was an early writer whose model of three approaches to workforce diversity was influential. The way the field sees diversity, experiences it, and understands it has been greatly influenced by Hofstede, Roosevelt Thomas, Cox, Harrington and other scholars in related fields of social inquiry despite scholarly critiques of this work.

Equal employment opportunity and affirmative action (EEO/AA)

> Affirmative action is somewhat of an albatross because some people still think of it as preferential treatment. Until the dominant culture in an organisation gets over that state of mind, things will be tough.
>
> (Sheldrich, cited in Galagan, 1991: 40)

It is beyond the scope of this chapter to chart the historical development of equality of opportunity in employment and affirmative action (EEO and AA), situated as it was, and continues to be, within national legislative and legal frameworks. Even so, drawing on Lewin's (1951) theory of change it is possible to attribute EEO/AA legislation and activism as making a significant contribution to the 'unfreezing' of organisational approaches to human resource planning and development. EEO and AA made, and continue to make, a significant contribution to developments in the field of diversity leadership and management as organisations experienced the turbulent impact of economic globalisation. Ensuring that organisations are compliant with local legislation in their dealings is now considered a necessary part of business for any large organisation (see for example Appelbaum and Fewster, 2002).

Generally, EEO and AA training programmes are designed to inform and train designated staff in organisations on the legal requirements regarding such things as recruitment, promotion, discrimination, reportable offences, privacy, and so on. Training is conducted by a person who is knowledgeable about local laws who ensures that the organisation understands its liabilities with regard to those laws. Designated staff in an organisation are responsible for ensuring that there are established policies and procedures with regard to dealing with EEO issues that arise. It is a very common approach to use training to communicate to all staff about their obligations under law such that if the organisation is accused of breaching its obligations, it can demonstrate that it has done everything possible to ensure its compliance with the law. A trainer, usually with an 'off the shelf' training package, will deliver a workshop for designated EEO or diversity staff which informs of their responsibilities.

Staff training for EEO compliance is normally conducted 'in house' with the designated staff responsible for the communication and implementation strategies (Barclay, 2000). For example, with regard to transparency in recruitment processes it would be those staff involved in recruitment processes. For something more general such as sexual harassment or bullying, workshops might be conducted for all staff to ensure that they understand their rights and responsibilities under the local laws.

Valuing diversity or managing diversity?

What had begun in the 1960s as a demand from unrepresented and under-represented women, minorities and immigrants to a fair and equal opportunity to secure employment had, by the 1980s, been substantially refocused into an argument between social justice imperatives which asserted the value of human diversity, and the importance of changing personal biases (for example, see Appendix A) and corporations looking to manage the human diversity in their workforces towards the maximisation of profit and the achievement of organisational goals (for example, see Appendix B).

'Valuing diversity' training – becoming aware of, and changing, personal bias

Workplace training in EEO and AA compliance raised many issues about the personal biases held by people that they brought to work with them. As identified above, organisational development and human resource development personnel are often given the responsibility to 'make something happen' to address the personal biases of staff, commonly to reduce conflict between identifiable groups. Historically, this has been a difficult area for trainers. Caudron (1993) provides a good example of the field in the early to mid-1990s when 'Valuing Diversity' was popular as an organisational change approach to diversity. She raised the issue that there are no professional standards for trainers, so anyone could 'hang out their shingle and become a diversity consultant' (Caudron, 1993: 51). Karp and Sutton (1993) argued that training people to value diversity did not necessarily help achieve organisational goals. They were critical of the fact that often trainers are women or from minority groups. They also pointed out that training programmes were often guilt driven, that the programmes usually had a specific set of values, and that how something is said is more important than what was intended (Karp and Sutton, 1993: 30–1). In general, the focus of 'Valuing Diversity' training was often shaped by local issues, with representatives of the 'minority' seeking to change the attitudes of the dominant 'majority', and was primarily geared to raising awareness of diversity without having the power to necessarily do anything to change the organisational culture.

Commonly, a 'Valuing Diversity' training process would combine group work, individual work and one-on-one coaching, to develop personal diversity skills, within the work and/or life context of the participant (see, for example, Appendix A). There was a strong focus on having participants understand why they feel the way they do about people who are different from them, with an inbuilt assumption that increased awareness of diversity issues would have a direct, and beneficial, flow on into the workplace. 'Valuing Diversity' training programmes were focused on the individual rather than the organisation and were often resisted by the majority who saw no reason to change and resented their privileges being challenged and eroded.

Training for the management of diversity – linking diversity to organisational goals

In 1990, R. Roosevelt Thomas Jr, President of the American Institute for Managing Diversity, wrote in the *Harvard Business Review* a paper titled 'From Affirmative Action to Affirming Diversity'. He argued for an 'openly multicultural workplace that taps the full potential of every employee without artificial programs, standards, or barriers' and focused on a system level approach to training as a way to modify the 'company's culture, vision, model, assumptions, and systems' (Thomas, 1990: 192).

The contribution of Jones *et al.* (1989) in the influential *Training and Development* journal is an early example of the shift from EEO/AA to a business approach to the management of diversity. From a business perspective, they explained that:

> The workforce diversity issue has no relationship to the old affirmative action and EEO programs. Affirmative action and EEO were equity issues. In an era where there were plenty of people to choose from, the question before society and employers was whether the selection of employees for jobs or promotions was discriminatory. Now the issue is not social justice. It's employer demand. The employer has to hire a certain number of people. Minorities, women, older workers, and others are in the pool as an absolute percentage of the people that the employer needs to hire from. So he [sic] has to look at a whole series of different issues.
>
> (Jones *et al.*, 1989: 13)

Organisations began to move away from the EEO and AA approach. The issue became 'why would an organisation promote diversity rather than simply complying with anti-discrimination laws?' Cox (1991) argued that, 'To capitalize on the benefits and minimize the costs of diversity, organizations of the 90s must be different from the organisation of the past' (cited in Cox and Tung, 1997: 7). Cox and Blake (1991) made an early attempt to move away from 'valuing diversity' for its own sake, instead arguing that diversity had to be harnessed to the business bottom line – profit. Galagan (1991: 40) reported that, 'a new wave of diversity programs is building in corporate America. The new programs differ from past efforts in one significant way: they treat diversity as a business issue – one that affects a company's performance' (see also Argyle, 2002).

A large amount of printed materials about diversity practice and training appeared in trade magazines and professional training and development journals during the 1980s and 1990s. Predominantly, case studies were used to demonstrate, in key dot points, how an organisation could become more efficient and effective in its leadership and management of diversity. There is an extensive record of tips, lists and tricks of the trade for the development of diversity training. A number of key questions are asked of a diversity related business plan, such as:

- Does diversity management have a strategic fit with the overall business plan?
- How will improved diversity management benefit the business?
- By how much will improving diversity management decrease expenses?
- By what margin will good diversity management give us a competitive edge?
- What are the on-going costs to maintain good diversity management in my company?
- Does it help the business know more about its customers' needs?
- Most importantly, does improved diversity management give the business a commanding market share lead?

Diamante *et al.* (1995) and Robinson and Dechant (1997) provide insight into the arguments made for building what became known as the 'Business Case for Diversity' in the late 1990s. Robinson and Dechant identify 'cost savings and winning the competition for talent as being strong arguments for the pursuit of diversity initiatives' (1997: 22). They argue that diversity *mismanagement* results in higher turnover costs, higher absenteeism rates and lawsuits on sexual, race and age discrimination, while diversity management will result in improving marketplace understanding, increasing creativity and innovation, producing higher quality problem solving and building effective global relationships.

Cassell and Biswas (2000) argue that the 'Business Case' approach proved to be an effective and popular way for organisations to begin to think about diversity, linked as it became to organisational effectiveness.

An analysis of the literature reveals some common underlying themes that shaped training. There was a strong focus on building the business case within the organisation. There are many anecdotal accounts of organisations having a champion who empowers the OD or HRD unit to develop 'something' about diversity that links to corporate goals. The internal personnel then develop a strategic business plan (see Appendix B for an example). As noted in Appendix B, this process can take a long time to achieve the necessary organisation-wide 'buy-in'.

The 2000s have witnessed a 'refreezing' of human resource planning, training and development with the ascendancy of the business case over the EEO/AA and personal awareness approaches to diversity (see, for example, Cox, 2002). Critics such as Thomas (2001) argue that driving diversity through a business management model has not dealt with the underlying tensions that diversity in the workforce bring, and Thomas points to the significant increase, in the US, of lawsuits brought by individuals and groups against organisations for discriminatory practices despite the claims of those supporting the 'Managing Diversity' approach that their interventions would substantially decrease such risks.

In addition, the business case for investing in diversity has proved difficult to make when using the above questions. Hansen (2003), for example, argues that 'for years the (diversity) industry has claimed that diversity programs yield higher performance and greater productivity, but the evidence offered is largely anecdotal or based on limited data collected through questionable methods' (Hansen, 2003: 28). The critique of diversity management training has been slow but persistent, owing predominantly to the fact that so little is known about how training is conducted and how its effectiveness can be measured. Thomas (1999), Hansen (2003) and Kochan *et al.* (2003) argue for effective measurement of diversity training outcomes to evaluate the contribution that diversity training makes, for example, to increased profit, greater customer share, reduced litigation and greater market respectability.

Certainly, it can be argued that much of what is done in diversity training is not quantifiable but diversity training is exposed in the 'Managing Diversity' approach to the same bottom line accountabilities as any other expense against profit. In this approach, 'diversity' has been corralled into the overall organisational strategy, as part of a growth strategy, a resource security strategy or a risk management strategy. The attention to pedagogy and content seems expedient at best.

Emerging diversity human resources development (HRD) professional and diversity training

Analysis of the literature over the past 25 years shows that a number of pathways to EEO/AA and diversity training are available in most multinational organisations around the world (see Figure 10.1).

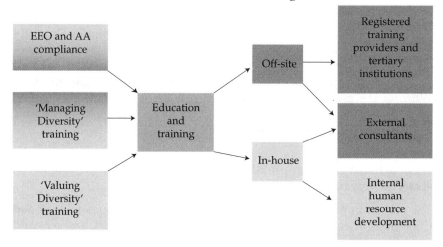

Figure 10.1 Diversity education and training pathways

Diversity training has become a global multibillion dollar industry in its own right (Hansen, 2003). No formal qualifications are required for trainers and the choice of trainer, consultant, consultancy company or course by an organisation will reflect the overall approach that they have chosen to take to diversity within their organisation. Roberson *et al.* (2001) provide a rare analysis of diversity training that is research based, such is the newness of this field. They found that diversity training is rarely subjected to evaluation, relies on feedback from participants, there is no measurement on how the training influences the behaviour of the trainees and little is known about how group composition affects training. Focusing specifically on training group composition, they found that 'trainees with prior experience of diversity training responded most positively to training groups homogenous with respect to racioethnicity and nationality; trainees without prior experience with diversity training were generally unaffected by training group composition' (Roberson *et al.*, 2001: 871). The design of diversity training programmes, while the pedagogy and content are difficult to access, can be more generally analysed through professional and trade magazines. Such analysis suggests that the provision of diversity training continues to be shaped by the market rather than by a sustained educational approach to pedagogy, curriculum and evaluation.

Conclusion

Historically, there have been three approaches to increased diversity in the global workforce, EEO and AA, and valuing and managing diversity. These approaches are not mutually exclusive and it is possible to identify aspects of all three in organisational and in human resource development programmes. The last 25 years has witnessed a burgeoning of diversity management professionals, and literature on diversity training. Diversity training, a largely disregarded field of adult education, has been pivotal in the education of the global workforce, grappling with the social, political and economic upheavals that have been produced by globalisation. Whether the management of workforce diversity continues to develop as a profession or is a temporary phenomenon of global economic reorganisation is yet to be determined.

Appendix A: An example of a 'Valuing Diversity' strategic development plan

The outline in Table 10.1 is drawn from a planning document developed through a series of workshops involving all the managers, workers and executives of a medium-sized multinational company based in Australia. Each section of the document was drafted by small groups of people drawn from the various levels of the organisation (making what is known as a vertical cut). The various contributions were then drawn together and a combined full draft again discussed by all staff. This process was facilitated by an external consultant working with internal HRD personnel. Once the Valuing Diversity plan was agreed, a training programme was developed by the external consultant to workshop each section as appropriate. The entire process was undertaken over an 18-month period.

Table 10.1 A Valuing Diversity plan

Vision and values	Outline of priority areas
Quality Policy Statement	Priority Area 1 – Data collection
Cultural diversity in the organisation	Priority Area 2 – Customer service
Principles	Priority Area 3 – Staff/Human Resources
Objectives of the cultural plan	Priority Area 4 – Technology development and resource allocation

Appendix B: An example of a business case for managing diversity

Table 10.2 A business case for managing diversity

Business strategy	People objective	Diversity linkage
Growth	Increase the talent within the enterprise	Attract, develop and retain the best talent for XYZ
Globalisation	Increase the organisational competence to operate effectively across diverse countries and cultures	Leverage multicultural differences to increase business value; develop multicultural sensitivity and competence
Shareholder value	Drive business results through high levels of organisational performance	Organisational capability relies on maximising talent; an inclusive and supportive environment drives high level commitment and utilisation of all employees
Operational excellence	Establish people systems and a work environment which support the concepts of OD	OD strategy depends on our ability to tap the discretionary efforts of all employees through their commitment and using the full capabilities of every individual
Customer satisfaction	Establish a responsive organisation capable of consistently adding value to our global customer base	Diversity creates a more adaptable, flexible and responsive organisation

References

Adler, N. (1983) 'Cross Cultural Management: Issues to be Faced', *International Studies of Management and Organisation*, 13, 1–2: 7–45.

Appelbaum, S.H. and Fewster, B.M. (2002) 'Global Aviation Human Resource Management: Contemporary Recruitment and Selection and Diversity and Equal Opportunity Practices', *Equal Opportunities International*, 21, 7: 66.

Argyle, N.J. (2002) 'From Affirmative Action to Diversity: Managing Human Resources for Productivity', *Public Performance and Management Review*, 25: 324.

Barclay, D. (2000) 'The Changing Role of the EEO Professional', *Diversity Factor*, 8: 37.

Cassell, C. and Biswas, R. (2000) 'Editorial: Managing Diversity in the New Millennium', *Personnel Review*, 29: 268.

Caudron, S. (1993) 'Valuing Differences isn't the Same as Managing Diversity', *Personnel Journal*, 72: 58.

Cox, T. (1991) 'The Multicultural Organization', *The Executive*, 5: 34.

Cox, T. (2002) 'Taking Diversity to the Next Level', *Executive Excellence*, 19: 19.

Cox, T.H. and Blake, S. (1991) 'Managing Cultural Diversity: Implications for Organizational Competitiveness', *The Executive*, 5: 45.

Cox, T.H. and Tung, R. (1997) 'Multicultural Organizations Revisited', in *Creating Tomorrow's Organizations*, New York: John Wiley.

Diamante, T., Reid, C.L. and Giglio, L. (1995) 'Make the Right Training Move', *HR Magazine*, 40: 60.

Encarta: 'Diversity'. Available at: <http://encarta.msn.com/dictionary_/diversity.html> (Accessed 1 August 2006).

Galagan, P.A. (1991) 'Tapping the Power of a Diverse Workforce', *Training and Development Journal*, 45: 38–44.

Hansen, F. (2003) 'Diversity's Business Case: Doesn't Add Up', *Workforce*, 82, 4: 28–32.

Harrington, L. (1993) 'Why Managing Diversity is So Important', *Distribution*, 92, 11: 88.

Hofstede, G. (1980) *Culture's Consequences: International Differences in Work-Related Values*, Beverly Hills, CA: Sage.

Hofstede, G. (1983) 'National Cultures in Four Dimensions: A Research-Based Theory of Cultural Differences among Nations', *International Studies of Management and Organization*, 13, 1–2: 46–74.

Hofstede, G. (1984) *Culture's Consequences: International Differences in Work-Related Values*, Abridged edn. Beverly Hills, CA: Sage.

Hofstede, G. (1985) 'The Interaction between National and Organizational Value Systems', *Journal of Management Studies*, 22, 4: 347–57.

Jones, R.T., Jerich, B., Copeland, L. and Boyles, M. (1989) 'How Do You Manage a Diverse Workforce?' *Training and Development*, 43, 2: 13–21.

Karp, H.B. and Sutton, N. (1993) 'Where Diversity Training Goes Wrong', *Training*, 30, 7: 30.

Kochan, T., Bezrukova, K., Ely, R., Jackson, S., Joshi, A., Jehn, K., Leonard, J., Levine, D. and Thomas, D. (2003) 'The Effects of Diversity on Business Performance: Report of the Diversity Research Network', *Human Resource Management*, 42: 3–20.

Lewin, K. (1951) *Field Theory in Social Sciences*, New York: Harper and Brothers.

Roberson, L., Kulik, C. and Pepper, M. (2001) 'Designing Effective Diversity Training: Influence of Group Composition and Trainee Experience', *Journal of Organizational Behavior*, 22: 871.

Robinson, G. and Dechant, K. (1997) 'Building a Business Case for Diversity', *The Academy of Management Executive*, 11: 21.

Thomas Jr, R.R. (1990) 'From Affirmative Action to Affirming Diversity', *Harvard Business Review*, 2: 107–17.

Thomas Jr, R. R. (1996) 'Redefining Diversity', *HR Focus*, 73: 6.

Thomas Jr, R.R. (1999) 'Diversity Management: Some Measurement Criteria', *Employment Relations Today*, 25: 49.

Thomas Jr, R.R. (2001) 'Diversity Tension and Other Underlying Factors in Discrimination Suits', *Employment Relations Today*, 27, 4: 31.

United Nations: 'Millennium Forum'. Available at: <http://www.un.org/millennium/declaration.htm> (Accessed 1 August 2006).

Wikipedia: Diversity. Available at: <http://en.wikipedia.org/wiki/Diversity> (Accessed 1 August 2006).

Wikipedia: Diversity – Business Context. Available at: <http://en.wikipedia.org/wiki/Diversity#Business_context> (Accessed 1 August 2006).

Wikipedia: Globalization. Available at: <http://en.wikipedia.org/wiki/Globalization> (Accessed 1 August 2006).

11 Organizational learning

Competence-bearing relations and breakdowns of workplace relatonics

Marianne Döös

Contextualized in Swedish work-life, this chapter deals with issues that may be assumed to confront several OECD countries. The underlying problem concerns which opportunities for everyday learning and competence development are offered in working life. A reorganization at one's workplace during the last year is the reported experience of 45–50 per cent of the Swedish workforce in various sectors. The organizational changes have, to a decisive extent, been poorly executed in light of their consequences for the competence and learning of employees and the organization. The aim of this chapter is to contribute to the forming of concepts and actionable understanding from an organization-pedagogic stance. A distinction is made between arranging learning occasions and organizing for learning in everyday settings. Relatonics is a concept that raises the concept of relations to an organizational level and takes argumentation to the level of the core task of the organization and organizational learning. Workplace relatonics are defined as the overall existence of the interactive processes between the human beings who bear the competencies of the workplace. Increased understanding is created of the importance of organizing work for learning, and the dangers of frequent reorganizations are highlighted. The concepts also aim at facilitating interdisciplinary exchange.

Introduction

Through qualifying experiences people slowly learn what is normal for a job, what the job-related problems are, and how they can be resolved. People find out who is good at this or that, and whose knowledge is available when an answer is required, or an argument needs to be presented. Under favorable circumstances, learning results in individuals who become and stay knowledgeable, and organizations that are viable and economically sound.

This chapter aims at affording concepts constructive for exploring the prerequisites for competence in organizations. The intent is to make a contribution to ways of understanding that can qualify the handling of learning processes in working life. The argument takes its point of departure from knowledge about the processes of individual and collective learning, and introduces *relatonics*, a concept to explain learning at the organizational level. Relatonics concerns the inter-related existence of ongoing relational processes that bear and develop competencies between people in the workplace (Döös 2004).

Competence is regarded as a means of competition between organizations (see, e.g., Dixon 2000; Nonaka 1996). To a growing extent, it seems to be competence that determines success, and competence can be improved via critical analyses of conditions for learning and skills development. The discussion assumes that an individual's competence is both stable and changing. Individuals take their knowledge and expertise with them from one context to another. Such know-how is personal and can be carried to new places and situations, where it is made available and can be put to use. In other words, this discussion assumes that know-how is closely linked to a particular individual. Individuals possess competence, i.e. the ability to apply their experience in specific contexts that call for action, such as problem-solving at work. But this is only half the truth. What is more or less the opposite is equally important, namely that know-how and competence are not an individual phenomenon but are existent in relations between human beings. Working in cooperation with others, individuals can overcome their own limitations, and find solutions to problems they could not have tackled alone. Many tasks carried out in modern organizations require the ability to comprehend, think and understand. This means that access to other competent people is likely to have become increasingly important.

Contextualized in Swedish work-life, this chapter deals with issues that may be assumed to confront several OECD[1] countries. The underlying problem concerns which opportunities for everyday learning and competence development are offered in working life. The focus is on the learning processes of people who have already developed considerable skills and know-how, i.e. on the further development of competencies by people who already know their jobs. A brief introduction to the Swedish work-life context and current conditions for competence is followed by an organization-pedagogic highlighting of concepts utilizable when connecting experiential learning to the organizational level. These concepts are: thought network, competence-bearing relation, workplace relatonics and organizing (work) for learning.

The Swedish context

Looking back at the last 15 years of the welfare state in Sweden, there have been dramatic ups and downs. There has been overheating in the economy, as well as deep crisis in the bursting of the IT bubble, and lately gradual recovery. Sweden's way of organizing welfare presupposes high employment. In *Year Book 2006* (Olofsson and Zavisic 2006), two general problems are identified: ever fewer people must provide for ever more;

and there is a growing problem of exclusion, where it has become more difficult for entrants to gain a foothold in the labor market, and for persons on sick leave to re-enter. Difficulties in getting a job apply especially to people of immigrant background. The state of the country is characterized by problems due to a lack of job opportunities, involuntary part-time working and high sickness absenteeism. There is a major increase in sick-leave periods and an increasing proportion of psychiatric diagnoses. At the same time, Sweden has the highest labor-force participation in Europe, especially with regard to women.

During the 1990s, employment grew in parts of the service production sector, in particular in knowledge intensive services, local manual service production and tele-support. The proportions employed in other branches of the economy declined during the same period, especially in branches concerned with the handling of goods. Generally, employment is decreasing in operations dominated by large workplaces (Giertz, in Abrahamsson *et al.* 2002).

Sweden shows "remarkably higher levels of psychosocial occupational-health problems than other EU countries" (Olofsson and Zavisic 2006: 29); and an increasing proportion report that they "find it hard to sleep at night because thinking of the job keeps me awake". Since increasing long-term sick-leave is at least in part linked to stress and burnout, the psychosocial work environment and organizational change have become the subject of much discussion.

Most of the leadership philosophies and trends that have had an impact in Sweden since the 1990s have come from the US, e.g. Lean Production and Total Quality Management (Björkman 1997) – and they tend to be adapted, in a somewhat improvisory manner, to local circumstances (Furusten 2001). However, Swedish work-life is also characterized by organizational forms involving teams and autonomous co-workers (Sisson 2000). For a number of years, participation and Japanese Kaizen-influenced continuous improvements were key words in Swedish work-life research (see, e.g., Nilsson 1999).

One major change is that organizing in the form of projects has become ever more prevalent. This entails that individuals are compelled to take greater responsibility for their personal development and careers, and sometimes also for their corporate undertaking's business risks (Olofsson and Zavisic 2006). Projects can be categorized into client-oriented business projects, product development projects and projects focusing on change to the work organization, i.e. to ways of organizing and working (Söderlund 2005). Companies dominated by product development projects tend also to have many organization-change projects. Accordingly, many projects are linked to reorganizations, and also to relatively brief life-spans in terms of organizational structure. Bäcklund (in Abrahamsson *et al.* 2002) takes the view that the work ethic that used to consist in predictability and reliability now involves changing jobs and taking risks. That is, the individual continuously "positions himself or herself in a network of *opportunities*, not in a specific job" (Abrahamsson *et al.* 2002: 221, author's italics). This gives rise to an uncertainty that according to Bäcklund, with reference to Sennett, involves the "corrosion of character".

At an international level, Sweden comes across as successful with regard to levels of competencies and educational opportunities for adults (Aspgren, in Abrahamsson *et al.* 2002). Requirements for simpler forms of work have increased, and a high-school qualification is demanded within most occupations. Many jobs are temporary, and university students who take on unskilled tasks as a sideline "enter a labor force that the lowly educated need for establishment in adulthood" (Arnell, in Olofsson and Zavisic 2006: 57). A challenge to Swedish working life lies in the supply of competencies for the future, not least because of major pension withdrawals. At the same time, a great proportion of skills development is now expected to be conducted in the course of the performance of work tasks.

Consequences for learning and competence in Sweden

Recent reports focus on the problem of work intensity, showing that too high a level of work intensity is not only harmful to individuals, but also has a negative impact on the results achieved by the organization, and entails costs due to a loss of know-how and knowledge (Docherty *et al.* 2002). There is increasing interest in issues involving sustainability, which – by contrast with intensity – involve the dependence of competitive organizations on ensuring that human resources are not consumed, but are, instead, (re)generated and allowed to grow. Learning has become accepted as a key phenomenon in modern working life. Researchers caution, however, that work learning studies must highlight dissimilarities in types of operations for conclusions to be drawn about competence demands, work conditions, work organization, management principles, work environment, and so on (Giertz, in Abrahamsson *et al.* 2002).

One tendency is that, for a variety of reasons, conditions for learning have deteriorated in recent years. In 2002, 45–55 per cent of employees within the total range of sectors reported that there had been a reorganization in their workplace over the preceding year (Döös 2005). This has been the situation for several years, in the private sector as well as the public. In practice, it is likely to be unclear to people where the boundary lies between a reorganization and, for example, the start of a new project. In both cases, it is the task of the individual to learn to get to know new co-workers and utilize the specialist competence of others, while at the same time maintaining one's own: "Every person's competence is exposed to competition in the case of each new project" (Arvidsson and Ekstedt, in Olofsson and Zavisic 2006: 96). Project organizing is contrasted with the "permanent organization", which is said to be a "prerequisite for transferring the knowledge gained in a project to any future project by transforming project members' private expertise into common organizational competence" (ibid: 90). Thus, the permanent platform and the project-based organization within an undertaking must somehow be coordinated and function alongside each other.

An organization-pedagogic perspective

The theoretical basis for this chapter is an experiential learning perspective founded in action and interaction. It involves the adoption of a context-oriented approach, developed at the Department of Education at Stockholm University in Sweden over a period of 30 years (see, e.g., Ohlsson and Döös 1999). In brief, learning is defined as a situated process of knowledge construction grounded in action, with the learner as an active constructor of knowledge and know-how. To learn implies changing one's ways of thinking and/or acting in relation to the task one intends to perform. This means that learning is linked to the potential for action, and enhances the carrying-out of intended tasks. Learning involves transactions between individuals and their environment (Kolb 1984). In recent years, efforts have been made to find ways of integrating this tradition with other contextual approaches. Organization pedagogics deal with how people organize themselves in developing social order, knowledge and identity (Döös *et al.* 2006).

Everyday learning within work tasks is closely related to the level of relevant competence that is being developed. In today's Swedish workplaces, many people are obliged to work quickly. This is achieved by performing tasks in minimum time, and by avoiding unnecessary initiatives and conversations, i.e. at the expense of realizing the workplace's positive learning potential. Where there is a choice between short-term and long-term solutions, the emphasis is on short-term efficiency. Accordingly, it may be asked what people actually learn at work in terms of quality and content, and whether it is relevant to the organization's operational task, i.e. its core task, such as taking care of children in the case of a day-care centre, lending books in a library or making cars in the automotive sector.

Theoretically rooted empirical studies in varying sectors during the 1990s and thereafter have generated robust knowledge about the processes of experiential learning, both for individuals (see, e.g., Bjerlöv 1999; Döös 1997) and at group or collective levels (see, e.g., Döös and Wilhelmson 2005; Granberg and Ohlsson 2005). Part of the organization-pedagogic undertaking is to take process knowledge of individual and group learning to the organizational level. In what follows, the above-mentioned four main concepts of relevance to this endeavor are considered.

Thought networks develop in small steps

Although many people think of learning as something quick and radical, empirical studies demonstrate that it is usually a small-scale process involving confirmation and more of the same, rather than gaining new knowledge and insights (Bjerlöv 1999; Döös 1997). One experience is added to another, constructing and confirming the everyday normality of a work task. Due to such normality, differences and deviations gradually emerge. The small steps and incremental changes in understanding are termed as "qualifying experiences" when Döös (1997) emphasizes the significance of a preceding action to the subsequent actions. This highlights that it makes a difference in terms of learning when a subsequent action is modified by the action that immediately preceded it.

An individual's understanding of something may be described as a thought network (Döös 1997). Thought networks are linked to situations and are action-related. A study of operators' learning while handling disturbances in automated production (ibid) concluded that the thought network couples the operator's analysis of the current situation to action via a characteristic of the situation that indicates possible courses of action. They are living (re)constructions, cognitive structures, open to change through the questions the individual poses, and as a result of the actions involved in performing the task. Thought networks are borne individually, but can also be more-or-less shared, and even connected and partly merged (Döös *et al.* 2005).

A study of learning in the telecoms sector[2] concluded that there was a lack of awareness of learning processes in the organization on the part of both management's and employees' thought networks. Thus, the learning processes were not intentionally organized for, or facilitated by, design. Interactions, work methods and competence-bearing relations were concealed from a learning point of view, and were simply regarded as work. Competence-bearing relations and the relatonic thus were simply left to their own, instead of being attended to and supported by management.

Competence-bearing relations

In addition to the fact that individuals carry their know-how from one setting to another, this knowledge also arises and survives in interpersonal relations in the workplace. In a competence-bearing relation, a single individual is capable of more than he or she can achieve alone. The presence of and de facto access to others shape and sustain the know-how. The telecoms study provided examples of this. In conversations between two highly expert engineers a switching process emerged, in which their ideas hooked on to each other's – a kind of "zipper talking" – in the course of a problem-solving session in front of a computer monitor. Understanding evolved simultaneously and jointly through shared commenting, interpreting and concrete task-performing. This may be seen as a process of the merging of the two experts' already well-developed thought networks. A merged thought network emerges and becomes existent in a relation, i.e. through interactions, conversations and (in this case) the experimentation required. The network exists, figuratively speaking, in between individuals, but is ready for use when needed.

Being able to continue to think and act jointly on the basis of an already-achieved level of competence calls for access to other competent persons. People see, hear and do things together. Buber (1953/1990) emphasizes the "lingering" consciousness that results from any conversation. The interest here lies in the residual knowledge residing in recurrent access to other individuals, who themselves are also knowledge-constructing agents. These are the colleagues in whose company you have thought, worked and gained experience, and who know accordingly what the shared words, allusions and solutions represent. You have jointly and communally lived through the reasons why you do what you actually do in the workplace. These are processes, based on participation, that require trust and confidence if they are to operate at a deeper level (see, e.g., Döös *et al.* 2003).

Workplace relatonics

The concept of relatonics takes relations up to the organizational level, moves on from a focus on relations between two or more specific individuals and elevates the level of argumentation to the core task of the organization and organizational learning. As a result, the concept remedies the weakness of the term "relation", which tends to be associated with private interpersonal contact. A relatonic is defined as the *composite existence of the interactive processes between human beings that bear the competence of the workplace* (organization). It is a dynamic structure of ongoing relational processes that carries and develops competencies.

As a phenomenon, there is a relatonic in all workplaces, which varies in quality in terms of its effectiveness with regard to the operative task. The contexts in which a relatonic emerges, changes and becomes important involve more or less well-functioning variants of cooperation. In a discussion of the "collective mind" of an organization, Weick and Roberts (1993/2001) point to individual competence being as necessary as it is insufficient. Interpersonal skills are a necessity, and cooperation is essential to the development of understanding in an organization. The phenomena of reasoned action and collective mind are developed in frequent mutual relations, and under circumstances in which operations are not conducted solely on a routine basis. In what Weick and Roberts call "heedful performance" (with reference to Ryle) each action is modified by its predecessor, indicating that the individual is still learning. Reasoned action involves active utilization of one's own and others' thought networks, and taking into account, noting and being mentally prescient of circumstances. As in "qualifying experiences" it allows a recent experience to make a difference, and thereby to affect subsequent action.

After a (major) reorganization, people in a workplace will start to build up new relations and new shared (thought) networks. At the organizational level, this means investing in a new relatonic. The building-up processes take time, and the old relatonic is squandered. This entails a substantial leakage of competence, where there is insufficient return on previous investment. From the perspective of relatonics, such leakage is not due to resistance to change; rather, it is a consequence of broken competence-bearing relations. Individuals no longer know where to turn in order to find competent answers to each other's questions. There is an impending risk that competence-bearing networks of relations will be torn apart in the course of reorganization processes.

Researchers' attention and some empirical studies point to organizational aspects as dangers for individuals, their health, their competence, and finally for the organization's competence. To exemplify, Sennett (2003) describes how today's flexible working life makes people and organizations dysfunctional and disoriented. Brödner and Forslin (in Docherty *et al.* 2002) refer to work intensity resulting in competence loss hazardous to the performance of organizations, and Wikman and Marklund (2003) conclude that the increase in sick-leave clearly is related to impaired psychosocial work conditions. Relationships between restructuring changes at workplaces, and individuals' motivation and wellbeing have been found in studies of burnout (Eriksson *et al.* 2003; Hasselgren 2004). In a study of home care workers, Astvik (2003) stressed the importance of relations and found non-constructive strategies with consequences for the quality of work task execution. The conditions for competence after a major reorganization of a public authority are described through the narrative of a senior employee (Döös 2005). The reorganization turned out to have severe consequences for fundamental tasks of the activity, consequences only occasionally noticed by management.

Human beings are not objects that can be transferred into a new setting (as several reorganizations seem to presume), and then interact with their competencies intact. If individuals repeatedly lose the people in which they have invested working relationships, their situation becomes tough and strenuous, which is likely to have a harmful impact on both individual and organizational competence. If this happens time and time again, people tend to adopt a lower level of ambition, accept lower standards of performance and lose interest. A situation may develop in which sloppiness is permissible, and where dissatisfaction with the quality of one's own work intermingles with a demand to endure an incompatible shifting between being regarded as a participant and being treated as an object. Such conflicting logics are assumed to bode ill for human beings, their learning and their competence.

Organizing (work) for learning

A distinction of importance to relatonics is that between *arranging learning occasions* and *organizing for learning* in everyday settings. The former is reserving time in an arena separated from everyday work tasks with the explicit aim of learning (e.g. a course or seminar). The latter is much different: organizing work tasks and their performance in a way that supports "qualifying experiences" and "heedful performances" in the everyday work situation.

Thus, organizing for learning means establishing conditions for continuous work flow that favor development of competence. Organizing for learning, for example, involves arranging individual work tasks so that they form a meaning-bearing entity for individuals – an entity that affords reason for relating (Stacey 2001) and reasoned action (Weick and Roberts 1993/2001). Another aspect of organizing for learning lies in designing various types of work processes that afford communication as well as joint action where people see each other in action (Larsson 2004). Larsson and Löwstedt (2002) describe this as organizing an operation so that learning is put into a system. The basis for systematic learning of this kind is:

> a structure that provides frequent opportunities to meet, a content to the meetings and gatherings that are permeated by joint reflection about experiences, and also a method of working that makes manifest the knowledge and experience in action of individual colleagues.
>
> (ibid: 111, my translation)

There is a gray zone open for reflection and definition concerning the distinction between arranging learning occasions and organizing (work) for learning. Work-team lunches and communal morning meetings are two examples of occasions that are deliberately arranged. At first sight, they do not form part of regular work tasks. No-one is looking after patients, nothing is being manufactured and no books are being distributed to borrowers. In this sense, they are sideline activities. On the other hand, there is clear evidence that such types of gatherings have a crucial impact on learning at work (Larsson and Löwstedt 2002), and might be regarded as examples of organizing (work) for learning. These kinds of phenomena involve organizing that is closely linked to both work and core operations, and to the people participating in the activities. They are not separated from everyday work, and do not take place in a specific arena; rather, they represent an everyday scene. People continue to be part of their joint meaning context (Ohlsson and Döös 1999), and remain in their specific action environment. On such occasions, decisions may be taken that apply to the communal workplace; issues and problems can be raised that involve thinking together; and accounts may be heard that make it easier to understand the realities in the action environment in a similar manner. The regularity of such meetings also means that participants may expect to have an opportunity to exchange a few words with people they need to get hold of. Such gatherings might be regarded as part of organizing (work) for learning, and thus be conceptually termed as *organized gatherings*.

The term *'arranged learning occasion'* may be reserved to refer to opportunities in which there is spatial separation between the specific environment and its meaning context, i.e. when an individual leaves the workplace to attend a course or seminar away from the meaning context and relations in the workplace. This involves a separation from the relatonic of the home organization, and thus creates a transfer problem on the individual's return to the workplace, when he or she tries to bring new knowledge and insights back and put them to use in the workplace.

Discussion

The need for the concept of relatonics and the associated reasoning about organizing (work) for learning and competence-bearing relations have emerged in a situation in which researchers into learning have considerable knowledge about experiential learning during the performance of work tasks. Transforming knowledge on learning and relations from the individual and collective levels to the organizational sphere is partly a question of establishing links between learning theories and other more traditional disciplines in the organization-development field, e.g. business administration. As Shani and Docherty (2003) have stated, the literature on individual learning in organizations runs in different disciplinary streams (such as educational, psychological and organizational behavior research) to those on literature of organizational learning (such as economics, organization change and development research). Inter-disciplinary exchange may be facilitated by concepts that work at the organizational level but integrate research from the field of experiential learning among adults, such as the concept of "relatonics". The current understanding however calls for more elaborated scientific knowledge and for practical examples.

Reorganization puts competence at risk

When competence is one-sidedly regarded as an individual characteristic, important questions regarding competencies existing in relations are excluded, both when it comes to current operations and to change and reorganization processes. Consequently, factors that are crucial to the quality of core operations and organizational efficiency remain in the shadows. In particular, there is need for awareness of the repercussions that reorganization often has upon the competence-bearing processes in the workplace.

In a functioning relatonic, co-workers know where the competencies lie, and who is good at what.[3] Who is good at what is linked to who performs particular tasks – since this is where you learn, and maintain and develop what you are good at. Experiencing frequent reorganizations, reorganizing tasks and changing the individuals who perform them give rise to the risk that co-workers no longer know whom to turn to when problems arise. Perhaps the person no longer even exists; the knowledgeable one has been transformed into a shoulder-shrugger who just knows a little about everything.

Interplay and relations are more or less dynamic. Relatonics may be both functional and counter-productive. Certain relations come to a standstill, and may conserve, even promote, evil. Other relations develop, and are a source of creativity and new ideas. Good relations take time to build, but may be instantly destroyed in the course of a reorganization. Human willpower, commitment, know-how, cooperation, competence, ability and feeling are key aspects of what we refer to as an organization. The degree of success with which people manage to organize themselves for the tasks they are to perform determines the quality of the outcomes achieved. This is an obvious point, but, in practice, it involves many challenges.

Changes are certainly required in organizations, but to achieve better results from core operations, attention could be paid to relatonics, and to establishing conditions that promote relatonics – organizing for learning and competence-bearing relations. This approach is aligned with the initiatives of Illeris and associates (2004) to create opportunities for "learning through a development of the workplace as a learning environment" (ibid: 139) and associated with the concept of learning by design (Shani and Docherty 2003).

Notes

1 The Organization for Economic Cooperation and Development, which groups 30 member countries, including Canada, the USA and most western European states.

2 The study concerned the learning processes of software development engineers working at the knowledge frontier of the telecom sector, at the interface between tele- and datacom within one company, Ericsson, Sweden. Special focus was upon the relation between individual and collective learning, i.e. how the knowledge was gained, interacted and transacted in and between teams. Data was collected during 2000 in four software-engineering teams, through semi-structured interviews, reflection groups and observations. Four researchers worked in close collaboration (Döös and Wilhelmson 2005; Döös *et al.* 2005).

3 This has, for example, been demonstrated in an ongoing study of a Swedish bank.

References

Abrahamsson, K., Abrahamsson, L., Björkman, T., *et al.* (eds) (2002) *Education, Competence and Work*, Lund: Studentlitteratur (in Swedish).

Astvik, W. (2003) *Relating as a Primary Task: Prerequisites for Sustainable Caring in Home-care Services*, Arbete och Hälsa 2003: 8, Stockholm: National Institute for Working Life (in Swedish).

Bjerlöv, M. (1999) *Learning in Work Based Discourse*, Arbete och Hälsa 1999: 1, Solna: National Institute for Working Life (in Swedish).

Björkman, T. (1997) '"Management": a fashion industry', in Å. Sandberg (ed.) *Management for All: On Discontinuities in Perspectives on Corporate Management*, pp. 58–85, Stockholm: SNS Förlag (in Swedish).

Buber, M. (1953/1990) *Between Man and Man*, Ludvika: Dualis Förlag (in Swedish).

Dixon, N. (2000) *Common Knowledge: How Companies Thrive by Sharing what they Know*, Boston, MA: Harvard Business School Press.

Docherty, P., Forslin, J. and Shani, A.B. (eds) (2002) *Creating Sustainable Work Systems: Emerging Perspectives and Practices*, London: Routledge.

Döös, M. (1997) *The Qualifying Experience: Learning from Disturbances in Relation to Automated Production*, Arbete och Hälsa 1997: 10, Solna: National Institute for Working Life (In Swedish).

Döös, M. (2004) 'Workplace relatonics: on everyday learning and competence in relations', *Arbetsmarknad & Arbetsliv*, 10, 2: 77–93 (in Swedish).

Döös, M. (2005) 'The life conditions of competence: on competence and relatonics in organizations', *Synopsis*, 7: 1–21 (in Swedish).

Döös, M. and Wilhelmson, L. (2005) 'Collective learning: on the significance of interaction in action and a common action arena', *Pedagogisk forskning i Sverige*, 10, 3/4: 209–26 (in Swedish).

Döös, M., Wilhelmson, L. and Hemborg, Å. (2003) 'Shared leadership as a possibility', in L. Wilhelmson (ed.) *Renewal in Swedish Workplaces*, Stockholm: National Institute for Working Life (in Swedish).

Döös, M., Wilhelmson, L., Backlund, T. and Dixon, N. (2005) 'Functioning at the edge of knowledge', *Journal of Workplace Learning*, 17, 8: 481–92.

Döös, M., Granberg, O., Ohlsson, J. *et al.* (2006) 'Organization pedagogics: a round table on development in and of organizations', NFPF, Örebro, 2006-03-09 – 11 (Conference paper).

Eriksson, U.-B., Starrin, B. and Jansson, S. (2003) *Burnt Out and Emotionally Emaciated*, Lund: Studentlitteratur (in Swedish).

Furusten, S. (2001) *Consulting in Legoland: The Jazz of Small-scale Management Consultation in the Improvisation on Standards*, Stockholm: Score.

Granberg, O. and Ohlsson, J. (2005) 'Collective learning in teams', *Pedagogisk forskning i Sverige*, 10, 3/4: 227–43 (in Swedish).

Hasselgren, H. (2004) *From Pleasure in Work to Sick Leave: Preschool Employees on Long Sick Leave Reflect on the Relationship Between Ill Health and Work Related Stress*, Linköping: Linköping University (in Swedish).

Illeris, K. and associates (eds) (2004) *Learning in Working Life*, Roskilde: Learning Lab Denmark, Roskilde University Press.

Kolb, D. (1984) *Experiential Learning*, Englewood Cliffs, NJ: Prentice-Hall.

Larsson, P. (2004) *Conditions for Change*, EFI, Handelshögskolan (in Swedish).

Larsson, P. and Löwstedt, J. (2002) 'Shouldn't we invest in knowledge management: on organizing systems for learning', in J. Löwstedt and B. Stymne (eds) *Scenes from a Company*, pp. 93–116, Lund: Studentlitteratur (in Swedish).

Nilsson, T. (ed.) (1999) *Continuous Improvement*, Solna: National Institute for Working Life (in Swedish).

Nonaka, I. (1996) 'The knowledge-creating company', in K. Starkey (ed.) *How Organizations Learn*, London: International Thomson Business Press.

Ohlsson, J. and Döös, M. (eds) (1999) *Pedagogic Interventions as Conditions for Learning*, Stockholm: Stockholm University.

Olofsson, J. and Zavisic, M. (eds) (2006) *Year Book 2006: Paths to a More Open Labor Market*, Stockholm: National Institute for Working Life (in Swedish).

Sennett, R. (1999/2003) *The Corrosion of Character*, Stockholm: Atlas (in Swedish).

Shani, A.B.R. and Docherty, P. (2003) *Learning by Design*, Malden: Blackwell Publishing.

Sisson, K. (2000) *Direct Participation and the Modernisation of Work Organisation*, Dublin: European Foundation for the Improvement of Living and Working Conditions.

Söderlund, J. (2005) *Project Management and Project Competence*, Malmö: Liber (in Swedish).

Stacey, R.D. (2001) *Complex Responsive Processes in Organizations*, London: Routledge.

Weick, K. and Roberts, K. (1993/2001) 'Collective mind in organizations: heedful interrelating on flight decks', in K. Weick (ed.) *Making Sense of the Organization*, Oxford: Blackwell Business.

Wikman, A. and Marklund, S. (2003) 'Interpretations of the development of work related sick leave in Sweden', in C. von Otter (ed.) *Outside and Inside Swedish Working Life*, Stockholm: National Institute for Working Life (in Swedish).

12 Learning imperialism through training in transnational call centres

Kiran Mirchandani and Srabani Maitra

This chapter focuses on the work-related learning of call center workers in transnational call centers in India. Drawing on 48 interviews with workers, we explore their experiences of the training they received. We highlight the ways in which training programs in Indian call centres facilitate workers' learning of both the product for which they provide service and of the "hidden curriculum" (Casey 1995: 78) of service work which includes the social and cultural messages of imperialism. These are the rules, codes and symbols that people learn through emulating Western accents, learning about their customers' lifestyles and masking their work locations. Through this analysis, we contribute to understandings of the ways in which learning for the global workforce is embedded within the social context of post-colonialism which characterizes global subcontracting chains.

Introduction

Saskia Sassen argues that analyses of global processes in terms of international trade and investment have produced a "rather empirically and theoretically 'thin' account" of the ways in which "the global economy needs to be implemented, reproduced, serviced, financed" (2001: 190, 192). Sassen notes that, "the global economy cannot be taken simply as given, whether what is given is a set of markets or a function of the power of multinational corporations" (2000: 217). Instead, the focus on the micro-processes through which global economies are sustained allows for analyses of the ways in which diverse groups of workers play varied and active roles vis-à-vis transnational corporate and financial practices. This chapter explores one such micro-process of globalization – employee training. We highlight the ways in which training programs in Indian call centres facilitate workers' learning of both the product for which they provide service and of the "hidden curriculum" (Casey 1995: 78) of service work which includes the social and cultural messages of imperialism. These are the rules, codes and symbols that people learn through emulating Western accents, learning about their customers' lifestyles and dealing effectively with the (often racial) outbursts of angry customers.

Through this analysis, we contribute to understandings of the ways in which learning for the global workforce is embedded within the social context of post-colonialism, which characterizes global subcontracting chains.

Theories of workplace learning (which is also often referred to as learning at work, or work and learning) can be broadly classified into those which focus primarily on the individual as learner, and those which focus on the micro-processes within which learning occurs. Through the focus on the individual as learner, theorists have documented the multi-faceted nature and forms of workplace learning and explored the differences in the learning which individuals engage in. Authors have focused, for example, on the varied circumstances in which workers engage in formal, non-formal, informal, incidental, social and critical learning (Foley 1999; Garrick 1996; Illeris 2003; Newman 2000; Marsick 1988). Forms of learning are distinguished in terms of whether the learning is conscious and deliberate, whether it occurs within the context of a structured educational program (Newman 2000), and whether it serves to challenge the status quo (Bratton *et al.* 2003; Foley 1994). Much of what is known about workplace learning has been developed through qualitative case studies with workers, such as Foley's (1999) analysis of learning amongst environmental activists, Beckett and Hager's (2000) study of professional workers, Wells' (1998) interviews about mentorship amongst women entrepreneurs and Boud and Middleton's (2003) exploration of learning amongst members of workgroups. While these case studies have provided rich ethnographies of the everyday lives of workers, and allowed theorists to document differences in learnings by women and men occupying a variety of class positions, there is a striking absence in this literature of discussions of learning in the context of global economic regimes. In fact, with few exceptions (such as Westwood 1984; Hart 1983; Fenwick and Mirchandani 2004) there has been little analysis of the ways in which workplace learning is racialized, and how racialization functions as a form of stratification in relation to gender and class.

In this chapter, we explore the ways in which work-related learning is situated within the contemporary social and economic context of globalization. Butler notes that capitalist work relations underlie the very conceptualization of work-related learning. She argues that

> despite the multiplicity of approaches to understanding and experiencing work, the contemporary framing of work in work-related education discourses and texts tends to both interpret and so represent work in its capitalist garb as paid work in the labour market
>
> (2001: 63).

As theorists such as Bhattacharya *et al.* (2002), Sassen (1998) and Bergeron (2001) have noted, contemporary capitalism is characterized not only by the commodification of labor but also by the globalization, feminization and racialization of the work force. We highlight the ways in which training programs in Indian call centres facilitate workers' learning of both the product for which they provide service and of the implicit imperialism in cross-border front-line service work. The focus of this chapter is on workers' accounts of their learning via the formal training which is provided by employers to enable workers to perform the tasks required by their jobs. In the sections below we analyze the ways call centre operators are taught to emulate Western accents, learn about their customers' lifestyles and deal with angry and frustrated customers with humility and patience.

Methods

In recent years, India has installed reliable high-capacity telephone lines as well as broadband Internet services and Voice Over Internet Protocol (VOIP) lines in most of its major cities. As a result there are now over 500 foreign companies who outsource work to about 300 phone-based call centres in India. Examples of companies which use India-based call centres include British Airways, TechneCall, Dell Computers, Citibank, GE, HSBC, British Airways, Cap Gemini, Swiss Air, America On-Line and American Express. The main incentives for companies to locate centres in India are low wages relative to the West, and the large English speaking labor pool. This paper draws on interviews conducted from 2002 to 2004 with groups of call centre workers in New Delhi and Bangalore, India (see also Maitra and Sangha 2005; Mirchandani 2004a; 2004b; forthcoming).

In-depth qualitative interviews were conducted with 48 call centre workers serving mainly American, British and a few Canadian or Australian clients. Much of the interviews were spent probing respondents' experiences of their jobs. Rather than an interest in the generalizability of results, this project serves to gain understandings of "the meanings that respondents associate with events, and that allow respondents to present their perspectives in their own words" (O'Neill 1995: 334).

Call centre workers were contacted via friends and colleagues in India; 27 male and 21 female workers were interviewed. Respondents were, on average, 22 to 25 years of age. One man and one woman were married, and another woman was engaged to be married – all other respondents were single. There were only a few differences in the educational levels of women and men in the sample – 15 of the women and 23 of the men had Bachelors degrees while four of the women and two of the men had Masters degrees. Workers earned between Rs 5,500 and Rs 20,000 (C$150–800) per month depending on levels of seniority in the company, with the exception of one male worker who had seven years of work experience and earned Rs 30,000 (C$1,200). Of the remaining workers, the average pay of the women and the men was the same. A significant portion of salaries was tied to performance incentives.

Training in call centres in India

Call centre workers (or "agents" as they are frequently called) are provided with intensive training prior to beginning work. The use of the term "agent" to refer to call centre workers evokes an image of an independent, skilled worker, although the work itself is structured to be highly routinized and scripted. Newly recruited agents (both male and female) receive paid training for between two and eight weeks. The training consists of two parts: 1) training about the process or product, and 2) training about providing service, or soft skills training on language and accent, culture and customer care.

Process training

All newly recruited workers are given training about the various aspects of the particular process/product. For example, if an agent is dealing with insurance claims, he/she is expected to know every detail about the history of the insurance company as well as its policies, claim processing systems and clientele. During the training, workers are given a sense of the various kinds of inquiries that they might get once they hit the production floor. As part of this training, agents are given scripts, which include answers to various problems their clients may face as well as greeting and call-ending procedures. Agents practice reading those scripts to prepare themselves and they are told that they must adhere to the script while actually talking to their clients on the phone. Agents are expected to follow the predefined script when answering queries from customers and they are told that any deviation from the script is grounds for reprimand: "We know the script, the customer asked this, we have to say like this. We used to get script for that."

In addition to the training workers receive at the start of their appointment, there is also an expectation that workers will engage in continual upgrading while they are on the job. This upgrading is provided online in some companies. An interviewee explained the process:

> [The company] has online trainings, so you just have to just log on to the web site and take the training. You can take the training yourself. So we had like CBTs like computer based trainings ... so they had given us all the access, [the company has] like a huge web site launch from ... so you just of the web site and get more information on [the company], products or how to do ... we also get ... apart from the regular training, they also send us separate training, email writing skills, we do most of our work on emails too, so they send us on emails, writing skills training.

However, the responsibility of undertaking online training lies mainly with the agents and they are sometimes reprimanded if they forget to check out the online services provided by the company from time to time.

At the same time, little time is set aside for workers to engage in on-the-job training during the workday. The training requirement often results in work intensification for many workers, who often have to stay past their regular shift to review the alerts on their unpaid time.

Providing "service"

The ability to provide service is seen as the core of the training which newly hired agents receive. This involves communicating effectively (that is, speaking in a customer-centred accent), learning about customers' lifestyles and dealing effectively with customer anger and frustration. As one worker points out,

> [it doesn't matter] if you have technical expertise or not. It's all about how you speak good English, how you communicate stuff to the people.

Acculturation and accent neutralization

Communicating "effectively" in the context of transnational call centre work involves learning to speak in a Western accent. Thus an important part of the training consists of what is known as an "Accent Neutralization Process" or "Voice Training Program". Rather than "neutralizing" accents, however, the focus of the training is clearly on encouraging the development of an American or British accent. Agents are taught how to pronounce letters like "o" or "r" with an American or British tone. Respondents note,

> I underwent voice and accent training, it is again was for three weeks, ... the rolling of the tongue, the 'r' sound, so that they do feel like that the call is coming from, so that they don't feel that the call is coming from outside US.
>
> [W]hat they do is they give you like small things like a couple of words, a few words that US people speak, in a different way. So instead of we saying 'talking' they say 't'auking'. So there is a difference. So they kind of teach us these small kind of ... they give small tips. This is how you talk. So that the American should understand you.

To perfect their accents, agents listen to taped conversation and practice speaking with an accent. An interviewee explained:

[T]hey have like all the words, used to have a check out graph, like this is the way you're speaking in this way and this is the word they speak in America in this way, and they have sentences and stuff like verbal recordings so we could listen to the conversations those were already there before. So that way we used to acquire like how to speak to customers ... We had to start off just from this line we had the manual like, hi! This is such and such, how may I help you to have more online experience? And then we used to make a little change in the accent like we used to say hi! This is so and so, how may I help you to have an even better online experience? [interviewee at this stage speaks with an accent] You know a little bit of change in the accent. This used to be the first sentence we used to start up with.

If an agent is found to be totally incapable of conversing with a customer, he/she might be moved to a different process altogether, for example a chat-based or a web-based process (often earning a lower salary).

The training given to the call center workers not only involves diction and accent, but also a crash course in American or British culture by imparting knowledge about literature, festivals through audio visual aids such as video, CDs, movies, etc. Agents are often made to watch popular TV shows such as *Friends* or movies like *Shakespeare in Love* or *My Fair Lady* to get an idea about American or British culture. Workers noted:

[I]f I am working with a UK based process, I need to understand the British culture a bit. I need to know a little bit about British literature [or] British theatre because ... if I start talking about Shakespeare all of a sudden and you don't know anything about Shakespeare you cannot contribute to that ... . So in the US scenario you need to be kind of understanding their cultures, holidays, why do they have Halloween, why do they have Thanksgiving, why do they have Memorial Days?

Masking identity

Acculturation training also involves adopting a Western name and masking the geographical location on the part of the agent, to make clients feel comfortable and to assure them that they are in fact talking to an agent from their own country. Thus under this process Kusum becomes Kelly who is trained to say that she is located in Simonton, Texas. An agent commented on this:

Especially the typical call center types ... don't tell them that we are in India. They totally avoid it ... because the customers are in Simonton in Texas. That's where our main office [X]. So we tell them we are in Texas. So sometimes people say where are you? Because of the accent ... obviously a little bit difference will still stay. Even after the training and stuff. They still understand. This is not a typical American. So they will ask you … 'Where are you?' right now I am in US. I am in Simonton.

One respondent said that some call centers even have giant TV screens showing the weather in different US cities, so that the agents can use the information on the screen to make small talk with the caller.

> Call centre agents are taught to take on a "Western persona" in order to better serve clients in the West. Alpa Shah, Research Manager, Frost and Sullivan says for example, "acting skills are required since an agent in India could be required to play the role of Colorado resident, one that skis in his free time. The goal of this strategy is to make callers more comfortable by eliminating any cultural barriers."
> (Sucha Vivek, Call Centers: Hello India! Monday, 27 August 2001)

Thus one of the reasons provided to justify the extensive language training is the need for customer identification.

"Good" customer service

In addition to Western accents and culture, call centre agents are also trained on how to provide good customer service – this involves being very humble, skilful and patient when talking to clients. They are given various tips on how to offer impeccable service to the foreign clients. A worker described the process:

> [B]asically it has to be like when you go to the training you know, [trainers tell you] you just have to listen to the customer first and then you have to answer. First listen to the customer and then say. Don't interrupt the customer, let the customers know what he wants to say and then you underline what his problem is and then speak.

Providing "good" customer service also involves dealing with irate customers. While irate calls are a mainstay of customer service work in any country, interviewees in Indian call centers commented that they face abuse from their American or British clients that have a racial overtone and is often triggered by anger over outsourcing and job loss. When asked about the kind of training given to deal with irate customers, an interviewee described aspects of that training:

> Soft skill training [to deal with irate customers, include training about] how do you pacify them, how do you defuse them, what kind of power statements that you can use to help them out and we also have all those power statements listed out in front of them [agents]. So

whenever they [agents] have an irate customer and they can just take a look at it and speak those sentences to the customer.

Thus agents are trained to give rote answers swiftly in clear English, which has been "neutralized" from any strong accent to deal with racial abuse at work. Examples of defusing statements typically include requests to irate customers "not to use [any] abusive language otherwise [the agents] gonna disconnect the call, [and] if it still continues ... just cut the call", or agents are told that they should let the customer "vent whatever they want to say" and then "once they are cool ... try and make them understand". Power statements include usage of words of encouragement such as wonderful, excellent, good job.

As part of their training, workers are told to think that customer abuse is a response to their professional rather than personal identities. An interviewee explains:

[W]e have to just see the customer. We have to take the company to consideration. We have to give a good service for the customer. That's matters, whether ... he is irate or he is abusing us it really doesn't matters. We have taken this job. We have to do the job properly. That's what it matters.

Another interviewee emphasized:

I think it is really important for all of us to realize that if he's [irate customer] yelling or shouting he is not shouting at you. If I am working for the process, I am not the process owner so it should not directly hurt me.

In these ways, workers learn to manage their emotions in order to construct customer abuse as a normal and everyday part of their jobs.

Conclusions

Appadurai notes that globalization is "inextricably linked to the current workings of capital on a global basis; in this regard it extends the earlier logics of empire, trade, and political domination in many parts of the world" (2000: 3). The analysis in this paper reveals that training programs for call centre workers represent an extension of the imperialist as well as economic relations of colonialism. As "clients" and "employers", transnational corporations define the nature, timing, norms and structure of work and workplaces in India, thereby trying to legitimize acculturation in terms of what might be regarded as normative codes at the level of the global. Workers have little discretion in their work – as one respondent notes:

[Y]ou have to manage ... we have to manage ... if you don't manage you will lose your job. [Y]ou have to manage. Consistently you have to perform.

This "performance" refers not only to the need to gain familiarity about the product for which workers are providing service so that they can meet stringent production targets but also to learn to become particular kinds of people. Adkins refers to this as the "culturalization of economic life that involves a stylization of work, workplace identities, production processes and products" (2001: 669). Much of the work-related learning of call center agents in India is structured by the globalized subcontracting regimes within which their jobs are situated. Workers learn strategies to combat customer backlash in the West against offshored jobs. They simultaneously deal with the racism and exclusion often also experienced by immigrant workers in the West.

The subcontracting of call centre work in India represents a "globalization from above" in terms of the language and cultural imperialism which is fostered through extensive training programs that workers are required to undergo. Transnational call centers are engaged in "language trafficking" which is the spread of particular types of English throughout the world (Swales 1997). As Phillipson (2001) notes, English is a key instrument used by transnational corporations to break down national barriers. Under the guise of promoting a "neutral" English that can be understood by Western clients, a regime of sameness is enforced. What is hollowed out is the contextual nature of cultural practices where mass-produced cultural images are allowed to proliferate in the name of representing the ideal of "Americanism" or "Britishness". As a consequence, workers in Bangalore or New Delhi can be trained, via the sustained artificiality of such devices as the giant screen announcing the climates of various US cities, to become call centre workers who can serve customers just as if they were living and working in the West. They are made malleable and adaptive to unfavourable working conditions while being bombarded with an exalted image of "global" culture which in fact has its locus in the west. Prasad and Prasad note that training programs are often "organizational locations for the construction of otherness through the systematic transformation of images about self and the other that markedly echo the legacy of colonialist discourses" (2002: 65). Indeed, training programs serve to assimilate workers into American society while they remain in India, creating an Indian diaspora within the "homeland".

Acknowledgements

This project was funded by the Shastri Indo-Canadian Institute and the Social Sciences and Humanities Council of Canada (Grant Number 410-2002-0554). We would like to thank the interview participants for their enthusiastic and generous involvement with the project despite their busy schedules.

References

Adkins, L. (2001) 'Cultural feminization: "money, sex and power" for women', *Signs*, 26, 3: 669–95.

Appadurai, A. (2000) 'Grassroots globalization and the research imagination', *Public Culture*, 12, 1: 1–19.

Beckett, D. and Hager, P. (2000) 'Making judgements as the basis for workplace learning: towards an epistemology of practice', *International Journal of Lifelong Education*, 19, 4: 300–11.

Bergeron, S. (2001) 'Political economy discourses of globalization and feminist politics', *Signs: Journal of Women in Culture and Society: Special Issue on Globalization and Gender*, 26, 4: 983–1006.

Bhattacharya, G., Gabriel, J. and Small, S. (2002) *Race and Power: Global Racism in the Twenty-first Century*, London: Routledge.

Boud, D. and Middleton, H. (2003) 'Learning from others at work: communities of practice and informal learning', *Journal of Workplace Learning*, 15, 5: 194–202.

Bratton, J., Mills, J.-H., Pyrch, T. and Sawchuk, P. (2003) *Workplace Learning: A Critical Introduction*, Peterborough: Garamond.

Butler, E. (2001) 'The power of discourse: work-related learning in the learning age', in R.M. Cervero, A.L. Wilson and Associates (eds) *Power in Practice: Adult Education and the Struggle for Knowledge and Power in Society*, San Francisco, CA: Jossey-Bass.

Casey, C. (1995) *Work, Self and Society After Industrialism*, London: Routledge.

Fenwick, T. and Mirchandani, K. (2004) 'Race, gender and networks in portfolio work: difficult knowledge'. Paper presented at the 45th Adult Education Research conference, Victoria.

Foley, G. (1994) 'Adult education and capitalist reorganisation', *Studies in the Education of Adults*, 26, 2: 121–43.

Foley, G. (1999) *Learning in Social Action: A Contribution to Understanding Informal Education*, London: Zed Books.

Garrick, J. (1996) 'Informal learning: some underlying philosophies', *Canadian Journal for theStudy of Adult Education*, 10, 1: 21–45.

Hart, M. (1983) 'Educative or miseducative work', *Canadian Journal for the Study of Adult Education*, 7, 1: 22–35.

Illeris, K. (2003) 'Workplace learning and learning theory', *Journal of Workplace Learning*, 15, 4: 167–78.

Maitra, S. and Sangha, J. (2005) 'Intersecting realities: young women and call centre work in India and Canada', *Women and Environments International Magazine*, Spring/Summer: 40–2.

Marsick, V. (1988) 'Learning in the workplace: the case for reflectivity and critical reflectivity', *Adult Education Quarterly*, 38, 4: 187–98.

Mirchandani, K. (2004a) 'Practices of global capital: gaps, cracks and ironies in transnational call centres in India', *Global Networks*, 4, 4: 355–74.

Mirchandani, K. (2004b) 'Webs of resistance in transnational call centres: strategies agents, service providers and customers', in R. Thomas, A.J. Mills and J.H. Mills (eds) *Identity Politics at Work: Resisting Gender, Gendering Resistance*, London: Routledge.

Mirchandani, K. (forthcoming) *Gender Eclipsed? Racial Hierarchies in Transnational Call Centre Work*, Social Justice.

Newman, M. (2000) 'Learning, education and social action', in G. Foley (ed.) *Understanding Adult Education and Training*, St Leonards: Allen and Unwin.

O'Neill, B. (1995) 'The gender gap: re-evaluating theory and method', in S. Burt and L. Code (eds) *Changing Methods: Feminists Transforming Practice*, Peterborough: Broadview Press.

Phillipson, R. (2001) 'Global English and local language policies what Denmark needs', *Language Problems and Language Planning*, 25, 1: 1–24.

Prasad, A. and Prasad, P. (2002) 'Otherness at large: identity and difference in the new globalized organizational landscape', in I. Aaltio and A.J. Mills (eds) *Gender, Identity and Culture in Organizations*, London: Routledge.

Sassen, S. (1998) *Globalization and Its Discontents*, New York: New Press.

Sassen, S. (2000) 'Spatialities and temporalities of the global: elements for a theorization', *Public Culture*, 12, 1: 215–32.

Sassen, S. (2001) *The Global City: New York, London, Tokyo*, Princeton, NJ: Princeton University Press.

Swales, J.M. (1997) 'English as Tyrannosaurus Rex', *World Englishes*, 16, 3: 373–82.

Wells, S. (1998) *Women Entrepreneurs: Developing Leadership for Success*, New York: Garland Press.

Westwood, S. (1984) 'Learning and working: a study of women on the shop floor', *Studies in the Education of Adults*, 16: 3–19.

Part III

Work, working life and working identities

13 Working on identities

*Clive Chappell, Hermine Scheeres and
Nicky Solomon*

Central to understanding the post-industrial, post-bureaucratic workplace is a recognition that organizations need to be flexible and responsive in their structures and operations. In other words, the very nature of what it is to be a contemporary organization now involves ongoing change. We suggest that any focus on change at the macro level often overshadows the micro processes that simultaneously constitute and are constituted by these macro level changes. In this chapter we suggest that macro level changes in the workplace always entail, and may even be said to rely on, changes in the micro processes of work and the ways that individuals do their work. Through our description of aspects of two Australian workplaces – one a further education college and the other a large manufacturing company – we illustrate the effects of the changes that workers experience when being asked to 'do things differently' in their everyday work practices. We argue that through the changed work practices they need to learn to become different workers; that is, to develop different understandings of their work roles, to construct different relationships with others in their workplace, to conceptualize their knowledge and work skills differently, to change their understanding of who they are at work; in short, they are doing identity work.

Introduction

Central to understanding the post-industrial (Block 1990), post-bureaucratic (Heckscher and Donellon 1994) workplace is a recognition that organizations need to be flexible and responsive in their structures and operations. In other words, the very nature of what it is to be a contemporary organization now involves ongoing change. The kinds of changes most often outlined, discussed and written about in management and organizational texts are those associated with economic restructuring: the adoption of a global orientation; a shift of business functions to remote sites; a reduction in the size and composition of the workforce; and a reorganization of the remaining workforce into cross-functional, team-based, work units. We contend that a focus on changes at the macro level can often overshadow or obscure the micro processes that simultaneously constitute, and are constituted by, these macro level changes.

In this chapter our point of departure is that macro level changes in the workplace always entail, and may even be said to rely on, changes in the micro processes of work and the ways that individuals do their work. What we are concerned with here is what this means for workers. We suggest that when workers are asked to 'do things differently' in their everyday work practices they are also being called on to become different workers; that is, to have different understandings of their work role, to have different relationships with others in their workplace, to conceptualize their knowledge and work skills differently, to change their understanding of who they are at work; in short, they are doing identity work.

Our discussion draws on writers who take a discursive approach to identity (re)formation and argue that identities are always in the process of 'becoming' (Foucault 1988; Gergen and Kaye 1992; Hall 1996; Usher *et al.* 1997; Rose 1998). Identities are also understood as conditional and contingent constructs, "increasingly fragmented and fractured; never singular but multiply constructed across different, often intersecting and antagonistic, discourses, practices and positions" (Hall 1996: 4). Identities therefore are being produced in a variety of sites, including workplaces. From this perspective all of our workplaces are sites of identity construction where competing and intersecting technologies of governing operate (Foucault 1980). Consequently, our working identities emerge from the shifting and sometimes conflicting interplay of technologies that circulate at work.

Identity work then is imbued with tensions and struggles. Much of the struggle around identity is a struggle for closure, a desire to 'be' a specific kind of individual, such as, for example, an effective team leader or a committed teacher. This struggle for closure leads to a homogenizing and over-determined process of identity (re)formation (Hall 1996; Usher and Edwards 1994; Bhabha 1994) which in turn leads to an engagement with issues of power and positioning, and a way of understanding identity in terms of subjects and subjectivities. For Hall (1996), identity refers to:

> the meeting point, the point of suture, between on the one hand the discourses and practices which attempt to 'interpellate', speak to us or hail us into place as the social subjects of particular discourses, and on the other hand, the processes which produce subjectivities, which construct us as subjects which can be 'spoken'. Identities are thus points of temporary attachment to the subject positions, which discursive practices construct for us.
>
> Hall (1996: 6)

The suturing of a subject to a subject position is not a simple process of hailing a subject into place through the hierarchical or hegemonic operations of power. Rather, it includes people recognizing their investment in a subject position, and enacting their productive power to capitalize on this realization. It incorporates an acceptance of selves that are able to act as well as be acted upon differently in different contexts – the inter-relation of technologies of the self with technologies of power. Identities can therefore be seen as the positions that the subject takes up: a kind of naming or location for subject positions at some point in their life and/or work trajectory.

In this chapter our aim is to illustrate how our working identities or the positions that as subjects we take up at work are a result of the interplay of technologies of the self and technologies of power. What is particularly interesting, from our point of view, is that economic restructuring entails the restructuring of the *workforce* as well as the *workplace*; it involves the restructuring of working identities, working knowledges and working relationships. Our focus therefore, is on the micro level of workplace restructuring. We are concerned with the ways that workers at two different sites, a shop floor and an educational institution, construct and reconstruct working identities from the discursive resources available to them. We present two snapshots. The first involves the identities of vocational education and training teachers in publicly funded colleges. The second focuses on the identities of workers in a manufacturing organization.

Working knowledge and vocational teachers

The policy discourses of new vocationalism that began in the late 1980s (OECD 1988, 1989, 1991) continue to dominate the educational policy environment of many countries. This is accompanied by the new knowledge discourses that draw attention to an "un-ruliness of knowledge" (Stronach and MacLure 1997) and to an increasing number of new partnerships, alignment and networks that work across educations and work sectors contributing to a realization of the relationship between work, education and the economy. In many ways these developments can be seen as favouring or promoting work-focused education over other forms of education. Vocational education is, after all, the education sector that has always laid claim to a close and explicit relationship with the world of work. Further Education (FE) in the United Kingdom, Technical and Further Education (TAFE) in Australia and Community Colleges in the United States, for example, have all, in different ways, constructed an educational identity through course provision based on the foregrounding of vocational knowledge, skill development and learning for work. At the same time Vocational Education and Training (VET) has also constructed vocational educators as industry experts who pass on their vocational expertise to students in the various courses offered by vocational institutions. In addition, VET has also usually deployed knowledge discourses that privilege practical, applied, contextualized and interdisciplinary knowledge over knowledge that is theoretical, 'pure', general and disciplinary knowledge. (Gibbons *et al.* 1994 discuss the former as Mode 1 knowledge and the latter as Mode 2 knowledge.)

Recent policy positions of a number of governments (DETS 2005; DfES 2005; SFEU 2005), suggest that reforms to this sector of education that began in the 1980s continue. Furthermore, the changing nature of work and the organization of work, together with predictions of chronic skill shortages brought on by ageing populations, have renewed government interest in education and work. The need to retain and retrain older workers, to increase the engagement of young people in vocational studies, the central role of industry and business in VET/FE decision making and the development of new ways of learning (Moynagh and Worsley 2003), are all high on the policy agenda in many European countries and Australia.

Overall, the argument of governments is consistent. Continuing economic development and social cohesion rely more than ever on a vibrant, high quality VET/FE sector, capable of rapidly responding to new skill demands, new labour market conditions, new contexts for learning and the increasing expectations of a diversifying group of clients of the system. One of the outcomes of this broad agreement is that there is increasing recognition by all governments that improving the quality of practices in teaching, learning and assessment is crucial if the sector is to respond to the new challenges that now confront it.

Recent policy reforms, while continuing to promote vocationalism, have also at the same time demanded major reforms to the ways in which VET is organized, delivered and funded. Workplace learning is promoted over classroom or college learning. Government policies demand more market-focused, commercially-oriented business practices in vocational institutions. New competitive practices in a privatized vocational education and training market have emerged and industry delivered and accredited vocational training programmes are encouraged.

While not denying the impact of these policy-driven changes on public vocational education institutions, the argument pursued here is that these institutions and the teachers that work in them also face unsettling times, brought on by the emergence of new knowledge discourses. These new discourses not only undermine traditional discourses that once worked to construct this educational sector, but also work to change the educational identity of its teachers.

The effects of new knowledge discourses on the identities of one group of vocational education and training teachers working in the institution of Technical and Further Education (TAFE) in New South Wales (NSW), Australia are examined here. This examination is based on recent research involving an analysis of how teachers talk about their work in this educational institution.

When teachers speak of their work in TAFE they place a great deal of importance on the industrial experience they bring with them to the institution. They commonly speak of 'knowledge of industry', 'workplace knowledge', 'technical competence', 'knowledge relevant to industry' and their 'practical experience' of work. They talk about bringing 'real-world' examples to the learning process, or as one teacher put it:

> TAFE pays me for my practical knowledge and skills gained through my work experience. Students in our courses aren't interested in theory, but want to know if it works in practice. I always have to make this connection and use real case studies and examples to illustrate what I mean.

By emphasizing the practical over the theoretical, applied knowledge over academic knowledge, experiential knowledge over disciplinary knowledge and contextualized knowledge over generalizable knowledge TAFE teachers construct an identity distinct from the identities of other educators, for example, educators in the academy. TAFE teachers generally lay no claim over the disciplinary knowledge of the academy that grounds much of the curriculum in higher education and indeed curricula in schools. Rather they claim specialized vocational knowledge and expertise gained through their experiences in particular industries and occupations. And unlike teachers in the higher education sector they make no claim to new knowledge production but rather the application and use of existing knowledge at work.

However, the talk of TAFE teachers also reveals that this claim to specialized, vocational knowledge and its application is deeply problematic. TAFE teachers speak consistently of the need to 'keep up to date' with industry and to maintain their 'industrial expertise'. Many also explain this need in terms of maintaining credibility with students.

> I'm really scared that I will lose the relevance and currency of my practical experience. I'm just really scared about my credibility with the students; you know five years down the track and I haven't worked in the industry for five years.

This commonly expressed view suggests that teachers believe that their legitimacy as teachers, particularly in the eyes of students, is dependent on their industrial expertise. In effect they use their industrial experience to mark them as distinctive. Moreover, they see this industrial knowledge and experience as conferring legitimacy on their occupational identity. The discourse of industrial expertise therefore does similar discursive work for TAFE teachers as disciplinary knowledge does for teachers working in schools.

This similarity however is only a partial one. In the world of the TAFE teacher the ability to 'keep up-to-date' is given additional importance because many TAFE students are not only learners but are, at the same time, workers. Thus they are able to make an immediate and on-going evaluation of the industrial expertise of the TAFE teacher. Students in their working lives can test the utility and currency of the vocational knowledge and skills that TAFE teachers share with their students immediately. It is in this sense 'practical' knowledge and is judged not in terms of its claims to generalizable 'truth' as in the case of discipline-based subjects but rather its performativity in the workplace. Consequently, a TAFE teacher's credibility as an 'industry expert' is always open to question and further compounded by her location in an educational site rather than an industrial workplace.

This educational location puts pressure on the discourse of industrial expertise that TAFE teachers use to construct a legitimate educational identity. This is a site characterized by discourses different from those that circulate in modern workplaces. These educational discourses therefore work to formalize 'industry knowledge' by deploying traditional curriculum technologies that compartmentalize knowledge into subjects, hierarchies, sequencing strategies and levels of achievement. They impose particular pedagogical and assessment practices into the learning process. And through these disciplining discursive practices they attempt to re-construct the contextualized knowledge of work into the generalizable vocational knowledge of particular occupations.

As a consequence TAFE teachers' identities are in some senses fashioned across the discursive space that constitutes working knowledge as different from traditional knowledge. TAFE teachers use the discourses of working knowledge to construct a legitimate occupational identity that is different from the identity of teachers working in other education sectors. However, their location within modern education also means that TAFE teachers draw on the educational sense making constructions to legitimise their identity as professional educators. They undertake teacher-training programmes that foreground traditional curriculum practices. They are encouraged to theorize their pedagogy through the discourses of educational psychology, sociology and academic research. All of these discursive practices have themselves been based on traditional views of knowledge that privilege knowledge that is formal, theoretical, generalizable and foundational.

The working knowledge that TAFE teachers bring with them to their educational practice contributes to the struggle currently being experienced by them. Such knowledge is constructed through the curricula and pedagogical practices within institutions still utilizing traditional discourses of knowledge. This knowledge and its manifestations sit uncomfortably side by side with the new knowledge necessary in the rapidly changing workplace.

Changing identities in response to changing work is not confined to educational work/ers. Indeed, the old boundaries of other workplace practices are blurring in similar ways – what used to count as valuable knowledge and accepted modes of knowledge production in these contexts is being relocated and restructured as new working knowledge. As we describe in the second snapshot, outside the walls of traditional educational institutions other kinds of working knowledge are also emerging and developing. As education, training and work become ever more inextricably linked, organizations and enterprises are including, as part of their (re)structure, people with specific expertise to be workplace educators and/or selecting and developing their own workers for these roles.

Working knowledge and industry workers

In this second snapshot we turn to workplace facilitators who have been drawn from within the ranks of their own organizations. These employees may have worked for years on a production line, or they may have been leading hands or supervisors. Now they are involved in moving from the production line to the meeting room – a shift from doing work to talking work. The shift to this site of work and learning by workers, and the valuing of new kinds of knowledge by managers and employers, is constructing new identities. This (re)formation of social relations and identities coupled with new knowledge and modes of knowledge production are the focus of ongoing negotiation in the workplace.

The same globalizing forces outlined in relation to the education site are at work in the final case study. To become more globally competitive, a focus on developing an appropriate workplace culture has been emerging. This 'culture', or new work order as it has been called (e.g. Gee *et al.* 1996), has a shared vision amongst employees as a central principle. All workers must be committed to the corporate culture, everyone understands the big picture: the company goals and the current productivity targets and levels. Vertical communication patterns and structures are now accompanied by horizontal ones. For example, now there are meetings in which employees from different levels come together to discuss the day-to-day organization of work, quality control, productivity levels, and generally problem solve. The 'work as talk' discussion in this section is an important kind of knowledge work affecting all employees and highlighting the complex roles of facilitators as they are charged with organizing and developing teams and leading regular team meetings.

Teams, team work and team meetings are central to the new consultative and participatory processes. At the same time, organizations are increasingly identifying and developing themselves as learning organizations (Marsick and Watkins 1999) where employees are expected to learn to be effective team members who can successfully participate in activities and interactions newly added to their job descriptions. The construction of the competent worker, therefore, includes knowledge, skills and attitudes that foreground social relations as much as the physical work of the production line. Problem-solving, consultative committees, quality circles, formal and informal on the job training, etc. all involve more and more talk. The textualization or languaging of the workplace is a significant shift in industrial work practices and works to discursively construct and value new kinds of work-related knowledge.

This snapshot draws on research into a manufacturing company's implementation of participatory and consultative practices as a frame for investigating how employees are struggling with new ways of 'being' (du Gay 1996). The workplace consists of approximately 800 workers in Sydney, Australia. It is a non-unionized site where up to 70 per cent of the production line employees are from language backgrounds other than English and where about 30 per cent of the workforce is casualized. The company brought in a new management team eight years ago to restructure the previously family-run organization. Management followed a now-accepted pathway of developing a mission statement and a set of core values, that is, the establishment of a new culture; a way of thinking whereby particular social identities of workers are constructed, and related social practices which they were expected to learn, demonstrate and value, are outlined (Gee *et al.* 1996). The mission or goals of the workplace could only be attained if work practices were inscribed as part of the identity of each of the workers – the values of the workplace are the values, thus part of the 'being', of each worker.

A major change was the creation of a new section or department comprising a manager and five facilitators whose function was to set up, organize and develop workplace teams. The five facilitators had been leading hands under the old system and their changing subjectivities as they assume very new work roles involve ongoing struggles as they are positioned in specific ways by management and by co-workers as well as consciously repositioning themselves. Within the organization's hierarchical structure the unit constitutes a separate wing with a middle-level manager and facilitators imbued with responsibilities and accountabilities. At the same time there is confusion among the members about both their position and power. One of the facilitators explains their position in the organizational structure as:

> The unit manager comes under the production manager so he's higher than the plant manager, and we're supposed to come under him, but we are not higher than the team leaders. I don't think we're higher than the people on the floor. I think mostly my level's there on the factory floor.

and

I don't think the plant manager has any authority over me ... well, he sort of does.

And further, commenting on the operators' perception of their relationship with the facilitators:

I think I get confused as to what they see me as ...

For management, questions about power and confusion regarding the unit are non-existent. It is a much simpler story: the creation of a new unit with specific functions working towards the common goal of improved productivity. They employ discourses of commodification (of knowledge) with which they are familiar in a manufacturing industry, and apply them to the production of the new worker. Thus, the new workers of the unit need some new things – in this case, new Mode 2 (Gibbons *et al.* 1994) knowledge regarding participatory and problem-solving activities as outlined in contemporary management and organizational change literature. A large consultancy company is called in to provide a package of new knowledge in the form of train-the-trainer programmes. The consultancy company, an organization which audits the workplace, develops company-specific materials and training programmes and carries out the training, works closely with them as a knowledge packager and transmitter. The emphasis is on a rational and linear development from a state of ignorance through a set of procedures towards enlightenment – a production pathway. The mode of knowledge production is very glossy: slick manuals and PowerPoint presentations carrying the essential message that it is up to each individual to act, to learn, to make a difference. The workers are perceived as free and active subjects who have individual choices. There is little understanding of the complexities of the cultural baggage brought into the workplace each day by each employee. This is the pattern set up for the facilitators which they in turn are expected to use in their facilitation roles. Management is in the business of making the process appear as simple and efficient as possible (just as they do with the production process).

However, for the unit manager and the facilitators the story is a different one. As they struggle with their own identities, there is a recognition that the human production line working towards the alignment of selves and work is not necessarily one with glitches which must be straightened out or solved by following the procedures in training manuals, but rather it could be seen as a site of on-going discursive construction of how and what to be in the new workplace. They constantly question and comment on what is going on. They go about their jobs in the contemporary moment albeit within the parameters and constraints of a unit which sees itself as 'without power'. Rather than simply reflecting a pre-given social world, they themselves 'actively make up a reality, and create new ways for people to be at work' (du Gay 1996: 53). As the members struggle with ways of being and the construction of subjectivities that are credible and comfortable, they know it is possible to work with uncertainty and multiplicity, that is, in a more post-modern way. Their discourses include cries of confusion about their 'real place', but they actively use this as a flexible position whereby they try out the new and different. It is the difference between the plant manager's definite position that:

> what happens here on the shop floor ... myself or my team leaders are responsible. We are the owners – they (from the unit), are there as a tool to help us get to our final destination

and the facilitator's view that:

> the responsibilities aren't clear. The roles are not clear cut – perhaps they need to be a bit blurred because they are breaking down boundaries, old strict demarcations, but it does make things difficult.

The facilitators see possibilities in hybridity. They are central players in the breaking down of boundaries; they are active subjects rejecting the fixed parameters and binaries of the 'old' work order, including notions of strict, linear pathways. This recognition of uncertainty is what may lead to outcomes that had not been envisaged. In the unit, the facilitators are not a neat fit with clear lines of power and responsibility; however, to see this position as a (re)location with the potential to open up a third space for different approaches to work, is part of the struggle for developing subjectivities that engender both feelings of insecurity and liberation.

Conclusion

Restructured workplaces and the discursive practices that bring these new workplaces into being privilege new forms of knowledge. The academic monopoly over knowledge production has been broken with all work sites becoming sites of knowledge production. As the two snapshots in this chapter demonstrate, the discursive practices that construct these new forms of knowledge have, amongst other things, disrupted the working identities of vocational teachers and industry workers. However, this disruption has manifested itself in quite different and site-specific ways. What counts as legitimate working knowledges, and what counts as legitimate working identities in local workplaces, are far from settled.

References

Bhabha, H.K. (1994) *The Location of Culture*, London: Routledge.

Block, F. (1990) *Postindustrial Possibilities: A Critique of Economic Discourse*, Berkeley, CA: University of California Press.

DETS (Dept of Education Training and Science) (2005) *Skilling Australia: New Directions for Vocational Education and Training*, Canberra: AGPS.

DfES (2005) *Skills: Getting on in Business, Getting on at Work, Part 1*, Norwich: Department for Education and Skills.

du Gay, P. (1996) *Consumption and Identity at Work*, London: Sage.

Foucault, M. (1980) *Power/Knowledge: Selected Interviews and Other Writings, 1972–1977*, Brighton: Harvester Press.

Foucault, M. (1988) 'Technologies of the Self', in L. Martin, H. Gutman and P. Hutton (eds) *Technologies of the Self: A Seminar with Michel Foucault*, Amherst, MA: University of Massachusetts Press.

Gee, J.P., Hull, G. and Lankshear, C. (1996) *The New Work Order: Behind the Language of the New Capitalism*, Sydney: Allen and Unwin.

Gergen, K.J. and Kaye, J. (1992) 'Beyond narrative in the negotiation of therapeutic meaning' in S. McNamee and K.J. Gergen (eds) *Therapy as Social Construction*, London: Sage.

Gibbons, M., Limogoes, C., Nowotny, H., Schwartzman, S., Scott, P. and Trow, M. (1994) *The New Production of Knowledge: The Dynamics of Science and Research in Contemporary Societies*, London: Sage.

Hall, S. (1996) 'Introduction: who needs identity?', in S. Hall and P. du Gay (eds) *Questions of Cultural Identity*, London: Sage.

Heckscher, C. and Donellon, A. (1994) *The Post-bureaucratic Organization: New Perspectives on Organizational Change*, Thousand Oaks, CA: Sage.

Marsick, V. and Watkins, K. (1999) *Facilitating Learning Organizations: Making Learning Count*, Aldershot: Ashgate.

Moynagh, M. and Worsley, R. (2003) *Learning From the Future: Scenarios for Post-16 Learning*, Hertford: Learning and Skills Research Centre.

Organisation for Economic Co-operation and Development (OECD) (1988) *Structural Adjustments and Economic Performance*, Paris: OECD.

Organisation for Economic Co-operation and Development (OECD) (1989) *Education and the Economy in a Changing Economy*, Paris: OECD.

Organisation for Economic Co-operation and Development (OECD) (1991) *Technology in a Changing World*, Paris: OECD.

Rose, N. (1998) *Inventing Our Selves: Psychology, Power, and Personhood*, Cambridge: Cambridge University Press.

SFEU (2005) *Future Focus Report*, Stirling: Scottish Further Education Unit.

Stronach, I. and MacLure, M. (1997) *Educational Research Undone: The Postmodern Embrace*, Buckingham: Open University Press.

Usher, R. and Edwards, R. (1994) *Postmodernism and Education*, London and New York: Routledge.

Usher, R., Bryant, I. and Johnson, R. (1997) *Adult Education and the Postmodern Challenge*, London: Routledge.

14 Fashioning subjectivity through workplace mentoring

Anita Devos

Mentoring programmes have been introduced across a range of settings as a preferred model of professional development. A large number of Australian universities, for example, have introduced programmes to support their women staff, with mentoring now a key feature of academic development. These programmes generally involve the pairing of a more and a less experienced member of staff to transfer and build knowledge, and support career development.

In this chapter I consider the role that workplace mentoring plays in shaping the subjectivities of women as academic workers, with reference to interviews conducted with two women academics. Mentoring, I argue, has a number of productive effects. In addition to learning new skills and knowledges or developing new networks, mentoring also produces knowledges of the self. This piecing together of the self, or 'identity work', is never complete but is iterative and contradictory, as the women negotiate their positions within the discursive terrains of academic life. Self-regulation is central to this process of (re-)shaping the self at work.

This research is significant as it applies contemporary theories of subjectivity to the study of workplace mentoring. It develops the theoretical foundations of mentoring and builds new ways of thinking about workplace mentoring as a site of learning.

Mapping the mentoring phenomenon

The last decade has witnessed a dramatic increase in interest in mentoring globally across contexts and industries. Mentoring is seen to play a critical role in building the skills and attitudes necessary for people to be successful in their lives and careers. Whether you are a community health worker in a Pacific nation, an aspiring manager in a global corporation, an unemployed teenager in an English city, or an African-American academic in an Ivy League university, mentoring is advocated as the key to social participation, and personal and professional advancement.

In spite of the growing literature, there is not a large body of work that expands or develops theoretical concepts in mentoring, with much of the literature based on evaluations of individual projects, and concerned with demonstrating success to stakeholders. Claims are made about the advantages of mentoring with a small critical literature that discusses harmful or problematic relationships, or the wider relations of power within which these relationships take shape (Colley 2001).

In this chapter, I build on the field through an analysis of two women's mentoring relationships using Foucault's theories of governmentality and subjectivity (1988, 1992). My aim is to explore the role mentoring plays in shaping women's understandings of themselves at work. This work forms part of a larger project on mentoring and women academics in Australian universities. In recent years a number of universities have introduced planned mentoring programmes for their women staff. These programmes provide access to information and support that women do not otherwise enjoy, and position women for promotion and other opportunities. This is against the backdrop of the continuing low representation of women in senior positions (QUT Equity Section 2004; Carrington and Pratt 2003).

The chapter opens with some background on mentoring in higher education, after which I outline my theoretical position. Through an analysis of interviews I conducted with two women academics, Michelle and Karen, I develop the argument that mentoring has a number of productive effects. It produces working knowledges and skills, but also produces particular sorts of organizational subjects for the time and the place. This is significant given the increasingly central role mentoring occupies in the suite of work-based education practices being deployed globally. I do not suggest here that the subjects produced in and through mentoring in any one site are homogenized, or that the processes of subjectification in mentoring always work. Instead I argue that mentoring necessarily shapes subjectivity, within the discourses at play in any given context.

The role of mentoring

Mentoring has long been part of academic life, as experienced academics have advised and supported graduate students in the development of their research (Marshall *et al.* 1998). In many fields, students are inducted into the research cultures of their discipline and the institution through their supervisor and in the context of a research team. Maack and Passet (1993) argued the main difference between mentoring in academic and corporate settings is that in academia there are many critical relationships with people who are outside the daily work environment. Many academics relate firstly to discipline networks nationally and internationally, rather than to their university. In a large-scale, longitudinal study of new academics in the United States in the 1990s, the researchers found that mentoring (individual relationship) and collegiality (relationships with many) are two ways in which new faculty are socialized into a new institution (Bode 1999: 121).

Marshall *et al.* suggest the more recent interest in *formal* planned mentoring programmes in universities has developed '... in response to the more competitive environment in which universities operate, and the requirement for more accountability and performance appraisal' (1998: 1). This proposition draws attention to the institutional work done by mentoring within the context of contemporary neo-liberal university governance. Mentoring socializes, teaches and plays a role in improving organizational performance.

Mentoring as a technology of governing

A number of commentators have noted how new forms of workplace governance and regulation and new work demands create new forms of subjectivities (Rose 1999 {1989}; du Gay 1996). The management of the subjectivity of workers becomes a central task of contemporary organizations, with the goal of creating active subjects who will be more productive (Usher and Solomon 1999). Over recent decades the demands of performativity (Lyotard 1984) have reshaped the goals of educational institutions in terms of economic imperatives (Usher and Solomon 1998: 2), leading to a scenario in universities where efficiency is the new bottom line (Blackmore and Sachs 2001: 45).

Professional development has assumed a critical role in driving and supporting agendas of the performative university. This work-based education invariably involves an element of self-formation and change, containing 'implicit theorisations concerning the nature of the self, its development or capacity for change and the way the self relates to others or to society more generally' (Chappell *et al.* 2003: 9).

This recent work on work and subjectivity draws heavily on Foucault's theories on the formation of the subject (1992). Foucault traced a range of texts that elaborate rules and opinions about how one should behave, arguing these texts serve as devices that enable individuals to 'question their own conduct, to watch over and give shape to it and to shape themselves as ethical subjects' (Foucault 1992: 16). Foucault described as 'technologies of the self' those technologies

> which permit individuals to effect by their own means or with the help of others a certain number of operations on their own bodies and souls, thought, conduct and way of being, so as to transform themselves in order to attain a certain state of happiness, purity, wisdom, perfection, or immortality.
>
> (Foucault 1988: 18)

He described these 'operations' as techniques or the ways in which the individual is governed by both the state and by him or herself (Foucault 1991). Technologies of the self are the practices by which individuals may situate and define themselves by becoming tied to a particular identity (Foucault 1983).

Rose (1999 {1989}) argues the new forms of subjectivities that characterise contemporary workplaces have developed alongside a culture of liberal freedom which celebrates values of autonomy and self-realization. Within this culture humans are 'obliged' to pursue their autonomy and self-actualization, to make their life meaningful 'as if it were the outcome of individual choices made in furtherance of a biographical project of self-realisation' (ibid: ix). In workplaces, technologies such as performance appraisal systems and training programmes provide the means for subjects to come to 'understand' and act upon themselves within the discursive context of their workplaces, creating order, knowledge, and ultimately, power effects (Townley 1994). Self-regulation is central to this task, wherein workers see congruence between their own and the organization's goals and regulate themselves accordingly (Usher and Solomon 1999: 156).

In his study of a knowledge-intensive unit undergoing change in a large corporation, Deetz (1998) suggested knowledge-intensive organizations are characterized by high levels of autonomy and self-management; rely primarily on individual and collective forms of intellectual capital; and rely more heavily on normative forms of control, exercised through self-surveillance and self-control rather than by the exercise of sovereign power by management. The products of most work processes in such organizations are hard to measure and are based on intrinsic characteristics:

> The often hidden and mysterious work, plus the absence of a clear physical product with measurable characteristics, leaves identity to be acquired from the projection of the subject rather than drawn from the product or work activity.
>
> (Deetz 1998: 157)

In the following sections, I explore the ways in which mentoring shapes the subjectivities of two women academics, Karen and Michelle. In particular, I investigate the ways the women produce and enact their desired subjectivities in and through mentoring, and the place of self-regulation in that process.

Karen: 'I've run out of excuses now'

> She {her mentor, Susan} didn't really crack any whips over me or anything, but just being in that formal relationship with her made me feel … it's time to really get some stuff happening. So, I made myself a timetable for getting stuff done, and so I did.

And later

> this {sending papers off to journals} might have all happened even if it hadn't been for the mentoring relationship. ... But I really felt like just having the University allocate funds, basically, to set up this structure, really motivated me, and made me feel like, 'OK, it's time to do something. I'm running out of excuses now!'

Karen is a senior lecturer in a social science faculty. She had worked as an academic for around 14 years and had had a few significant mentors over this time. In this quote, Karen explains the role Susan played in her academic work. Susan became her mentor as part of a 12-month women's mentoring programme at one university. In this passage Karen is quick to assure me that Susan did not exercise power over her when she says, 'she didn't crack any whips'. However the exercise of disciplinary power as a function of the mentoring relationship is evident in Karen's own self-regulating *as an effect* of that relationship ('just being in that relationship ...'; 'So I made myself a timetable for getting things done'). In her disavowal of sovereign power by her mentor (power *over* ...) Karen effectively disavows the operation of power at all. She asserts it was 'just being in that formal relationship' that led her to 'get stuff done'. In doing this Karen disguises the operation of disciplinary power (power *to* ...) that operates through mentoring, disciplining her (self) within the discursive formations of academic work and careers. The disavowal allows Karen to reassert herself by implication as the self-managing subject.

Karen reproaches herself as having been an insufficiently active subject particularly in regards to research, declaring 'I'm running out of excuses now!' It is worthwhile noting that at the time to which she referred Karen was working full-time following her return from leave after the birth of her second child. In the two years prior to her leave she was one of a small number of staff setting up a new degree programme in a new school. Her comments reveal her active self-disciplining in the performative university. Karen actively took on her performance as a researcher as her project, enlisting Susan's help in the task of (re)producing herself as the disciplined researcher.

Karen identified herself as a feminist and she had been active on feminist issues in her faculty. She remarked in our interview:

> That's a lot of what you get from mentoring, knowing it's not just you. Knowing that the experiences that you're having have some sort of basis in the outside world, and that it's part of a system and you can help to understand the system better.

The issues confronting women and other minority group members in higher education are well documented and are not the subject of this chapter. Of importance here though is the way the systemic factors that limit women's participation in research are disguised within the discourses of the performative university, in which low research output is framed in terms of the shortcomings of individual women. On the one hand, Karen laments she is not more productive as a researcher, and on the other, she identifies the problem in terms of those systemic issues.

In the following passage, Karen explains why she asked Susan to be her mentor. Here she works the discourses of the performative university while also highlighting the importance of role models for women:

A: So, why did you choose Susan?

K: She struck me as someone really solid and centred and caring. Like, a really serene sort of person ...

I'd just met her a couple of times, and I just thought, you know, if she has gotten where she is – because she was an Associate Professor ... while being this ... very stable, gentle-seeming sort of person, she must really have some clues! About the way that I'd like to be living my life, too. ... I'd like to get ahead and not be ... a maniac, which a lot of people are! Let's face it, a lot of women are, who get ahead. They get ahead by being perfectionists and difficult and all those things. A lot of men are, too, obviously, but ... you need to be that little bit more difficult to break through as a woman. ... I didn't want to be that kind of person. I saw myself as someone more like Susan. I wanted to be more ... calm and serene and centred, and just – {pause} quietly achieving.

One of the first issues Karen discussed with Susan was some negative teaching evaluations in her first semester back from maternity leave. Karen alternates between the distress the evaluations caused her, and the tone of the disciplined researcher, reporting she had 'made a timetable for getting stuff done ... those papers just sitting there, just waiting to be sent off', and 'did it'.

I asked Karen to define mentoring:

It's about supporting people to do what they want to do. ... it can be making alternative suggestions about: 'Maybe you don't want to do what you think you want to do!', ... like a paternalistic sort of role. ... I think if you get too far out on that ... then it's not mentoring any more. I think it really does have to be within a context where the mentee sets the agenda ... and the mentor's job is, 'OK. Here's how you achieve that!'

Here Karen asserts a distinction between mentoring as a form of paternalism and mentoring as a type of self-directed learning (Devos 2004). She implies mentoring embodies self-directedness *and* direction by others, in so doing drawing attention to mentoring as a site of governmentality in which the subject is both governed and self-governing.

Michelle: 'I do all the things that you're supposed to do'

> I think of myself as a teacher, but I do a lot of research as well. I publish,
> I do administration and I do public service. I do all the things you're
> supposed to do as an academic.

Michelle is a senior lecturer in a humanities faculty. She has had a number of male and females mentors in her career, including informally in her workplace and discipline, and formally through a women's mentoring programme. In the quote above, Michelle presents herself as a self-managing subject, speaking through the discourses of academic work in the performative university.

At our interview, Michelle told her story of going to university in her twenties after several years spent working and travelling. She excelled as a student with a string of 'high distinctions' – the top grade possible. The 'self' she constructs in this story is of a brilliant young student destined for academic life. From time to time this story is interrupted with glimpses of a different story, characterized by ill health and performance pressures. During her first couple of years as an academic, Michelle suffered serious stress because of her heavy workload, and her position as the only woman academic in her department. Through these years her commitment to her career project did not falter but was in fact strengthened:

> I'm very dogged, and I continued to publish and I continued to run
> projects even though I was worked to death. … And when I'd publish
> something I'd say 'publication against the forces of oppression'!
> [laughs] So, and I just thought 'Fuck it! You're not going to stop me
> publishing!' And, so, I'd be doing my publications with money from
> my grant, and I'd write a nice application, I'd get money for research
> projects, I had to run the bloody projects!

This was by her account a very painful time yet it takes second place within her primary narrative of achievement. She continued to suffer with anxiety about sustaining her performance, with the worry that 'something would slip … irrecoverably' leading her to start taking sleeping pills. Deetz (1998) noted the shift that has occurred in the new discursive regimes of contemporary workplaces. Whereas previously work was designed for sustaining the body and supporting external relationships, now the reverse is the case: 'The company is integrated into the self, leaving one's body and non-work relations as oppositional' (ibid: 166). As in Michelle's case, the primary expressed concerns are that the body, or social needs or families, do not let the employee do more work better. The response is to medicate the body to mask the symptoms of stress and fatigue.

Michelle submits herself to the regimes of her workplace and of academia more generally through her uptake of the position of enterprising academic, pursuing research grants and international networks. She talks about the importance of women's networks at her workplace and their role in sustaining her as an academic, noting the ways in which these networks and friendships can change the culture of the workplace or temper some of its worst features. But the pleasures of these networks are activated *as a consequence of* the violence she experienced, and of her positioning as an enterprising academic within her field.

In her account, she refers indirectly to her complicity, or the complicity of all women, in sustaining the culture of performativity, when she states, 'well, in a sense, you self-exploit in the beginning because you want to do everything so well ...'. She exposes her actions upon herself as the active self-managing subject, normalizing and universalizing her experiences by her use of a tense other than the first person: 'well, *you* self-exploit ... because you want to do everything so well'.

Michelle, like Karen, is engaged in identity work of constructing her understandings of herself through her accounting of her experience. Her investment in *not* seeing herself as exploited in the present is strong, in spite of the evidence of her extraordinarily high workload at the time of our interview. Yet to diffuse this tension she compares her present situation with her early years in the job.

Michelle repeatedly displays her initiative in managing her own conduct, and self-regulating within the terms of the regimes of academic work and the careers discourse (Grey 1994; Savage 1998). This self-regulation occurs in the face of her at times profound unease with her positioning, the effects on her wellbeing, and, like Karen, in tension with her feminist analysis of gender issues in higher education.

Michelle stresses the importance of women role models, especially as a graduate student, and the importance of women colleagues now as an academic. She also refers to her sense of responsibility as a successful woman to act as a role model for other women coming through whom she now mentored. She speaks about three women role models in her field when a graduate student, each of whom she described directly or indirectly in relation to men. The first of these she describes as 'some men are frightened of her'; the second she described as having a successful academic husband and subsuming her career to his until they divorced; and the third she described as a 'very lady-like lady – you know, published but not as published as she should be'. All three are defined in terms of their marital status or their relationship to a feminine ideal.

These remarks echo Karen's description of her 'serene, caring' mentor, offering different insights into the question of women, gender performativity (Butler 1999 {1990}) and academic success. For Karen and Michelle their women mentors offered important role models. They provided different takes on what it means to be a successful woman academic, and different ways of understanding and conducting oneself institutionally and within a disciplinary network.

Fashioning the self in mentoring

In this chapter, I drew on interviews with two academics to illustrate the ways in which mentoring acts as a technology through which women self-regulate within the discursive formations of academic work, gender and careers. Karen and Michelle are engaged in ongoing identity work, assembling and reassembling themselves according to the demands of subjectivity in the performative university. The women's ongoing self-management reflects the iterative and continuous nature of the project of the care of the self, where 'each day we make ourselves anew in fresh formulations' (Hutton, 1988: 134). Contradictions or tensions may be talked over the top of or quarantined, or become the subject of critical engagement with others such as through women's networks, as was the case for both Karen and Michelle. This identity work then is a rocky road, frequently contested within the women's own accounts.

My reading here highlights the ways mentoring activates self-regulation by the mentee (and possibly by the mentor too). Karen and Michelle are moved to manage their conduct in particular ways in light of the understandings of academic work they draw from mentoring and from their discursive contexts. Parallel stories of stress and struggle are contained within their accounts through the women's sustained and strategic self-regulation within their mentoring relationships and as academic workers more generally. For Karen and Michelle, mentoring contributed to the formation of new working knowledges, new networks and strategic plans for their futures. However these knowledges are enacted through technologies of self-regulation.

Some of the knowledges produced may be transgressive in that they invite the mentee to form new and critical understandings of her environment and of her positioning within that. It is important then that mentoring is not construed as a hegemonic process that merely turns out docile bodies. The subjects produced are active and politicized in their own self-constitution.

This reading of mentoring is significant because it offers fresh conceptual insights into the technologies of the self and of the workplace through which workers build and regulate their identities. It challenges current thinking on mentoring in two ways, namely by illustrating the identity work performed in and through mentoring; and secondly, through locating this work within its political contexts.

References

Blackmore, J. and Sachs, J. (2001) 'Women leaders in the restructured university', in A. Brooks and A. Mackinnon (eds) *Gender and the Restructured University*, Buckingham: Society for Research into Higher Education and Open University Press.

Bode, R.K. (1999) 'Mentoring and collegiality', in R.J. Menges and Associates (eds) *Faculty in New Jobs: A Guide to Settling In, Becoming Established, and Building Institutional Support*, San Fransisco, CA: Jossey-Bass.

Butler, J. (1999 [1990]) *Gender Trouble: Feminism and the Subversion of Identity*, New York: Routledge.

Carrington, K. and Pratt, A. (2003) *How Far Have We Come? Gender Disparities in the Australian Higher Education System*, Canberra: Information and Research Services. Department of the Parliamentary Library.

Chappell, C., Rhodes, C., Solomon, N., Tennant, M. and Yates, L. (2003) *Reconstructing the Lifelong Learner: Pedagogy and Identity in Individual, Organisational and Social Change*, London: RoutledgeFalmer.

Colley, H. (2001) 'Righting rewritings of the myth of mentor: a critical perspective on career guidance mentoring', *British Journal of Guidance and Counselling*, 29: 177–95.

Deetz, S. (1998) 'Discursive formations, strategized subordination and self-surveillance', in A. McKinlay and K. Starkey (eds) *Foucault, Management and Organization Theory: From Panoptican to Technologies of Self*, London: Sage Publications.

Devos, A. (2004) 'The project of others, the project of self: mentoring, women and the fashioning of the academic subject', *Studies in Continuing Education*, 26: 67–80.

du Gay, P. (1996) *Consumption and Identity at Work*, London: Sage.

Foucault, M. (1983) 'The subject and power', in H.L. Dreyfus and P. Rabinow (eds) *Michel Foucault: Beyond Structuralism and Hermeneutics*, second edition, Chicago, IL: University of Chicago Press.

Foucault, M. (1988) 'Technologies of the self', in L. Martin, H. Gutman and P. Hutton (eds) *Technologies of the Self: A Seminar with Michel Foucault*, Amherst, MA: University of Massachusetts Press.

Foucault, M. (1991) 'Governmentality', in G. Burchell, C. Gordon and P. Miller (eds) *The Foucault Effect: Studies in Governmentality*, Hertfordshire: Harvester Wheatsheaf.

Foucault, M. (1992) *The History of Sexuality Volume 2: The Use of Pleasure*, London: Penguin.

Grey, C. (1994) 'Career as a project of the self and labour process discipline', *Sociology*, 28: 479–97.

Hutton, P.H. (1988) 'Foucault, Freud and the technologies of the self', in L. Martin, H. Gutman and P. Hutton (eds) *Technologies of the Self: A Seminar with Michel Foucault*, Amherst, MA: University of Massachusetts Press.

Lyotard, J.F. (1984) *The Postmodern Condition: A Report on Knowledge*, Manchester: Manchester University Press.

Maack, M. and Passet, J. (1993) 'Unwritten rules: mentoring women faculty', *Library and Information Science Research*, 15: 117–41.

Marshall, S., Adams, M. and Cameron, A. (1998) 'Mentoring academic staff: lessons from the field'. Paper presented at the Annual Conference of the Higher Education Research and Development Society of Australasia (HERDSA), Auckland, New Zealand: HERDSA.

QUT Equity Section (2004) 'Advancing the AVCC Action Plan for Women: cross-institution comparisons based on 2003 DEST data'. Brisbane: Queensland University of Technology.

Rose, N. (1999 {1989}) *Governing the Soul: The Shaping of the Private Self*, London: Free Association Books.

Savage, M. (1998) 'Discipline, surveillance and the "career": employment on the Great Western Railway', in A. McKinlay and K. Starkey (eds) *Foucault, Management and Organization Theory: From Panoptican to Technologies of Self*, London: Sage Publications.

Townley, B. (1994) *Reframing Human Resource Management: Power, Ethics and the Subject at Work*, London: Sage Publications

Usher, R. and Solomon, N. (1998) 'Disturbing the ivory tower? Educational research as performance and performativity', Paper presented at the Annual Conference of the Australian Association for Research in Education, Adelaide, Australia: AARE.

Usher, R. and Solomon, N. (1999) 'Experiential learning and the shaping of subjectivity in the workplace', *Studies in the Education of Adults*, 31: 155–64.

15 Negotiating self through changing work

Stephen Billett

This chapter discusses how individuals' sense of self mediates the impact of work transformations brought about by economic and social globalization. It proposes that through work and working life, individuals' sense of work self is shaped through negotiation between social and personal imperatives. Therefore, understanding the impact of globalization on work requires going beyond accounts of social theorizing and 'objective' accounts of changes and their impacts to include workers' subjective experiences. Using case studies of transformations in five individuals' work lives, these changes are shown as being not necessarily disempowering and dehumanizing, but potentially serving workers' personal and work-life goals. Central to effectively negotiating these transformations is the exercise of individual agency and intentionality directed towards maintaining and remaking their selves through working life.

Changing work and changing workers

In every testimony to the experience of de-humanizing pressures of modern industrial society, there is also a testimony to a contrary sense of self, of personal identity, of being human; of what it is or might be like to be in control of our own lives, to act in and upon the world, to be active human agents. So, in the name of our personal identities, our personal hopes and projects and longings, in the name of ourselves, we resist.

(Dawe 1978 cited in Knights and Willmott, 1989: 535–6)

Economic globalization is transforming not only the kinds of work available, but also the micro processes that constitute the work individuals engage in and come to identify with as workers. In the final quarter of the last century and, so far in this century, there have been transformational changes in the kinds of work available, how work is practised and performance requirements for work (Billett, 2006b). Transformations in global economic activity, technology and the cultural needs (e.g. McBrier and Wilson, 2004) have rendered participating in work more turbulent. Indeed, much is made of the disempowerment and anxiety caused by the turbulent and uncertain nature of contemporary work (e.g. Giddens, 1991; Bauman, 1998; Beck, 1992). Clearly, some of these changes can be disempowering and dispossessing. However, the impact of globalization, whilst ubiquitous, may not be as uniform, universal, equally severe or pervasive as some accounts suggest. To understand these changes and their impact upon individuals requires going beyond 'objective' measures of work transformation, changing patterns of employment and participation of work, as important as these are, to include the subjective experience of those who work and negotiate these changes. Only through understanding the consequences of these changes upon individuals can assertions about their impact be made with confidence.

Claims about the negative impacts of globalization emanate most strongly from accounts that might be described as social theorizing, which are admittedly speculative. They are often premised in theoretical accounts or aggregated quantitative data that have sought to identify patterns of impacts across populations of workers. These accounts are premised on propositions within the authors' theoretical (Giddens, 1991) or ideological stance (Beck, 1992) or their observations of the past and speculations of the future (Bauman, 1998). These accounts extend from meta-analyses of changing societal conditions, through to those explaining how individuals and society come together in working life. The social structuring of work and its legacies are a common starting point, with individuals by degree being viewed as captive, subjugated or resistant to those structures. For instance, in the risky and uncertain era of late modernity, individuals are held to have become 'enterprising selves' (Rose, 1990; Du Gay, 1996) engaging in self-regulation and acting inconsistently with personal preferences. To secure continuity and advancement in employment, individuals are claimed as directing their personal agency and intentionality and subverting their real selves (Grey, 1994). Such perspectives privilege the social world encountered in work life and positions it as objective and comprising potent institutional facts (Searle, 1995) to which individuals are inherently posterior.

All this underpins claims about the anxiety-ridden and uncertain contemporary times, thereby supporting Bauman's (1998) view that a continuous and logically coherent working life is now less available, making continuity of work skills and identity problematic. Certainly, the period since the mid-1970s has featured increased global competition, pressure on labor productivity and the deployment of management practices to achieve increased levels of productivity in many western economies (Carnoy, 1999; Handel, 2005). Carnoy suggests that with intense global competition, work is being reorganized around 'the centralised management, customised products, and work differentiation ...' (Carnoy, 2001: 306). One consequence is to make work more sub-contracted, undertaken by part-time and temporary workers, while core work becomes more broadly skilled and conducted by teams (Billett, 2006b).

Another consequence is the separation of workers from stable work and occupations that enjoyed acceptance and provided secure work identities in modern industrialized societies (e.g. Carnoy, 2001). More so, many new jobs are held to be contingent, fixed term and part-time (Carnoy, 1999), making work insecure. Yet, the impact of these changes is unlikely to be uniform, instead differing in character and degrees and at different times and places, across and within countries. For instance, some kinds of work (e.g. garment, automobile and steel production) were exported from some countries to others or intra-nationally. These kinds of employment migrations are having a particular, and sometimes, devastating, effect upon the communities as either the losers or beneficiaries from such changes. Some forms of work, such as the face-to-face services (Shah and Bourke, 2003) comprising much of professional employment, are relatively immune from being exported, although still subject to other kinds of changes. So the impact of work life is different across categories of employment and across and within countries. From empirical evidence, Handel (2005) proposes that job security and internal labor markets eroded in the 1990s. Yet, he qualifies that the effect fell disproportionately on white-collar and more educated workers, thereby narrowing the insecurity gap between more and less privileged workers.

However, the appraisal of the changes to and impacts of work is largely through aggregated measures, rather than more subjective accounts of an individual's experience of work (Handel, 2005). Consequently, conceptions of what constitutes good work and an effective working life are premised by these accounts, rather than those accommodating and articulating individuals' subjective experience of these changes. In Pusey's (2003) study, more nuanced accounts of individuals' views about changing work emerge. For instance, focus groups identified middle Australians' 'struggle for recognition' within social hierarchies: both 'as moral worthy people deserving respect ... for what they do for others' (ibid: 92) and as wanting a decent living standard. Therefore, to understand globalization's impact upon workers requires understanding its consequences from their perspectives. Otherwise there is a contradiction between claims and method, i.e. imposing a subjugating set of claims without engaging with and seeking to understand those about whom claims are being made. Certainly, it seems important to go beyond measures of work transformation, changing patterns of employment and participation of work as 'objective facts' and engage the subjective experiences of those who work. For instance, Noon and Blyton (1997) claim most people in all occupations would continue to work for personal reasons, even if they had no financial need. This suggests either wholesale social subjugation (i.e. the individual becomes socialized to engaging in work) or individuals finding meaning and sense of self within their work which is personally sustaining, or some combination of the two perspectives. Regardless, greater clarification of individuals' roles and motivations are required.

Work, change and subjectivity

It follows that the impact of changes brought about by globalization needs to be understood from personal or subjective viewpoints. The imperative here is not to confound or counter the pessimistic accounts provided above, but to offer more comprehensive and grounded accounts of these impacts. This includes both material impacts upon individuals' sense of selves as workers. Pusey (2003: 2) concludes that 'For nearly everyone work is a social protein, a buttress for identity and not a tradeable commodity', thereby indicating the need to go beyond material impacts and understand those associated about the self. Certainly, in studies examining the lived experience of contemporary workers (e.g. Somerville and Abrahamsson, 2003; Fenwick, 2002, 2004; Billett *et al.*, 2004; Billett and Pavlova, 2005; Somerville, 2002) a complex pattern of social and personal imperatives emerges. That is, an intertwining and negotiation between the press of the social world (i.e. changes to work activities) and personal agency and intentionality shapes how individuals view their work, their sense of self as workers and, consequently, how they gauge the impact of change.

Indeed, transformations in work stand as points where this intertwining and negotiating can be appraised. Participation in work requires individuals to apply what they know (i.e. their cognitive experience) in construing, constructing and enacting what is required when conducting their work tasks (Billett, 2006a). Moreover, this process is necessarily negotiated. The suggestion of the social (e.g. the clues and cues, interpersonal interactions, exhortations, etc.) is rarely so comprehensive or compelling to be faithfully expressed or secured. Even if motivated to be faithful to that suggestion, individuals necessarily construct meaning from what they encounter and perceive. So despite work situations providing rich repertoires of clues and cues for performance and social partners to observe and engage with and be monitored by (i.e. forms of social suggestion), these encounters are construed and constructed through individuals' subjective experiences. Central to this negotiation is individuals' sense of self that is shaped by how they perceive the world (i.e. their gaze) and the discourses that they have access to and can deploy (Billett, 2006c).

Moreover, individuals' personal circumstances and trajectories are such that what for one individual is an opportunity to expand their role and sense of self, for another is a threat to their competence and self. Further, inevitably, participation in work involves the active remaking of the activities and practices that constitute paid work. This remaking consists both the process and outcome of individuals' active construal and construction of changing work tasks and interactions. So, except perhaps in the most compelling of circumstances (e.g. the removal of a form of work, loss of employment) transformations to work provide opportunities for workers to engage with, interpret and negotiate work activities through their personal intentions and agency. So even if individuals wanted to be uncritical and passive, in the on-going negotiating of meaning and remaking work these personal attributes inevitably are exercised. Yet, individuals are unlikely passive recipients of the social suggestion (Valsiner, 2000). Therefore, the remaking of work in the face of transformations provides spaces for negotiation between the personal and social with individuals' sense of self mediating these negotiations, and being potentially reshaped through these processes (Billett *et al.*, 2005). However, the scope, extent and purchase of these negotiations and their consequences are distributed unevenly across workers.

To elaborate the centrality of human subjectivity – the conscious and unconscious thoughts and emotions (Weedon, 1997) in negotiating the impact of globalization, the next section illustrates and discusses accounts of the work-life histories of five individuals engaged in different kinds of paid employment, albeit each subject to work change premised on globalized events or imperatives (Billett, 2006a). In each instance, these workers' sense of self about work guided and mediated these negotiations and their impacts. For four of these workers, these negotiations led to supporting or elevating their standing in the workplace. In the fifth instance, it was the over-exercise of self through personal agency that led to an unsatisfactory outcome for that individual. By different degrees, for each worker, there is evidence of a negotiated interdependence between their needs and the affordances of the workplace, and individuals' subjectivity. Yet in terms of volition and intent, in each instance, these five individuals' exercise of agency at work was directed towards 'being themselves'. This emphasizes the salience of individuals' subjectivity in working life and the remaking of transforming work. This suggests change in capacity and subjectivity is neither a product of social suggestion or individual agency alone but of an ongoing and differentiated negotiation between the personal and social imperatives. Consequently, the micro-social processes comprising inter- and intra-personal reveal the impact of globalization on work, working life and working identities.

Negotiating transformations in working lives

The investigation described and discussed here identified bases by which five individuals engaged in and negotiated their work lives through processes of change. Data were gathered through a series of sequenced tape-recorded conversations occurring every two months over a year. The aim was to map changes in working life, subjectivities and decision-making. To appraise and validate analyses of the data, its initial analysis and tentative deductions were discussed with participants in subsequent interviews.

The participants were selected by their engagement in diverse kinds of work, modes of engagement with work and diversity of work histories. There was no attempt to select participants who were well-positioned to exercise personal and autonomous agency. The participants were as follows. Ken was an information and communications technology manager within a state government department, with particular responsibilities for electronic security across the department. Carl was a commission-only insurance broker. He worked as a sole operator business within a large brokerage company. Lev worked as an electronics engineer in a large multinational corporation that designs and manufactures rail transportation systems. Lyn worked part-time in a wholesaler in the metropolitan wholesale fruit and vegetable market. Commencing at 2:00 am, she worked two or three days a week, continuing until the day's orders were complete and dispatched. Mike was a supervisor and customer service coordinator in a large automotive vehicle dealership, working across the workshop and sales departments and with customers. Collectively, these individuals engaged in diverse forms of work that have distinct performance requirements and means of engaging in work.

Transformation across working lives

Each participant's work histories included work transformations either before or during the period of the study. Carl, the insurance broker, was a professional sportsman before becoming an insurance broker. So there was a transformational change between his original and current career. Ken, the information technology unit manager, grew up in and remains part of a Christian community. His early work was church-related. Subsequently, he worked in retail, restaurant management and pest-control work before developing expertise with electronic security systems. Lev learnt electronic engineering in the Russian military and was then employed as an electronic engineer in the Russian rail system. Upon migrating to Australia, he worked as a night-time hospital orderly because of his poor English proficiency. He described this as demeaning. However, when his English language competence improved, he gained employment as an electronic engineer. Lyn, the worker in the fruit and vegetable market, had previously worked in shops, cars sales yards and factories while being sole caregiver for her three children. Mike's move into a supervisory role in the mechanical workshop was relatively recent. He had been a motor mechanic throughout his working life, including being a road-side service mechanic assisting motorists whose vehicles had broken down.

So, each of these five workers had experienced significant work-life transformations. Only Mike had had a continuous vocational focus as a motor mechanic. The others, by degree, had experienced discontinuities or transformations in their working lives and occupational identities. For Lyn, the fruit market work represented an emerging work identity that was uncertain and immature. Yet, she was quite intentionally seeking to transform her identity – the social projection and embodiment of self – from being seen primarily as a caregiver to her children to that of a worker. These diverse and meandering working-life trajectories illustrate instances of the ongoing processes of making and remaking occupational identities and personal subjectivities through work-life histories. These are now likely increasing in frequency and degree as work-life transforms. Also, these personal trajectories and the subjectivities illustrate the distinct premises that individuals bring to their work and their negotiation of work transformations.

Transforming work

As noted, each of these workers had experienced transformation in their work in recent times, which continued during the yearlong investigation. These transformations were the product of or analogous to impacts of a globalized economy. Yet, instead of being disempowering and marginalizing, as some accounts predict (Bauman, 1998; Beck, 1992; Rifkin, 1995), these five individuals largely adapted well to the impact of the transformation in their working life. Indeed, rather than being an impediment, these changes were often instrumental in bolstering their standing in the workplace, career progression and sense of self as workers.

Legislation introduced to regulate the financial industry required greater transparency when advising clients about insurance quotes. This transformed Carl's work. Each quote was now required to be documented more fully and meticulously and took far longer. Because of the additional work and relatively low return, small quotes and policies became less attractive to Carl and are now processed by clerical employees. Carl's preference had always been to work on high-value insurance policies and with large policyholders and, importantly, to build and maintain relations with these clients. Under these new work requirements, he was successful in directing more attention to these kinds of projects, which suited his personal and work preferences and were more profitable. Moreover, the more comprehensive documented procedures assisted Carl to refute the claims of malpractice by a disgruntled client who claimed Carl had failed to insure a property that was subsequently destroyed. The more meticulous record-keeping processes provided clear evidence that no agreement had been concluded with this client. So, these transformations to his work ultimately served Carl well for his preferred business and the probity of his practice.

Ken's permanency and enhanced status in information technology work were secured because of heightened global concerns about security. Establishing, operating and maintaining informational technology-based security systems became indispensable to his employer. Because of his early itinerant working life, Ken's primary work goal was to secure well-paid and superannuated employment until retirement. The arising need for heightened levels of security in his department and elsewhere assisted him to achieve his goal of well-paid and superannuated employment.

The electronics engineer, Lev, experienced both sides of globalization. He had held a technical position in a large multinational company, which centralized its maintenance work elsewhere, thereby rendering him redundant. However, he then gained employment in a better paid and more prestigious job in the multinational transport corporation. The downturn and crisis in the global aviation sector following the 2001 attacks on New York and Washington deleteriously affected this corporation. However, because he worked in the division associated with rail transport, Lev was spared redundancy again, unlike others elsewhere in the corporation. Moreover, the corporation's shift in focus to rail transport during a downturn in aviation work served to secure his employment.

Lyn worked to secure and develop a niche role as a new employee at the fruit and vegetable market. The workplace was turbulent and had high employee turnover. Transformations in this workplace included staff leaving and a new task of exporting fruit and vegetables by airfreight to Papua New Guinea. These changes provided opportunities to establish roles and a particular identity for Lyn. Indeed, her employment was seemingly buoyed by her interest in and competence to undertake new tasks, including managing the export orders, which made her solely proficient in customs processes. This new work requirement (i.e. export orders) bolstered her place in the work team and granted her a particular role and workplace identity. This was personally significant as she sought to establish an identity outside of being seen as a caregiver to her children; her sense of self was transformed as she undertook new roles and projected her new identity as a worker.

Mike's role in coordinating relations between clients and workshop staff arose out of global competition: automotive manufacturers' lengthening of warranty periods for purchasers of new vehicles. For dealerships, the purchase of a new vehicle is now the beginning, not the end, of the relationship with customers. The vehicle has to be maintained over the warranty period. Automotive mechanical work now makes interacting with and maintaining clients a key workplace goal. Positive relations might lead to the purchase of another new car at the end of the warranty. Mike's combination of automotive and inter-personal skills, and values required to address this work change, secured him promotion. These values were closely aligned to his professional interests of automotive engineering and customer service, and his personal preferences and enjoyment in helping clients. So these transformations to automotive mechanic work served to meet needs associated with his sense of self as a worker and extended his work identity to include that of a supervisor.

For these five workers, work transformations brought about through global factors were negotiated in ways that were consistent with or bolstered their senses of self. Only one participant experienced major disappointment over the 12-month study. This arose when Lev, on returning from a training course, became too agentic and wrote to senior managers advising them of his ability to improve their work areas' productivity with his newly acquired knowledge. This seemingly brushed up against and contravened the workplace's norms and practices, and his invitation was treated with silent dismissal. His exuberant agency led not to his desired promotion, but to being reassigned to other work duties. Later, his employment was terminated. So, the transformations that impacted these five individuals' work broadly served or had the potential to buttress their employment and standing, that is they assisted rather than inhibited these individuals' work goals. So despite the work status differences in the five cases (i.e. professional, technical, managerial, trades and manual), all had invested their work with identification and attachments (needs for meaning, sense of competence, belonging, etc).

Of course, the experiences reported here and consequences for individuals may not be typical. Elsewhere in the transport corporation where Lev worked were job losses, career truncations and dislocations. Yet, these five randomly selected workers' experiences question claims that work transformations brought about by globalization necessarily lead to disempowerment, marginalization and anxiety. The relationships between work changes and these individuals' continuities included acting to and negotiating those changes. Moreover, these negotiations were premised not on denying the self, but on salient bases for these individuals' sense of self and were directed by personal imperatives of 'being themselves'.

Negotiating self through changing work

In different ways, all five participants claimed that their working life was merely a means to an end. Through work transformations, these five individuals exercised their agency in intentional efforts to 'be themselves'. This was the case even in intentionally transforming that self as opportunities arose (i.e. Lyn), analogous to the enterprising self, but directed towards goals of their making, not the workplace. Yet, this was more readily achievable for some than for others. For Ken, his family and church community and relative lack of interest in the specific work activities meant that workplace conflicts were less significant to him. He worked around a new boss's agenda, for instance. However, Lev's sense of self was violated by having his suggestions for work improvement summarily dismissed. So although both Ken and Lev worked in large organizations that exercised regulatory practices (Bernstein, 1996) the impacts were relational, having less impact upon Ken than Lev. These two individuals' sense of selves about work shaped how, and for what purposes, they engaged with work, and how they negotiated change at work.

In sum, by different degree, there was evidence of interdependence and intertwining between the personal and workplace imperatives in negotiating workplace transformations. These individuals' capacity to exercise their agency at work was aligned with how they valued that work and identified with it and negotiated a place for themselves. These individuals were not passive in the face of these transformations; they resisted these changes through negotiation and the exercise of securing a self consistent with their personal trajectories. This suggests that, in part, understanding and managing the effects of globalization are locatable in how individuals' sense of self are exercised and negotiated. Hence, whilst the objective facts of transforming work conditions and the availability of work brought about by globalization needs to be understood, their consequence and impacts can only be fully apprehended through a consideration of their impact in terms of workers' subjective experience and negotiation of those changes.

References

Bauman, Z. (1998) *Work, Consumerism and the New Poor*, Buckingham: Open University Press.

Beck, U. (1992) *Risk Society: Towards a New Modernity*, London: Sage.

Bernstein, B. (1996) *Pedagogy, Symbolic Control and Identity: Research Critique*, London: Taylor and Francis.

Billett, S. (2006a) 'Exercising self through working life: learning, work and identity', in A. Brown, Kirpal, S. and Raumer, F. (eds) *Identities at Work*, Dordecht: Springer.

Billett, S. (2006b) *Work, Change and Workers*, Dordrecht: Springer.

Billett, S. (2006c) 'Work, subjectivity and learning', in S. Billett, T. Fenwick and M. Somerville (eds) *Work, Subjectivity and Learning*, Dordrecht: Springer.

Billett, S. and Pavlova, M. (2005) 'Learning through working life: self and individuals' agentic action', *International Journal of Lifelong Education*, 24: 195–211.

Billett, S., Barker, M. and Hernon-Tinning, B. (2004) 'Participatory practices at work', *Pedagogy, Culture and Society*, 12: 233–57.

Billett, S., Smith, R. and Barker, M. (2005) 'Understanding work, learning and the remaking of cultural practices', *Studies in Continuing Education*, 27: 219–37.

Carnoy, M. (1999) 'The great work dilemma', in J. Ahier and G. Esland (eds) *Education, Training and the Future of Work 1*, London: Routledge.

Carnoy, M. (2001) 'The family, flexible work and social cohesion at risk', in M.F. Loutfi (ed.) *Women, Gender and Work*, Geneva: International Labour Organisation.

Du Gay, P. (1996) *Consumption and Identity at Work*, London: Sage.

Fenwick, T. (2002) 'Lady, inc.: women learning, negotiating subjectivity in entrepeneurial discourses', *International Journal of Lifelong Education*, 21: 162–77.

Fenwick, T. (2004) 'Learning in portfolio work: anchored innovation and mobile identity', *Studies in Continuing Education*, 26: 229–46.

Giddens, A. (1991) *Modernity and Self-identity: Self and Society in the Late Modern Age*, Stanford, CA: Stanford University Press.

Grey, C. (1994) 'Career as a project of the self and labour process discipline', *Sociology*, 28: 479–97.

Handel, M.J. (2005) 'Trends in perceived job quality, 1989 to 1998', *Work and Occupations*, 32: 66–94.

Knights, D. and Willmott, H. (1989) 'Power and subjectivity at work: from degradation to subjugation in social relations', *Sociology*, 23: 535–58.

McBrier, D.B. and Wilson, G. (2004) 'Going down? Race and downward occupational mobility for white collar workers in the 1990s', *Work and Occupations*, 31: 283–322.

Noon, M. and Blyton, P. (1997) *The Realities of Work*, Basingstoke: Macmillan.

Pusey, M. (2003) *The Experience of Middle Australia*, Cambridge: Cambridge University Press.

Rifkin, J. (1995) *The End of Work: The Decline of the Global Labor Force and the Dawn of the Post-market Era*, New York: G.P. Putnam.

Rose, N. (1990) *Governing the Soul: The Shaping of the Private Self*, London: Routledge.

Searle, J.R. (1995) *The Construction of Social Reality*, London, Penguin.

Shah, C. and Bourke, G. (2003) 'Project 2000–02: changing skill requirements in the Australian labour force in a knowledge economy', Working Paper No. 48. Melbourne: Centre for the Economics of Education and Training.

Somerville, M. (2002) 'Changing masculine work cultures', in J. Searle and D. Roebuck (eds) *Envisioning Practice: Implementing Change*, Gold Coast: Australian Academic Press.

Somerville, M. and Abrahamsson, L. (2003) 'Trainers and learners constructing a community of practice: masculine work cultures and learning safety in the mining industry' *Studies in the Education of Adults*, 35: 19–34.

Valsiner, J. (2000) *Culture and Human Development*, London: Sage.

Weedon, C. (1997) *Feminist Practices and Post-structural Theory*, 2nd edition, Oxford: Blackwell Publishers.

16 Identity formation and literacy development within vocational education and work

Glynda A. Hull and Jessica Zacher

Within the US, as well as internationally, workers are now continually asked to retool their skills while nation states look for ways to achieve or retain competitive economic advantages. In the United States, federal policy has shifted over the last two decades from job creation to job training, and the lion's share of funding for adult education and literacy programs now goes toward work-related education and skills development. In this chapter, we illustrate how US workplaces and vocational programs are important sites not only for skill development but also for identity construction, although they are not often recognized as such in the educational or policy literature. Using data drawn from ethnographic studies of work and job training, we illustrate and examine the promotion and enactment of identities, as well as the role of literacy, broadly conceived, in the process. We ask how such a focus might inform conceptions of growth and change in adulthood.

Introduction

In this chapter we illustrate how United States workplaces and vocational programs are important sites not only for skill development, but also for identity construction, although they are not often recognized as such in the educational or policy literature. To argue this point, we draw on ethnographic and qualitative data from two projects carried out over a period of approximately ten years at two California sites. In these studies, we examined the literacy requirements of new and traditionally organized workplaces in the Silicon Valley and the literacy and technology learning requirements of a vocational program designed to provide intensive training on information technologies and life skills.

Many of the participants in our studies were recent immigrants and still struggled with English, while others had been born in the United States and had struggled to succeed in mainstream schooling situations. Most would be categorized as "low income," and virtually all were looking for opportunities to redesign their life chances, to start fresh, to get new jobs, or simply to improve themselves (cf. Greene, 1990; Inbar, 1990). As literacy researchers, we were concerned with literacy's role in this process of self-improvement and development, as were the employers, workers, teachers, and students with whom we worked. However, as we reanalyzed the data from both of these projects in our ongoing attempts to understand the relationships between identity and literacy (see also Hull *et al.*, forthcoming; Zacher, forthcoming), we found that particular understandings of identity construction (e.g., Giddens, 1991; Hall, 1996; Holland *et al.*, 1998) afforded us greater understandings of the underlying goals of job and workplace training, as well as the goals of students and workers in such programs.

Job training program shifts in the United States

Job training programs are now ubiquitous in the US, having garnered for several decades enthusiastic bipartisan support from the US Congress, culminating in comprehensive legislation, most recently the passage of the Workforce Investment Act (1998). However, interest in worker training and retraining is also an international phenomenon, as nation states look for ways to achieve or retain competitive economic advantage. Such job training programs and vocational offerings are sometimes considered second chances for education – designed, that is, with a social justice orientation in mind and offered as assistance to individuals who have been poorly served educationally and who consequently need help to change careers, reverse paths, or attempt something once again. With its thousands of community colleges, its vast system of vocational training, and its equally vast, if largely uncoordinated, collection of remedial programs, adult basic education, and literacy classes, the United States would seem to epitomize a society that values a second chance for every citizen (cf. Grubb and Kalman, 1994).

However, some would argue that a genuine second chance philosophy has never been at the center of much of US educational policy (cf. Oakes, 1986; Varenne and McDermott, 1998); job training programs are almost always under-funded, marginal, and limited in their success. Studies of adult basic education classes have consistently shown that students do not remain in these programs long enough to appreciably improve in reading (Porter *et al.*, 2005). More worrisome still, large-scale studies of job training (i.e., 20,000 people over four years) have demonstrated no significant effects in terms of employment and wages (Lafer, 2002). In fact, Lafer argues that the current federal emphasis on job training is a kind of political subterfuge, an effort to direct attention away from the fact that there are not enough well-paying jobs, regardless of the kinds of training workers may receive. Up until the Regan administration in the 1980s, Lafer points out, federal policy had supported job creation; however, with Regan's economic policies came a shift in federal emphasis from job creation to job training, a focus that continues to this day.

Employers, workforces, and identities at a crossroads

Significantly, a parallel shift has occurred in the focus of job training and its measurement of success. According to Lafer (2002), current employers frequently direct their complaints about the American workforce not toward their deficiencies in cognitive skills, but toward their values and behavior: discipline, punctuality, loyalty, and work ethic. Both in the US and internationally, job programs have increasingly begun to address such attitudinal barriers by providing instruction in what are popularly called "life skills" (Perrow, 2000). It is perhaps not surprising that a well-documented discourse focusing on worker deficits soon began to accompany calls for worker retraining, or that this discourse lapsed regularly into varieties of ethnic, racial, gender, and even generational stereotyping (Hull, 1993). One of the more infamous calls to action around worker deficits was based on the worry that our near-future US workforce was likely to be "nonmale," "nonwhite," and "nonyoung" (quoted in Hull, 1993; cf. Rose, 2005). Similar worries about worker deficits and a future minus qualified workers were a part of the culture at our two research sites, Teamco, a Silicon Valley company, and City Jobs, a technology-training job program (both names are pseudonyms).

It is at the complex nexus of global economic competition, US policies on job training, and doubts about the quality of the US workforce that we situated our analysis of the identity work undertaken by employers, employees, teachers, and students at Teamco and City Jobs. Over the course of our research in these contexts, we came to think a great deal about identity and development in adulthood, building on theoretical traditions that envision human development as a process of continual identity construction and the exploration of possible selves. This conception places considerable emphasis on language as a key developmental tool, especially the role of narrative in constructing a self and the notion of self as a story.

Identity and adult agency in our studies: definitions and ideas

Drawing from ethnographies of personhood, social theory, and socio-historical research on literacy, learning, and human development, we conceptualize identity as enacted and agentive. We see identity enactment occurring via specific channels, highlighted in particular moments, and visible in certain spaces and places. More specifically, identity is enacted through and mediated by language and other cultural artifacts (such as the job interview skits that students practiced at City Jobs, or the presentations to management made by in-work teams at Teamco) (cf. Vygotsky, 1978; Cole, 1996). Identities are amalgamated from past experiences, available cultural resources, and possible subject positions in the present and future (cf. Eisenhart, 1995; Hall, 1996); we saw students and workers draw on a variety of past experiences to create their current selves. Identities are also articulated through story or narrative (cf. Ochs and Capps, 2001; Bruner, 1994) and continuously revised (Giddens, 1991); indeed, it was as we listened to and later analyzed City Jobs students' life narratives that we saw such self-articulations.

In both of the studies represented here, it was clear to us that identities index social positions and a person's privilege or lack thereof in relation to that of others (cf. Holland *et al.*, 1998; Goffman, 1959). As identities are also inseparable from learning, especially the mastery or acquisition of expertise (cf. Lave and Wenger, 1991; Wenger, 1998), being positioned as a student at City Jobs, or a work team member at Teamco, indexed participants in certain ways and afforded them differing experiences of job skill acquisition. From such a perspective, identities allow the possibility of agency or the capacity to direct or influence one's own behavior and life path (cf. de Certeau, 1984; Holland *et al.*, 1998).

Throughout our research and analysis, we saw identities enacted most intensely during performative moments (Urciuoli, 1995; see also Hull *et al.*, forthcoming). On these occasions participants were called upon to publicly perform or enact an identity for an audience, including, for example, certain classroom or workplace presentations, graduation speeches, or other ceremonies. Lastly, identities are always influenced by and enacted in, across, and against particular places, spaces, and landscapes (cf. Mitchell, 2002; Soja, 1996). Thus, we turn below first to the workplace (Teamco), and then to the job training program (City Jobs), the local contexts within which adult students attempted to enact new selves.

Workplace training: issues at Teamco

The data reported in this section come from a larger ethnographic study (Hull *et al.*, 1996) of two circuit board assembly factories over a four-year period. In this study, we hoped to develop a view of how workplaces were changing under the pressures of global competition by examining the textual practices that play such a prominent role in the new work. At issue here was a new conceptualization of literacy, one that went beyond a notion of basic skills to incorporate something of the "higher order" thinking processes that many people believed then and still assert are at the heart of transformed workplaces and successful competition in a globalized world (Barton, 2000). "Is there a new literacy in new workplaces," we wanted to ask, "and if there is, how can we describe it, and how can workers best acquire it?" Further, we learned from this research that the project of creating new capitalist workplaces also requires shaping workers' identities; that language and literacy practices are intimately connected both with the work of such factories and with shaping workers' identities; and that adult workers exhibit a range of responses to attempts to shape their identities and attendant literacies.

Teamco had embarked on a quality enhancement program centered on self-directed work teams. In this form of work organization, we found that literacy saturated the world of electronics assembly, that there was a vastly increased demand that workers at all levels be able to deal with alphabetic texts and other forms of representations during their shifts, and that not only supervisors but all workers were required to monitor productivity and quality through detailed record-keeping and data analysis. For example, workers on the manufacturing floor were expected to physically manipulate circuit boards and sometimes manually affix components to the boards, but they were also increasingly asked to operate and monitor robots that did this work more efficiently and accurately than humanly possible.

At the same time, as this work began to be mediated by literacy in quite fundamental ways, workers increasingly came to be judged in light of their performance around literacy and language-saturated activities. Our research eventually identified over 80 categories of literate activity among front-line workers, which we divided into seven overall groupings. These categories greatly extended the usual notions of basic skills as decoding or encoding simple texts (see Hull, 1999). Another remarkable finding, given the tenor of the times in the mid-1990s, was that despite the fact that the workforce was comprised mostly of recent immigrants, many of whom were still learning English or settling into the country, these adults were able to manage the massive, complex, multimodal and multi-representational literate demands of their work. They were able to do so in large part because they worked in teams, due both to the new organizational structure of the company, and the informal ethnic networks that existed throughout the shop floor.

In fact, the most important variant in terms of workers' engagement with the new culture of teams, teamwork, problem-solving, and paperwork had to do, not with literacy per se, but with accepting or rejecting the working identities being promoted by the company. It has become almost a commonplace to say that producing and regulating identities is a major aim for today's global companies (cf. Carnoy and Castells, 2001), and that, more than ever before, workplaces influence the social identities that workers develop. We found this to be the case, but also found much variation in workers' responses to their company's notion of an ideal worker as a self-directed team-player, a problem-solver, and a symbol analyst. Some rejected or ignored the model, others embraced it, and still others turned it to their own purposes; these responses of course also influenced workers' engagement with literacy practices (cf. Hull, 2002). We in fact identified several categories of engagement and identification in relation to the company's model of an ideal worker. These ranged from "unengaged and unidentified," to "engaged and resistant," to "engaged and transformative," to "engaged and identified." Here we will briefly illustrate one end of the spectrum, "unengaged and unidentified," by introducing Loi, who rejected the notion of teamwork. A Vietnamese woman in her 50's, she had been in the United States five years at the time of our interviews with her.

In one particular interview (conducted in Vietnamese by a member of our research team who was fluent in the language), Loi initially adopted the party line regarding self-directed work teams (SDWTs), claiming teams were good not only for the product, but also for the company and "for everyone." Asked whether she saw any drawbacks in the program, she offered an interesting hedge: "No … but there *could* be." Then, after again stating that she had no opinions on SDWTs or the classes that workers were required to take in order to learn what the company described as the principles of teamwork (e.g., accepting change), she offered an account of *other* people's opinions:

> The majority, most of the workers here don't like "SDWT." "They, they look like Communist. Yeah, they look like" – All – most the people say like that. A majority, the great majority, everywhere, in every building I hear the same thing. Study, making them study is an act of extreme pressure, forcing them to study. They study because they are forced to. They don't like it. So they don't think it is something they should put any effort into.

She added that this forced "studying" was nothing new, that her co-workers had already experienced this in Vietnam, and "because of fear of communists they ran over here," only to meet up in the workplace with what seemed to her to be the Viet Cong's teacher.

Loi's history as an immigrant from Vietnam who had negative experiences with communism and attendant ideas of collective study and work clearly shaped her present notion of being a worker at Teamco. Loi, then, represented a segment of workers at Teamco who, for a variety of reasons, distanced themselves from the identity of self-directed worker and therefore took part in team-related and literacy-intensive activities only peripherally. She steeled herself against participating in anything that would in any way compromise her view of herself as a person free from imposed ideologies. Certainly, some of her co-workers were enthusiastic about the self-directed work teams, but Loi's silence and marginal participation in team meetings were often taken by supervisors and team coordinators as a sign that she and other reticent and disengaged teammates had not "grasped" the concept of teams due to their lack of formal education.

Vocational training programs: issues at City Jobs

Having observed the sometimes brutal working conditions of high-pressure entry-level work in the electronics industry, we searched for exemplary vocational programs, and we turned up several that promised to train low-income residents of Oakland, just 30 miles away from the Silicon Valley, for high tech, high-paying jobs. City Jobs, the program we chose to study, had a social justice focus and represented itself as helping to "close the digital divide." Through intensive technical training and also regular instruction in what were called "life skills," City Jobs intended to prepare economically disenfranchised area residents to become IT (information technology) technicians, computer professionals who would then be able to give back to the community.

The data referred to in this section came from 18 months of fieldwork at City Jobs, primarily participant observation and interviews (see Hull *et al.* forthcoming). From this research we learned that vocational programs, like new capitalist workplaces, also focus on shaping workers' identities as much as they focus on imparting skills and knowledge. Students in these programs, like their counterparts in the workplaces we studied, had a range of responses to these attempts to shape particular selves. Again, as at Teamco, language and literacy practices were integral parts of the vocational curriculum, even when not acknowledged. Last, adult students attended the vocational program for a range of reasons, only some of which converged with the goals of the program. While the program marshaled a range of helpful experiences and resources for participants, the job-training enterprise was also fraught with unexpected tensions, complexities, and obstacles, many of them connected to issues of identity and representation.

The first finding we discuss here is that contradictory conceptions of students resulted in mixed messages about identity and development. On the one hand, for example, students were told by Ken, the charismatic founder and director of City Jobs, that they were "all geniuses" in at least one thing, and possibly two, and that the challenge was to figure out what these things were. Yet, in the course of our data analysis, we found seven times as many negative labels for students, and comments about them, as positive labels. Promotional flyers characterized the students whom City Jobs wanted to serve as "under-skilled," "poverty-level," "disadvantaged," "at-risk," "welfare-based," "unemployed," and "low-income." In speeches, promotional materials, and in conversations with visitors to the program, Ken often described his students by singling out characteristics and circumstances that focused on their needs. He mentioned, for example, that most had never left the neighborhood even to go across the Bay to San Francisco, while others were orphans or had criminal records, and most had few "options."

The director positioned himself and his program as offering strategies, knowledge, and skills that would make change possible for students. A central text in this enterprise was Stephen R. Covey's popular book, *Seven Habits of Highly Effective People* (1990), which offered "insights about adapting to personal and professional change" as well as ways to change "self-defeating behaviors". A second contradictory discourse arose from the tension between the stated social justice goals of the program and the capitalist-centered texts and autobiographies students were asked to read and study. Several students braced against the push to develop such identities, and eventually began to voice their skepticism about Ken's belief in them and also about the impact of City Jobs on their futures.

Our second finding was the mismatch between the literate demands of IT training and participants' notions of what the work would be like. City Jobs focused on technical training, knowledge, and applied skills, but most of what had to be learned was mediated by print. Ken and the directors and teachers of other technical job training centers were worried about the literacy demands from the start; they saw reading as a real hurdle in a technical curriculum offered to students who, according to Ken, read on average at a seventh grade level. One frustrated instructor remarked that in the IT world, "there's just no way around it. You just have GOT to read." She went on to explain that the technical manuals were dry and dense, and that the certification testing targeted "college educated and self-motivated people."

Except for the small bit of help we provided or marshaled on how to read the real texts (our recommendation, in lieu of Ken's proposed strategy of simplifying the texts), students were left to swim on their own. Most seemed to accept the reading and the technical tomes as part of the IT world, but for many students, the text-saturated nature of the program was a big disappointment. In one student's memorable words: "It ain't what I thought it was gonna be. It's just a whole bunch of protocols and definitions to me ... I thought we was gonna be fixing viruses and stuff like that. It's still the same paper and pencil stuff." It is not surprising, then, that at the end of the program, although almost all of the students felt more confident around computer hardware and software, 90 percent were not able to pass the literacy-laden certification tests that are the coin of the realm in the IT world.

A third finding speaks to the ways in which participants accepted, rejected, modified, and ultimately made their own the notions of being a good worker that were promoted in the program. To illustrate this identity construction process, we'll introduce one of the students, Amy, an African-American woman who began the program enthusiastically, hoping to get in on the "dot.com" phenomenon. Initially, she eagerly adopted the philosophies of work and workers promoted in the program, including the *Seven Habits*. However, by mid-program, the heavy workload, dissatisfactions with the curriculum, and a growing suspicion that there would not be high-paying jobs at the end of the line all began to take their toll. Amy had trouble picking up the discourse of the program. She inferred that learning the "lingo," as she put it, was more difficult for her because she was a woman, since she saw some men in the program talk the talk more easily.

Amy's deep desire to enter the field was not enough, and as the months progressed and the technical curriculum grew increasingly more complex, we observed a decline in her self-confidence and in her hopes for passing the technical certification tests. "At first I *expected* to pass the tests," she told us, "Now I'm just hoping I *might* be able to pass them." Though she continued to want a job in the industry, she was timid about applying, fearing she did not have the skills. At the graduation, Amy produced her own version of the *Seven Habits*; "Habit #5 was 'teach yourself to read'," she intoned. And then she paused for this punch line: "Teach yourself to read so you can understand why you're not employed!" Despite her sarcasm, Amy remained positive about her experience at City Jobs, even though she did not enter the IT field but moved instead to working toward a teaching credential in elementary education.

Conclusion: identity and literacy development across contexts

Our work has highlighted the centrality of identity as a construct for thinking about adult students. We have illustrated how certain identities recruit certain literacy practices, and conversely, how certain literacy practices in tandem with new technologies can recruit especially powerful representations of self, which may in turn guide actions and behaviors. At Teamco, for instance, particular literacies were required and resisted in various conditions. Our findings from the Teamco site are also a reminder of the ways in which much work, even at the entry level, now has a literate overlay. Finally, the Silicon Valley study, like other research that has examined entry-level positions firsthand (cf. Gowen, 1993), brings home the extreme economic struggles of people who must start out at this level.

Particular notions of self as workers, people, and citizens were promoted at City Jobs as well as at Teamco, and at both sites students did not adopt the promoted versions of who they might become, but seemed to try them on for size and then reject or rework them as they were able. At City Jobs, proficiency in certain kinds of literacy practices, though assumed by the program and necessary for IT certification, did not enter into most students' notions of themselves as workers at all, and were not a regular part of the curriculum.

To attempt to bring identity development as the fostering of possible selves into the arena of adult education and adult literacy is a large task, when in the US there has been a huge investment in instrumental skills that can be measured and that lead toward recognizable valued outcomes, like GEDs, TABE scores, or some indicator of workplace readiness (Belzer and St. Clair, 2003). How might we measure and report, not to mention explain the importance of, changes in understandings of self? Yet to ignore adults' identity projects, their attempts to fashion a self that they view as possible and desirable, is to risk losing their engagement in both school and work, a truth that many adult literacy educators have known all along. There is no better time, as the field moves toward more narrow understandings of literacy, teaching, and learning, to find individual and collective ways to go against the grain. After all, that is what our adult students do as they find their ways to our classes again and again despite great odds.

References

Barton, P. (2000) *What jobs require: Literacy, Education, and Training, 1940–2006.* Policy Information Report. Princeton, NJ: Educational Testing System.

Belzer, A. and St. Clair, R. (2003) *Opportunities and Limits: An Update on Adult Literacy Education.* Columbus, OH: Center on Education and Training for Employment.

Bruner, J. (1994) 'The remembered self', in U. Neisser and R. Fivush (eds) *The Remembering Self: Construction and Agency in Self Narrative.* Cambridge: Cambridge University Press.

Carnoy, M. and Castells, M. (2001) 'Globalization, the knowledge society, and the network state: Poulantzas at the millennium', *Global Networks,* 1(1): 1–18.

Cole, M. (1996) *Cultural Psychology: A Once and Future Discipline.* Cambridge, MA: Harvard University Press.

Covey, S.R. (1989) *Seven Habits of Highly Effective People.* New York: Simon & Schuster.

De Certeau, M. (1984) *The Practice of Everyday Life.* Berkeley, CA: University of California Press.

Eisenhart, M. (1995) 'The fax, the jazz player, and the self-story teller: how *do* people organize culture?', *Anthropology and Education Quarterly,* 26(1): 3–26.

Giddens, A. (1991). *Modernity and Self-identity: Self and Society in the Late Modern Age.* Cambridge: Polity Press.

Goffman, I. (1959) *The Presentation of Self in Everyday Life.* New York: Doubleday.

Gowen, S. (1993) *The Politics of Workplace Literacy.* New York: Teachers College Press.

Greene, M. (1990) 'Revision and interpretation: opening spaces for the second chance', in D. Inbar (ed.) *Second Chance in Education.* London: Falmer Press.

Grubb, N. and Kalman, J. (1994) 'Relearning to earn: the role of remediation in vocational education and job training', *American Journal of Education,* 103(1): 54–93.

Hall, S. (1996) 'Introduction: who needs identity?', in S. Hall and P. du Gay (eds) *Questions of Cultural Identity.* London: Sage.

Holland, D., Lachicotte Jr, W., Skinner, D. and Cain, C. (1998) *Identity and Agency in Cultural Worlds.* Cambridge, MA: Harvard University Press.

Hull, G. (1993) 'Hearing other voices: a critical assessment of popular views on literacy and work', *Harvard Educational Review,* 63(1): 20–49.

Hull, G. (1999) 'What's in a label? Complicating notions of the skills-poor worker', *Written Communication,* 16(4): 379–411.

Hull, G. (2002) 'Enacting a self', in J. Searle and D. Roebuck (eds) *Envisioning Practice: Implementing Change.* Proceedings of the 10th Annual International Conference on Post-compulsory Education and Training. Brisbane: Australian Academic Press.

Hull, G., Jury, M., Ziv, O. and Katz, M. (1996) *Changing Work, Changing Literacy? A Study of Skill Requirements and Development in a Traditional and Restructured Workplace.* University of California, Berkeley: National Center for Research in Vocational Education and National Center for Study of Writing and Literacy.

Hull, G., Jury, M. and J. Zacher (forthcoming) 'Possible selves: literacy, identity, and development in work, school, and community', in A. Belzer (ed.) *Quality in Adult Basic Education: Issues and Challenges.* Mahwah, NJ: Lawrence Erlbaum. Publication expected in 2006.

Inbar, D.E. (1990) 'Introduction: the legitimation of a second chance', in D.E. Inbar (ed.) *Second Chance in Education.* London: Falmer Press.

Lafer, G. (2002) *The Job Training Charade.* Ithaca, NY: Cornell University Press.

Lave, J. and Wenger, E. (1991) *Situated Learning: Legitimate Peripheral Participation.* Cambridge: Cambridge University Press.

Mitchell, W.J.T. (2002) 'Space, place, and landscape', in W.J.T. Mitchell (ed.) *Landscape and Power*, second edition. Chicago, IL: University of Chicago Press.

Oakes, J. (1986) *Keeping Track: How Schools Structure Inequality.* New Haven, CT: Yale University Press.

Ochs, E. and Capps, L. (2001) *Living Narrative: Creating Lives in Everyday Storytelling.* Cambridge, MA: Harvard University Press.

Perrow, M.E. (2000) 'Learning in transition: youth development in post-apartheid South Africa'. Unpublished Doctoral Dissertation, University of California, Berkeley.

Porter, K., Cuban, S., Comings, J. and Chase, V. (2005) *"One day I will make it": A Study of Adult Student Persistence in Library Literacy Programs*, NCSALL Report. New York: MDRC.

Rose, M. (2005) *The Mind at Work: Valuing the Intelligence of the American Worker.* New York: Penguin Books.

Soja, E.W. (1996) *Thirdspace: Journeys to Los Angeles and Other Real – and Imagined – Places.* Malden, MA: Blackwell Publishers.

Urciuoli, B. (1995) 'The indexical structure of visibility', in B. Farnell (ed.) *Human Action Signs in Cultural Context.* Lanham, MD: Scarecrow Press.

Varenne, H. and McDermott R. (1998) *Successful Failure: The Schools America Builds.* Boulder, CO: Westview Press.

Vygotsky, L. (1978) *Mind in Society: The Development of Higher Psychological Processes.* Cambridge, MA: Harvard University Press.

Wenger, E. (1998) *Communities of Practice: Learning, Meaning, and Identity.* Cambridge: Cambridge University Press.

Zacher, J. (forthcoming) 'Social hierarchies and identity politics: what a Bourdieuian analysis adds to our understanding of literacy practices and multicultural curricula', in A. Luke and J. Albright (eds) *Bourdieu and Literacy Education.* Mahwah, NJ: Lawrence Erlbaum.

17 The power and price of English

Educating Nepalese people for the global workforce

Ram Ashish Giri

Nepal has been contributing to the global workforce since the treaty with the British East India Company in 1815, when recruitment began of selected Nepali youth to serve in British and Indian regiments around the world. In recent times, Nepal's contribution to the global marketplace in industries such as world tourism and hospitality, as well as to the workforce of the world and to regional bodies, has been significantly lauded. The mix and level of knowledge and skills required to be a functional member of a global workforce will differ from industry to industry. However, workers need to have the ability to integrate and apply their academic, technical and practical knowledge and good communication skills to interact and work cooperatively within global teams. While the place of English in educating Nepalese for the global market place is undeniable, there are a number of challenges, and a debate about the controversial role of English in the Nepalese community. This chapter explores from a language education, particularly English language education (ELE) perspective, some of the challenges facing global workforce education at the policy, culture and education levels. In Nepal, as ELE embraces the sustainability agenda, the great culture divide it creates has received a lot of attention especially in the wake of recent political conflict. The chapter analyses the impact of the emerging policy dimension to the role of English in educating Nepalese for tomorrow's market place.

Introduction

What we earn depends on what we learn.

>   (Bill Clinton, quoted in Tye and Tye 1992)

Reports on Nepali education, particularly English language education (ELE), have mainly blamed the Rana regime (1846–1950 AD) for the way they introduced the English language to Nepal, for keeping it exclusively for themselves for so long, and for depriving the average Nepali of its benefits. A number of articles, especially in the last three decades, have criticised the controversial segregative role English has played in the Nepalese community in favour of the ruling elites and the hegemonic control it has provided for them over Nepalese society in general and education in particular. I do not dispute the malevolence of their restrictive ELE policy, nor do I support the control they exercised over education, but these reports, by either fault-finding or criticising the much-condemned autocratic regime for their restrictive ELE policy, are either naïve or inaccurate. I argue that the so-called "democratic" governments have not done much for educational development either. The system of education, for example, remains to date as old-fashioned, product- or knowledge-based, teacher-centred and examination-dominated as it was some 50 years ago. The concept of educational development, in the modern sense of the term, did not exist then, nor does it exist now. It is high time Nepalese academia stopped blaming the Rana regime or the governments thereafter, broke through the (internal) colonial mentality or the infrastructure of the arrogant eliticism, and worked towards developing an educational system which is based on the social, economic and occupational demands of the nation and the region.

Education is a reflection of social, political and linguistic realities. Relative to time, the model of education adopted in Nepal, for example, either is an instrument of caste or class survival or exhibits subservience to the political will. Language choice is also appropriated to either endorse the inherited model or perpetuate existing choices.

The advantage English language education exerts on Nepal is widely accepted. All sections of the population, for example, are keen to send their children, despite their exorbitant fees, to any school promising education in English. The virtues of English and its contribution to socio-economic and educational progress have been perceived differently by different sections of population. While its role in educational quality and economic progress is indisputably perceived to be instrumental, it is also considered as a barrier to social progress and equitable economic development.

How does Nepal educate its people for the global industries? What knowledge and skills are paramount for them? What role does English play in their education? What challenges or threats does it pose to the Nepali community? What implication does it have on ELE in Nepal? These are some of the questions this chapter attempts to answer.

Historical context

It is not certain when English was adopted in Nepal. Seventeenth-century Malla kings, who had elaborate trading arrangements with Tibet and North India, were believed to have literacy in English (Pradhan 1982, Awasthi 1995) and used it as a lingua franca to carry out their transactions (Morris 1963). Similarly, European missions, founded in the late seventeenth century and early eighteenth century, trained Nepalis to assist with their activities. This was the beginning of English as the language of workforce education, though at a miniscule level. A landmark in this direction was the commencement of recruitment of Gurkha soldiers as a part of the famous Sugauli Treaty in 1815. Education of the Gurkha soldiers, who served in large numbers in the First and Second World Wars in several Asian, Middle East and European countries, took place in the medium of English. Two centuries later, the recruitment of the Gurkhas continues but with one basic difference. Functional ability in English used to be developed after their selection. It is a pre-condition and an important selection criterion now.

ELE took a different approach when Jung Bahadur Rana, the first Rana Prime Minister, visited Britain in 1950 where he learned amongst many other things the power of language and its ability to create superiority. The Ranas already believed that they were a superior race and the one destined to rule. English became the quintessence of their supremacy (Stiller 1993: 84). Upon Jung Bahadur's return, he ordered that Rana children be taught English. An exclusive English medium school was set up in Kathmandu in which children of the ruling elites received ELE. English soon became the symbol of status, power and privileges, and a means to segregate people between the rulers and the ruled. In the next 100 or so years, the Ranas used ELE as a strategy to strengthen the power structure by maintaining the caste-/class-based population. Some 16 decades later on, the division between the rulers and the ruled continues and ELE is playing a major role in it.

English in Nepalese workforce education

English was unfortunately not adopted as an instrument for development in workforce education. In the Nepali education system, it was in fact used as a tool to create a class of home-grown educated workforce who would in turn use its power to dominate, segregate and govern.

The first schools and colleges established at the beginning of the twentieth century were affiliated to and followed the education system of British India which was based on the Macaulian pattern of education which emphasised English education to form a class of persons who believed in and/or supported the superiority of race (Shrestha 1983, Di Bona 1989). The graduates of these initial schools, anglophiles in their taste and attitude, held important positions in most service sectors. English, as their preferred means of communication, became an important part of their power and superiority.

Planning workforce education involves a number of steps – to identify areas of demand of workforce in various employment sectors nationally as well as regionally; to specify required communicative and work skills and knowledge of the fields and accordingly develop educational and training packages; to develop infrastructure with adequate expertise and training facilities; to set up a mechanism for the promotion and mobilisation of workforce; and finally, to keep the workforce up-to-date with the recent trends and development in the areas of their employment. However, modern Nepal has remained entangled in decades of educational experimentations and is yet to fully realise these steps and found a system of workforce education which would adequately contribute to the national as well as regional demands of the workforce.

Under pressure from rapid development and modernisation elsewhere, a modest effort in formal workforce education in Nepal began in the final years of the Rana regime with the establishment of a technical training school in 1942 and introduction of what was called 'the basic education' in 1947. The aim of these schools was to provide vocational and technical training to graduates who would fulfil the need of low-level workforce in the development sectors. However, due to resentment from the urban elites, these schools were later converted into 'English schools'. The elites protested the nature of education in these schools which they said 'hindered academic development of their children' (Manandhar 1990: 37).

In the post-Rana period, acute shortage of workforce was the main obstacle to the national development. Consequently, secondary level vocational education was considered to be the best way to involve the local population in the national development. Following the recommendations of the National Education Planning Commission (1954), the first multi-purpose high school was set up in Pokhara, 200 km west of the capital city of Kathmandu. By the end of 1970, 29 multipurpose schools for agriculture, trade and industry, secretarial science, education, and home science had been established in various parts of the country. The type of vocational courses offered at a given school depended upon the needs of the local community. Though vocational education was a viable means of providing the local population with necessary developmental skills, its use on a national scale was not considered seriously. And due to the lack of financial resources, required expertise, infrastructure and above all a sustainable long-term approach to workforce education, these multi-purpose schools were abolished with the introduction of the New Education System Plan (NESP) in 1971.

The NESP (1971–75) adopted a pyramid structure of workforce education which consisted of basic level workforce at the bottom of the structure climbing upward with middle level workforce, high level workforce and specialised/research level workforce at the top. Government departments, such as the National Vocational Training Centre and the Centre for Technical Education and Vocational Training, educated the basic level workforce in areas such as mechanics, agriculture, nursing, health and cottage industry, whereas the middle and higher level workforce (such as Engineering, Science and Technology, Forestry, Agriculture, Commerce and Education) was produced by the institutes affiliated to Tribhuvan University.

The NESP downplayed the importance of English in developing the workforce. As a result, workforce education suffered a serious quality set back and has been struggling to revive ever since. The political instability of the post-NESP period, and the recent political turmoil has crippled the development process. As a consequence, social issues such as education have remained unattended. This, however, has created an opportunity for the private sector to set up and operate workforce education institutes with English as a lingua franca.

To sum up, given the strategic geographic location, scenic attraction and tremendous interest of the international community, Nepal could have easily been developed as a hub of regional/global diplomacy, economic and educational activities. Global workforce education with English as its lingua franca could have been given priority. This could have played a prominent role in the development of tourism and hospitality, travel and transportation, health resorts and health farms, regional and international diplomacy. However, development and modernisation have remained stagnant and as a consequence, global workforce education, except for a few private institutes, has not prospered as expected.

English as a language in workforce education

English as a language of workforce education is accorded a high place in Nepali education. However, ELE is treated differentially in the two different school systems. Quality ELE, even in the twenty-first century, remains inaccessible to most people.

Upon the abolition of the Rana regime through a popular movement in 1950, Nepal embarked on experimentation with political democracy and planned formal education. Planning fell into the hands of a few anglophiles and elites educated in English medium 'westernised' schools, who, because of their hierarchical neo-colonial background, made a conspiratorial choice of educational goals and approaches which strengthened their social hierarchy and maintained their status quo (Shrestha 1983).

As a direct consequence of this planned inequality (Tollefson 1991), discrepancies in the quality of ELE in urban elite schools and other schools persisted. The deteriorating state of ELE in the public schools created a congenial opportunity for Nepali anglophiles to set up a private school system. In this way a dual system of public vernacular Nepali medium schools and private English medium schools emerged, which has created two-tier citizenship in the country, perpetuating already existing class-divisions and power structure.

Henceforth, the government and educational planners have included English in the educational curricula as a compulsory subject without giving much thought to what repercussions it might have for a mostly illiterate population or what role it could play in enhancing the development process. Despite the fact that English was accorded a high place in education (25 per cent of total curricular weightage) and was recognised as the most important means to learning, considerations about its role and status took a back seat in the planning process because governments in the post-Rana period either deliberately ignored it or remained engaged on other issues. Quality ELE, as a result of this, remains inaccessible to most people. Planned and functional workforce education, therefore, became an illusion for the average Nepalese people.

English as a language of education

The pattern of education in Nepal when it commenced in the nineteenth century was, as can be deciphered from the discussion above, essentially that of the British schools in India. Therefore, the medium of instruction as well as of examination was English until the 1971 reform. Even after the establishment of the School Leaving Certificate (SLC) board in 1933, English remained compulsory as a medium of instruction as well as of examination.

In the wake of Nepali becoming the national language in the 1950s, the question of medium of instruction in education remained controversial. A survey conducted by the first National Education Planning Commission in 1954 revealed that on average, nearly half of Nepal's population wanted English to remain as the medium of instruction. Throughout the 1950s and 1960s English remained the language voluntarily opted for by SLC candidates as a medium of instruction and examination (Sonntag 1980). Similarly, Subba (1980), conducting a survey at the higher education level almost 30 years after the first survey, revealed findings that 'English is the preferred medium of instruction in most disciplines at Tribhuvan University'. She also claimed that even after the 1971 reform, during which English was replaced as the medium of instruction in most subjects, it remained as the most preferred language in education (ibid: 86), especially at the higher level.

In the twenty-first century, English is the only medium of instruction in most private schools and colleges (about 8,500 of them) and it alternates with Nepali in most urban public schools. It remains as the only language of information at all levels of education. This is because knowledge of English is viewed as critical to professional and vocational success for individuals and for Nepal as a whole.

English is a vital part of mother-tongue education. A number of mother-tongue schools have been set up throughout the country the purpose of which is to provide early primary education in the language of the local community and to promote their language and culture. However, parents, realising that the local languages do not have the same value for employment, trade and education as English, demand that English be included in the curriculum right from the initial years of education. Most mother-tongue schools, therefore, offer English from Year One to attract enrolment. English has thus become indispensable in the Nepalese education: without it education in the first language is neither possible nor practical (Eagle 2000).

The previous sections illustrate that English is a lingua franca and the core of education at all levels. In private schools and colleges, it is the only medium of instruction. It is the second language in major disciplines of higher education. The sections also indicate the choice of English as the preferred means of education and that the decision to keep it to urban elite schools might have been deliberately made with a view to creating a division in the Nepalese population.

English as a lingua franca outside formal education

Outside formal education, the situation is not much different. English is the second most used and sought after language in the media, academic activities, libraries, administration, diplomacy and business, higher-level academic and research activities, economy and white-collar professions (Dahal 2000). English has always been an important part of the Nepali media. In recent years, it has become the dominant language in print and electronic media, television and radio. It is estimated that materials or programmes in English occupy more than 20 per cent of all media space and time. According to Verma (1996), about 25 per cent of daily newspapers are English newspapers. Similarly, public and private radio stations as well as TV channels devote a significant amount of time to programmes in English.

A new breed of people has emerged because of English, people with a new culture; a culture of reading, viewing and appreciating English. Subscribing to English media does not only indicate economic prosperity, it also denotes modernity and high social status. In Nepalese society, English has a prominent place. Apart from being a 'prestige' language and status symbol, it has also become a basis of upward social mobility. As such, as the quotations below suggest, it enjoys a special status in all aspects of social life:

> English is the second most widespread language in Nepal in terms of popularity, education, and use. It is spoken at all socio-economic levels, by both literate and non-literate people.
>
> (Eagle 2000)

> In Nepalese context, English functions as the language of prestige …
> [and] a means of upward mobility.
>
> (Yadava 2005: 157)

English has become synonymous with being 'educated'. Parents, who are illiterate, take pride in listening to their children chant the English alphabet or recite rhymes and songs in English. People with proficiency in English are perceived to be cultured, civilised and modern. Those who lack it are 'backward'.

At the regional and global levels, English is the only language of communication. Only a handful of Nepalis (just over 1,000 of them; CBS 2002) speak English as their first language. However, a large number of people speak it at their educational institutions and workplaces. High ranking officers of the army and police, teachers and staff of private schools/colleges, doctors and engineers, use English for their professional interactions. Similarly, people working for national and international banks, business enterprises, international organisations and diplomatic agencies speak English. Communication in most prominent hotels in most urban cities of Nepal is carried out in English. Supporting the view that it is fast becoming an alternate language of communication, Greenbaum (1996) finds that:

> in the last few decades, English has been filling at least some of the functions of a second language in a country that has several indigenous languages.
>
> (Greenbaum 1996: 242–3)

English has thus become the language of employment, professional development and economic success. Ability to speak/use English helps with educational, socio-economic and professional gains. It provides access to world expertise and open information. English has become a lingua franca in most crucial sectors to the point that any educated Nepali is, in a real sense, deprived of all sorts of opportunities if he or she does not know English. English in Nepal, as in the global world today, has become synonymous with the development of critical sectors. It supports political, economic, military and linguistic development (Khaniya 1990) and functions as an instrument for the nation's empowerment and modernisation (Subba 1980). Lack of it means isolation, less competitiveness and less educational advancement.

Even buffaloes speak English

Perhaps the most illustrious contribution English has made to a development sector of Nepal is to the tourism industry. In tourism, the largest industry in terms of foreign currency earning and employment, English functions as its backbone as well as a liberator or equaliser for the people involved. In the tourist resort of Pokhara (especially lakeside Pokhara), as in many other tourist centres, people sometimes joke that 'even the buffaloes there speak English'. Of course the saying in itself means nothing. However, it is indicative of how English has broken all barriers (castes and classes) in this community and how it has played a constructive role in the lives of all concerned. In the administrative hierarchy of tourism, people are placed according to their ability, experience in the field and knowledge of English as its lingua franca regardless of their caste or class background.

English for survival in the global workforce market

It is a fact that English provides a socio-political and economic competitive edge. More and more countries in Asia today are adopting and even stressing ELE in order to remain or become dominant in their neighbourhood or to have a competitive advantage over their neighbours. In South Asia, English was originally adopted as a political manipulation. However, it has become an economic necessity for most countries today. At an intra-national level, for example, in the northern states of India that are socio-politically and economically behind the rest of the country and where the status of English has been fiercely debated at times, English is back on the agenda in recent years, as they want to catch up with the rest of the Indian states. At the regional level, globalisation and, therefore, global English as political and economic terms, develop from below rather than from above for English is not only the language of technological, economic and educational resource, it is also the language of preference as well as of resistance. In other countries of the region, however, globalisation has been inflicted from above, so that global English, as a political weapon, supports the ruling elites' hegemonic control of the process (Sonntag 2003). India is, thus, in an advantageous situation and, therefore, has a competitive edge so far as the status and role of English as the language of global workforce education is concerned, as desire and motivation for ELE comes from the grassroots level.

In Nepal, however, a mixture of globalisation-from-above and globalisation-from-below can be seen operating, especially in recent years. As discussed earlier, globalisation of workforce and practice of English in global education was adopted as a top-down process. While it has a class implication and therefore a basis of elitism, English in global workforce education can be seen as a result of the standard and quality of the global workforce as perceived by the global workforce education agencies in Nepal. English in this sense is considered as an economic liberator or equity provider rather than an enslaver.

Nepal never has been and is unlikely to be, not in the foreseeable future anyway, a competitor in economic terms in the region. However, it does aspire to rise from the status of one of the poorest nations of the region, or of the world for that matter, to become comparable to any emerging nation. It also aspires to modernise its educational and developmental practices. Therefore, the workforce it produces is crucial for what it can achieve from them. One of its aspirations is to produce a quality workforce for intra-national, regional and global marketplaces. Today, Nepal not only contributes to the demand for national and regional workforces, but it also supplies a skilled and semi-skilled workforce to car manufacturers in

Korea and Japan, the tourism and hospitality industry in North America and Europe, and to education, security and other trade organisations around the globe. The workforce working in these countries not only brings in much-needed economic gains, it also provides equally important exposure, experiences and expertise. English as the medium of training and a lingua franca of global workforce education is, therefore, more for Nepal's survival as a developing country than for its competitive edge in the region.

The global marketplace requires global knowledge

Though the concept of globalisation is not new, it has been a slow but inevitable process in global workforce education. It is a slow process because, in spite of the fact that national borders have become fluid, and economic models share similar basic orientations, the culture is yet to acquire a global dimension, and politics remains stubbornly local. It is an inevitable process because education demands changes and the changes that are taking place in education through the dramatic development in the information and communication technology cannot be prevented by local dimensions.

Workforce education trainees of the twenty-first century will face an altogether different world order when they graduate from their schools or institutes. They will deal with people from diverse ethnic, gender, linguistic, racial and socio-economic backgrounds. They will experience serious health problems, inequities among less-developed and more-developed nations, environmental deterioration, overpopulation, transnational migrations, ethnic nationalisation and the decline of nation-state. The new age will challenge their emotional, intellectual and physical well being. Global workforce education, then, has to free itself from the limitations of national and cultural dimensions and aim at equipping them with the attitudes, knowledge and skills they need to become competent, responsible and human citizens of their community, state, nation and the world. It will have to help them acquire the sensitivities, tolerance and respect for all human beings to live harmoniously in an independent world.

The epigraph of *'What we earn depends on what we learn'*, given in the beginning of the chapter captures the importance of the type of global workforce education required. Today's workforce education has to prepare all professionals with adequate knowledge of all sorts to deal with their involvement in the worldwide working systems. It requires five interdisciplinary dimensions:

- perspective consciousness (appreciation of other images, views, thinking, etc.),
- environmental awareness,

- cross-cultural awareness,
- systemic awareness (familiarity with local and international systems and how they link in patterns of interdependence), and
- awareness of options or choices.

The workforces of the world, no matter what field they work in, have become more mobile physically as well as electronically. A medical doctor trained in Nepal can work in an African country. Similarly, a mineworker from Africa can train and work in Nepal to dig or develop mineral projects. Being a member of a global workforce thus involves communicating his or her own point of view at the same time as being able to understand and appreciate others. The only way this has been possible is through English.

Education for the global workforce constitutes *'global literacy'*, *'global competencies'* or *'global skills'*. Global workforce education providers, therefore, apply a global approach to coaching and evaluating employees' performance. The slogan *'Think globally; act locally'* succinctly summarises their approach to workforce education. The global market and global workforce requires a lingua franca, and English has definitely assumed and established itself in that role already.

As a lingua franca of the global market, English is not only a marker of modernity, but it is also a guarantor of prosperity. As a consequence, countries like Nepal take extreme measures to ensure it is learned. They privilege ELE at the expense of other curricular areas. A good performance in English is an essential requirement for a place in the global workforce.

The price of English

Privileging English for workforce education has not always brought good results. Despite some positive outcomes, Nepal has paid a heavy price for it. The discussions above indicate that English has played a powerful role in Nepal. It has been the most popular language in education, the only means to the world body of knowledge, and a key to access electronic as well as printed information. It has played a significant role in modernising the developmental process in certain fields, especially tourism. It is because of English that the Nepalese people have been able to contribute to a number of important world fronts such as world peace and security, tourism and hospitality, and regional diplomacy.

The Nepalese people, however, have paid a heavy price for the benefits they have received from English. It has become an important means to colonialise the minds of millions of Nepalese, who for one reason or another do not have access to quality ELE. It has become a basis of power and privileges for a handful of the ruling elite who have used it to create a monopoly and status quo. English has thus become a cause of social division (Kerr 1999). That is to say, it has not united people for building the nation; rather it has divided them into the groups of rulers and the ruled. Therefore, it does not empower the average Nepali, rather it enslaves them.

The dominance of English, apart from creating divisions in the population, has also brought threats to local languages and cultures. As a consequence of the value added to English, most local languages and cultures are either dead or dying at an alarming rate. Attempts have been made in recent years to preserve some indigenous languages and cultures through the introduction of mother-tongue education at the primary level. However, because of the non-existence of a clear language policy at the government level, mother-tongue education has largely been a ritualistic exercise, and without the inclusion of English, it fails to attract enrolment.

The heaviest price the Nepalese people have paid is in the field of local language and culture. The perceived value of English, and its popularity in all aspects of Nepalese life, has been responsible for what may be termed 'cultural anarchism'. More importantly, as Malla (1968) observes below, it has divided the cultural mind of the Nepalese people:

> My first few books of initiation exposed me to a linguistic maze of emotionally unknown quantities. By the time I was learning to discover myself in this emotional maze, picking up a few clues here and a few clues there, a totally bewildering factor enters into the emotional landscape of my lonely childhood. This was English – the architect of my divided life.
>
> (Malla 1968: 243)

Over-emphasis on English right from the initial stage of education has displaced people emotionally as well as culturally. To quote Malla again:

> This was what in my time was called The First Book. ... The first sentence in the book was a potent magic incantation. Learning thereafter began with 'I go' = [ma janchhu]. An English word was equated with a Nepali word; an English sentence with a Nepali sentence. An emotionally unknown quantity was equated with another. But the present indefinite sentence, 'I go', was in itself symbolical. Since the day I learnt to recite that sentence in English, I have been 'going' – going further and further from where I began, from my home, my language, my culture, my land, from my roots, if you will. But whither?
>
> (Malla 1968: 244)

Conclusion

Despite the controversies surrounding it, ELE has already made its place in the Nepalese society and workforce education. As a lingua franca and a second language in several key sectors in Nepal's development, it has the potential of playing a constructive role in developing national, regional and global workforces. What is needed is careful planning, giving English its due recognition in national policies, allocating adequate resources and ensuring efficient implementation of policies.

English has power because it creates a 'culture of power'. Nepal, however, has paid a very high price for it. It is yet to be seen how and when Nepal bails itself out of the culture of power that English has inflicted upon it.

References

Awasthi, J.R. (1995) 'A Linguistic Analysis of Errors Committed by Nepali Learners of English'. Unpublished PhD Thesis. Department of Linguistics, University of Hyderabad.

CBS (2002) *Vital Statistics*. Kathmandu: Central Bureau of Statistics, HMG/Nepal.

Dahal, R.K. (2000) 'Language Politics of Nepal', *Contributions to Nepalese Studies*, 27(1): 155–90.

Di Bona, J. (1989) *Critical Perspectives on Indian Education*. New Delhi: Bahri Publications.

Eagle, S. (2000) 'The Language Situation in Nepal', in R.B. Baldauf and R.B. Kaplan (eds) *Language Planning in Nepal, Taiwan and Sweden*. Sydney: Multilingual Matters.

Greenbaum, S. (1996) 'Afterword', in R.J. Baumgardner (ed.) *South Asian English: Structure, Use and Users*. Chicago, IL: University of Illinois Press.

Kerr, R. F. (1999) 'Planning and Practice: Factors Impacting on the Development of Initial Education in Nepal with Special Reference to English Language Teaching'. Unpublished PhD Thesis. School of Education. Melbourne, Victoria University.

Khaniya, T.R. (1990) 'Examinations as Instruments for Educational Change: Investigating the Washback Effects of the Nepalese English Examinations'. Unpublished PhD Thesis. Edinburgh, University of Edinburgh.

Malla, K.P. (1968) *The Road to Nowhere*. Kathmandu: Shajha Prakashan.

Manandhar, T.B. (1990) *Educational Changes and Employment: Educational Development in Nepal*. Kathmandu: Ministry of Education, HMG Nepal: 33–71.

Morris, J. (1963) *A Winter in Nepal*. London: Rupert Hart Davies.

Pradhan, R. (1982) 'Pratap Malla's Inclination towards Arts, Music and Literature', *Centre for Nepal and Asian Studies (CNAS) Journal*, 9(2): 65–80.

Shrestha, R. (1983) 'English as a Second Language/English as a Foreign Language Distinction: Its pedagogy and the Nepalese Context', *Contributions to Nepalese Studies*, 11(1): 45–59.

Sonntag, S. (1980) 'Language Planning and Policy in Nepal. 48', *ITL: Review of Applied Linguistics*, 46: 71–92.

Sonntag, S. (2003) *The Local Politics of Global English: Case Studies in Linguistic Globalisation*. Oxford: Lexington Books.

Stiller, L.F. (1993) *Nepal: Growth of a Nation*. Kathmandu: Human Resource Development Research Centre.

Subba, S. (1980) 'The Medium Question in Nepalese Higher Education', *Contributions to Nepalese Studies*, 7(1–2): 71–95.

Tollefson, J.W. (1991) *Planning Language, Planning Inequality, Language Policy in the Community*. London: Longman.

Tye, B.B. and Tye, K.A. (1992) *Global Education: A Study of School Change*. New York: State University of New York Press.

Verma, Y.P. (1996) 'Some Features of Nepali Newspaper English', in R.J. Baumgardner (ed.) *South Asian English*. Chicago, IL: University of Illinois Press.

Yadava, Y. (2005) 'The Politics of Language Planning in Nepal's Multilingual Contexts: Its Implications for the Terai'. Paper presented to the Conference on Nepal Terai: Context and Possibilities. Kathmandu, Nepal, Social Science Baha and B.P. Koirala India–Nepal Foundation.

Part IV

Challenges for work-related education

18 Brain drain and the potential of professional diasporic networks

Fazal Rizvi

Brain drain has long been regarded as a major problem for the countries of the Global South, which has been compounded in recent years by the intense global competition for skilled labor. Various schemes designed to make 'staying at home' more attractive for skilled emigrants have failed to address the problem. Recognizing that in the era of globalization the prevention of the transnational mobility of skilled workers is neither possible nor desirable, a more radical alternative to the problem of brain drain has been proposed that relies heavily on the idea of 'diasporic networks'. This strategy is based on the assumption that recent developments in technology and globalization now make it possible for skilled workers to emigrate yet remain connected, through various networks, to their country of origin, and still make a contribution to its social and economic development. This chapter discusses this 'diaspora option', and asks to what extent it represents a way forward in arresting the brain drain problem. It argues that the potential of this policy option cannot be fully realized unless professional diaspora networks are underpinned by a range of support mechanisms in which education plays an important role in preparing people to develop the capacity for working in transnational spaces in ways that are both systematic and productive.

> The process that has come to be called 'globalization' is exposing a deep fault line between groups who have the skills and mobility to flourish in global markets and those who either don't have the advantages or perceive the expansion of unregulated markets as inimical to social stability and deeply held norms.
>
> (Rodrik 1997: 12)

In his eloquent statement, Rodrik suggests that the current dynamics of the global economy have accentuated the asymmetry between two categories of people: those who are highly skilled workers, who can take their skills where they are most wanted, and those for whom mobility is at best uncertain, elastic and often hazardous. This suggests that it is no longer useful to consider migration as a generalizable phenomenon. Patterns of transnational mobility vary considerably, and depend markedly on the changing nature of not only the skills of the people who wish to move but also the global labor market and the nature of work itself. Despite relatively free movement of capital, no country now welcomes mass migration, but insists on being highly selective. Unskilled migrants and refugees are discouraged, often in ways that are highly punitive, whereas 'business' migration is welcomed, especially in areas where there is a shortage of skills. Most of the OECD countries now have developed policies and programs to attract skilled workers, mainly from the developing countries (OECD 2001).

This has compounded the problem of 'brain drain' that the poorer countries of the Global South have long had to endure. International organizations such as International Labor Office and UNESCO are not unaware of this problem, and have proposed a range of policy solutions to address it. Their solutions have included bilateral agreements, tax schemes and other strategic investments to make 'staying at home' more attractive. But, realizing that such policy solutions do not always work, they now propose a more radical alternative that relies heavily on the idea of 'diasporic networks'. They suggest that developments in technology and globalization now make it possible for skilled workers to emigrate yet remain connected, through such networks, to their country of origin, and still make a contribution to its social and economic development. In this chapter, I want discuss the idea of professional diasporic networks, and ask to what extent these represent a way forward in arresting the problem of 'brain drain' from the Global South to the Global North. I want to argue that the potential of this policy option cannot be fully realized unless diaspora knowledge networks are underpinned by a range of support mechanisms, in which education plays an important role in preparing people to develop the capacity for working in transnational spaces in ways that are both systematic and productive.

Though a contested term, the idea of 'brain drain' is widely used to refer to a one-way flow of highly skilled people who move from their country of origin to another country, often in search of a better job, pay or living conditions. Scholars such as Salt (1997) argue that the term 'brain drain' has been used synonymously with the movement of human capital where the net flow of expertise is unidirectional rather than modal. According to Giannoccolo (2004), the use of the word 'brain' alludes to any skill, competency or attribute that is a prospective asset, whereas the word 'drain' refers to the intensity with which the most talented people leave their country of origin at a substantial rate to pursue their careers elsewhere.

For several decades now, brain drain has been viewed as an intractable problem undermining the developmental efforts of the poorer countries of the Global South. Many of these countries invest heavily in educating their citizens in anticipation of their support for development projects only to find that they are unable to prevent many of their skilled workers from pursuing professional careers abroad. Skilled workers leave 'home' for a wide variety of reasons, some personal and others professional, including the fact that the poorer countries often do not possess the physical or economic infrastructure in which graduates are able to use their skills and knowledge. It is estimated that about one-third of all scientists born and educated in Africa, for example, work in foreign laboratories, a massive drain on both talent and investment that poorer countries can ill afford (*Economist* 2002)

Various policies have been introduced by developing and developed countries alike to stem this flow, ranging from imposing strict restrictions on visas to offering attractive salaries to those prepared to return (see Johnson and Regets 1998). So far, however, they appear to have made relatively little impact, especially in the context of an intense global competition for skilled labor. It is now widely admitted that the global circulation of skilled workers cannot be prevented even if it were considered desirable. As a result, attention is now being paid to the ways in which this movement might be turned into a developing country's advantage. One of the more promising lines of thinking revolves around the idea of 'professional diasporic networks'.

The idea of 'professional diasporic networks' suggests the possibility of creating infrastructures around which emigrants are able to actively participate in the development of their country of origin without having to physically live there. Such an approach accepts that emigration of skilled workers, broadly defined as those in possession of a tertiary degree or extensive specialized work experience, is inevitable, but insists that the developing countries can nonetheless utilize their skills and knowledge. In this way, a 'professional diasporic network' emerges as an expression of a direct relationship between knowledge and development. International organizations, such as UNESCO, have accordingly promoted the creation of such networks, working with a new discourse of 'knowledge for development'.

To understand how this so-called 'diaspora option' (Meyer and Brown 2003) has become a realistic possibility, it is important to consider how the contemporary processes of globalization are transforming the traditional concepts of migrancy and transnationality. Indeed, several researchers (for example, Papastergiadis 2000) have pointed out that 'migration' may no longer be an accurate term to understand the mobility of skilled workers. This is so because migration has the connotations of permanency or long-term stay, whereas their movement tends today to be intermittent and short-term, and involves multiple points of identification. For many such workers, a single homeland can no longer be considered as the unique reference for defining their socio-cultural identity. Their identity now depends on how they view, maintain, activate and reproduce their relationship with their country of origin, conditioned by their use of new information and communication technologies and their transnational networks, both personal and professional.

One of the salient characteristics of the contemporary globalization processes is the intensification of the flows of capital, goods and services, as well as ideas, cultural symbols and people. As Castells (1999) argues, globalization has changed the spatial organization of the world from a 'space of places' to a 'space of flows.' These flows are mainly organized through networks of the most varied kinds, such as intergovernmental organizations (IGOs), transnational corporations, NGOs and diasporic communities (Held and McGrew 2000). It is with an understanding of these flows that we can begin to understand how economic, social and cultural relations associated with brain drain are assuming new forms and have varied outcomes, and therefore require new policy responses.

Global networks are facilitated mostly by the developments in transport and communication technologies that have engendered a 'much more compressed view of space and time' (Carnoy 2002: 3). Nowadays we can observe an increasing material integration of space obtained through rapid forms of mobility. These forms, both physical and virtual, bring 'different time zones together and connect them in real time' (Aneesh 2006). Furthermore, connections promote and strengthen social networks and eradicate barriers to international mobility. Thus, networks can be seen as catalysts in lowering the barriers as well as promoting the movement of highly skilled workers but still retaining the possibility of connections across national boundaries.

New transport and communication technologies not only foster the conditions for extensive migration, but also, and perhaps more importantly, 'allow the constitution of a production and management system spread all over the world yet working on real time and working as a unit through the combination of telecommunications, fast transportation, and computerized flexible production systems' (Castells 1999: 47). However, while new forms of production and management are widely diffused in the global economy, 'they do not include all territories and do not include all people in its workings' (Castells 1999: 132). To be more precise, dominant sectors in developed and developing countries are connected to the hegemonic networks of the global economy in an ever-changing hierarchy in which positions are not fixed, but are determined according to the market 'value' of what they produce and to their influence upon the global processes of production and consumption. At the same time, 'segments of countries and regions' are disconnected from this global economy (Castells 2000).

Concomitantly, the processes of integration in the current wave of globalization entail both new forms of labor and economic practices around the world. Aneesh (2006) contends that these forms of labor become a part of the networks of capital integration. As mobility of different types becomes a common feature, the global mobility of labor, and particularly of highly skilled workers, increasingly depends on networks. In the same way the possibility of individuals to be recruited in certain occupations depends on their capacity to operate through networks. Also, the economies of states and territories (local, national or regional) depend increasingly on global flows created and maintained by groups of individuals through social networks.

Hence, in the hope of utilizing and benefiting from these flows and networks, individuals are forced to expand their understanding of globalization and must work outside the confines of set geographical regions. Accordingly, brain drain can no longer merely be defined in terms of geographical boundaries, especially in a context of a global economy that neither is totally global nor can be considered completely national (Aneesh 2006). Rizvi (2005: 189) argues accordingly that 'in an age of globalization, the key issue has become not where people are physically located but what contribution they are able to make to the social, cultural and economic development of the countries with which they identify'. This implies that brain drain cannot simply be measured through a set of economic data, constructed around national categories, because that tells only part of the story. In addition to an understanding the economic affects of transnational flows, it is also necessary to comprehend how brain drain reconstitutes the nature of cultural and political relations, as well as of professional identities, that span across national boundaries.

What this account suggests then is that 'the development effects of migration not only entail remittances and investments, but also include an important socio-political dimension. Through such social and political investments, migrants can contribute to shaping a better societal climate in countries of origin in general' (Haas 2005: 5). Despite this recognition, most recent literature on brain drain continues to focus exclusively on its economic effects. Most recent studies debate, for example, the effects of remittances on the economic growth of less-developed countries, overlooking the importance of considering social and cultural considerations as well, and of elaborating how social networks are central to understanding the changing dynamics of skilled mobility.

Networks have of course always been central to and have provided avenues for the migration process itself. In his historical overview of immigration into the United States, Tilly (1990) emphasizes that it is the 'networks that migrate'. 'By and large', Tilly says, 'the effective units of migration were (and are) neither individuals nor households but sets of people linked by acquaintance, kinship, and work experience.' Networks connect migrants across time and space. According to Boyd (1989: 641), 'once begun, migration flows often become self-sustaining, reflecting the establishment of networks of information, assistance and obligations which develop between migrants in the host society and friends and relatives in the sending area. These networks link populations in origin and receiving countries and ensure that movements are not necessarily limited in time, unidirectional or permanent'. Social networks play a crucial role in helping migrants find jobs and accommodation. But they are also important in circulating goods and services, and in providing continuous sources of social and economic information, as well as psychological support. They guide migrants into or through specific places and occupations. In this way, migration can be conceptualized as a process of network building.

Of course, the formation and operations of particular migrant networks are deeply affected not only by information and opportunities but also by their social position and power. Aiawa Ong (1999) has shown, for example, how middle-class emigrants from Hong Kong, in contrast to working-class ones, use different kinds of networks for different kinds of purposes in arranging their movement and resettlement abroad, and in retaining links with Hong Kong. According to Shah and Menon (1999) high occupational groups rely more on networks of colleagues and professional organizations and less on kin-based networks. Gender relations are also deeply implicated in the formation of networks and in the ways they are accessed, managed, sustained and utilized to derive social and economic benefits.

This discussion suggests that there is considerable variety in the forms of relational and structural arrangements embedded within migrant networks. As Vertovec (2002: 3) notes, 'social ties in pre-migration networks are related to factors affecting which people migrate, the means of migration, the destination (including locality, accommodation and often specific job) and future prospects for physical and occupational mobility'. He quotes Meyer (2001) in suggesting that 'connections with earlier migrants provide potential migrants with many resources that they use to diminish the risks and costs of migration: information about procedures (technical as well as legal), financial support, job prospects, administrative assistance, physical attendance, emotional solidarity'.

Migration theorists have long recognized that migrants maintain contact with people in their countries of origin through correspondence and the sending of remittances. Yet early sociologists of migration focused largely upon the ways in which migrants adapted themselves to their place of immigration through processes of assimilation and integration. But this research always assumed nation-states to be self-contained, with fixed cultural borders. Even the theories of multiculturalism worked with a similar assumption, even if they rejected the idea of assimilation. However, with globalization has come the realization that the cultural boundaries of nation-states were never entirely fixed and have become increasingly porous; and with advances in technologies, the logic of assimilation of people into spaces that are somehow largely immutable has become increasingly hollow.

This has led to a new approach to migration studies that recognizes the links migrants often maintain to people, traditions and causes outside the boundaries of the nation-state to which they have moved. As Vertovec and Cohen (1999) indicate, this new approach underscores the numerous ways in which transnational networks today are different and more intense than their earlier forms. There have emerged, they argue, new patterns in transnational mobility, by which people now create and circulate in transnational communities, or what Appadurai (1996) calls 'diasporic spaces'.

According to Portes (1997: 812), these spaces comprise 'dense networks across national borders created by immigrants in their quest for economic advancement and social recognition. Through these networks, an increasing number of people are able to live dual or even multiple lives. They are often bilingual, move easily between different cultures, frequently maintain homes in two countries, and pursue economic, political and cultural interests that require their presence in both'. This transnationality is of course enhanced by newer, cheaper, and more efficient modes of communication and transportation, which enable 'globally "stretched" patterns of activity' (Vertovec 2002: 4) affecting a variety of social relations across the diaspora. These relations include various forms of economic exchange, political mobilization, cultural communication, information sharing and the formation of professional links.

This is not to deny that various forms of transnationalism have always existed through chain migration, regular communications among split families, sending of remittances, as well as transnational labor markets. However, there is something new about the contemporary labor practices, which GATS/WTO and numerous professional associations are now seeking to 'internationalize', that is, develop guidelines for training, accreditation, ethics and standards (Robertson 2006). The transnationalization of the labor market has encouraged new services for labor recruitment, movement and job placement. These services have been provided by specialist agencies that take care of bureaucratic rules and regulations that surround the recruitment of highly skilled people. In the IT industry, Khadria (2001) notes, the agency work known as 'body shopping' is often sanctioned by governments and corporations alike, precisely at a time when the pejorative idea of 'people smuggling' has been to applied to those who arrange the movement of refugees and unskilled people.

This illustrates how the networks utilized by skilled workers often tend to be of a different nature, and have different outcomes, than those characterizing low or unskilled workers. The differential networks characterizing various kinds of workers influences, first of all, the ways in which skilled migrants are recruited. Higher education is a foremost source of skilled migrant networks. Indeed countries like Australia have increasingly sought to align their educational and immigration policies. Ziguras and Law (2006) have shown how Australia now views international students as attractive migrants who are not only prepared to invest in their own higher education but also play an increasingly important role in ensuring the continuing supply of new student-migrants.

My own research (Rizvi 2005) indicates that networks developed by international students often serve to encourage colleagues and friends from the home country to join them in Australia. They also attract other skilled people to enter the migration stream through their own ad hoc networks of colleagues and project collaborators, and through, as I have already noted, the work of recruitment and relocation agencies. This movement has been accelerated by the intense global competition for particular skills. In the area of IT, for example, until recently worldwide opportunities and competition for skilled workers were stimulated by the globalizing nature of the work that was fluid in terms of skill requirements, was not linked to particular cultural contexts, was dominated by the English language; and was based on on-the-job experience as the most important means of acquiring human capital or becoming multi-skilled. As Iredale (2001: 13) points out, it thus involved a high degree of mobility across spaces and had considerable potential for return migration and investment. Importantly, also, transnational networks of such skilled workers do not merely represent bi-national patterns of movement. As Vertovec (2002: 7) notes, 'they regularly entail the mobility of workers throughout an international arena'. It is possible, for example, for a Hong Kong IT worker to work, at one time or another, in mainland China, the UK and the USA as well as in Hong Kong. This suggests a pattern of 'brain circulation' rather than brain drain.

Under the conditions of 'deterritorialization' (Tomlinson 2000), the international mobility of skilled people is both a consequence of and a necessary stimulus to sustain the processes of economic and cultural globalization. The increasingly globalized knowledge economy demands that there be circulation of knowledge workers and brokers. This is as important for the developed countries as it is for the developing economies. If this is so then it is suggested by a number of recent scholars, such as Meyer and Brown (2003), that for the developing countries to benefit from the knowledge economy, the physical location of people is immaterial, so long as the developing economies are able to draw upon their expertise, regardless of where they live.

Meyer and Brown call this the 'diaspora option', underlining the need to create links through which skilled emigrants could still be effectively and productively connected to their country of origin. They argue that a crucial advantage of the diaspora option is that 'it does not rely on a prior infrastructural massive investment, as it consists in capitalizing already existing resources. It is thus at hand for any country which is willing to make the social, political, organizational and technical effort to mobilize such a diaspora' (Meyer and Brown 2003: 3). It is with this recognition of networks resulting from skilled-worker circulation that many analysts and policymakers have tended to look beyond the discourse of 'brain drain', and to consider notions of the globalization of human capital and to think of the professional labor market as both flexible and globally mobile. This has led to the popularity of the notions of brain exchange and brain circulation.

The idea is to accept the fact that many skilled workers want to migrate for personal, familial and career development, but their skills can nevertheless be utilized to support the development aspirations of their home country. Indeed, diasporic knowledge networks are deemed crucial to realize such aspirations. A number of schemes have thus emerged over the past decade or so, developed both by international organizations and by transnational networks of expatriate professionals, to forge a new 'knowledge for development' so that skilled emigrants can continue to play an effective and productive role in their home country's development, even without any physical temporary or permanent return.

It is argued that this can be facilitated by what Meyer and Brown (2003) call 'distant cooperative work' within the professional diaspora networks. Although some networks of this kind have existed in one form or another in the past, attempts are now being made to make them more systematic, dense and productive. The United Nations Development Program (UNDP), for example, supports many such initiatives with a program called TOKTEN (Transfer of Knowledge Through Expatriate Nationals). TOKTEN has created databases of people and assists skilled expatriates to engage in various development projects. Another form of diaspora knowledge networks involves on-line mechanisms for information exchange and recruitment among occupational professionals. For example, Siliconindia.com has been created to enable IT workers and businessmen of Indian background to remain connected with each other and contribute to the developments in India.

From the point of view of the developing countries, the diaspora option has several advantages. It enables a country to have access not only to their skilled citizens no matter where they reside but also to the socio-professional networks in which they have become inserted abroad. Their transnational networks can be useful in attempts to build a locally based enterprise by connecting them to a far-reaching 'research and technico-industrial web'. The resultant long-distance networks among local and foreign-based professionals can provide important channels throughout which run flows of capital, skill, managerial know-how and information. Such knowledge networks can also direct considerable foreign investment towards the developing countries, as has been the case in India. Much of India's recent economic growth has arguably been facilitated by IT workers in the United States, who have helped create India's vast IT industry by encouraging American companies to outsource some of their work.

Put in these terms, the diaspora option emphasizing 'brain circulation' seems highly promising. However, while it is true that the notion of 'brain drain' needs to be re-thought, the idea of brain circulation does not escape many problems of its own. For such circulation is often characterized by its sporadic, exceptional and limited nature. As Teferra (2003) points outs, most networks have a short life span, and fail to become systematic, dense and productive. Among those in the network who have not had extensive opportunities to travel and live abroad there remains a great deal of resentment towards those who have; and the attitude of emigrants towards their own country of origin often appears arrogant and patronizing. But beyond these social and technical problems, there is a more fundamental issue: that the transnational space within which brain circulation takes place is not a neutral one, but is characterized by uneven distribution of opportunities and asymmetrical flows of power.

The notion of brain circulation appears to rest on an assumption that the new knowledge economy is potentially less exploitative of developing countries than was the old economy. While it is true that the globally integrated knowledge economy requires the development of greater transnational collaboration, and mobility among skilled workers, it is still based on modes of capital ownership and production that are inherently unequal. The substitution of the concept of brain drain with brain circulation does not solve this problem. Under the conditions of globalization and deterritorialization, it is clear that the notion of 'brain drain' needs to be re-conceptualized in more contemporary terms, because issues of global inequalities now presents themselves in markedly different ways. Inequalities are no longer linked to the modernist conception of national development but are located within patterns of transnational flows not only of capital but also of people, information and skills. These flows reshape social identities, and require not only new ways of thinking about relations between globally mobile skilled workers and their social obligations to their communities but also about the ways in which the potential of professional diasporic networks can become sustainable and more effective in addressing the problems of global inequalities surrounding the production and utilization of knowledge.

For this to happen, the networks themselves need to address the issues of asymmetries of power, and the unidirectional flows of knowledge. If the diaspora option is a more contemporary policy response to the problems of global inequalities, then professional diasporic networks cannot simply be viewed as a way of contributing to further capital accumulation but as a serious attempt at addressing the question of whose interests are served by the globally-oriented labor market. This important task cannot be adequately undertaken without recourse to an international education that helps high skills diasporic workers to understand how contemporary processes of globalization have altered the landscape in which they work, and that it may now be transnationally organized but only under social conditions that are inherently unequal. Workers located within the diasporic networks need to recognize that while the volume and speed of intercultural exchange has increased at an unprecedented rate, creating greater possibilities of trade, transfers of technology and cultural cooperation, globalization has also created new forms of inequalities and that the global labor market is as harsh on the poorer communities as were the local economies.

Never before therefore has there been a greater need for intercultural understanding and communication, predicated not on essentialist conceptions of cultures, but based on a need to explore the dynamics of professional interactions across national boundaries. New ways of thinking about economic and cultural exchange are necessary, involving conceptions of others and ourselves that are defined relationally, as complex and inherently dynamic products of a range of historical processes and the contemporary cultural economies of global interconnectivity. Epistemologically, all cultural understanding is comparative because no understanding of others is possible without self-understanding. If this is so then it is important for networks to understand their own social conditions of work relationally and reflexively. Just as corporations are encouraged to become learning organizations then so too must professional diasporic networks. Without such a commitment they are unlikely to be sustainable and realize the potential they clearly have for working productively for the developmental aspirations of their country of origin.

References

Aneesh, A. (2006) *Virtual Migration*, Durham, NC: Duke University Press.

Appadurai, A. (1996) *Modernity at Large: Cultural Dimensions of Globalization*, Minneapolis, MN: University of Minnesota Press.

Boyd, E. (1989) 'Family and Personal Networks in International Migration: Recent Development and New Agendas', *International Migration Review*, 23(3): 638–70.

Carnoy, M. (2002) *Sustaining the New Economy: Work, Family and Community in the Information Age*, New York: Russell Sage Foundation.

Castells, M. (1999) 'Flows, Networks, and Identities: A Critical Theory of the Informational Society', in M. Castells, R. Flecha, P. Freire, H.A. Giroux, D. Macedo and P. Willis (eds) *Critical Education in the New Information Age*, Lanham, MD: Rowman and Littlefield, pp. 37–64.

Castells, M. (2000) *The Network Society*, Oxford: Blackwell Publishing.

de Haas, H. (2005) 'International Migration, Remittances and Development: Myths and Fact', *Global Migration Perspectives*, 30. Centre for International Development Issues, Radboud University, Nijmegen, The Netherlands.

Economist (2002) 'Outward Bound', September 26.

Giannoccolo, P. (2004) 'The Brain Drain. A Survey of the Literature', Working Papers 20060302 (revised 2006), Università degli Studi di Milano-Bicocca, Dipartimento di Statistica.

Held, D. and McGrew, A. (eds) (2000) *The Global Transformation Reader: An Introduction to the Globalization Debate*, Cambridge: Polity Press.

Iredale, R. (2001) 'The Migration of Professionals: Theories and Typologies', *International Migration*, 39: 7–24.

Johnson, J. and Regets, M. (1998) 'International Mobility of Scientists and Engineers to the US: Brain Drain or Brain Circulation?', National Science Foundation Issue Brief No. 98-316.

Khadria, B. (2001) *The Migration of Knowledge Workers*, New Delhi: Sage.

Meyer. J.-P. (2001) 'Network Approach versus Brain Drain: Lessons from the Diaspora', *International Migration*, 39: 91–108.

Meyer, J.-P. and Brown, M. (2003) 'Scientific Diasporas: A New Approach to the Brain Drain', Management of Social Transformations, Discussion Paper No. 1, http://www.unesco.org/most/meyer.htm.

OECD (2001) *S&T Labour Markets: Highly Skilled Globetrotters: The International Migration of Human Capital*, Paris: Organization of Economic Cooperation and Development.

Ong, A. (1999) *Flexible Citizenship: The Cultural Logics of Transnationality*, Durham, NC: Duke University Press.

Papastergiadis, N. (2000) *The Turbulence of Migration*, Cambridge: Polity Press.

Portes, A. (1997) 'Immigration Theory for the New Century: Some Problems and Opportunities', *International Migration Review*, 31: 799–825.

Rizvi, F. (2005) 'Rethinking Brain Drain in the Era of Globalization', *Asian-Pacific Journal of Education*, 25(2): 175–93.

Robertson, S. (2006) 'Brain Drain, Brain Gain and Brain Circulation', *Globalization, Societies and Education*, 4(1): 1–6.

Rodrik, D. (1997) *Has Globalization Gone Too Far?*, Washington, DC: Institute of International Economics.

Salt, J. (1997) *International Movements of the Highly Skilled*, Paris: OECD Occasional Paper 3.

Shah, N. and Menon, I. (1999) 'Chain Migration through the Social Networks: Experience of Labor Migrants in Kuwait', *International Migration*, 37: 361–80.

Teferra, D. (2003) *Scientific Communication in African Universities: External Assistance and National Needs*, London: RoutledgeFalmer.

Tilly, C. (1990) 'Transplanted Networks', in Yans-MacLoughlin (ed.) *Immigration Reconsidered*, Oxford: Oxford University Press.

Tomlinson, J. (2000) *Globalization and Culture*, Cambridge: Polity Press.

Vertovec, S. (2002) 'Transnational Networks and Skilled Labour Migration', paper presented at Ladenburger Diskurs 'Migration' Gottlieb Daimler und Karl Benz-Stiftung, Ladenburg, 14–15 February.

Vertovec, S. and Cohen, R. (eds) (1999) *Migration and Transnationalism*, Aldershot: Edward Elgar.

Ziguras, C. and Law, S.-F. (2006) 'Recruiting International Students as Skilled Migrants: the Global Skills Race as Viewed from Australia and Malaysia', *Globalization, Societies and Education*, 4(1): 59–76.

19 Social technologies at work

Bernard Holkner

Communication technologies are essential to the operations of global organizations. They enable texts and discourses to cross the boundaries of time and space. When we train and support workers to operate in these environments we are concerned with agreed understandings of how technologies are to be used, and what kinds of knowledge is valued by the organization. This chapter discusses an approach to work-related education in which the objective is to better manage the social and political implications of using these technologies. From this perspective, their use necessarily implies complex relationships between people and systems. Particular emphasis is given to emerging social software, which although grounded in informal and social applications, provides particular opportunities for workers and their organizations to contextualize and order knowledge. These methods recognize the interdependence of workers, their ongoing connectedness to their work and managing large bodies of texts in a range of media.

Introduction

The global workforce is made possible with communication technologies of different kinds. A significant part of workplace education for information technology professionals is generally understood to be teaching people to use specific technological systems. Less attention is paid to the impacts and broader potentials of communications technologies at work. In this chapter, I argue that the major challenge for work-related education with regard to ICTs is not mastery of the technological system, no matter how complex it might be, it is helping people to understand the social and political implications of the technologies they use, and will come to use in the future, within their own work contexts.

Organizations which rely upon workers globally distributed in place and time make use of information and communication technologies (ICTs) to overcome these boundaries, paying attention to the efficient use and reuse of a range of texts, each with its own context and history. Within global corporations, information technology professionals develop or select methods for managing organizational knowledge based upon available software, purpose-built software like Knowledgebases, Groupware, Group Decision Support Systems (GDSS), Computer Supported Cooperative Work (CSCW) as well as commonly accepted systems like email and databases recruited from 'everyday' applications. Elsewhere in this volume, authors discuss the impacts of technologies in broader terms, while this chapter discusses the social impacts with a focus on the technologies themselves. My argument is that the exact nature of a knowledge text and how it is used between people collaborating or in any of the other subtle relationships of work should be exposed for analysis by workers as well as by management and researchers. This discussion of ICT-enabled texts and their movements is based on better understanding socio-technical networks and some emergent technologies. It takes a particular view of the differences in how knowledge can be conceptualized by management and workers.

ICTs and the global workforce

There are two aspects of the education of the global workforce that ICTs influence. First, workers need, and are required, to be skilled in the use of organizational applications of technologies in communicating and in handling data in the companies for which they work. Second, workers need to learn about, and continue to develop over their working lives, sophisticated understandings of the ways that ICTs inflect working relationships and the meanings that can be made from data by other workers and systems. The first of these is of course a recognized organizational imperative. The second is more subtle, and critical to the workers themselves as they move within and between organizations, and negotiate their working lives.

Workers are connected by the rules of organizational structures. These connections enable and facilitate work and the coordination of work activities. When organizations employ information and communication technologies, both the work and the ways to work are governed by the rules of work practice and additionally by the systemic rules of software. Let me give an example. As I write this, a particular unwanted feature of web browsers is that after loading they will place the keyboard cursor into the first text box of a loaded screen. So, with *Google* as my starting page the cursor is conveniently placed in the search box, since that's all that I'm likely to do with that page. However more times than not, I load the web browser with the intention of viewing some other website. While the browser loads, I can place the cursor into the navigation text box, but if I do this before *Google* has completely loaded, part of my typing is moved into the search window. I learn not to be angry that I have to retype. I learn also that there are rules in the software that probably make good sense. But not to me. After all could it not detect …? These software rules may be either deliberately (as in this case), or unwittingly introduced, but in terms of my work they impact in ways that make me change or adapt my preferred or other learned processes to make it possible to cooperate with the software. As it turns out, in most situations like the one above, it's even difficult to know where to go and complain. Is this a feature of the browser or of the web page?[1] Someone programmed it and it has a surprising impact on my work, but I don't know them or how to find them. So when generic software, in-house software and work practices all impact on workers we become compliant in accepting 'the way it's done'.

In this chapter, I will use the combination of understanding systems, technologies and knowledge to lead up to an analysis of some emerging technology applications and their potential to contribute to global work and to joining up global workers.

Technologies, knowledge and work

Technologies help us and our work places to be organized. We are not incapable of choosing a movie, contacting friends, setting a meeting time and place or refining those arrangements when circumstances change, but for people separated in time and space, leaving signs, or asking our friends to join with our current purpose is made easier with telephones, appointment books, alarms and lists. Communication seeks to overcome time inconvenience and separation in space and purpose. Communication, information technologies and data perform roles in global work that are regulated by systemic rules that are defined by organizations and software and by practices that are 'local' only in the sense that they are grounded in organizational culture.

From the point of view of workers and technologies, knowledge is not a synonym for information (Wilson 2002). Information is contextualized data. For my purposes, knowledge can be regarded as the individual's and the group's use of that information. It is particular to an individual, and can be argued as demonstrated in action. We might ask then, 'How does this knowledge become organizational knowledge?' There are familiar techniques for building databases of experience, product behaviour, and even 'scripts' used by call centres to resolve customer enquiries. In practice, workers are usually not isolated, and while knowledge is highly contextualized to individuals and groups, it is critical to the 'team' charged with gathering, refining, storing, evaluating and applying this material. New advances in indexing and retrieval of relevant material aim to release people from tedious and difficult sifting of data (Iyengar *et al.* 2002) and yet the reliance upon systemic rules remains unchanged.

So how do these connected workers understand their reliance on colleagues, software, hardware and the relationships that necessarily bind them? It's easy to explain a slow network or faulty workstation, even when one has no idea what or where it is, or indeed who (if anyone) is responsible for its repair. To effectively describe connected workers in computer-mediated and distributed workspaces needs clarification of the scope of the transactions and awareness of the actors (people and machines) engaged. A *knowledge network* is a particular way to label the intended harmony of people and machines which are gathered around projects where effective information handling and context translates to purposeful knowledge. These networks extend beyond organizations and workplace teams, but most importantly, they are dynamic in membership and power relations (Holkner and Farrell 2005). The tension for organizational structures is that these generally refer to lines of reporting. Technology is understood as simply the means by which communication is made and data is stored. Increasingly, workers are expected to adopt and engage with computer and communications hardware and software as business needs and operational efficiencies change, and yet the complexities of working with technologies are less transparent as systems become more sophisticated. Workers are generally expected to engage with complex networks of these kinds through software training, but as far as the human dynamics involved at all stages, most would be unaware of the cast, their roles, or even the potentials of connected co-workers.

I have more than once required the services of a tow truck to rescue my parade of poorly maintained vehicles. Some years ago I listened in to the tow truck driver speaking with his depot via two-way radio.

DRIVER: Fifty
OPERATOR: Fifty
DRIVER: FJ to Eltham
OPERATOR: Fifty

Busy two-way radio networks necessitate brief conversations. The last time I called for a tow truck, the driver had available my name, telephone, address, vehicle details and nature of the problem displayed on the terminal in his cabin. He pressed a button on the terminal to convey that he was driver 276 (fifty), and taking my neglected wreck to the repairer (FJ to Eltham). Systematizing the rescue process with software and hardware has simultaneously improved information flow, replaced an entire overcrowded voice communication network and, it can be argued, removed opportunities for local knowledge or impulsive assistance from co-workers. Now that there is no apparent need for a radio operator at the tow truck depot, neither is there an opportunity for a connected worker to advise that the Eltham repair shop is now closed. Similarly, when the local volunteer fire brigade's communication network was centralized, the opportunities for the radio operator to give directions, 'the fire must be behind Tommy's hut' or advice, 'I think there may be gas cylinders in that shed ...' were lost. This 'local knowledge' is replaced by an accurate map reference or hazard code if one is available in the database. These systems can unfortunately be less helpful since they might require someone distracted by reading a map or a hazard guide in the fire engine.

Computer systems can be programmed to register events including logging people's uses of time, the people that they routinely communicate with and patterns therein and the texts that they create, read and share. It is particularly interesting to consider the impacts of computer systems automatically harvesting, summarizing and contextualizing data in situations where workers have only limited understandings of what may have been 'lost' or modified in this kind of translation. From a worker's point of view, accessing a corporate 'knowledgebase' gives a necessarily limited view of others' actions and resources. With the context removed or at least limited, and a 'best fit' answer, it becomes impossible to trace information back to its sources. Certain technologies have been able to challenge contemporary views of knowledge, literacy (in certain new genres) and work. The advents of writing, printing and the digital age for example, each refined what was considered to be knowledge, who was able to gain it and how that could be done. Near-future technologies have the same potential to create new work practices and impact on social systems. *Audio mining* is the description given to technology which has essentially grown from voice software. With some dedication, it is possible, even helpful, to train a computer to recognize voice instructions and to take dictation. With audio mining, mature databases will be able to contain all of the speeches and radio or television utterances of the broadcasting population. Now the possibility of retrieving conversations and speeches has to be considered alongside the techniques of digitizing voice (W3C 2001). Essentially, a public database might be interrogated along these lines:

> Anything that was said by Nicholas Negroponte in relation to technology and leisure.

or

> Search all of the UNESCO files and speeches for views about language in the workplace. Now refine this to material from African continent delegates. Give me the results in original audio as well as transcript.

If we consider the same technologies applied to workers' training presentations and telephone conversations, the need for a new literacy emerges. Moreover, the opportunities for highly directed searches for information, sources of information and most significantly, improved contexts, change the nature and potential of texts in workplaces. Techniques for the helpful and accurate retrieval of these texts are significantly more sophisticated than common search engines, and the design of semantic indexing and similar methods deserves considerable attention by workplace educators and researchers alike.

The ambiguity of what organizations need to know

The 'need to know' is both an imperative and a condition. From an educator's point of view, organizations require timely and detailed information about their products, services, operations, workers' needs, to name several. Their uses of technology to these ends are actually simple in that information, while subject to shifting time, can be easily gathered and stored. In another context, organizations have fundamental requirements to be fulfilled so that they can make a claim of knowledge. To pursue this, we might regard the ambiguity as claims: *'We can say that we know that!'*

In this first instance, an organization establishes its needs in order to qualify as a knowledge manager or broker. Staff, technology, policy (systems) are gathered together and arranged so that their services are recognizable as knowledge. This comprises the tacit and explicit knowledge, and variations between these descriptions (Nonaka 1994): *'We need to know that.'*

In this case, there are data and procedures that are necessary to enable an organization to function. Organizations need data to create information and then knowledge, and this data is just as likely to be about the conduct of the organization and its systems, and implementation procedures as it is targeted data of and about the nature of the information that they need to do their work.

In terms of technology these needs are quite different. In the first instance, organizations need to be convinced and to convince their network of associates, clients and other stakeholders that their business is knowledge and that they are effective and proactive in that pursuit. In the second, organizations build a culture of awareness of the scope of the data that they value that can be transformed to knowledge and of the socio-technical systems that are necessary for them to function.

Databases of techniques, experiences and problem resolution are typical 'tools' of global organizations. They are necessary as organized documents and yet the step to describing them as components of an organizational knowledge actor network is a long one (see Edwards and Nicoll, Chapter 24, this volume). Understanding the complex relationship of technology and connected workers implies comfort and flexibility in the social structures that are necessary for them to work. A particular genre of technology, 'social software', used variously to locate and communicate with people with similar interests, provides an alternative means of approaching the same (working) problems, this time from the point of view of workers.

As an example, I have selected three 'social' technologies to discuss as contrasting in approach to business applications: the blog, the wiki and instant messaging. After providing brief accounts of these technologies I will discuss the implications of employing them in globally distributed workspaces.

Blogs

A blog (Weblog) is essentially an online diary that the author makes available to the internet public. These are subscription-based information resources, identified by the intersecting interests of their authors and readership. Using the protocols of RSS (Really Simple Syndication), individuals are able to receive regular updates on the work and thoughts of others who become members of loose networks. While it's possible for readers to attach comments to blog entries, these interactions are typically conversational rather than purposeful in a work sense. Nevertheless, the time-stamped experiences together with the strong sense of the author's connection and ownership can give the texts a particular credibility. Trust in the quality of the text is embedded in some knowledge of the author's history, but also in the fact that the blog entry has been a voluntary act motivated by interest in communicating. For the most part, blogging is considered an 'after hours' pursuit conducted enthusiastically, sometimes with an agenda to more fully discuss a work issue. The website cyberjournalists. net (http://www.cyberjournalist.net/cyberjournalists.php) refers to the blogs of respected mainstream media journalists – *j-blogs* – which can be the source of more detailed and critical discourses than were published in their employment. Even if we consider the unregulated nature of blogs, and the potential for bias and poor research, their potential as worthwhile sources is evident (Roth 2004). Blogs specifically designed for knowledge management, knowledge weblogs or *klogs*, have limited currency in workplaces, usually as shared notebooks that are officially sanctioned but clearly regulated.

It is notable that the extent of indexing of blog entries is limited to global search engines. In other words, it's difficult to identify specific useful texts as emanating from personal or business blogs where they exist. Any particular value in blog entries through their potential for improved connection with the author is lost unless that entry happens to be in the domain of a blogger whose postings are regularly perused.

In workplace settings, there will be blogs and similar discourses that are occasionally and informally accessed to solve problems just as there is an increasing although limited institutionalized application of blogs. The ability to search for blog entries, blog authors and to become familiar with the social networks that make them effective, is a fundamental requirement for workers to learn that is substantially different to keyword or text-based searching that is familiar to most ICTs at work.

Wikis

Considered 'an underground IT phenomenon' (Dickerson 2004), a wiki is a networked application designed for people to easily create and edit connected pages with complete freedom to change or even delete the work of others. In its original form, a wiki is open to the public where anyone is able to create series of connections, add materials and propose meanings without any regulation. In educational and work situations, wikis are controlled through login access and 'history' files so that damaged work can be restored, and authorship tracked. Notwithstanding the apparent risks of vandalism, these events are in fact not especially problematic, largely a result of the above controls. In practice, wikis rely upon the community of contributors in ways that are quite unlike traditional workplace knowledge management software. Wiki contributors are operating in an environment where loose connections to any existing pages are encouraged. Since the format of a page is not defined, these contributions can take the form of notes, anecdotes, statistics, links to formal data sources. These texts might include audio, video, or graphical materials, and would be automatically linked to other wiki pages with the same title. So a page represents an issue and the full extent of interconnection with other contributions will only be understood as each reader follows leads of interest. Naturally, since contributors are equally free to add to or change existing pages, they are never finished and revisiting an item of interest can produce improved or indeed worse results.

Documents are more easily created and edited than with established business knowledge management software, commonly described by vendors as 'solutions'. As an aside, it is interesting to observe that the term solution implies that it's possible and desirable to apply a product to the diverse information management tasks that would be required by organizations. While wikis are being increasingly used in business settings, there are perceptions that their experimental nature and the lack of an explicit management hierarchy makes them difficult to sanction (Goodnoe 2006). In fact these methods for documenting work activities are necessarily decentralized and reject traditional organizational structures. The true tension of collaborative development of working resources through a wiki exists in managing suitable system integrity, user securities, the desirability of anonymity and the users' perceived freedom to engage. Ideally, participants are enthusiastic in collaboratively building the resource.

At the time of writing, the indexing and search function of wikis for particular comments or coherent texts is limited to simple keyword Boolean searches. In a sense this is perhaps not a limitation since the strength of the wiki rests in the willingness of workers to work collegially, and to treat the materials as strongly connected to the community of authors.

Instant messaging

One of the least formal communication technologies, Instant Messaging (IM) finds its way from purely social applications to the workplace. IM is almost synchronous in nature, particularly on high-speed networks, although the temporal dimensions of IM are quite unlike other communications technologies. This may in part be due to the perception that this social communication is layered on top of a person's other pursuits, or work in the case where IM is used by workers.

When people use IM their interactions are dyadic, more like telephony than Internet Relay Chat (IRC) to which it owes some history. Unlike IRC, Instant Messaging doesn't rely upon people entering a cyberspace 'room' to converse with whoever is present. Its communities are created by individuals who select contacts they are prepared to associate with in this way. IM presents a particular kind of casual communication where creative spelling, abbreviation, emoticons and punctuation are used to reinforce the essentially social nature of the connection even when the issue under discussion is clearly business and important. Etiquette in IM is arguably more relaxed than email – possibly as a consequence of perceived privacy. It appears unique in tolerating long periods of absence without the kind of stigma that ignoring a telephone call might produce. IM is a communication activity on a multitasking layer that participants understand. It is used to negotiate availability, maintain a sense of connection and to suggest switching to other media (Nardi *et al.* 2000). These activities are perceived just as important as any information being passed.

Social software and working relationships

Considerable work goes into collecting databases and texts while developing work systems. Software and hardware recruited to these systems can also be designed with a range of contextual features to try and provide examples and indicators of reliability. In practice this means that organizations' systems are designed to adhere to rules which pre-empt workers' uses of information in terms of locating the solution, explaining the solution or problem, finding the part number or locating the correct consultant. Goals are necessarily distanced from workers who need them, but as long as workers support includes building awareness of the systems and how they are designed to work, the workers have a small amount of autonomy to protect them. Social software, in particular blogs, wikis and IM as discussed, describe and provide different or even democratic collaborative work, 'the opposite of Groupware since the former supports the desire of individuals to form groups to achieve personal goals' (Boyd 2003).

Moving and storing texts

The value of organizational knowledge rests in the texts, their contexts and the complex relationships between people and systems. Group ownership of information texts and a desire to support these with context and working relationships is critical to the texts becoming in any way useful. Workers who are loosely connected through systems need the confidence and skills in recognizing and maintaining the relationships as much as they need skills in operating software. The rise of IM for staying in touch with friends has brought about the expectation that people will multitask their current activities, work or leisure activities, on a computer along with the IM software. Individuals regulate how much time they will spend with each application, to what extent each can interfere or take priority over another. Compared with the traditional telephone, which is always permitted to interrupt most activities, multitasking work and communication or network building are much more under the control of the individual.

In this way work is made up of particular decisions about *how to work*. How can texts be stored with suitable context and connection? Moving texts through and across technologies brings about problems with time, end user literacy and the specific problems of texts in different media and formats. Work might involve answering an email or telephone while accessing information resources, helpdesk scripts or even expert co-workers. Further to this, is considerable awareness of the status and reliability of information texts which may have been selected or summarized by a computer from narrative or interviews into simple database entries.

Issues for knowledge and technology

Modern computer systems are perfectly capable of operating several software applications simultaneously, and experience shows that people are able to develop the skills of moving between these systems, moving documents between and through them, and summarizing or translating texts for people to receive in other media. When George, the marketing manager of a global high-technology medical products organization sends out important information to the company's field workers, he pays little attention to his co-workers' conditions of reception and will email large documents with detailed coloured images attached. George cannot understand that he has in fact developed a reputation for annoying behaviour by his friends as they find that they are unable to download the huge files into their company-supplied pocket computers. Similarly, when Tim, the IT manager, developed systems for telephone messages to appear automatically on field workers' pocket pagers he had no idea that workers would share strategies to avoid being overwhelmed by repetitious texts. Meanwhile, the training arm of this, and one would suspect many similar organizations, doesn't provide support for the *working use* of their technologies, but merely for their 'correct' mechanical operation. These examples alert us to the risks of overlooking the complexities of working with technologies frequently dismissed as concerns for IT training (Holkner and Farrell 2005).

Conclusion

Social software at work has the potential to locate knowledge in an extended range of contexts. It is critical that workers know something about the contexts in which their ICT-enabled texts arise: the person who developed the text, their narrative of experience, continuing discourses of others who comment on any text, and the broader network of individuals with shared interests. Furthermore, recognizing a worker's skill and autonomy in seeking support through social software is a way for organizations to give workers a stronger ownership of their work. Equally, this acknowledged unity of worker and knowledge gives a continuing connection with their intellectual work, and thereby improves workers' engagement with day-to-day problem solving. This implies responsibility for encouraging learning and ongoing support for workers engaged in knowledge work with ICTs. A large part of this support involves recognizing the place of worker identity in technologically mediated workspaces. Social software creates the promise of a different kind of global workplace and a different kind of global workforce in which individuals are placed in the foreground and their connections suitably valued.

Note

1 It is in fact a Javascript process written into the web page itself.

References

Boyd, S. (2003) 'Are you ready for social software?' Available at:<http://www.darwinmag.com/read/050103/social.html> (accessed 6 May 2006).

Dickerson, C. (2004) 'Wiki goes to work'. Available at:<http://www.infoworld.com/article/04/11/12/46OPconnection_1.html> (accessed 5 March 2006).

Goodnoe, E. (2006) 'Wikis at work'. Available at:<http://internetweek.cmp.com/shared/article/showArticle.jhtml?articleId=178601096&pgno=1> (accessed 7 April 2006).

Holkner, B. and L. Farrell (2005) 'The Network is Down'. Paper presented at the Researching Work and Learning Conference, Sydney.

Iyengar, G.H., H.J. Nock, *et al.* (2002) 'Semantic Indexing of Multimedia Using Audio, Text and Visual Cues'. Paper presented at the ICME 2002 – IEEE International Conference on Multimedia and Expo, Lausanne, Switzerland.

Nardi, B.A., S. Whittaker, *et al.* (2000) 'Interaction and Outeraction: Instant Messaging in Action'. Paper presented at the 2000 ACM Conference on Computer Supported Cooperative Work, Philadelphia: ACM Press.

Nonaka, I. (1994) 'A Dynamic Theory of Knowledge Creation', *Organizational Science*, 5: 14–37.

Roth, M.M. (2004) 'How Journalists See the Blogosphere'. Available at:<http://www.asc.upenn.edu/mmccoy/blogs.pdf> (accessed 14 March 2006).

W3C (2001) 'Voice Extensible Markup Language (VoiceXML) Version 2.0'. McGlashen, S. Available at:<http://www.w3.org/TR/2001/WD-voicexml20-20011023/> (accessed 3 April 2006).

Wilson, T.D. (2002) 'The Nonsense of Knowledge Management', *Information Research*, 8(1).

20 'Knowledge society' or work as 'spectacle'?

Education for work and the prospects of social transformation in Arab societies

André Elias Mazawi

This chapter examines how education for work policies are debated in the Arab states in relation to notions of a 'knowledge society'. It starts by positioning these debates over the backdrop of local and geopolitical contexts in relation to which competing notions of a knowledge society are constructed. A second part offers a review of some major education for work reforms. The review suggests that despite different contexts shaping their labour markets, the Arab states are implementing increasingly similar education for work policies along notions of a 'knowledge society' promoted by international development networks. It is argued that this is due to their differential location within trans-national labour flows and to their dependency on global financial markets. A third part investigates how, in this context, Information and Communication Technology (ICT) is seen as the carrier of a new ethic of education and work which would facilitate the emergence of an 'Arab knowledge society'. Yet, this part also suggests that notions of a knowledge society intersect with entrenched social cleavages, ultimately reproducing hegemonic notions of lifelong learning and education for work. The chapter ends with a reflection on the underpinnings of education for work in the Arab region.

Introduction

In a recently published book, *Building Knowledge Cultures*, Peters and Besley (2006: 117) point out that the notion of the 'knowledge society' emerged primarily as a 'policy construction' in which education is approached as 'a subset of wider economic policy'. Operating as a policy tool through which work is reconfigured around the processing of 'intangible capital', the knowledge society is characterised by new social hierarchies and multifaceted divisions of labour (David and Foray 2003; see response by Winch 2003). The notion of a knowledge society also signals a structural shift, from a political economy in which the state pro-actively intervenes in the market, to a political economy based on the 'responsibilising of the self'; an approach which erects the individual, in the words of Peters (2001), as a 'moral agent and its construction as a calculative rational choice actor' (p. 61). This 'duty to the self', states Peters (2001), 'legitimises the concepts of lifelong learning and entrepreneurship aimed at the production of flexible workers' and establishes 'the combined notions of "education for work" and "enterprise education" as modes of social participation' (p. 62).

The centrality of education for work, within the context of policy shifts towards a 'knowledge society', is of particular relevance to the case of the Arab states across the Middle East and North Africa. Two issues are raised in this respect. First, in most Arab states, the dominance of the public sector reflects the state's position as a major employer and provider of educational and employment opportunities (Kabbani and Kothari 2005: 52). Controlling educational provision *and* paid work is therefore central for the political legitimacy of the Arab nation-state, especially in the absence of established institutional mechanisms for political and economic participation (Murphy 2006a). Hence, deregulating the state's control over these resources, as part of shifts towards an entrepreneurial vision of a knowledge society, reconfigures not only the interface between education and work. Deregulation also reconfigures the very socio-political formations from which state-entrenched elites derive their power to control and allocate social and economic resources (Posusney 2003; Sadiki 1997; Tadros 2006), 'requiring a complex political and economic balancing act, as well as the confident support of the military' (Ehteshami and Murphy 1996: 769). If so, how do state policies concerned with education for work in the Arab states negotiate their way through this double-bind, with its underlying political tensions and embedded contradictions? How and to what extent do policies that seek to reconfigure the interface between education and work weave into the notion of a 'knowledge society' aspects of work which generate 'new' forms of political legitimacy?

Second, developing a meaningful approach to education for work hinges on the state's capacity to foster modes of individual subjectivity 'through and by the market'. These include the promotion of lifelong learning and worker flexibility, as modalities of civic and economic participation, and the introduction of Information and Communication Technology (ICT). However, Patterson and Wilson (2000: 85) observed that commentators and policy makers regularly make 'extravagant' and 'utopian claims' – 'untested empirically and limited logically' – about the contribution of ICT to equity and the circumstances under which ICT may deepen social inequality and exclusion. With regard to the Arab states, it remains unclear how market-induced subjectivities intersect with historically and culturally-situated social cleavages rooted in economic rentierism and state patronage, a patriarchal social order, and in class, religious and spatial identities. How does the intersection of markets and social cleavages shape education and work opportunities available to diverse social groups in Arab societies?

Because of its contradictory location in a globalising world economy, the Arab region offers an interesting context to examine how global and regional geopolitics, state-entrenched elites and social cleavages intersect around notions of a 'knowledge society'. This chapter starts by positioning the current debates on education for work in the Arab states over the backdrop of local and geopolitical contexts in relation to which competing notions of a 'knowledge society' are constructed. A second part offers a review of major education for work reforms. The review suggests that despite the different contexts shaping their labour markets, the Arab states are implementing increasingly similar education for work policies along notions of a 'knowledge society' promoted by international development networks. It is argued that this is due to their differential location within trans-national migrant labour and to their dependency on global financial flows. A third part investigates how, in this context, ICT is seen as the carrier of a new ethic of education and work which would facilitate the emergence of an 'Arab knowledge society'. Yet, this part also suggests that notions of a knowledge society intersect with entrenched social cleavages, ultimately reproducing hegemonic notions of lifelong learning and education for work. The chapter ends with a reflection on the underpinnings of education for work in the Arab region.

Debating the knowledge society in the Arab region

The notion of a 'knowledge society' is highly contested across the Arab region, along with that of globalisation. Some argue that the knowledge society offers a window of opportunity for broader social, political and economic development (UNDP 2003). Others argue that the knowledge society represents a facet of globalisation, a force which negates 'state, nation and homeland'. For them, it threatens to enclose Arab societies on the margins of an American-dominated world economy, as consumers of Western technology and know-how (see the analytical review by Tarabichi 2000). Others, still, posit that '[k]nowledge, education, and learning are central to the Islamic view of life and work' (Akdere *et al.* 2006: 356). For them, the notion of knowledge in society can be reclaimed, only if informed and transformed by an Islamic epistemology and praxis associated with Islamic communitarian foundations from which work draws its meanings (Halstead 2004: 521–2; Lubeck 1998).

One of the contentious aspects associated with the notion of a knowledge society pertains to discourses of 'knowledge deficit'. Circulated through documents such as the *Arab Human Development Report* (AHDR) annual series (UNDP 2003), these discourses are drawn upon by academics, policy makers, consultants, planners and observers who account for the 'failure' of Arab states to integrate into the global knowledge economy (see Sakr 2004). 'Knowledge deficits', it is argued, result from authoritarian, non-democratic and corrupt political systems, rampant poverty and illiteracy, centralised economies and failed industrialisation. Additional factors cited refer to the negative impact of dysfunctional cultural practices, such as the dogmatism of fundamentalist movements and social conformism more generally. According to this view, Arab societies must embark on an arduous 'cognitive journey' (UNDP 2003: 48) and build a viable knowledge society, the 'only way to lead the region into a renaissance' (p. 178).

Policies in this direction have been consistently encouraged by international non-governmental and semi-governmental organisations involved in setting up the development agenda across the Arab region. These called for a new approach to education for work to be adopted. For instance, the UNESCO-sponsored *Beirut Declaration on Higher Education in the Arab States for the XXIst Century* identified the promotion of lifelong learning as a regional priority, so that the Arab states 'achieve sustainable and global development' through education for work (UNESCO 1998). The Declaration further called for mechanisms in higher education to be established in order 'to allow [the] workforce in all fields to upgrade their skills and develop new competencies at regular intervals throughout their lives'. More recently, the authors of the UN-sponsored *Arab Human Development Report* (AHDR) identified knowledge 'as the road to development and liberation, especially in a world of intensive globalization' (UNDP 2002: 19). In their subsequent report for 2003, they called for the 'building of a knowledge society as a cornerstone of human development, a means to expanding people's capabilities and choices and a tool for overcoming human poverty' (UNDP 2003: 35). In the same vein, a World Bank publication articulated its vision with regard to the meanings attached to education for work in the Arab states. It emphasised that the 'knowledge-based society can only grow if every individual is keen, throughout his or her lifetime, to acquire new knowledge and to update knowledge acquired earlier'. It went on to state that in 'a freer and more open system, this makes it possible to adapt to new labor market conditions and to acquire the necessary mobility to "cover" the risks of participation in the globalized world' (Aubert and Reiffers 2003: 36–7). Western governments and political blocs, like the US and the European Union (EU), are also highly involved in shaping current policies concerned with education for work across the Arab region (see Dalacoura 2005; El Kenz 2005). This has been evidenced, for instance, with the announcement of the 'US–Middle East Partnership Initiative' and the US 'Greater Middle East Initiative' publicised by the US government in 2002 and 2004 respectively. The latter proposed reforms that will facilitate the 'building of a knowledge society' a 'Literacy Corps', the wiring of schools to the Internet, the introduction of 'Discovery Schools' and the bridging of 'educational deficits'.

In contradistinction, critics counter-argue that determining what counts as knowledge and work cannot be dissociated from the broader unequal power frameworks associated with Western colonialism and imperialism and which continue to affect Arab and Muslim societies (Pasha 2002). They maintain that knowledge should be understood, not as a marketable product, but as socially constructed, culturally immersed and historically-situated understandings and behaviours that underpin social and economic organisation and political action. They therefore argue that clarifying the intersection of power and knowledge is pivotal if Arab societies are to build a viable platform for social transformation; one which transcends Western hegemony and economic subordination through labour. This view led some writers to voice their concerns over American initiatives that aim to 'reform education and the tools of knowledge and information' across the Middle East and beyond. For instance, Labyadh (2004) views the knowledge society as a disruptive policy tool deployed 'to alter the components of the Arab and Islamic culture and identity'. For him, this version of the knowledge society seeks to 'organise the markets in favour of trans-national corporations, completely disregarding a genuine economic development of the [Arab] countries, their industrialisation and agriculture while providing priority to the freeing of trade and the limiting of the role of the state' (p. 140). This particular version of the knowledge society deepens the dependency of the Arab region on Western capitalist economies. Not only does it fail to offer a platform for national liberation and emancipation through work, but it ultimately institutes technological consumption as a proxy for productive 'work'. It thus maintains, according to this view, the economic marginality of Arab societies within global economic flows (Zyab 2002).

Repositioning education, knowledge and work

Over the last three decades, demographic transitions, regional political instability and persisting fiscal crises in the Arab states contributed to shift 'the policy focus from providing health and education for a young population, to facilitating employment and output growth' (Yousef 2004: 4). The growing emphasis on employment creation highlighted the role played by vocational education and professional training, at secondary and post-secondary levels, in ensuring an employability-driven education (Tzannatos and Handoussa 2001). Concerns have been further heightened by unemployment rates among the 15–24 age group, 'the highest in the world, estimated at over 25 percent in 2001', 'accompanied by the lowest labor force participation rates in the world, for both males and females' (Kabbani and Kothari 2005: 50). Hence, Kabbani and Kothari (2005) conclude that '[s]ubstantial improvements in educational attainment ... have not fully translated into better employment outcomes' (p. 51).

For many, the dominance of an 'academic' curriculum and the marginality of vocational programmes represent major fault lines underpinning anaemic economies and precarious labour markets across the Arab region. Enrolling less than 10 per cent of all secondary school students in the region (Kabbani and Kothari 2005: 34), and maintaining only weak links to higher education systems and the economy (Al Heeti and Brock 1997: 387–8; Heyneman 1997: 461), vocational education offers training mainly to drop-outs from academic programmes of study. Tzannatos (2000) more generally points out that, in most Arab states, vocational training 'is fragmented with too many systems running in parallel with [the] same purpose but with distorted and varied approaches without any coordination' (p. 13). He further indicates that vocational programmes 'focus mainly on pre-service training, and the cost-benefit to enterprises provides no incentive for them to provide in-service training', with a few exceptions, such as Tunisia (p. 13).

Reforms introduced in the Arab states in the field of education for work have targeted two major areas: vocational education and training and the restructuring of higher education linkages with the economy. With regard to vocational education and training, policies are concerned with the provision of market-oriented training in fields associated with skilled manual labour. The main consideration here is to boost the employability and entrepreneurship of secondary and higher education graduates as they transit into the labour market. Some writers have suggested that these reforms signal a shift from vocational programmes which 'target those who have dropped out of the education system for academic reasons' (Fakhro 2003: 10) towards professional training programmes which are part of 'a comprehensive strategy that links the education system with the training system, the public and private sector in view of emerging labour market requirement' (p. 22). Notwithstanding, a World Bank publication characterised these reforms as 'still too isolated, fragmented, and rigid' (Aubert and Reiffers 2003: 36).

At the higher education level, new forms of academic and semi-academic programmes of professional training emerged in many Arab states, geared towards responding to perceived labour market demands (Wilkins 2001). For instance, colleges of technology were founded, under different designations, such as Colleges of Technology in Saudi Arabia and Egypt, Higher Colleges of Technology (HCT) in the United Arab Emirates (UAE), and Higher Technological Institutes (HTI) in Tunisia. Colleges of technology offer employment-directed training. In the UAE, HCTs offer programmes in business, engineering, communication technology and health science. In Saudi Arabia, colleges of technology, first founded in the mid-1980s, focus on 'mechanical, electrical and production subjects which are the foundation of skilled manual jobs' (Mellahi 2000: 337). Subsequently, the 1990s witnessed the creation of new vocational and technical programmes which offer training under various forms of internships. In some Arab states, such as in Egypt, Morocco and Tunisia, experiments with 'contract training partnerships' of different types between private and public institutions were conducted. In other cases, programmes were offered either through distance education or through partnerships between universities and professional institutes. In Morocco, the National Charter on Education and Training (NCET) designated the years 2000 to 2009 as a decade of reform through 'lifelong learning, partnership with companies and communities, active learning methodologies, and universities as engines for development' (Cox *et al.* 2006: 92).

The second area in which education for work reforms were introduced pertains to the linkages between higher education institutions and labour markets. Seen as enhancing capabilities in the fields of scientific inquiry, technology transfer and integration, these policies are part of the broader restructuring of higher education and the economy. Guided by World Bank and IMF policies and characterised by 'a general tendency towards privatization and self-financing' (Charafeddine 2006: 172), these reforms have facilitated the emergence of 'types of learning closely associated to the market' (p. 174). Jordan, where private universities and post-secondary institutions have come to outnumber public ones, offers a particularly relevant illustration (Mazawi 2005: 159–79).

Nonetheless, Arab countries differ in terms of the national contexts the above policies seek to address. For Arabian Gulf states, which overwhelmingly rely on expatriate workers, representing in some cases over 90 per cent of their workforce, the major concern is to train their citizens in ways which facilitate their entrance into salaried jobs in the private sector (Nicks-McCaleb 2005: 326). The major aim is to 'nationalise' or 'indigenise' the labour force and replace imported workers who, in the words of one official, 'build our homes, repair our cars, fix our televisions and run the production lines in our factories' (Al-Sulayti 2000: 275). The dependence of the Gulf states on foreign labour, and the limited pool of qualified citizens, have resulted, for instance in the UAE, in a 'low skill level, a low provision of training, severe skills mismatch, low transfer of knowledge, weak efforts for local technological development, dependence on foreign technologies and productivity decline' (Muysken and Nour 2006: 976). Mellahi (2000: 337) reports that, in Saudi Arabia, colleges of technology, geared towards 'the production of highly skilled technicians and middle management to replace foreign workers in the private sector', have difficulty attracting students from among Saudi nationals into 'non-office skilled jobs such as mechanic and production engineering' because nationals 'overwhelmingly prefer specialties that have white collar job prospects' (p. 338). Generally, the attractiveness of vocational education and training for Arabian Gulf citizens remains quite low for reasons associated with state patronage, cultural belief systems and social class distinctions.

Somewhat differently, for Arab states located outside the Arabian Gulf, such as Jordan, Egypt and Morocco, education for work policies were affected by structural adjustment policies implemented under the aegis of the World Bank and the IMF. These policies evolved around the restructuring of the labour market, the consolidation of the private sector as the driving force of the economy, and the promotion of globally competitive knowledge economies (Posusney 2003). Here, the major concern is, in the words of Kabbani and Kothari (2005), 'creating enough jobs to accommodate entering cohorts' of younger workers into the labour market (p. 2), particularly among graduates with 'mid-levels of educational attainment' (p. 32). Diverting higher education graduates into the private sector is seen as a central mechanism that lessens reliance on occupational opportunities customarily offered within an already overburdened and overstretched public service.

Some writers have pointed out that education for work policies in higher education aim also to reverse the preference of nationals for the social sciences and humanities at the expense of science and technology and encourage them to opt for the latter. Yet, with an R&D investment not exceeding 0.3 per cent of GDP (Aubert and Reiffers 2003: 3), the majority of research organisations in the Arab states, about 65 per cent, are managed by ministries; less than a fifth is managed by universities and slightly over 15 per cent are autonomous or part of the private sector (Saleh 2002: 227, 231). Governmental institutions therefore leave little space for universities. Moreover, within the context of regional military conflicts and rivalries, intra-Arab collaboration in the area of research remains limited and weak (Saleh 2002; Zahlan 1999). To transcend this 'culture of bureaucracy and institutional fragmentation' which hampers initiatives for technological capability development and technology transfer, Saad and Zawdie (2005) proposed a shift from central planning to liberalisation according to the 'triple helix' model of innovation. The model, which they suggested for Algeria, is based on establishing 'a network of collaboration between firms, subcontractors, universities, research institutions and government institutions' in view of integrating science and technology in development policies. Other initiatives, for instance in Qatar, the UAE and Kuwait, led to the establishing of science parks, Internet cities, and industrial incubators (often with Free-Zone incentives) in an attempt to boost industry-based R&D, attract foreign direct investments, expand the capabilities of private sector companies, and generate local occupational opportunities for qualified nationals. These initiatives, undertaken by an organisational network partly or wholly sponsored by Gulf governments, are part of the restructuring of the interface between education and work. This said, at the regional level, the political fragmentation of the Arab states limits the possibilities of transformation of Arab economies. It institutionalises dependency on Western consultancies with the linkages between education and work being mediated by external factors over which the Arab states have little leverage. This fragmentation fuels not only high unemployment among the educated but also brain drain out of the region.

The 'new pedagogies of learning' and the construction of social inequalities

The repositioning of education, knowledge and work in the Arab states was accompanied by a critique of prevalent approaches to teaching and learning. Deemed 'traditional', these approaches were described as authoritarian, based on rote memorisation and negating the learner's agency in the construction of knowledge. Over this critique, ICT and more particularly the Internet came to be perceived by policy makers as a major tool which offers unlimited learning opportunities and enhances the skills and performance capabilities of individuals. For them, ICT carries not only a learner-centred educational 'ethic', but also an ethic of work and productivity, that which is associated with the training of a flexible worker and a self-directed citizen. For instance, Al-Gharrab (2003: 7) claims that ICT offers 'flexible learning [and] "continuing education" at any age and under any circumstances in this new era: the era of knowledge and learning organizations'. For Sa'igh (2001), '[e]lectronic education widely opens the door to on-the-job training and to self-learning, and can be widely and effectively used for conscientization, guidance and cultivation' (p. 21). Al-Hamad (2003) adds that '[a]dopting the right technologies and good work ethics are at the root of success in economic development' (p. 16). A position paper, circulated by the Arab NGO Network for Development (2004: 4) considers ICT as 'one of the more important tools to transfer, utilize, mold, and invest technology in the process of developing human capacities'. It emphasises that '[e]nhancing these technologies in all educational levels, focusing on the quality and content of educational materials, and the creation of virtual universities and libraries can contribute to the amelioration of educational systems and curricula'.

The introduction of ICT across the Arab region has also been associated with the expansion of distance learning initiatives, such as the foundation of the Arab Open University in Kuwait in 2002. This and similar initiatives seek to target 'those who work or have family commitments' so that they may study 'where they reside'. Also, universities are becoming more involved in continuing and lifelong education, a role once relegated to literacy campaigns and adult learning. They increasingly draw on conceptual components associated with the learning society discourse, as is evidenced by the proceedings of many regional conferences focusing on ICT. Yet, despite expectations to the contrary, the contribution of ICT to the enhancement of work-related training remains modest (Dutta and Coury 2003: 123, 125). With regard to Egypt, Warschauer (2003) suggests that the disjuncture between the 'rhetoric and reality of technology-based educational reform … limit[s] the impact of machines' in reforming education for work. ICT is seen by policy makers as having the inherent 'ability' to facilitate and transform existing modes of teaching and learning, promote 'autonomous learning' and institute 'equal opportunity for all' through the mere provision of equipment. Warschauer (2003) concludes that, as a result, 'ICT has not appeared to contribute in any meaningful way to reform and modernization of education'. Elsewhere, he further observes that the introduction of ICT was mainly 'part of a broader Westernization process'. It did not necessarily enhance democratisation and the emergence of the autonomous citizen (Warschauer 2004: 388).

The contribution of work-oriented distance education programmes remains limited too. On this, Alsunbul (2002) poignantly observes that distance education degrees obtained by citizens of Arab states from outside their countries are not recognised or accepted either by their government, the private sector or by Arab universities due to a 'chaotic accreditation' (p. 70). It may therefore be argued that, rhetoric to the contrary notwithstanding, lifelong education through distance learning has not provided Arab citizens with meaningful cross-border or cross-sector mobility, either in terms of enhancing their pursuit of educational opportunities or in terms of expanding their occupational outlets. Lifelong learning opportunities continue to reflect a rather narrow national and sectoral approach, marked by broader regional fragmentation, duplication and lack of coordination. This, of course, raises broader questions not only regarding the purchase and dissemination of technologically sophisticated infrastructures, or the building of a regional infrastructure, but also with regard to the relations between lifelong learning, social opportunities and social participation.

Moreover, the few studies available suggest that access to ICT is skewed in favour of men and social elites located in urban and metropolitan centres (Dutta and Coury 2003: 120; Kirchner 2001: 155; Wheeler 2003). Despite their greater access to educational qualifications, liberalisation and restructuring policies exact a much heavier price from Arab women compared with Arab men. With regard to Egypt and Jordan, the increasing deregulation of labour – within the combined context of structural adjustment policies and persistent patriarchal domination – result in less employment opportunities being accessible to women in certain private sector jobs (Assaad 2002; Miles 2002). Assaad (2002) explains that in a patriarchal social order, '[b]ecause educated young women were unable to increase their commuting rates to the same extent [as men], they were undoubtedly shut out of many private sector jobs' (pp. 19–20). In oil-exporting Saudi Arabia and other Gulf states, women's higher levels of schooling and training compared with men are met by policies and institutionalised practices which regulate women's exchange power, thus accentuating the mismatch between skills acquisition and effective access to work (Calvert and Al-Shetaiwi 2002; Mahdi and Barrientos 2003). Joseph (1996) observes that patriarchy continues to be 'woven throughout Arab society partly because of the fluidity between civil society and state, public and private domains, family and government' (p. 18). Thus, the expansion of ICT and distance education often operates in ways which maintain gender seclusion and the institutionalisation of distinct occupational enclaves for women in new and not less restricting ways. Some may claim that these institutional arrangements 'shield' women from competition with men. Others may rather consider them as determining the power of women to exchange educational resources for mobility opportunities, thus maintaining women in conditions of economic peripherality and subordination. More generally, however, writers have pointed out that, in many Arab states, political liberalisation – through the introduction of ICT, the privatisation of higher education and the initiation of shifts towards a 'knowledge economy' – was undertaken in as much as it enabled state-entrenched elites to retain 'a significant degree of control over the extent and nature of the political space' (Murphy 2006b; see also Wheeler 2003 with regard to Egypt).

Some concluding reflections: whither education for work?

'Work' currently stands at the centre of major restructuring initiatives across the Arab region, in relation to which education is perceived as a core policy tool. Education and work are associated with competing notions of a 'knowledge society' (or of knowledge *in* society) disseminated by local, regional and international development agencies and associations. How work is restructured, and how it is positioned in relation to knowledge and education, raises issues related to capacity-building and development, for sure. Yet, these issues are also part of larger dynamics embedded in intra-regional, geopolitical and global power relations. This chapter suggests that education for work reforms across the Arab region have become enmeshed in a complex imbrication of 'networks' composed of local, regional and global organisations which henceforward set the development agenda. In the words of Carnoy and Castells (2001), these 'networks' operate alongside the state as 'shared institutions ... enacted by bargaining and interactive iteration all along the chain of decision making' (p. 14). Policy makers and reformers manoeuvre therefore in an increasingly contested and fragmented terrain, caught betwixt and between competing development agendas, within a globalised and competitive world economy. While the deregulation of education and work seeks to trigger the generative capabilities of the 'national' economy, the state remains involved in asserting its control over (and regulation of) new spaces of work to preserve its very *raison d'être* in the process. The result is a dislocation between policy discourses which emphasise the centrality of education for work in the process of economic development, and the inability of the Arab state 'to penetrate society effectively' through taxation mechanisms imposed on work (Ehteshami and Murphy 1996: 756). According to Sadiki (1997), this dislocation narrows down the 'state's capacity for redistributive justice and equity that renders political authority *ipso facto* good and worthy of deference' (p. 143).

As the interface between education and work is being re-drawn, and competing notions of a 'knowledge society' eagerly contemplated by different constituencies, the Arab region has become extremely vulnerable since the mid-1980s, following the slumping of oil revenues. Characterised by internecine geopolitical rivalries, weakened economies, overwhelming dependency on foreign assistance and protection, and internally eroded political legitimacies, Arab economic 'growth has not only slowed down but has essentially collapsed', threatening 'social development gains achieved during the earlier high growth period' (Elbadawi 2005: 293–4). Within this context, the reforming of vocational and professional training, the alignment of higher education along market demands and the introduction of ICT, appear to have impacted economic growth and the alleviation of youth unemployment only modestly, at best. Moreover, states across the Arab region remain engaged with education for work reforms largely in the form of 'nationally' bounded projects, disconnected from geopolitical conflicts which ultimately impede the emergence of a meaningful regional development strategy.

One therefore wonders whether education for work reforms introduced in the Arab region do not operate, to use a term coined by Guy Debord (2005 [1967]), as a political 'spectacle', largely intended to satisfy demands by competing stakeholders with which the state is embattled to ensure its survival. From this perspective, it would seem as if education for work reforms represent, to use Debord's words again, a 'tautological' system 'which is both the meaning and the agenda of [a] particular socio-economic formation' (Thesis 11), stemming 'from the fact that its means and ends are identical' (Thesis 13). Such a personal reflection may be vindicated, perhaps, by the activism of a growing array of community-based associations which assume a greater role in the provision of work, development and welfare services in a variety of domains, as an alternative to the state. These associations often clash with the state over what funding sources are legitimate, which social and political agenda should be promoted, and what development stands for (Carapico 2002). For instance, Bayat (2002) points out that from the 1980s onward, 'Egypt's social Islam has become perhaps the most pervasive phenomenon in the region', accounting for one-third of all private voluntary associations in the country (p. 12) and providing services from schooling to health, from work opportunities to welfare and banking services. Similarly, Okruhlik (2002: 27) observed that Islamists 'have clearly been the most articulate and powerful of the various forces in Saudi Arabia. They are better organized and more cohesive than other social forces in representing their interests to the state'. Through their opposition and dissent, Okruhlik argues that 'Islamists began a national conversation about what it means to belong and about the relationship of state and citizen, and religion and state'

(p. 27). Differently from the corporate private sector, which the state seeks to co-opt and strengthen, these associations focus rather on community activism, social transformation and the promotion of social justice from a variety of competing epistemic standpoints, yet within a political view of the world which situates the citizen within broader intersections of culture, identity, community and self, however imagined (Bayat 2002; also, see the cases presented in Hautecoeur 2002).

The above reflection serves as an appropriate point of entry into the second issue raised in this chapter, regarding the intersection between market-induced and culturally-situated identities. The review suggests that education for work reforms, and particularly the introduction of ICT, are perceived by policy makers as facilitating the emergence of a new 'ethic': an ethic which reflects a new civic identity associated with an autonomous, flexible and economically productive citizen, or, to use Peters' (2001) words, an ethic which reflects a 'responsibilised self'. Yet, as the review in this chapter also suggests, the emergence of such an ethic is strongly compromised by existing gender, class and regional cleavages which are rooted in deeply-seated power differentials. The latter not only determine the range of social and mobility opportunities open to individuals and groups, but as pointed to more generally by Patterson and Wilson (2000), further operate as exclusionary mechanisms which recast existing cleavages, and their wealth and power correlates, in terms of differential participation rates in emerging labour market opportunities.

This conclusion raises a larger question, one which pertains to the epistemic foundations that inform notions of 'education for work' in the Arab region and beyond. If education is seen exclusively as 'a subset of wider economic policy', much along conceptions of human capital theory, then what has this conception of education abrogated that negates its expected transformative potential? Posed differently, it may be worthy to ask, what is educational about 'education *for* work' that could inform both the commitment of the state to social justice, and the commitment of differentially located individuals to exert, in Coulter and Wiens' (2002) rendition of Arendt's work, a 'visiting imagination' that creates a common ground for both spectator and actor to stand on and engage in broader social transformation?

References

Akdere, M., Russ-Eft, D. and Eft, N. (2006) 'The Islamic worldview of adult learning in the workplace: surrendering to God', *Advances in Developing Human Resources*, 8(3): 355–63.

Al-Gharrab, I.M. (2003) 'E-learning: introduction to non-conventional training', paper presented at the Second Arab Conference on Counseling and Training, 21–23 April, Al-Shariqa, UAE: Arab Institution for Administrative Development (Arabic).

Al-Hamad, A.Y. (2003) 'The Arab world: performance and prospects', paper presented at the Arab World: Performance and Prospects, Dubai, UAE: Per Jacobsson Foundation, September 21.

Al Heeti, A.G. and Brock, C. (1997) 'Vocational education and development: key issues, with special reference to the Arab world', *International Journal of Educational Development*, 17(4): 373–89.

Al-Sulayti, H. (2000) 'Education and training in the GCC countries: some issues of concern', in *Education and the Arab World: Challenges of the Next Millennium*, Abu Dhabi, UAE: Emirates Center for Strategic Studies and Research, 271–8.

Alsunbul, A.A. (2002) 'Issues relating to distance education in the Arab world', *Convergence*, 35: 59–80.

Arab NGO Network for Development (2004) 'Information and knowledge society: questions of development, trade, reform, and democracy'. Second Regional Preparatory Meeting for the World Summit on the Information Society (WSIS). Damascus, Syria: 21–23 November.

Assaad, R. (2002) 'Informalization and de-feminization: explaining the unusual pattern in Egypt', paper presented at the Conference on Rethinking Labor Market Informalization: Precarious Jobs, Poverty, and Social Protection. Cornell University, NY, 18–19 October.

Aubert, J.-E. and Reiffers, J.-L. (eds) (2003) *Knowledge Economies in the Middle East and North Africa: Toward New Development Strategies*, Washington, DC: World Bank.

Bayat, A. (2002) 'Activism and social development in the Middle East', *International Journal of Middle East Studies*, 34: 1–28.

Calvert, J.R. and Al-Shetaiwi, A.S. (2002) 'Exploring the mismatch between skills and jobs for women in Saudi Arabia in technical and vocational areas: the views of Saudi Arabian private sector business managers', *International Journal of Training and Development*, 6(2): 112–24.

Carapico, S. (2002) 'Foreign aid for promoting democracy in the Arab world', *Middle East Journal*, 56(3): 379–95.

Carnoy, M. and Castells, M. (2001) 'Globalization, the knowledge society, and the network state: Poulantzas at the millennium', *Global Networks*, 1(1): 1–18.

Charafeddine, F. (2006) 'Financing higher education in Arab countries: problems and challenges', in J. Tres (ed.) *Higher Education in the World 2006: The Financing of Universities*, New York: Palgrave, 168–75.

Coulter, D. and Wiens, J.R. (2002) 'Educational judgment: linking the actor and the spectator', *Educational Researcher*, 31(4): 15–25.

Cox, J.B., Al Arkoubi, K. and Estrada, S.D. (2006) 'National human resource development in transitioning societies in the developing world: Morocco', *Advances in Developing Human Resources*, 8(1): 84–98.

Dalacoura, K. (2005) 'US democracy promotion in the Arab Middle East since 11 September 2001: a critique', *International Affairs*, 81(5): 963–79.

David, P.A. and Foray, D. (2003) 'Economic fundamentals of the knowledge society', *Policy Futures in Education*, 1(1): 20–49.

Debord, G. (2005 [1967]) *The Society of the Spectacle*, trans. K. Knabb. London: Rebel Press.

Dutta, S. and Coury, M.E. (2003) 'ICT challenges for the Arab world', in S. Dutta, B. Lanvin and F. Paua (eds) *Global Information Technology Report, 2002–2003:*

Readiness for the Networked World, Oxford: Oxford University Press and the World Economic Forum.

Ehteshami, A. and Murphy, E. (1996) 'Transformation of the corporatist state in the Middle East', *Third World Quarterly*, 17(4): 753–72.

Elbadawi, I.A. (2005) 'Reviving growth in the Arab world', *Economic Development and Cultural Change*, 53: 293–336.

El Kenz, A. (2005) *Europe and the Arab World: Patterns and Prospects for the New Relationship*, London: Zed Books.

Fakhro, M. (2003) 'Globalization and equity in the Arab world', paper presented at the Fourth Annual Global Development Conference, Egypt: Global Development Network, 19–21 January.

Halstead, J.M. (2004) 'An Islamic concept of education', *Comparative Education*, 40(4): 517–29.

Hautecoeur, J.-P. (ed.) (2002) *Ecological Education in Everyday Life*, Toronto, ON: University of Toronto Press.

Heyneman, S.P. (1997) 'The quality of education in the Middle East and North Africa (MENA)', *International Journal of Educational Development*, 17(4): 449–66.

Joseph, S. (1996) 'Patriarchy and development in the Arab world', *Gender and Development*, 4(2): 14–19.

Kabbani, N. and Kothari, E. (2005) *Youth Unemployment in the MENA Region: A Situational Assessment*, Washington, DC: World Bank.

Kirchner, H. (2001) 'Internet in the Arab world: a step towards "information society"?', in K. Hafez (ed.) *Mass Media, Politics and Society in the Middle East*, Cresskill, NJ: Hampton Press.

Labyadh, S. (2004) 'What role for globalisation in the events of September 11 and the occupation of Iraq?', *Shu'un 'Arabiya* [Arab Affairs], 120: 122–41 (Arabic).

Lubeck, P.M. (1998) 'Islamists responses to globalization: cultural conflict in Egypt, Algeria and Malaysia', in B. Crawford (ed.) *The Myth of 'Ethnic Conflict': Politics, Economics and Cultural 'Violence'*, Berkeley, CA: University of California Press.

Mahdi, S.T. and Barrientos, A. (2003) 'Saudisation and employment in Saudi Arabia', *Career Development International*, 8(2): 70–7.

Mazawi, A.E. (2005) 'Contrasting perspectives on higher education governance in the Arab states', in J.C. Smart (ed.) *Higher Education: Handbook of Theory and Research*, 20, Dordrecht: Springer Science, 133–89.

Mellahi, K. (2000) 'Human resource development through vocational education in Gulf cooperation countries: the case of Saudi Arabia', *Journal of Vocational Education and Training*, 52(2): 329–44.

Miles, R. (2002) 'Employment and unemployment in Jordan: the importance of the gender system', *World Development*, 30(3): 413–27.

Murphy, E. (2006a) 'The state and the private sector in North Africa: seeking specificity', *Mediterranean Politics*, 6(2): 1–28.

Murphy, E. (2006b) 'Agency and space: the political impact of information technologies in the Gulf Arab states', *Third World Quarterly*, 27(6): 1059–83.

Muysken, J. and Nour, S. (2006) 'Deficiencies in education and poor prospects for economic growth in the Gulf countries: the case of the UAE', *Journal of Development Studies*, 42(6): 957–80.

Nicks-McCaleb, L. (2005) 'The impact of state funded higher education on neighbourhood and community in the United Arab Emirates', *International Education Journal*, 6(3): 322–34.

Okruhlik, G. (2002) 'Networks of dissent: Islamism and reform in Saudi Arabia', *Current History*, January: 22–8.

Pasha, M.K. (2002) 'Predatory globalization and democracy in the Islamic world', *Annals of the American Academy of Political Science*, 581(1): 121–32.

Patterson, R. and Wilson, E.J. (2000) 'New IT and social inequality: resetting the research and policy agenda', *The Information Society*, 16: 77–86.

Peters, M. (2001) 'Education, enterprise culture and the entrepreneurial self: a Foucauldian perspective', *Journal of Educational Inquiry*, 2(2): 58–71.

Peters, M. with Besley, A.C. (2006) *Building Knowledge Cultures: Education and Development in the Age of Knowledge Capitalism*, Lanham, MD: Rowman and Littlefield.

Posusney, M.P. (2003) 'Globalization and labor protection in oil-poor Arab countries: racing to the bottom?', *Global Social Policy*, 3(3): 267–97.

Saad, M. and Zawdie, G. (2005) 'From technology transfer to the emergence of a triple helix culture: the experience of Algeria in innovation and technological capability development', *Technology Analysis and Strategic Management*, 17(1): 89–103.

Sadiki, L. (1997) 'Towards Arab liberal governance: from the democracy of bread to the democracy of the vote', *Third World Quarterly*, 18(1): 127–48.

Sa'igh, A. bin A. (2001) 'Education for citizenship and the challenges for globalization in the Arab countries', report commissioned by the Arab League Educational, Cultural and Scientific Organization (ALECSO) Al-Riyadh, Saudi Arabia: King Saud University, Faculty of Education. http://www.alecso.org.tn/ anglais/pages/dirasa/dirasa-001.htm.

Sakr, N. (2004) 'UN analysis of aggregate Arab "knowledge deficit"', *The Political Quarterly*, 75(2): 185–90.

Saleh, N.A.M. (2002) 'Research management issues in the Arab countries', *Higher Education Policy*, 15: 225–47.

Tadros, M. (2006) 'State welfare in Egypt since adjustment: hegemonic control with a minimalist role', *Review of African Political Economy*, 33(June): 237–54.

Tarabichi, G. (2000) *From Arab Renaissance to Apostasy: Arab Culture and its Discontents in the Age of Globalization*, London and Beirut: Saqi Books (Arabic).

Tzannatos, Z. (2000) 'Social protection in the Middle East and North Africa: a review', paper presented at the Mediterranean Forum, Cairo, Egypt: March.

Tzannatos, Z. and Handoussa, H. (eds) (2001) *Employment Creation and Social Protection in the MENA Region*, Cairo: American University in Cairo Press.

United Nations Development Programme (UNDP) (2002) *Arab Human Development Report: Creating Opportunities for Future Generations*, New York: UNDP.

United Nations Development Programme (UNDP) (2003) *Arab Human Development Report: Building An Arab Knowledge Society*, New York: UNDP.

United Nations Educational, Scientific and Cultural Organization (UNESCO) (1998) 'Beirut declaration on higher education in the Arab states for the XXIst century', Arab Regional Conference on Higher Education. Beirut, Lebanon: 2–5 March.

Warschauer, M. (2003) 'The allures and illusions of modernity: technology and educational reform in Egypt', *Educational Policy Analysis Archives*, 11(38). http://epaa.asu.edu/epaa/v11n38.

Warschauer, M. (2004) 'The rhetoric and reality of aid: promoting educational technology in Egypt', *Globalisation, Societies and Education*, 2(3): 377–90.

Wheeler, D.L. (2003) 'Egypt: building an information society for international development', *Review of African Political Economy*, 30: 627–42.

Wilkins, S. (2001) 'Human resource development through vocational education in the United Arab Emirates: the case of Dubai Polytechnic', *Journal of Vocational Education and Training*, 54(1): 5–26.

Winch, C. (2003) 'Education and the knowledge economy: a response to David and Foray', *Policy Futures in Education*, 1(1): 50–70.

Yousef, T. (2004) *Unlocking the Employment Potential in the Middle East and North Africa: Toward a New Social Contract*, Washington, DC: World Bank.

Zahlan, A. (1999) *The Arabs and the Challenges of Science and Technology: Progress Without Change*, Beirut, Lebanon: Centre for Arab Unity Studies (Arabic).

Zyab, M. (2002) 'The threats of globalisation to the Arab homeland', *Al-Mustaqbal Al-'Arabi* (The Arab Future), 276 (Arabic).

21 Pedagogical approaches to work-related learning with special reference to the low-skilled

Knud Illeris

This chapter focuses on the special problems of low-skilled adults in relation to adult education. It is well known that, unfortunately, overall the low-skilled are participating in adult education programmes to a lower extent than other groups. The reason for this is partly that companies and nations do not seem very interested in investing in education for this group, and partly that the low-skilled themselves are not very inclined to take part in adult education. Based on three years' research in the area, the chapter discusses the psychological motives for the reservations and ambivalence of the low-skilled and suggests various ways to deal with the issue in practice – the main key being to build on the subjective needs for qualification and to avoid challenging feelings of inferiority, deficits, defeat and failures of the past.

Introduction

This chapter emerges from the three-year Research Consortium on Workplace Learning which was run by the Learning Lab Denmark from September 2001 to the end of 2004. The consortium involved eleven senior researchers and five graduate students, included sixteen empirical projects and, in addition to the project reports, published four edited books, several articles, a special issue of the *Journal of Workplace Learning* (Ellström and Illeris 2004), and a final book, *Learning in Working Life*, which also came out in an English edition (Illeris *et al.* 2004).

The special problem of the low-skilled

One of the main purposes of our consortium was to highlight the special problems of the low-skilled section of the workforce. It is well known that those who already have the weakest educational background also participate in organised continuing education and training to a lesser extent than other groups. It seems to be a consistent trend that the more previous education one has, the higher the probability of participating in organised adult education. This obviously makes the low-skilled more vulnerable in all contexts where educational level is important, and therefore they constitute one of the most fundamental, difficult and serious problems in connection with the issue of workplace learning.

This problem is rapidly increasing at present in the industrialised countries of the west, in line with the reduction in the share of jobs that can be performed with a limited education. The background is a relative decline in the labour-market share of industry and manufacturing and increasing automation within these occupations, and at the same time, rising demands for personal competences and computer qualifications in the expanding areas within the service, health and social sectors at all levels.

This reduces job openings for the low-skilled – and when unemployment is relatively high, this decline is enhanced by the better educated looking for jobs that are beneath the level of their qualifications. The question of educational standards thus becomes mixed with the more individual question of who has the right personal competences.

Thus the problems traditionally related to the low-skilled have increased in scope and content during the last twenty years. The field has become more complicated and varied, requiring particularly differentiated, flexible and sensitive openings and services, and this implies far-reaching demands for innovative thinking, engagement and flexibility, both politically and administratively, and in the business sector, from the top to shop-floor level.

The subjective feeling of ambivalence

In relation to any kind of formal education or training it is characteristic of most low-skilled individuals that they are subjectively deeply ambivalent about any kind of formal education or training. They want, and they do not want, to participate at one and the same time. When my colleagues and I interview such people, whether at workplaces or in educational settings, we have observed that in general they know very well that what they need in order to obtain a stable job situation is formal education or training. But at the same time they strongly wish that this was not the case (Illeris 2003b, 2003c).

It is evident that most of the low-skilled did not do very well at school. They have had nine or more years of everyday experience of not being good enough, they have often been humiliated and marginalised, and they wished to leave school as soon as they possibly could. Very few of them feel any desire to return to a situation that would remind them of all their failures and humiliations – and probably also repeat them. On the other hand, it becomes more and more obvious that this is the only way out of their vulnerable situation.

Thus the low-skilled nearly always have a rather clear awareness of their need for more general education, in areas such as reading, written skills, arithmetic and mathematics, foreign languages, computer skills and general social and cultural orientation. But the forces pulling in the opposite direction – their lack of self-confidence in terms of education and the unpleasantness of going back to school – are usually stronger. For this reason they need a special incentive, a relevant opening that links up with their own needs, and the reduction of the social, practical and financial barriers, not least the experience of humiliation.

The need for subjective anchorage

Educational initiatives for the low-skilled today seem to be more varied and confused than before. If this is to be handled seriously, that is as something other than making the statistics look good and perhaps resolving the situation for a few of those who have the strongest resources, there is a need for radical initiatives that consistently take their starting point from the low-skilled, and respect their situation as they experience it. Nothing much happens if those who are to learn are not met with something that is meaningful for them on the basis of their own premises (Illeris 2004a).

Some kind of subjective anchorage seems to be the key to activities and measures that can provide a broader breakthrough. It must be realised that the majority of the low-skilled, in different ways, are in situations where they are not open directly to traditional educational initiatives. They do not really believe in them, they have bad experiences of not being able to live up to what is expected, and they usually have repeatedly experienced what it means to be rejected, not feel respected, etc.

But, simultaneously, relevant initiatives must also move things along, because it is precisely the current situation and the way the individual relates to it, that is the problem. A sustainable solution thus presupposes an educational angst that must be overcome, some type of breakthrough, an identity defence that must be opened, or perhaps some dreams and goals that must be found somewhere in what is experienced as a great unstructured vacuum.

These are processes that psychologically go deeper than what is generally understood as learning (Illeris 2004b). Nevertheless in the great majority of cases, competence-developing initiatives are the best way forward, because the development of better and more practically relevant competences are an important part of what is necessary to escape from the situation. However, it must be accepted at a political, administrative and practical level, that the development of relevant competences for this group is directly connected to some deep and demanding psychological processes that cannot be disregarded if progress is to be made.

This does not merely require respectful understanding of the situation as the person in question experiences it. It also requires an accepting firmness that stays with the social realities, in the face of justified insecurity and unrealistic wishful thinking. Being educated for places for which they are not needed helps nobody, but if they are to go for something where they are needed, they must want it themselves. The psychologically liberating and the socially relevant qualifying processes must be united in one practical process (Illeris 2003a).

Therefore these functions must be undertaken by people who can manage this duality. These people can be difficult to find and it may be necessary to take action in this area from the point of view of both education and salary. In addition, time and relevant opportunities in relation to the labour market must be available. Overall it must be accepted that such processes cannot be successful over a broad area if there is no willingness to accept the subjective needs of those concerned and to invest the necessary resources. After all, there is a lot of money to be saved at the other end each time the process succeeds and what was a painful and costly problem becomes a qualified workforce.

If we want to tackle the problems of the low-skilled in the breadth and complexity they have today, we must realise that it does not help to invest in minimum solutions. Half-baked solutions will only result in new problems with even greater human and economic costs. In the following, I shall try to approach in more detail what is important for tackling these problems at the practical level.

Contacts and the way in

The low-skilled who are in the labour market often already have, as mentioned, a sceptical approach to anything that reminds them of teaching and school, and at the same time workplaces are also often reluctant to involve them in special learning initiatives. It is of crucial importance to introduce openings and incentives that directly respond to this scepticism and blocks off the low-skilled from general education and skills upgrading, not least in such areas as reading, writing, arithmetic and computer skills, and likewise general information about work-relevant and social subjects.

In the first place it is a matter of establishing contacts with the sceptical workers and employees so they can contribute to thematising the needs for learning that most of them actually express in the studies conducted in the area. There would seem to be a need for personal contacts that can be experienced as loyal and respectful, whereas contacts experienced as coming from above, from management or public authorities, do not usually have the best chance of being successful. Experience has shown that outreach activity by interested co-workers, union representatives, health and safety representatives or people who themselves work with continuing education at shop-floor level stand the best chances of getting a relevant dialogue going (Illeris *et al.* 2004). But this requires time, engagement and a certain amount of experience as to how it can be done. Therefore the resources must be present to upgrade such contact persons and to provide for the necessary time and the practical opportunities needed.

In one of our projects we had remarkably good experiences and results with adult educators contacting unskilled workers in local industrial enterprises. But we also learned that this requires that the educators have time for individual talks with the workers, have relevant offers prepared in advance and are willing to adjust them in accordance with the needs expressed by the workers and, consequently, that there is special earmarked funding available for such contact activities (Illeris *et al.* 2004). If the funding must be provided by the general operating costs of the institution, it seems to be almost a law of nature that this is not sufficient for the task to be successful.

However, many of the low-skilled that need training are not employed. Actually, the majority of adult education participants in Denmark have been placed, referred or sent to attend the education programme in question by public authorities or agencies, and this has usually not been a positive experience. In the course of my research I have been rather shocked to observe the proportion of participants in adult education programmes who felt they had been "placed" there and who had no reasonable prior knowledge of what the course aimed to achieve (Illeris 2003b).

Without doubt, part of the background for this is that the referring bodies work under considerable time pressure and are subject to very tight limits as to the amount of time they are allowed to allocate to each client. The outcome is that these bodies are forced to consider their task completed as soon as a client has been admitted into an education programme.

This situation is, however, doubly disempowering for the participants: first, they feel that they are under compulsion or pressure when they approach these authorities, and second, they feel that then they are not even shown reasonable individual concern. For counselling in this context to be ethically defensible and practical as well as economically appropriate, it is of decisive importance that it is provided until the individual in question psychologically "accepts the result". There is a need for a dialogue that takes its point of departure in the individual's own premises, as well as for time for the individual to ponder the issues, discuss it with others with whom they feel confident, get used to the idea, find the subjectively positive aspects of the situation, and first and foremost accept entering into the project actively and wholeheartedly.

The decisive importance of division of responsibility

It is also of decisive importance that the point of departure of planning is that the participants are adults, i.e. humans who both formally and in reality are responsible for their own actions and decisions. Of course, this applies also to their learning. Actually, the element of adult training programmes that participants react most strongly against is that this responsibility is not respected. Perhaps they do not even respect it themselves. But all this disrespect seems mainly to stem from the fact that we have all acquired some notions of learning from our schooldays in which it is precisely the distribution of responsibility that is different because the students are children.

The question of division of responsibility is fundamental when we are concerned with adult education and training. Once we have realised this, we also have the key to understanding many apparently irrational matters, ranging from general planning to all sorts of minor and major practical details at floor level. Part of this is that it is the learners themselves who basically perceive this as natural and legitimate even though, at the same time, they more or less consciously react against it.

Therefore it is not so simple, in that we just decide that adult education and training within a certain given framework is the learners' responsibility. Those who manage such training programmes must make an active effort not to assume the responsibility, an action which rather paradoxically also involves them having to accept responsibility for "returning" responsibility to the learners. This is not as uncomplicated as it may immediately sound. In practice, it has proved to be a highly difficult process, which very often involves surmounting deeply rooted resistance, and it therefore requires perseverance and determination from both sides (cf. Illeris 2004a).

First, it is always difficult for leaders and instructors to surrender their position of power voluntarily and even actively. In addition, assuming responsibility for not assuming responsibility appears both paradoxical and contradictory. However, this *is* exactly what is required. Furthermore, the situation may in practice be highly sensitive and emotional, and there is a very fine line between the learners' responsibility for their own learning and the leader's responsibility for providing the optimal conditions and input for this learning.

In existing programmes, the learners may easily be perceived as irresponsible just because they hesitate to assume responsibility for what they ultimately experience as what others have decided for them. It may well be that in many cases they would have decided the same thing or something similar themselves, but they have seldom had the opportunity for this because the culture dictates that most important decisions are made by others on their behalf. It may also be that they find it difficult to make decisions themselves when they have the opportunity, but this is, after all, exactly what the development of competence to a large extent is meant to produce. Therefore the leaders must not react to such problems by merely assuming responsibility, but on the contrary hold the learners to the fact that it is their responsibility.

Finally, the learners' taking responsibility for their own learning in no way means that there will be less responsibility for the leaders and instructors. On the contrary, it may be even more demanding in terms of responsibility when, in many everyday situations and details, leaders and instructors must constantly decide what may reasonably be considered the learners' own responsibility, and what the company or the instructor may and must assume responsibility for, instead of just fulfilling the traditional, responsible role that everybody is so familiar with.

The time, place and context of training and education activities

When planning the learning activities it is also important to constantly incorporate and respect the strained relations that many of the low-skilled have with school and education activities. At the start especially, both physically and from the point of view of content, everything must take place as close as possible to the daily place of work, and it also creates security if it takes place together with co-workers whom one knows well and trusts.

For those who are employed in larger enterprises, it will often be possible to place training activities in locations at the workplace, sometimes even combined with activities directly connected to production or other work. Other courses with unemployed participants or a mixed composition of participants may circulate between locations at school and various relevant workplaces, which will allow the participants to experience various work environments.

In general it is always important to take into account the fact that for learners who may often be fundamentally ambivalent, such practical features as time and place may easily be decisive for their attitude. It is much easier to accept loss of time and a lot of travel if participating in a programme that one has chosen voluntarily and maybe with enthusiasm. In Denmark we have quite a few examples of vocational training courses that take place at or close to the workplace at the end of the workday and with a fifty-fifty share of work time paid by the employer and leisure time relinquished by the workers. This is experienced as a "fair deal" and thus provides a good starting point and climate for learning.

Learning content and methods

With respect to the content and methods of the learning activities, it is important to range widely. Part of the problem for the low-skilled is often to see and understand the work in a larger context, to experience that it is performed in other ways at other places, to gain insight into what triggers and determines the changes that take place, to have the opportunity of asking questions and expressing doubt and resistance, to themselves try – for example through projects or the like – to be proactive in relation to their own work situation and work function, and to see that the experience and qualifications they have can be important and used as a starting point for learning more. It can be an almost euphoric experience for this group to realise that learning initiatives can also be something where one can make active use of one's experience, where one can play a part in deciding, and where what one contributes is not irrelevant.

One Danish example is a training programme at a large sugar factory where the participants prioritised teaching in the "soft" subjects like communication, active listening and coaching. At the same time the participants typically emphasised that being allowed to deal with subjects and problems from their own everyday work life was positive and different from what they had previously experienced during their time at school. That anyone "could be bothered doing something just for us" was quite a different and surprising experience that strengthened the self-confidence and self-awareness of many.

Very often workers' educational and training needs are not formulated clearly and unambiguously. Neither the enterprise's nor the employees' needs are something that can merely be "uncovered". Valuable training options rather emerge from a process in which the wishes of management, the needs of the employees and what an educational institution can offer, must be developed and adjusted to each other. This is often experienced as time consuming, but it gives the processes a solid anchorage for all parties involved and is also of importance for the implementation and subsequent follow up (Jørgensen 2004).

However, the most important need for qualifications for the low-skilled are generally in basic subjects such as writing, reading, languages and computer skills. This is usually also recognised by the learners themselves. But the more school-like teaching that is a necessary part of these subjects is precisely what they more or less consciously try to avoid. It was therefore a remarkable feature of the example mentioned above that when the participants had "broken the ice" by projects closely connected to their work situation, it was easier for them later to come to terms with a more traditional teaching situation and take up the more school-like subjects.

On the pedagogical level, it is important that the division of responsibility discussed above is translated in practice into real participant direction, that it is the participants who control the process in interaction with the instructors' qualified and loyal assistance and support. Another important pedagogical principle is problem orientation, in that the point of departure for the learning activities is taken in broadly defined thematic areas and problem fields that the participants find important in relation to the targets of their training programmes. This increases the possibilities for active, relevant learning. In general, participant direction and problem orientation are best practised through such pedagogical forms as action learning (Yorks *et al.* 1999) and project work (Illeris 2004a).

Evaluation and certification

Parallel with, and at the end of, training courses there is, as a rule, one or more form of monitoring and evaluation of the participants' activities and qualifications. Such monitoring and evaluation is in its source and essence a societal necessity, in that society must ensure that persons have specific skills to handle specific functions or to be accepted into further education. At the same time, it can be of great significance for the individual that he or she can get her/his qualifications formally approved, practically in regard to status, and psychologically as an acknowledgement that can provide identity and generate self-confidence.

The traditional forms of evaluation must be considered an obsolete reflection of industrial society. Through attendance monitoring and exams, participants are placed in opposition to the "system" as a powerful adversary, in the same way as in the labour conditions seen in industrial employment. The concern is with conformity and submission to external power-based demands and not the joint promotion of personal development and its realistic evaluation.

Naturally, the power aspect cannot be eliminated, but it is not impossible to find forms in which it assumes a less dominant character and respects the adult participants' experience to a higher degree, even though they also experience a certain duality between the wish for self-direction and the wish for obtaining formal approval.

Generally, the common attitude among adult training participants in Denmark today is that they would like to have documentation for completed education programmes, which not only testifies to satisfactory participation but also includes certification of the qualifications they have acquired. Though they show willingness to accept that as a learner one must have one's qualifications tested, there is widespread scepticism towards having this take place through an examination in the traditional sense. Many low-skilled learners have had painful experiences with exams, and indicate, among other things, that they involve heavy and irrelevant psychological pressure, that the evaluation is unfair, that too much depends on luck and coincidence, etc.

On the other hand, it is not easy for the participants to clearly express possible alternative ways of evaluating, as must be done in order to make it possible to document the competences acquired. However, it is a widely held view that evaluation must be carried out by the leaders or instructors with whom the learners have daily contact, because it is only they who have the background to know what the learner actually knows and is able to do and understand. In terms of learning, the concern is to find evaluation forms that support, and not inhibit, the participants' independence, responsibility, cooperation, etc., and thereby also their competence development.

References

Ellström, Per-Erik and Illeris, Knud (eds) (2004) 'Workplace learning: Scandinavian perspectives', *Journal of Workplace Learning*, special issue, 16(8).

Illeris, Knud (2003a) 'Workplace learning and learning theory', *Journal of Workplace Learning*, 15(4): 67–178.

Illeris, Knud (2003b) 'Adult education as experienced by the learners', *International Journal of Lifelong Education*, 22(1): 13–23.

Illeris, Knud (2003c) 'Low skilled adults' motivation for learning'. Paper presented at the CEDEFOP Conference on Lifelong Learning, Thessaloniki, June 2–3. Online. Available at:<http://www.ruc.dk/upload/application/pdf/3c5bf3cc/thessaloniki.pdf> (accessed 30 October 2006).

Illeris, Knud (2004a) *Adult Education and Adult Learning*, Melbourne, FL: Krieger Publishing.

Illeris, Knud (2004b) 'Transformative learning in the perspective of a comprehensive learning theory', *Journal of Transformative Education*, 2(2).

Illeris, Knud *et al.* (2004) *Learning in Working Life*, Copenhagen: Roskilde University Press.

Jørgensen, Christian Helms (2004) 'Connecting work and education: should learning be useful, correct or meaningful?' *Journal of Workplace Learning*, 16(8): 455–65.

Yorks, Lyle; O'Neill, Judy; Marsick, Victoria J. (1999) *Action Learning: Successful Strategies for Individual, Team and Organizational Development*, Baton Rouge, LA: Academy of Human Resource Development.

22 Gender matters in IT

Skills hierarchies and women's on-the-job learning

Shauna Butterwick, Kaela Jubas and Hong Zhu

The information technology (IT) field is a fruitful context within which to examine the relationship between work and learning given the rapid pace of change in the field and the constant demand to learn new skills. This discussion focuses on gender, work and learning grounded in an investigation of women who for the most part began their IT work in Canada without formal credentials. We explore their alternative learning pathways illustrating how women can do well in the knowledge-based economy. Their stories challenge the taken-for-granted notion that formal credentials are required for such jobs and illustrate that intuitive, artful approaches to solving IT problems are quite effective. Their stories also tell of encountering sexism and the need to learn not just IT-specific skills, but how to negotiate the gendered politics of the workplace.

Introduction

By bringing a gender lens, this discussion offers a counter narrative to dominant notions about educating the global workforce. In particular it challenges the lack of differentiation and notion of a generic worker and training strategy. While the dominant discourse about working in IT claims that workers must acquire formal training, almost all of our study participants entered IT without such credentials and learned their skills informally and on the job. While in many IT training programmes theoretical knowledge and linear problem solving pathways dominate, our study participants valued training that was more practically oriented and were quite successful in solving IT problems with intuitive and artful approaches. Our participants found IT to be a good place for women to work, but they also had to learn, in addition to their IT skills, how to deal with sexist attitudes. These findings are further explored in the discussion below which begins by outlining the study's feminist orientation, briefly describing the IT field in Canada, and noting previous research that has explored women's participation in IT training and workplaces.

Women learning and working in IT

A feminist epistemology frames this discussion and our study. This orientation sheds light on some assumptions about educating the global workforce and about the learning pathways to and within the IT field. As Huws (2000: 345) has argued, '[t]he transition to the knowledge society must … be set against a strongly differentiated background. "Men" and "women" cannot be seen as homogeneous categories but must be studied in their specific situations, where occupational and regional variables play a major role.' Our approach has been informed by the work of feminist theorists, such as Smith (1987), who calls for research which begins with women's everyday lived experience, in order to better understand the social and ruling relations immanent in and extending beyond the everyday. Such an approach, as Naples argues (2003: 84), can 'help to transform traditional categories of analysis that originate from dominant groups.'

This study builds upon and extends existing knowledge of women's experiences in IT training and workplaces. Like other countries, Canada is undergoing a transition in which IT is playing an important and increasing economic and societal role (Bowlby and Langlois, 2002). As Habtu (2003) notes, there is still much to be explored in relation to who works in the IT field and what tasks they perform. It was only in 2001 that Statistics Canada began collecting information about IT workers; at the time, 2.6 per cent of Canada's labour force (or approximately 406,700 people) were located in the IT sector with women making up one quarter (28 per cent). When the notion of IT jobs is expanded beyond programming and software engineering, women's participation is much higher; almost half of business analysts, help desk staff, and administrators are women, and in areas such as technical communications, they are the majority of workers as website developers and IT trainers and the like (Panteli *et al.*, 2001; Lahey, 2002; Selfe and Hawisher, 2002; Habtu, 2003). Furthermore, research has found that many women working in these feminized niches do not have formal IT credentials (Millar and Jagger, 2001). Countering the notion that formal IT credentials are necessary to work in IT, a gendered lens reveals that 'the field of information technology is a roadway with many on-ramps' (Turner *et al.*, 2002: 16).

Women's experiences in IT have also been influenced by the boom (1997 to 2000) and bust (2001) years of the IT industry (Bowlby and Langlois, 2002). Over the course of 2001, the bust of the sector had a particularly strong impact on workers with the lowest levels of education and women, as they experienced the greatest threat of job loss (Bowlby and Langlois, 2002; Bowlby, 2003).

The studies mentioned above, together with research that outlines women's low participation in traditional computing science university programmes, indicate that women are acquiring their IT skills through alternative pathways (Millar and Jagger, 2001; MacInnis, 2003). Research on IT curricula can help to shed light on women's reluctance to participate in formal training. Many programmes, particularly those in university, emphasize theory over practice, technical over 'softer' interpersonal and communication skills, and rational-linear problem-solving over developing intuition (McDill *et al.*, 2000; Turkle and Papert, 1990). This hierarchy of skills persists, despite a recognition that the abstract approach to programming evident in computing studies leads to 'impoverished notions of electronic literacy' (Selfe and Hawisher, 2002: 241). Efforts have been made to introduce alternative approaches to the IT curriculum, some of which have increased women's enrolment (e.g. Margolis and Fisher, 2002). Despite these efforts, a gender hierarchy persists in which men's technical expertise is considered superior (by both instructors and students, male and female), even when women outperform their male peers (Henwood, 2000).

We have built upon these inquiries and focused our investigation on the work and learning histories of women who, for the most part, entered the IT field without formal credentials, examining their approaches to learning, whether these informally acquired skills are recognized and rewarded, and their general views of working in the IT field.

Exploring women's informal learning pathways to IT jobs

This project[1] is a partnership between community-based and academic feminist researchers. ACTEW (A Commitment to Training and Employment for Women), an umbrella organization of training agencies based in Toronto, initiated the project when its members noted women's increasing participation and the issue of IT credentials. Between 2003 and 2005, using a snowball sampling technique, we gathered the work and learning histories from 75 women who live and work in and around Vancouver, Victoria and Toronto, Canada. Our participants' ages ranged from 24 to 60 years. Most were white, middle class and able-bodied women[2] of European ancestry. Overall only a small proportion had children, and no participants had young children; those with children (who were now grown) were in their late forties and early fifties. All had some post-secondary education and most had university degrees, mainly in the social sciences. Almost all the women, once they began working in IT, had also participated in some short-term formal IT training either on or off the job. Our participants worked in diverse occupational niches, from positions typically associated with the IT field (e.g., network administration, programming and software engineering, and web development and design) to those often omitted from accounts of the field (e.g., technical writing, project management, and secretarial work).

In the following discussion we focus on several aspects of the work and learning histories we have gathered, outlining in particular some key findings which challenge assumptions about educating the global workforce. Given the space limitations of this chapter, we cannot offer contextually detailed portraits of all our participants. To give some sense of the kinds of work and learning histories gathered, however, we begin with a longer narrative from Laura[3] whom we interviewed in 2003. At that time, Laura was 50 years old, married with no children, and working as a business analyst in government.

Laura's story

INTERVIEWER: Can you tell us about your background, education and how you started working in IT?

LAURA: In my case, I completed various undergraduate courses, mainly in arts, but do not have a degree. In my early years of high school I actually belonged to a computer club, so it was the kind of thing that interested me even though I ended up going on to other interests. After some post-secondary courses, I did a number of different things including working as a claims officer. It was via that job that I got into IT. The IT area needed more staff and so they held an internal competition that offered on-the-job training. This was about 25 years ago, back in the days of punch cards with very few people actually in the field. They offered a course which was essentially text-based along with a video tape. The rest of the training involved doing tasks of increasing complexity. Within the IT department, some resisted other areas of the company moving into IT, especially the people who didn't have a degree, who weren't from IT, and happened to be female. Unfortunately, I ended up working for one of these people. He often gave me incorrect information, led me down the wrong track, and in some cases deliberately sabotaged me. His behaviour was quite apparent to other people around me who would tell me how to handle this kind of a situation.

INTERVIEWER: Please describe for us how you approach learning IT on the job.

LAURA: For me, I keep all the information I've gathered and approach a problem intuitively. I go more directly to the solution and have all of that background more closely at hand and draw on it relatively unconsciously. I bring to problem solving all of my life experience. While I can go right to the heart of the solution, the words for the explanation might not be there. It's very clear what needs to be done, but because the appropriate jargon is not necessarily being used, and the path is not being explicitly demonstrated, it ends up affecting credibility. The other kind of things that present obstacles for me in learning are available time and competing tasks because it's relatively rare to have time that can be devoted strictly to learning. It has to be done in the context of doing a number of other activities.

INTERVIEWER: What resources do you use; what supports your learning?

LAURA: A lot of my learning experiences occur at home. In order to stay current, I find that this ends up needing to become my hobby as well. I spend $600 to $1000 a year on computer-related books. One of the main sources of information for me is also the internet. Within our union contract we can take a minimum of five days of training per year and often I take more training than that.

INTERVIEWER: Are IT jobs good jobs for women?

LAURA: Early on, when it was a new area it was good; everyone was valued and had status. Now that's less so. I've seen the numbers of women decrease over the years. Credentials are now becoming very important.

IT: a road with many onramps

Our study participants' work and learning histories challenge notions that formal IT credentials are key to accessing IT jobs and that career paths into IT are linear. Several participants, like Laura, explained how their first formalized IT learning took place in the workplace, often provided by their employers. For older participants in particular, these 'back and side door' points of entry occurred at a time when the IT field was in its infancy, with fewer IT training programmes in existence. While knowledge of IT is still essential for working in the field, these women's accounts illustrate that these skills can be effectively acquired through informal and on-the-job learning. Participants' work histories looked something like a 'snakes and ladders' game; women had begun working post-high school and after university in other kinds of work, often in such feminized clerical fields as office administration.

In Laura's case, although she had been interested in computers early on, her first few jobs were mainly in some form of office administration. Laura made a conscious choice (likely informed by her earlier interest in computers) to seize the chance to enter the field, and her IT career grew from there. Another participant of similar age, who also did not have a post-secondary credential, first encountered computers when she was a clerical volunteer working on a community newspaper and then later, when working in a temporary clerical position. In both situations, her interest and aptitude were recognized and in the latter situation, her employer provided on-the-job training. 'He said that I had an aptitude for the computer and got me specialized Word training [with] their computer consultant [who] showed me a lot of stuff about keeping a network and installing software and working my way through'.

Other participants can be considered the 'accidental IT worker' as their stories speak of a less conscious choice to move into IT. As IT began to be increasingly used in many workplaces, they found themselves having to learn in order to cope; many became the office IT expert. 'I ended up being the director's secretary, but he didn't need one so I got to do other things and at that time we were just starting with the internet ... I got trained in Front Page ... basically everything grew up around me and I became the expert.' One participant shifted to IT after taking a government-funded course when she was unemployed. 'I got lucky that I got laid off because I was able to take this course with government support.'

Their stories illustrate that women can do well in IT without beginning with formal IT credentials, although, as discussed in the next section, many did eventually participate in IT training. While they recognized the value of an IT credential, many were critical of these programmes, particularly when a theoretical orientation was emphasized over practical application.

Effectiveness and support for formal IT training

As noted, once they began working in IT, many of the participants attended short-term workshops and some took longer certificates and diplomas in IT. Many noted that rapid changes in IT development made finding a relevant training programme difficult. While Laura, who worked in a unionized site (which was not the case for most of our participants), received support for her IT training, she also noted that to keep up, she often took more training than that which was funded and spent considerable time and money on self-study. Many noted, as did Laura, that it was often difficult to find time to focus on learning a specific IT skill, given the pace and demands of their work, and they also recognized that the pace of change made on-the-job learning essential.

Many of our participants did get some kind of employer-supported training, most of it on the job, while fewer women were supported to take time off work for training. 'The business allowed me to take the time to do [courses] and they encouraged a couple of other courses that they paid for.' One participant who had taken the plunge and paid for an expensive IT certificate at a polytechnical institution had mixed reviews about the return on her investment. 'I would say that overall the program wasn't a huge success in terms of job placement at the end. Certainly wasn't as rosy a picture as they like to give people with your $16,000.' Another participant, who was self-employed, wanted to take further training but her status as a consultant made this difficult. 'When you're thinking about whether you can pay the rent all the time, you're not thinking about furthering your education'.

Several participants were very critical of the kind of education they encountered in formal training settings. 'They had a little course talking about CPM which was the first of very many disappointing computer courses. Most of them are totally useless, they don't talk to what you really need, they talk theory.' Another participant, who took training from a private IT agency, found the instruction was very poor. 'I felt that I didn't get too much out of having an instructor teach me the course. I didn't feel there would have been too much difference in learning the materials [on my own].'

While many participants were critical of formalized training that was theoretically oriented and that required they follow a linear problem solving pathway, they also commented on how the credential helped them gain entry to jobs. 'I think from an employer's point of view, they want to see that you've been through some sort of a formal educational program. And really that was what I felt the benefit of the program was giving me that formalized qualification.' Other participants experienced closed doors because they did not have the IT credentials employers were looking for, despite their informally acquired skills. 'I was laid off in the recession of 92 ... I couldn't get a job in IT because I didn't have formal training.' This participant then sought out some formal training and worked her way up from help desk to a management position, but when she faced another layoff, she decided to leave IT. 'Then I got laid off again for heaven sakes and decided time for change and that's why I embarked on this [new] business.'

Another older participant explained the challenges of IT workers who began working when there was little IT training offered and, who, as a result, were self-taught. 'We're from this generation that knows a lot but not quite everything. There are very few [technical] courses offered for people at the sort of level we're at and [who] want to learn more, because most of those people ... are basically self-taught.'

Our study illustrates the paradox of formal IT training. The credential helps them get jobs and promotions, however, the training is sometimes irrelevant to the real demands of their jobs and having a credential does not protect them from lay offs.

Informal, social and intuitive learning

While participants were critical of the limitations of theoretically driven formal training, all embraced the learning imperative of IT and engaged in ongoing, informal, collaborative and intuitive learning processes. They gradually built a base of IT knowledge by 'scaffolding' existing understanding, watching and interacting with others, and using their intuition as they encountered new problems. Observing others was frequently mentioned as key to learning IT in the early stages. 'I would consciously try to observe other people and see what kinds of things they were doing and try to make a note of them ... people I perceived as being successful [and] trying to figure out what it was they did in order to become successful.' While they engaged with a lot of self-directed learning, that process also involved interactions with other colleagues or friends.

I took some books out of this library, went home and started creating [web] pages ... I created this little site and then it was more or less practice. I just practiced on my own time. And Fran and I were talking back and forth. So we would talk and she was really interested in the graphics end of it. So as she got into graphics I would pick things up from her so I didn't have to do so much on my own because there's a lot of fiddling with graphics.

Many were like Laura who described her problem solving as intuitive and a process that drew upon many different aspects of their life experiences, not just their IT work. Participants offered different definitions of intuition – from 'gut feeling' to 'a pre-verbal instinct that you somehow have to articulate to yourself,' to 'something that you feel is right, based on what you've done before when you have encountered similar problems, without really thinking about it' to 'thinking wild' to 'I have no idea where to start and my body just goes, and, oh ... this is exactly what I'm looking for.'

These informal, social and intuitive approaches stand in stark contrast to the dominant discourse on work and learning which tend to emphasize formal training and conceptualizes learning as an individualistic and linear process.

Surviving the gendered politics of IT

While learning IT skills was important to their success in the IT field, participants also spoke about lessons they learned about themselves and how to effectively address the gendered politics of IT. IT work had been a good move to make for most participants given the decent salary, diversity of jobs and constant challenge to deal with changes in IT development. While it was described as a good place to work, many participants also told stories of discrimination and harassment using phrases such as 'the boys' club' to characterize the IT field. Laura's story of the sexism that she encountered was matched by that of another participant, who described a difficult conversation with a client. 'This one particular day I call him back and we're chatting. He said to me "Oh, you're one of those" and I said "What do you mean?" He said "You're one of those one in 100,000 women who think".' This participant developed specific strategies to address sexism, which involved presenting herself as strong and assertive. These efforts, however, sometimes led to more encounters with sexist beliefs. 'I'm a strong woman and they can sense that ... They need, for their own personal comfort, to have a woman who is not going to come up with too many ideas [of her own].' Another participant commented on the importance of continually assessing each new encounter, an approach she felt most men did not have to develop. 'A woman is automatically not to be trusted and will be tested, whereas [with] a man moving into the same space, there would be an assumption of skill and confidence.'

Another participant, the only woman in an IT software development company, had to routinely negotiate the masculinist IT culture. As a minority, she learned to keep silent in the face of sexist jokes. 'It's still such an "old boys" network. I mean, you go into a software company and the programming department is likely to be 80 percent men. What do they joke about? They joke about, you know, they make offensive sexual comments. And as a woman, you … end up being uncomfortable. But what can you say?'

Conclusion

Our study captures stories of women who are successfully working in IT without formal credentials and how they take initiative with their learning. Their experiences illustrate how informal learning is key to developing and maintaining IT skills, and the effectiveness of artful and intuitive approaches. The IT field appears to value their contributions and to some extent support their alternative approaches to learning. Our work confirms the findings of existing studies, and expands our understanding of women's role in IT by exploring how and what they learned. As Lipsett (2000) has argued, women's approaches to technology and learning are an asset, and 'multifaceted competencies, including the communication and social skills required for team and project organization are becoming strategically more important … women can be proactive in adjusting to new realities by honing these skills' (ibid: 327).

It is important to also recognize that, at times, our participants' informally acquired IT competence was challenged, as was their social location as women. At certain moments, a skills and gendered hierarchy was in operation, one which positioned technical over social skills, and formal learning over informal learning. To help understand this tension, we return to feminist theory, particularly Smith's (1993) understanding of an important dialectic where women are the subjects and active creators of their experiences, as well as being objects of the social relations which organize contemporary capitalist operations.

The now massive productive apparatus of capital that depends upon, services and produces the material dimensions of the social relations of femininity, also depends upon and must be responsive to women's active participation. Women are not just the passive products of socialization; they are active; they create themselves. At the same time, their self-creation, their work and the uses of their skills, are coordinated with the market (Smith, 1993: 161).

Our study draws attention to the deeper and more nuanced understanding of educating the global workforce that emerges when attention is given to the specific context of work and learning using a gender lens.

Notes

1 We are one of 12 case studies that are participating in a research network focusing on the 'Changing Working Conditions and Lifelong Learning in the New Economy' which is known by the acronym WALL (Work and Lifelong Learning). It is funded by the Social Sciences and Humanities Research Council of Canada (SSHRC).
2 Only one of our participants indicated that she had a disability.
3 Laura is a pseudonym as are any references to specific work sites. Her narrative is made up of a compilation of excerpts from one interview.

References

Bowlby, G. (2003) 'High-tech: two years after the boom', *Perspectives on Labour and Income Statistics Canada*, Catalogue 75-001-XIE, November 2003: 14–17.
Bowlby, G. and Langlois, S. (2002) 'High-tech boom and bust', *Perspectives on Labour and Income, Statistics Canada*, Catalogue 75-001-XIE, April 2002: 12–18.
Habtu, R. (2003) 'Information technology workers', *Perspectives on Labour and Income, Statistics Canada*, Catalogue 75-001-XIE, July 2003: 5–11.
Henwood, F. (2000) 'From the woman question in technology to the technology question in feminism: rethinking gender equality in IT education', *European Journal of Women's Studies*, 7: 209–27.
Huws, U. (2000) 'The changing gender division of labour in the transition to the knowledge society', in K. Rubenson and H. Schuetze (eds) *Transition to the Knowledge Society: Policies and Strategies for Individual Participation and Learning*, Vancouver: University of British Columbia, Institute for European Studies.
Lahey, L. (2002) 'Band of sisters' [electronic version], *Computing Canada*, 13 December: 26.
Lipsett, B. (2000) 'The impact of the knowledge-based economy of women's participation', in K. Rubenson and B. Schuetze (eds) *Transition to the Knowledge Society: Policies and Strategies for Individual Participation and Learning*, Vancouver: University of British Columbia, Institute for European Studies.
McDill, M., Mills, S. and Henderson, Y. (2000) 'Tracking the gender barrier: a 1990s follow-up study' (Draft/preprint), Presentation from New Frontiers, New Traditions (6th Annual Conference), St John's, NF, 6–8 July 2000. Available <http://www.ccwest.org/DBSearchEngine/Conf2000Papers/McDillMoyra.pdf> (accessed 15 January 2004).
MacInnis, P. (2003) 'The gender gap' [electronic version], *Computing Canada*, 6 June: 26.
Margolis, J. and Fisher, A. (2002) *Unlocking the Clubhouse: Women in Computing*, Cambridge, MA and London: MIT Press.
Millar, J. and Jagger, N. (2001) *Women in ITEC Courses and Careers: Final Report*. Available <http://www.dfes.gov.uk/research/data/uploadfiles/ACFE89.pdf> (accessed 7 January 2004).
Naples, N. (2003) *Feminism and Method: Ethnography, Discourse Analysis, and Activist Research*, New York: Routlege.
Panteli, N., Stack, J. and Ramsay, H. (2001) 'Gendered patterns in computing work in the late 1990s', *New Technology, Work and Employment*, 16(1): 3–17.

Selfe, C. L. and Hawisher, G. E. (2002) 'A historical look at electronic literacy: implications for the education of technical communicators' [electronic version], *Journal of Business and Technical Communication*, 16(3): 231–76.

Smith, D. (1987) *The Everyday World as Problematic: A Feminist Sociology*, Toronto: University of Toronto Press.

Smith, D. (1993) *Texts, Facts, and Femininity: Exploring the Relations of Ruling*, London and New York: Routledge.

Turkle, S. and Papert, S. (1990) 'Epistemological pluralism: styles and voices within the computer culture', *Signs: Journal of Women in Culture and Society*, 16(1): 128–57.

Turner, S.V., Bernt, P.W. and Pecora, N. (2002) 'Why women choose information technology careers: educational, social, and familial influences'. Paper presented at the Annual Meeting of the American Educational Research Association, New Orleans, LA, April 1–5, 2002. Retrieved from Educational Resources Information Centre (ERIC Document Reproduction Service No. ED 465878) (accessed 17 December 2003).

23 Women and their knowledge managing the 'other economy'[1]

Maria Clara Bueno Fischer and Clair Ribeiro Ziebell

This chapter is about the ways that women learn, through their lives and through their experiences – informally and incidentally, and also in non-formal education. Two case studies of women's learning through community and social action, in formal and non-formal work activities and in solidary[2] enterprises in the South of Brazil are presented and analysed. Through their life experiences, the women acquired not only skills and knowledge, self-awareness and social and political understanding but also ways of thinking and acting that support the current oppressive social relations. Such learning is relevant to their performance in solidary enterprises and can help to explain the ambiguous and contradictory outcomes.

Introduction

The 'other economy' is an umbrella term coined by a Brazilian author, to describe diverse forms of organizing the economy that have emerged in Brazil and elsewhere as an alternative to the capitalist economy.

> Labelled as solidary economy, social economy, new cooperativism or self-managing firms, these are innovatory economic practices associated to new values and principles that are opposed to [capitalist] economic and ecological predatory economic practices and to those that produce [social and cultural] exclusion.
>
> (Cattani, 2003)

A number of inter-related concepts are associated with the 'other economy': associativism, self-management, social capital, fair trade, co-operation, local development, moral economy, popular economy, social emancipation, solidarity-based market and others. To establish a solidary economic enterprise was the original aim of the people we interviewed.

> Solidary economic enterprises include different modalities of economic organisation. It comes from workers' free associations, on the basis of principles of self-management, co-operation, efficiency and viability.

> Agglutinating individuals excluded from the [formal] labour market, or moved by the force of its values and searching collective alternatives of survival, the solidary economic enterprises develop activities in the production, services, commerce and credit sectors
>
> (Gaiger, 2003: 135)

It is very hard to establish an enterprise based on the principles of solidarity. It is necessary to get financial support; to commercialize products and services; to develop collective and horizontal management; to understand and to deal with social human relations; to know the country's legislation and also to implement it; to face unfair competition with 'false' co-operatives; to have infrastructure; to acquire education and qualifications related to the focus of the enterprise; to surpass gender asymmetries and to struggle for adequate public policy.

As is well known, both men and women from *popular sectors*³ constitute the oppressed pole of our unequal and patriarchal society and it is these de-humanized people who are becoming the main protagonists of the 'other economy'. We believe that there is a unique value in studying *women's* performance in solidary economy enterprises and the way it has been influenced by their previous experience and learning. Using two case studies, we present and discuss women's skills and knowledge, self-awareness and social and political understanding and, at the same time, the ways of thinking and acting that support the current oppressive social relations generated through women's daily life and work experiences. Such learning is relevant to understand their performance in solidary enterprises and helps to explain the ambiguous and contradictory outcomes that occurred.

The case studies

We interviewed women from a service sector worker co-operative (enterprise A) and a worker (pro-cooperative) association producing herbal remedies and healthy homemade foods (enterprise B). The first is situated in São Leopoldo and the other in Canoas, both suburban areas of Greater Porto Alegre in the South of Brazil.

Enterprise A was established in a context of local unemployment with the support of the local community, social workers, community workers from the local university and the assistance of the national metal worker trade union which is a confederation member of the Brazilian CUT – one of the national trade union centres (CNM/CUT). Workshops about sustainable development organized and sponsored by the metalworkers' leaders were a key element in the choice of co-operativism as a way to face unemployment. A group of twenty people – men and women – started a worker cooperative but only seven women and one man remained in the business when we undertook our research

A group of fifteen women created enterprise B. A community education course called 'Multiply' for urban women, funded by the government and organized by some activist women with the support of a local union member of CNM/CUT, motivated them to establish the enterprise. One of the course's expected results was to organize activities for women from the local community who were trapped in domestic routines. A very active woman, called here Carla, led a group to establish a *women's* pro-coop association based on their own ideas. Later, as members of this association, they attended a sixty-hour course, sponsored by the same union, which was designed to help people who are involved in the implementation and management of solidary enterprises.

Enterprise A does not function any more as a co-operative based on the principles of solidarity and democracy. Nowadays the co-operative statute is just a formal document. It is much more a kind of small business in the service sector. In enterprise B, even with the limits of their practice where they struggle to maintain regular collective meetings for democratic discussion and definitions, the ends and the means of the business are a better life for the workers and the community. In this sense enterprise A is becoming, in practice, a business based on alienated labour relations, unlike enterprise B where women are pursuing labour relations based on the values of co-operation and democracy.

The relative failure of enterprise A and the comparative success of enterprise B, regarding the coherence of their intentions to become a solidary enterprise and the actual outcome, and our curiosity to understand the ways in which women make sense of their current and previous experiences and how they relate these to the contents of institutionalized provision and courses, led us to ask women about their learning throughout their life and work experiences. Our main hypothesis was that this would help us to understand more deeply the limits and the possibilities of their performance in the enterprises.

Women's learning in the local community

The theoretical framework developed in this chapter has three dimensions: a broad conception of education and learning; an emphasis on the relationship between people's current behaviour and representations and their previous learning experience; and, also, the role of gender relations in shaping social practices. Our knowledge of what constituted prior learning for the women comes from the interviews we conducted with them and the workshops we ran.

Many of the women interviewed have been involved in several caring and organizing activities at home and in the community where they live. They have also participated in social and community educational activities promoted by the local church, unions, the urban social movement and

Non Governmental Organizations (NGOs). In these very lively situations they have learnt and developed their knowledge.

Some of the women participated in a local housing movement that offered a significant learning opportunity and was recognized as such in the interviews. They identified positive results and learning about collective organization, occupation of abandoned houses, bargaining and also the advantages of collective action and of sharing knowledge in order to achieve social rights. Specific political and instrumental skills – the '*how to*'s – were learnt: how to co-ordinate groups; how to create proposals for collective demands and make collective and/or individual decisions; how to reach consensus; how to encourage people to develop the desire and the disposition to keep fighting for their rights; how to plan actions taking account of tactics and strategies; how to act in identifying and considering the co-relations of force and, therefore, the specific interests of people and groups; how to identify ways to fight to defend themselves and how to learn to face tensions when there is no consensus. They also learnt how to recognize and deal with what is at the same time both democratic and, on the other hand, authoritarian management. They also cited learning to overcome the fear of giving a public speech, valuing their own opinion and learning how to maintain enthusiasm and initiative in hostile situations. They faced the challenge to be coherent in their public activities. Their discourse and their actions were (and still are) checked continually. They are expected to provide reliable information and to be responsible in their use of public and community resources. All these requirements provide valuable learning experiences.

According to more than one respondent, Basic Christian Communities (CEBs) are the sites where important learning took place. In these communities they had developed values relating to autonomy and solidarity and they recognized the importance of these. They gave some examples of the kind of values they were referring to: 'to instruct people how to fish and not simply to receive fish'; 'what you learn you must teach others, not simply keep it to yourself'; 'to live in community' and 'to give and to receive'.

Women learned through non-formal education activities how to fight to build more symmetrical gender relations. Some of the respondents had attended Popular Legal Promotors (PLP) and Gender Leadership courses and highlighted the contribution that these made to their performance in the enterprises. In the PLP[4] courses, women learn how to defend each other in situations of social and gender inequality, violence and prejudice. In the Gender Leadership courses they critically reflect on gender relations in order to construct more equal social relations in the workplace, in the family, in groups, social movements and the organizations in which women participate. This course is promoted by the local university in partnership with the Women's Education Network of Sao Paulo. These non-formal education activities are inspired by Popular Education principles and methodologies.

Formal education was not recognized as preparing them for working in co-operatives; neither was school seen as a rich site where children and young people were educated about the solidary economy. Nevertheless, some of the respondents attended basic adult education courses developed by the CNM/CUT.[5] Women were conscious of the requirements employers have today for formal education qualifications and some of them, although involved in solidary enterprises, still wanted to get a formal job. But accreditation, as we know, also has a social value beyond the demands of the current labour market. This was made clear to us when, for example, at the end of the Gender Leadership and PLP courses, we witnessed the women's satisfaction in receiving a formal certificate. But this is another subject and does not relate to the role of school in supporting the development of the 'other economy'. What should be noted however, is that the Brazilian federal government is supporting adult education courses whose purpose is to educate people in income-generation strategies within the general framework of the 'other economy' (Kruppa, 2005).

Women's learning in work situations

We asked women about their learning in work situations they were involved in either before, or even concomitant to, their involvement in the enterprises.

First, we noted that all of them had developed some specific skills at home: cooking, making natural medicine, embroidery and sewing. This knowledge was developed further and/or used in social communitarian actions for income generation – for example in the enterprises – and in community care. To illustrate learning from their other experiences of work, we will use the examples of two women. Jane exemplifies how they move 'in and out' of the formal labour market, and the centrality of domestic work (in their own homes and outside) in their lives. Carla exemplifies the richness of what we call here *communitarian management* as well as the role that some women, not just in the cases presented here, have played in leading women's participation and liberation within the context of the 'other economy'.

Jane, from enterprise A, worked previously under formal labour relations in the shoe-making and air conditioning manufacturing industry. She had also worked as a domestic servant with and without a labour contract. In the shoe-making workshops she worked informally. Her evaluation of working in firms was positive because of the economic and social autonomy she achieved under formal labour relations which allowed her to receive legal social benefits and vocational qualifications. She learnt what she identifies as 'professional' knowledge and a Taylorist approach to management based on social division of labour and rigid hierarchy. She also emphasized the positiveness of certain of the social relationships and skills she learnt with the ladies of the houses where she worked as a domestic servant. For her, the sexual division of labour is fair when it is related to the physical effort demanded from the task.

Carla, from enterprise B, is the other illustrative case. She worked for a short time in formal job activities in the service sector. Her main previous and concomitant work activities to her duties at the pro-co-op association, were selling cosmetics, making and selling handicrafts and doing domestic work. As an informal seller she learnt good social communication and how to develop relationships. It was, however, her work in communitarian management that was fundamental to her and the site where she learnt the most. Her participation in the association resulted from her involvement with and in the community involving herself in one activity after another without a break. She is a typical example of an activist developing a *direct social network*, a concept we will discuss later in this chapter. This woman is a singular illustrative case of a conscious mediation between the world of production and the world of reproduction so important to the 'other economy'.

Relating previous learning to their performance in the co-op enterprises

When the women started the enterprises they had tacit learning related to the reproduction of life or to what is known as 'women's work', providing general services, embroidery, cooking, producing natural medicines and managing the daily life of a community (*communitarian management*). This is very common in enterprises of this kind. They had also learnt issues and 'ways of doing' related to management in the firms where they worked: quality control of products and processes; bureaucratic aspects and the processes of labour organization.

The case studies show differences between the transference of women's previous skills and ethical and social learning in the two enterprises. The ability to make handicrafts, significant for women of enterprise B, was not enhanced despite their desire to become 'professional' in making handicrafts. In enterprise A the women used, and improved upon, the skills they had previously developed in making homemade food and natural medicines. Women of enterprise B had difficulty putting into practice in the co-op what they had learnt and practised in the women's movement about gender relations, although they still maintain and developed them further in other social spheres. Something different occurred with women of the other enterprise as we will see later in this chapter.

Understanding the ambience of the development of women's tacit learning

Direct action was the main strategy of the Latin American women's movement in the 1970s and 1980s, especially for those located in the field of popular social movements. These emerged outside of the productive sphere and the conventional canals of political mediation in a context of a crisis of the (capitalist) state that generated huge social demands (Doimo, 1995). There is, therefore, a particular culture which is different or even a stranger to the traditional social relations that occur in the productive sphere. Women's action in the community today is still framed by this heritage.

Doimo's notion of *direct action network* helps us to understand the cultural characteristics of the community as a site of women's tacit and informal learning. She defines it as 'social nets that mobilise people who are disposed to have a continuous participation in social movements in a field informed by common values' (Doimo, 1995: 152). For her 'these nets emerge from personal relations and through manifestation of different interests and communication between groups of distinct nature and functions and have in the CEBs its founding matrix' (ibid: 155).

> nets (are) constituted by people who are disposed to use and participate continuously and concomitantly in struggles against the high cost of living, to get a day-care centre, followed by a battle for public health ... characterised as having a spasmodic behaviour.
>
> (ibid: 152)

People who participate in these networks learn to struggle and to develop consensus-reaching processes, regarding values that guide and regulate a specific way of behaving. She affirms that

> the participation of the individuals in these nets is based on the idea of the consensus and of the solidarity, that creates a space for charismatic leaders creating difficulties for the absorption of internal conflicts and then, it ends up excluding divergent voices
>
> (ibid: 156)

Acting in these networks produces a specific way of 'how to do and to be'. Charismatic leadership; difficulties in dealing with conflict and the almost spontaneous characteristics of their day-to-day action in the community, are some aspects of an informal education process the women of our case studies are immersed in. These are aspects that influence their way of participating in the process of generating the 'other economy'. Positive learning can also be identified in these nets, for example, the development of their capacity to implement and act in networks and the results they get from this. Their active involvement in the creation of collective forums and availability to participate in Popular Education activities such as PLPs and Gender Leadership courses are relevant examples.

Learning gender relations through life experiences influenced women's performance in the enterprises. The group of the worker co-op found themselves embedded in, and reproducing, social relations based on gender asymmetries: abuse of power, double shifts and unequal remuneration. A woman used to be the formal president of the co-op, but her husband assumed the presidency with the apparently passive agreement of the group. He, an authoritarian person, was a pensioner and former bank worker who knew the bureaucratic procedures required to run a business. He made a formal speech in favour of women's rights, imposing his leadership with the passive acceptance of the women. Why, with their rich previous experience and acknowledged learning about women's rights, did they not assert themselves in the face of this discriminatory act against them? They were asked to explain how the man took over and their answer was that it was fair as he had more time and experience.

Saffioti (2002) affirms that gender patriarchal relations persist in current capitalist social relations. She affirms that this matrix 'shapes deeply people's subjectivity' (Saffioti, 2002: 333). She refers, for instance, to the women's feeling of impotence. 'As gender crosses social life as a whole, it can be affirmed that women experience impotence every day deeply' (ibid: 135). More than men, they endure the impotence as they have been 'trained' for it.[6] Carreira *et al.* (2001) point out other interesting aspects related to this issue. They cite, for instance, women's belief that 'the' power isolates one person from another and that women are all equal. As a consequence they pursue consensus obsessively. Women tend to prioritize and to preserve relations between people at all costs. Such illuminating insights contribute to understanding women's subjectivity, which is culturally forged and still remains, creating barriers for women's autonomous action in social and private spheres.

The formal and legitimate leadership of enterprise B brought certainties, and learning which was more solid about the advantages of symmetrical gender relations. Such a perspective had been developed mainly on courses and activities for women in the local and regional community in which Carla had participated. She was the proponent of the enterprise. From the beginning, her proposals have been based on a feminist perspective of helping women who were imprisoned in daily domestic routines. The association is based in her house but she insists that it should be transferred to another place. She is a leader with the characteristics of a popular educator, always remembering what it means to establish a 'real' co-op and showing how to do this via practical actions: cultivating new projects; stimulating the group to establish networks and acquire the views of wider groups of women; searching for ways to commercialize the products, among other things. In the interview, several times she used the phrase 'how we are going to do this or that?'.

Some, however, said they would like to have the presence of men in the association to sell the products and that they would feel safer and more respected if that could happen. They also tended to depend on Carla to take decisions. So the patriarchal culture manifests itself again: specific tasks and conditions of social respectability are associated with men and also the women show signs of impotence when transferring power to others, not taking it fully in their own hands.

The notion of direct action networks and the category of gender allow one to understand some of the historic cultural barriers the women faced trying to become self-confident in running solidary enterprises and, at the same time, to identify cultural elements that are a positive assistance in implementing solidary enterprises.

Women's previous experience and skills were central to the establishment of both enterprises: their ability to take initiatives, their capacity to mobilize resources and to establish networks. But as enterprise A achieved formal and legal recognition, their previous learning became apparently inoperative or unimportant. The previous autonomous and emancipatory learning apparently vanished. The hegemonic capitalist and masculine perspective of organizing the labour process became very influential and ended up shaping the co-op's economical and political perspective. Women had difficulty in transferring emancipatory feminist learning to the sphere of production. They did not perform and act with the full capacity they had demonstrated in other spheres of social action.

Economy, politics and culture are intertwined human spheres that feed into each other and the results affect work situations. We could say that men and women have difficulty in overcoming the asymmetrical sexual division of work. Perhaps a re-conceptualization, representation, political and ethical understanding of women's and men's domestic and community management activities are necessary to overcome that historical limitation. It seems to us that the lack of such a social and cultural process by ordinary people as well as in the academic world creates economic and symbolic barriers for men and women to critically recognize learning originating in the sphere of the reproduction and transfer it into the sphere of production and vice versa. The success of the 'other economy' depends on this happening as it certainly would contribute to an emancipatory relationship between those spheres.

We have mentioned and discussed women's learning in formal work activities. They learned to give value to the regular wage and social benefits, associating them with better conditions to survive and to get social recognition. At first sight this could be seen simply as an alienated women's perspective but it can also be seen as an empirical recognition of working class historical rights. They know that work in a solidary enterprise does not necessarily mean a better economic alternative for everyone, but for the older and unemployed it represented an alternative to a very difficult economic and social situation. It represents to some people the concrete possibility of an income and, at the same time, to have their own business based in an emancipatory framework. But, again, previous informal learning in firms pressurizes the achievement of, for instance, a more horizontal relationship at work. The women who worked in firms experimented with the vertical hierarchy but did not participate as shop stewards or union representatives at the workplace. Such experience perhaps would help the development of a democratic management in a co-operative or other solidary kind of economic enterprise. As is discussed here, the workplace site is not a community site, and this must have something to do with the transference or not of learning from one experience to the other.

In this chapter we have identified what women learnt, during their lives, through their experiences, informally and incidentally, and also in non-formal education activities, in order to understand their performance in solidary enterprises. In order to do this, we analysed the sites where such informal learning was developed. The concepts of direct action network, gender and a broad education and learning concept were adopted to enrich our understanding of the complex issues involved in establishing emancipatory and solidary economic enterprises.

Our case studies show the richness and complexity of building the 'other economy' which include women and men well prepared to take the responsibility of running enterprises based on a very different perspective than the one they are used to within capitalist social relations. Conscious learning demands effort and time. They should become conscious of the informal learning that takes place due to the cultural weight of the heritage of our historical oppressive social relations. They also should be conscious of their positive informal and tacit learning in order to realize its value. This is a central condition for their role within current and future social relations that should surpass the perverse circle of current oppressive sexual division of work. Therefore one central task is the design of formal and non-formal education activities that take these issues into account.

In the context of our country, Brazil, with its precarious social and public state policy, we do not believe in the success of the 'other economy' but we know that every single struggle to establish solidary enterprise can be a step in this direction.

Notes

1 The state agencies FAPERGS and CNPq have sponsored this study.
2 'Characterized by or having solidarity or coincidence of interests' (New Shorter Oxford English Dictionary) [Editor].
3 'Working class' [Editor].
4 Popular Legal Promoters are women who take qualifications in national legislation and rights, with emphasis on women's rights, becoming

disseminators of the information received within their own communities, fortifying and characterizing feminine intervention in the development of equalitarian relations (ONG CECA – Ecumenical Center of Evangelization Qualification and Assessorship, 2003).

5 The current Brazilian legislation allows organizations from civil society to implement adult education courses, although they are certified by formal schools indicated by the state. The progressive trade union movement has taken this opportunity to innovate a curriculum combining a formal school syllabus with political issues concerning workers and community interests (Fischer and Hannah, 2002).

6 Saffioti (2002) recognizes that women do exert power but impotence takes advantage when woman face men or face 'their man'. This author's reflections were developed from an analysis of violence against women and, more specifically, domestic violence. Nevertheless they are fruitful for understanding our cases.

References

Carreira, Denise; Ajamil, Menchu; Moreira, Teresa (eds) (2001) *Mudando o mundo: a liderança feminina no século 21*, São Paulo: Cortez, Rede Mulher de Educação.

Cattani, Antônio David (ed.) (2003) *A outra economia*, Porto Alegre: Veraz.

Doimo, Ana Maria. (1995) *A vez e a voz do popular: movimentos sociais e participação política no Brasil pós-70*, Rio de Janeiro: Relume-Dumara.

Fischer, Maria Clara Bueno and Hannah, Janet (2002) (Re) 'Constructing Citizenship: the Programa Integrar of the Brazilian Metalworkers' Union', *Compare*, 32(1).

Gaiger, Luiz Inácio (2003) 'Empreendimentos econômicos solidários', in Cattani, Antônio David (ed.) *A outra economia*, Porto Alegre: Veraz, 135–43.

Kruppa, Sonia M. (ed.) (2005) *Economia Solidária e educação de Jovens e Adultos*, Brasília: INEP/MEC.

Saffioti, Heleieth (2002) 'Violência contra a mulher e violência doméstica', in Bruschini, Cristina and Unbehaum, Sandra G. (eds) *Gênero, democracia e sociedade brasileira*. São Paulo: Editora 34 Ltda. e Fundação Carlos Chagas.

24 The ghost in the network

Globalization and workplace learning

Richard Edwards and Kathy Nicoll

In this chapter we explore some of the ways in which globalization has become an actor in many workplaces in the world through the networking potentials of information and communications technologies, and the relationality and interconnectedness engendered by them. We focus on the ways in which globalization is realized in workplaces through texts and discourses and the flows of communication thereby supported. We argue that it is through such realizations that globalization is in part learned and vice versa. Drawing broadly on actor-network theory (ANT), we sketch some of the actants, relationships and performances that make these globalized practices possible and consider the learning enmeshed within the practices of such workplaces. The chapter is theory driven and illuminative.

Introduction

This chapter sets out to explore some of the ways in which globalization has become an actor in many of the workplaces of the world through the networking potentials of information and communications technologies (ICTs), and the relationality and interconnectedness engendered by them (Urry 2003). Globalization, and in particular global competition, has been positioned as a key driver for workplace change in recent years, impacting upon the nature and organization of work and the requirements of workers to more readily adopt a learning disposition to their labour. Messages for such change are carried in the policy-led discourses of lifelong learning, as well as the hyperbole of business gurus and in the popular media. They are not without opposition, of course, both academically and politically, but this has not stopped them from being powerful.

Our focus is on the ways in which these messages are rhizomatically entangled and *realized* in workplaces through the texts and discourses, the flows of communication, enabled by ICTs. We are not concerned therefore with how globalization is formulated as a context for workplace change, but with how it haunts the very practices of the workplace. It is through the practices of the workplace that globalization is realized in its many different forms. Thus, for instance, just-in-time technology supports the production and distribution of goods from one part of the world to another, based upon the computerization of data on patterns of consumption. In large multi-national companies, team-working across sites – which may embrace different languages and cultures as well as areas of expertise – networks workers into collaborative forms that shrink the globe. Globalization is thus a metaphor that is deployed within discourses for change, but it is also a nominalization of the practices that bring it forth. In different ways, the call-centre workers of India and Northern Ireland, the bean farmers of East Africa, the DELL customer services and sales workers in Glasgow and the Ford car workers in Geelong, take up and realize globalization through the practices of their workplaces.

Drawing upon actor-network theory (ANT), we sketch some of the actants, relationships and performances that make examples of such globalized practices possible, and consider the learning enmeshed within them. In the process, we explore the ways in which they become embodied in globalization itself, as actors in rather than simply an outcome of certain technologically enabled practices, and some of the implications of this. We point to ways in which globalization is realized through the entanglement of human and non-human actors, in particular ICTs, in the performance of work.

The chapter is in three parts. First, we outline the theoretical positioning informing our understanding. ANT has become influential across the social sciences in recent years. However, it is important to bear in mind that it has a longer history, and it is not a coherent theory as such, more a stimulating way of theorizing. Second, we sketch some of the ways in which globalization is taken up in the workplaces of today. Finally, we put forward some propositions regarding globalization and workplace learning that we consider important to take forward. The chapter is theory driven and illustrative. Inevitably, given length, only so much detail can be provided. The metaphors of the ghost and haunting are derived loosely from Derrida (1994), suggesting that globalizing practices have a troubling effect on existence. However, this is not a fundamental troubling. Just as the ghost paradoxically can never fully realize the past within the present, globalizing practices are never able to be fully realized, to fully relinquish their ghostly existence. This is not to suggest in any way that they do not have very real material and other effects.

Actor-network theory

ANT is part of the shift from individualized, psychological approaches to the understanding of knowledge-building to more social and cultural interpretations. Here there is focus on ontology rather than epistemology, wherein 'reality *is a relational effect*. It is produced and stabilized in interaction that is simultaneously material and social' (Law and Urry 2003: 5, emphasis in the original). The social is thus both enacted and real, what we have termed *realized*. Knowledge-building, or knowing performance, is taken to be a joint exercise within a network that is spread across space and time and includes inanimate – e.g. tools, pens, computers, software, mobile phones, charts, machinery – as well as animate objects. The symmetry between inanimate and animate objects in ANT arises because 'human powers increasingly derive from the complex *interconnections* of humans with material objects ... This means that the human and physical worlds are elaborately intertwined and cannot be analyzed separate from each other' (Urry 2000: 14, emphasis in original). To put this in other terms, 'the argument is that thinking, acting, writing, loving, earning – all the attributes that we normally ascribe to human beings, are generated in networks that pass through and ramify both within and beyond the body. Hence the term, actor-network – an actor is also, always, a network' (Law 2003: 4). To talk of the social then is to talk of the entwinements of the human and non-human. ANT therefore deconstructs the boundaries between society and the technical, nature and culture, etc. and, with that, the distinctions between the natural and social sciences (Law 2004). What happens in workplaces then is not simply the result of human intention or impersonal forces, but is the result of forms of connection, interaction and translation between different actants, which can always fall apart. In examining the actor-networks of specific workplaces we can point to practices referred to as 'action at a distance' (Miller and Rose 1993) that are translated into workplace practices. In this, ANT shares much metaphorically and intellectually with complexity theory in the natural sciences and chaos theory in mathematics (Urry 2003).

We see immediately the heuristic usefulness of ANT to a consideration of globalization and workplaces, as workplaces are workspaces to use Farrell's (2005) useful distinction. 'Physical work*places* [form] local nodes of a complex network of people, technologies and practices that constitute a potentially globally distributed work*space*' (Farrell 2005: 5, emphasis in the original). In other words, the workplace is inseparable from the interconnections that make the performance of work possible and which compress and construct time and space in particular ways. These may be manifestations of globalization and contribute to it. They entail humans and non-humans being both connected and translated in order that a specific workplace can continue to thrive.

> According to [the model of translation], the spread in time and space of anything – claims, orders, artefacts, goods – is in the hands of people; each of these people may act in many different ways, letting the token drop, or modifying it, or deflecting it, or betraying it, or adding to it, or appropriating it ... When no one is there to take up the statement or token then it simply drops.
>
> (Latour 1986: 267)

It is on the effectiveness of interconnection and translation that a workplace may then be evaluated in the production of information, knowledge, goods and services. A workplace only becomes such because of a series of actors being inter-related in ways that can be signified as work; it is a network effect.

Actor-networks are unstable, precarious. They 'expand, contract and shift configuration over time, and even the most stable and predictable of them are constantly being reappropriated and redefined by the nature of the flows that animate them ...' (Nespor 1994: 12). Workplaces therefore can be seen as intersections or nodes within actor-networks, in which actants and participation are ordered in the construction of time and space. The very ordering of this construction and the actants mobilized, embeds a regularity of working practices and with that knowledge. Knowing is a range of space-time distributions which constitute that ordering and mobilization. Thus, '"learning" should refer to changes in the spatial and temporal organization of the distributed actors/networks that we're always part of' (Nespor 1994: 11). An architecture or built environment of workplace learning starts to emerge for consideration. This may reside partly in the workplace, but extends beyond immediate relations as a container of work practices to embrace the complex networks and uptakes across space and time through which those practices become possible. They are mobilizations and translations of spatially and temporally distance settings in central positions and knowledge is their property (Nespor 1994). Workplaces are complex and contested organizational forms, which have to be constantly performed to exist. ANT therefore emphasizes the performative nature of work and learning as network effects.

It is through translation or mediation that networks are formed and may become simplified to the extent that they act as a unity, what some have called 'punctualizations' (Law 2003) insofar as they cease to look like, to be visible as, networks, and come to act as resources that can be used. Without such practices, there is no network.

> This, then, is the core of the actor-network approach: a concern with how actors and organizations mobilize, juxtapose and hold together the bits and pieces out of which they are composed; how they are sometimes able to prevent those bits and pieces from following their own inclinations and making off; and how they manage, as a result, to conceal for a time the process of translation itself and so turn a network from a heterogeneous set of bits and pieces each with its own inclinations, into something that passes as a punctualized actor.
>
> (Law 2003: 6)

ANT emphasizes the dynamic nature of practices and the actions through which things happen. It also provides a means of examining the ways in which action at a distance is realized, given the focus on the spatio-temporal and on mediation. As such, it is useful for examining the dynamics of workplaces in relation to the actant, globalization.

Globalizing workplaces – a ghostly presence?

The debates in and around globalization are many and varied regarding its existence, significance and desirability (Held and McGrew 2000, Edwards and Usher 2000). At theoretical and political levels there are those who are sceptical that globalization is occurring, or who are oppositional to its manifestation on the basis that it represents a form of neo-liberal economic colonialism. There are those who identify an emerging globalism from current trends, and welcome the potential cosmopolitanism this may bring. And there are those for whom it represents a complex set of emerging practices or processes, that compress space and time in ways that encourage increased hybridization, rather than any simple homogenizing of the globe. And then there are the questions of whether we discuss globalization as a thing or globalizing processes as action, or both given that each is only realizable through the other.

What cannot be denied is that globalization has been harnessed as a powerful discourse, both as an exigence for rationalizing certain forms of action and as a descriptor of the processes at play. As such, in some ways, globalization could be said to be a self-fulfilling prophecy, for insofar as it is used to guide our actions then so it will become. And this is the very view that ANT encourages us to take, as 'the global comes to constitute its own domains; it is continuously reconstituted through material-semiotic processes' (Law and Urry 2003: 7).

The workplace is a key nodal point through which globalizing work is done, given the economic and symbolic work of such spaces. But how is this achieved? We focus solely on the realization of globalization through translations afforded by communications technologies. This does not represent a form of technological determinism, as should be clear from the above. Neither globalization nor the uptakes of technology are determined by that technology alone, as anyone using a computer or mobile phone well knows. Not only is global connectivity possible through other means, but new technologies are entwined within those already existing. Thus, as Farrell and Holkner (2004: 136) suggest,

> Workspaces are hybrid, then, not just because they are constructed and mediated by a range of communication technologies but also because, when established and new technologies are brought together in these ways, their interaction creates new discursive resources, discursive resources that make available new working identities, values and practices and sideline others.

Farrell and Holkner (2004) draw upon the example of collaboratively constructed databases in a multinational textile company to discuss the negotiations of self and presence that take place for those communicating in this manner. Thus, the information on deadlines that is put into the database within the mending shed is read next door in the weaving shed, in the company head office in another city, as well as by suppliers and clients elsewhere in the globe. There is surveillance here for all concerned in negotiating certain norms for communicating and acting in this situation. There is also a realization of globalizing processes – space-time compression.

There is also a multimodality (Kress 2000) to the communication practices in play here. The supervisor in the mending shed still keeps her exercise book of information, in addition to contributing to the computerized database. People write notes for themselves as well as read and write emails. Instead of the much hyped 'paperless office' therefore, there is a proliferation of communications and texts. 'In the globally distributed, ICT-enabled workspace, work practice has to a significant extent become textual practice. [These] texts are the contexts in which we do our work, and ... these texts, like all texts, are contested sites' (Farrell 2005: 8). It is the multimodality of these practices that in part helps to ensure the continued connections, even when aspects of the technological network go down (Holkner and Farrell 2005).

Thus, alongside the complexity of relationships there is a diversifying of semiotic practices in workplaces. The 'crisis' of literacy much talked about by governments, employers and others is indeed tangible – not in the individual deficit ways in which it is usually framed, however. We witness not so much a crisis of basic skills – a lack – but a crisis of possibilities, of unfulfilled and perhaps unfulfillable potentialities. With the proliferation and hybridization of artefacts and genres of communication come many different possibilities for reading and writing the self and/with others, and the negotiations of languages and cultures that entails. What then is appropriate is multiplied, not reducable to a single standard. The ghost of globalization then has many personalities and representations. Thus Farrell's earlier (2000) framing of workplace literacy tutors as 'discourse technologists' itself has possibilities that go beyond any simple inculcation into the workforce of a global corporate culture. However, it remains the practices that focus on the lack that largely are taken up in addressing the multimodality of workplaces.

The database draws upon and collects other times and spaces within a central location. It represents therefore a geographical compression of time and space. It compresses by bringing activities of previous times and spaces of actor-networks into the present. In so doing it creates a new space and time, to make visible that which may then be acted upon. Law and Moser (1999) identify a project management spreadsheet as an actor that makes visible to the manager that which needs to be worked upon. Without this resource the manager could not manage, at least not in quite the same way. Thus, in ANT terms, the manager is an effect of other performances that are distributed across the actor-network: 'if we are concerned with Andrew-as-a-manager, then it turns out that he is an effect of a performance that is distributed *not only across his body, but also into a ramified network of other materials'* (Law and Moser 1999: 4, emphasis in original). It, the spreadsheet, allows the actor-network to become visible; for it to be seen that elements are in place and operating as they should be, and where adjustments are necessary for the future to go according to plan. It constructs a space/time within which distributed actors can act in accord with a particular logic.

This is not to attribute action to individual actors. The manager is not able to act without the vision imparted by the project management spreadsheet. She/he is thus materially heterogeneous, an assemblage, comprising both a human element and extensions of the actor-network; 'It is no longer easy to determine the locus of agency, to point at one place and to say with certainty that action emerges from that point rather than from somewhere else' (Law and Moser 1999: 4). Within the mending shed the actors are sets of extensions according to the elements that they take up and put down (human/scissor, human/sewing machine, human/spreadsheet, etc.). Each has its communicative requirements. This multimodality of communicative practices and assemblages points to the complexity of intersecting, overlaying and interwoven networks, where the actions possible are multiple. The human/spreadsheet acts to manage the future through the available representation.

Organizations are thus ordered performances, but this order is both materially and discursively heterogeneous and unstable. Agency is not determined but 'is spread between what we might think of as different logics of organization' (Law and Moser 1999: 4). Where a network acts with a logic of globalization, even though there will be slippage and deferral between this and alternatives, there will be a tendency for the materialization of texts (databases, spreadsheets, planning formulae, environmental scanning reports) and tools supporting increased punctualization. Texts and tools, themselves forms of punctualization, bring together information pertinent to an ordering logic, and ICTs play a powerful part in this. Thus, even though it may not be apparent, globalization can be said to be an actant in the workplace, a ghost constantly haunting the work and learning that is done there.

Such practices are increasingly usual in the day-to-day performances of work, either explicitly or implicitly. They both require and enable us to be multiply different, but also impose certain constraints. The networks are not completely open, but they can be subject to play, indifference and irony. They bring us into the presence of otherness (even of ourselves as possible assemblages diversify) even as they mediate the differences through the introduction of certain standards. As with the harmonization of railway gauges in the nineteenth century and its significance for nation building and trade, so in the twenty-first century the standardization of communications technologies and texts that bring aspects of the globe into view is modelling a certain global imaginary, a unity marked by difference.

To talk of globalization or globalizing processes as actants is to point to their capacity to compress space and time as they construct new conduits, bend space around themselves, make up elements that are dependent upon them, construct and require alternative languages, knowledge and learning. Such reconfigurations are realized both materially and representationally. Thus, the electronic database, accessible from the weaving shed, is one such process or element. Past, present and future work is accumulated as a particular centralized and collective reordering. Realizing globalization entails the production, distribution and reception of information and knowledge in this way, often in complex patterns of communication and connectivity. Within the workplace, the database acts in the reordering of activities even though there can be a degree of creativity for those involved. The possibilities for this are spread across different logics of orderings (Law and Moser 1999). There can then be a tension between organizational control and the action of actors within networks. This is not new in workplaces, but the challenges to globally distributed workplaces are greater. We are in the realm of controlled-decontrol and absent presences.

This is all very well but globalized networks and spreadsheets existed before the proliferation of ICTs. Why is it that networks become translated in this way? Effective ordering strategies are those that embed network relations within materials that are durable across time, create the possibility of transmitting immutable mobiles across space, anticipate responses and reactions, take effect within multiple locations and can themselves become relatively stable and multiplied (Law 2003). ICTs help strengthen and stabilize such ordering processes; they help punctualize actor-networks whether or not this is according to an explicit logic of globalization.

Ghost-busting or haunting the ghost?

We have argued that globalization is a ghost that haunts work and learning. How do we pursue this and the globalizing processes entailed so that they may be researched, when our approaches to research also help to realize that which we enact? Here research is an element within a globalizing actor-network even while it comments upon it (Law 2004).

The actor-networks within workspaces are systems of ordering through which organizations control and produce appropriate activity. Systems of electronic communication quite radically compress and reorder space and time. They join up peripheries within central locations to harness action to organizational and globalizing purposes and steer networks from a distance. With these are strategies of translation, attempts at ordering within workspaces, which help make globalizing processes durable, mobile and able to act at a distance. There are questions here then about what specific strategies regulate and delimit the space, and what activities they require. What are the struggles to negotiate and overcome these limits? Where do these ordering processes break down so that elements 'make off on their own' (Law 2003: 5) and with what consequences?

It is electronic communications that are often argued to bring forth a quantitative and qualitative shift in the potential of such systems. Some have claimed that electronic networks compress space and time to the extent that they have no space-time coordinates: 'electronic language ... is everywhere and nowhere, always and never. It is truly material/ immaterial' (Poster, in Nespor 1994: 27). For actor-networks to exist in realizable forms they require the relative stabilization of time and space and forms of punctualization to support and sustain this. Networks are complex, intersecting and intertwined at nodal points, in order that they make possible specific forms of flow. Parts of these must be deleted, or simplified, so as to conceal aspects from view. The worker cannot 'see' the programming codes that support the software that he or she is using, or the networks that made it possible and support it. The worker, in sending an email to a client, cannot see the actor-network that maintains institutional servers, firewalls, virus protection, and permits the compression of time-space which makes that action (almost) always a possibility. Punctualization makes up actants as network packages, which become taken for granted as routine resources within spaces of work and learning. The assemblages and subjectivities required within one network package may be quite distinct from those of others. And when punctualization breaks down, such as in the crash of a computer system, routine resources become visible as the actor-networks that realize them. Disciplinary power flows within a geometry that separates the insiders from the outsiders, knowers from unknowers, of packages. Literacy 'problems' emerge as communication flows do not exist across package boundaries; they are commonly inexplicable to those working outside them, and knowledge and literacies are not shared. In exploring globalizing processes in learning at work, we can then explore what is made visible and what punctualized in this way; what actor-networks are concealed, revealed and undermined by breakdown; what forms of assemblage and multimodality are required within and across them; and what potentialities are opened and closed in this. We can examine what is being multiplied as appropriate for packaging in order that conduits can be realized; what renegotiations of network, subjectivity, language and culture these entail and for whom; what literacy potentialities are formed, made possible and enacted in networks through which such globalization processes are at play.

Learning has not been taken here as a change in the psychological make-up of an individual or even of individual meaning constructed through social activities that are located in time and space. Learning is the changes in the spatial and temporal organization of distributed and interwoven actor-networks. Actor-networks learn. Time and space are made up within textual stories that may follow a logic of globalization, and these are embodied within such assemblages. Knowledge thus always takes material as well as representational forms. Returning to the example of the not-so-paperless office, the records for the mending shed are accumulated with those of others as electronic data. This is the accumulation of previous data representations anew. The new data sheets represent time and space – information is of past and current turnover of work, deadlines met and unmet, of mending sheds that are geographically and temporally dispersed – and, through this, knowledge is realized and the future can be calculated. Data is accumulated so that it can operate as a node at the intersection of networks, as a strategy for ordering and reordering. Implicit in the compression of globalizing processes, is the reconfiguration of space-time and learning.

The ghost of globalization then has many personalities and representations, which is carried into and through workplaces in different ways. Not least through the research narrative about globalization and workplaces of which this is an example. The extent to which the haunting is by globalization or by its spectre awaiting realization is then perhaps immaterial. Through a ghost busting or haunting of the spectre we have hoped to illuminate and in some small way unsettle its material effects.

References

Derrida, J. (1994) *Specters of Marx*, New York: Routledge.

Edwards, R. and Usher, R. (2000) *Globalization and Pedagogy: Space, Place, Identity*, London: Routledge.

Farrell, L. (2000) 'Ways of doing, ways of being: language, education and "working" identities', *Language and Education*, 14, 1: 18–36.

Farrell, L. (2005) 'The problem with "common knowledge" at work', paper presented at the Researching Work and Learning Conference, University of Technology, Sydney, December.

Farrell, L. and Holkner, B. (2004) 'Points of vulnerability and presence: knowing and learning in globally networked communities', *Discourse*, 25, 2: 133–44.

Held, D. and McGrew, A. (eds) (2000) *The Global Transformations Reader*, Cambridge: Polity Press.

Holkner, B. and Farrell, L. (2005) 'The network is down', paper presented at the Researching Work and Learning Conference, University of Technology, Sydney, December.

Kress, K. (2000) 'Multimodality', in B. Cope and M. Kalantzis (eds) *Multiliteracies*, London: Routledge.

Latour, B. (1986) 'The powers of association', in J. Law (ed.) *Power, Action and Belief: A New Sociology of Knowledge*, London: Routledge and Kegan Paul.

Law, J. (2003) 'Notes on the theory of the actor network: ordering, strategy and heterogeneity', Department of Sociology and Centre for Science Studies, Lancaster University, Lancaster, UK. Available at http://www.lancs.ac.uk/fss/sociology/papers/law-notes-on-ant.pdf (Accessed 4 March 2006).

Law, J. (2004) *After Method: Mess in Social Science Research*, London: Routledge.

Law, J. and Moser, I. (1999) 'Managing, subjectivities and desires', Lancaster: Centre for Science Studies, Lancaster University. Available at http://www.lancs.ac.uk/fss/sociology/papers/law-moser-managing-subjectivities-desires.pdf (Accessed 15 June 2006).

Law, J. and Urry, J. (2003) 'Enacting the social', Department of Sociology and Centre for Science Studies, Lancaster University, Lancaster, UK. Available at http://www.lancs.ac.uk/fss/sociology/papers/law-urry-enacting-the-social.pdf (Accessed 28 February 2006).

Miller, P. and Rose, N. (1993) 'Governing economic life', in M. Gane and T. Johnson (eds) *Foucault's New Domains*, London: Routledge.

Nespor, J. (1994) *Knowledge in Motion: Space, Time and Curriculum in Undergraduate Physics and Management*, London: Falmer Press.

Urry, J. (2000) *Sociology Beyond Societies: Mobilities for the Twenty-first Century*, London: Routledge.

Urry, J. (2003) *Global Complexity*, Cambridge: Polity Press.

Index